Social
Psychology
and
Cultural
Context

Cross-Cultural Psychology Series

SERIES EDITORS

Walter J. Lonner
Western Washington University

John W. Berry
Queens University

Many of the basic assumptions contained in standard psychology curricula in Western universities have been uncritically accepted for many years. The volumes in the **Cross-Cultural Psychology** series present cultural perspectives that challenge Western ways of thinking in the hope of stimulating informed discussions about human behavior in all domains of psychology.

Cross-Cultural Psychology offers brief monographs describing and critically examining Western-based psychology and its underlying assumptions. The primary readership for this series consists of professors who teach, and students who take, the wide spectrum of courses offered in upper-division and graduate-level psychology programs in North America and elsewhere.

EDITORIAL BOARD

Books in this series:

Social
Psychology
and
Cultural
Context

John Adamopoulos
Yoshihisa Kashima

Editors

CCP
Cross-Cultural Psychology

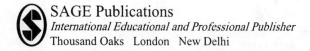
SAGE Publications
International Educational and Professional Publisher
Thousand Oaks London New Delhi

For information:

SAGE Publications, Inc.
2455 Teller Road
Thousand Oaks, California 91320
E-mail: order@sagepub.com

SAGE Publications Ltd.
6 Bonhill Street
London EC2A 4PU
United Kingdom

SAGE Publications India Pvt. Ltd.
M-32 Market
Greater Kailash I
New Delhi 110 048 India

Printed in the United States of America

Library of Congress Cataloging-in-Publication Data

Main entry under title:

   Social psychology and cultural context / edited by John Adamopoulos
and Yoshihisa Kashima.
   p. cm. — (Cross-cultural psychology series; v. 4)
   Includes bibliographical references.
   ISBN 0-7619-0637-1 (cloth: alk. paper)
   ISBN 0-7619-0638-X (pbk: alk. paper)
   1. Social psychology. 2. Ethnopsychology. 3. Context effects
(Psychology) I. Kashima, Yoshihisa, 1957- II. Title. III. Series.
   HM1033 .A33 1999
   302—dc21
                                                    99-6254

99 00 01 02 03 04 05 7 6 5 4 3 2 1

Acquiring Editor:	Jim Nageotte
Editorial Assistant:	Eileen Carr
Production Editor:	Diana E. Axelsen
Editorial Assistant:	Nevair Kabakian
TypesetterDesigner:	Christina M. Hill
Indexer:	Jeanne R. Busemeyer

Contents

FOREWORD

A careful analysis of the history of Western psychology and a thorough consideration of various efforts that preceded the advent of what is currently called modern, scientific psychology document that the role played by culture in human behavior has interested scholars in psychology and other disciplines for many generations (e.g., Cole, 1996; Jahoda, 1982; Jahoda & Krewer, 1997). How could different views of the world, different languages, different religions and cosmologies, and different ideas about the nature of the human mind *not* have intrigued the inquisitive theoretician and researcher? Yet despite this thread of continuity in the intellectual history of the discipline of psychology, organized and cooperative efforts by more than a handful of psychologists have been relatively recent. These efforts started to take shape in the mid-1960s, and by the early 1970s there was enough of a critical mass of like-minded psychologists around the world to usher in the institutionalization of cross-cultural psychology as a viable method of inquiry. Since then, this perspective has become a visible force in psychology both conceptually and methodologically, and its future seems secure even if there is some question about the exact course that it might take (Segall, Lonner, & Berry, 1998). As more people "discovered" ("rediscovered" may be more accurate) the importance of culture, it is curious why this interest has not been more pervasive over the years.

Although recent historical records on the matter are spotty and incomplete, a meeting that spanned the last days of 1966 and the first days of 1967 at the University of Ibadan in Ibadan, Nigeria, appears to be the first meeting that brought together a number of social psychologists from several countries. All of them were primarily interested in studying the role played by culture in psychology, and in particular the role played by key social psychological areas of research such as attitudes, prejudice, conformity, ethnicity, and so on.

Approximately 80 people, mostly from Africa, were in attendance. A central figure at that meeting was Harry Triandis, then just 39 years old. Among other accomplishments of that collection of scholars was their resolve to stay in touch through the *Cross-Cultural Social Psychology Newsletter,* which the participants agreed to initiate as a way to augment important future contacts and collaboration. Harry agreed to edit the *Newsletter,* which he did for a short time. The *Newsletter*'s mailing list became important to several people, including myself. Critical in the process that led to the inauguration of the *Journal of Cross-Cultural Psychology* in 1970, and a mark of his character and generosity, was Harry's voluntarily sharing with me that important list of several hundred names and addresses. He did not have a compelling reason to be so helpful, however. When I first contacted him, he was among about 10 (of approximately 300) who expressed doubts about inaugurating a journal of the type explained in letters seeking advice and support. A few years later, he was a pillar of support and encouragement, and he has been one of the key consultants over the years. These matters of historical record show that Harry was among the founders of institutionalized and organized cross-cultural social psychology. Because social-psychological topics dominate the cross-cultural literature, it follows that he has been a dominant and ubiquitous presence in the development and growth of cross-cultural psychology.

The affable Harry will tell you, however, that his editorship of the *Newsletter* (now the *Cross-Cultural Psychology Bulletin*) did not last long. After 2 years he relinquished the editorship, passing it along to Yasumasa Tanaka of Japan. The reason for this is that Harry's research, usually involving extensive international collaboration, was expanding. During that period, he was involved with numerous projects involving various facets of what he called subjective culture. These projects culminated in the 1972 publication of *The Analysis of Subjective Culture.* That book, which he coauthored with colleagues from Greece, Japan, and India, is among two or three other books that heralded the beginning of what has become a steady stream of books that in some substantial way focus on interrelationships between the phenomenon of culture and the multifaceted field of psychology. For instance, a book edited by Cronbach and Drenth (1972) was seminal in taking a close look at "mental tests" and what must be done to adapt them for use in other cultures.

The importance of subjective culture to Triandis's career and how he helped conceptualize and analyze it cannot be overstated. An important person in the early stages of his prolific professional development was psycholinguist Charles E. Osgood. Osgood's research on the measurement of meaning was broadly influential (Osgood, May, & Miron, 1975; Osgood, Suci, & Tannenbaum, 1957). Triandis, who went to the University of Illinois largely because of Osgood's pulling power, developed a number of ways to measure norms, values, beliefs, behavioral dispositions, and assorted other behaviors. Without exception, these studies were designed to measure the ways in which humans, because they have been socialized differently, cut up the pie of experience in unique and culture-centered ways. Now, approaching 30 years after the publication of his 1972 book, it appears that, while Triandis's approach was broadly cross-cultural, it was also congenial to the scope and aim of those who identify with cultural psychology. Essentially, the study of subjective culture is the study of how people construct meaning in their specific cultural context.

The Analysis of Subjective Culture was indeed influential. However, it was not until the late 1970s that Harry's efforts became even more central to the growing interest in cross-cultural psychology. Asked by Allyn and Bacon if he would be interested in heading an effort to publish several books in cross-cultural psychology, Harry agreed to look into the matter. By 1977 he had lined up several coeditors and more than 50 authors to prepare the six-volume *Handbook of Cross-Cultural Psychology*. Published in 1980, the *Handbook* became the signal publication event in the area, an event virtually guaranteeing that cross-cultural psychology was to be noticed as an intellectual force. That the second edition of the *Handbook*, with a broadened perspective, was published recently (Berry et al., 1997) is a tribute to Harry's earlier efforts.

As important as his influence was on cross-cultural psychology by way of numerous books and a small mountain of journal articles and other publications, Harry's strongest role has been that of teacher-mentor. During his long career at the University of Illinois, he has contributed substantially to the development of social and cross-cultural psychologists, as well as those in other disciplines such as business, management, and education. His legacy, which will have a multiplying effect on future generations, has many human faces. They include Josephine Naidoo from India (now in Canada), who was Harry's first Ph.D. student; John Adamopoulos and Yoshihisa Kashima, the coeditors of this volume; Harry Hui and Kwok Leung of Hong Kong; and a long and impressive list of active teachers and researchers. Through them, Harry's influence will spread and flourish like the branches of an olive tree from his native Greece. Similarly, collateral influences, such as his research with many collaborators and numerous coauthors, will continue to be felt in virtually all cross-cultural psychology efforts. The past 10 years or so have seen a sharp increase in the number of college and university courses throughout the world that focus on culture as a powerful force that shapes the thought and behavior of all humans. It would be most difficult to organize and teach one of these courses without mentioning Triandis's influence numerous times. It would be impossible to discuss individualism and collectivism, recently of captivating interest to many, without mentioning Harry's numerous contributions to that area of inquiry.

The well-deserved accolades for Harry continue to pile up, and these have been documented elsewhere in this volume. I will close my remarks by saying that I am extremely pleased that this book has been added to the cross-cultural literature, and I am flattered at having been given the honor of writing this foreword. My pleasure is enhanced by the fact that this important contribution to the literature appears in a series of books that John Berry and I coedit. It is a fitting tribute to Harry and adds yet another solid branch to a spreading tree that now has roots throughout the world.

—Walter J. Lonner
Western Washington State University

PREFACE:
A Dedication

A few years ago, a number of psychologists with broad interests in the analysis of culturally based phenomena met for a day of celebration at the University of Illinois, intellectual home of one of the modern pioneers of cross-cultural psychology, Harry C. Triandis.

Harry, ever youthful and vigorous, was staring at the start of another decade of his life—the age of wisdom (or, as some call it unimaginatively, the age of retirement). It was a good time to celebrate his many accomplishments and, above all, his significant contributions to the nascent field of cross-cultural psychology: Harry had pushed as much as anyone against an indifferent and often hostile crowd in psychology for the recognition of the important role of culture in psychological explanation.

Among the celebrants—in body or in spirit—were many former and current students of Harry's, colleagues and research collaborators from around the world, friends, and family. The theme of the day was how much Harry had given to so many people as a teacher and mentor, a scholar, a researcher, a colleague, a friend. Senior cross-cultural psychologists, looking back over their own distinguished careers, could trace the intellectual influence of Harry's work on their own research programs. Perhaps most important, a new generation of cross-cultural researchers could look to theoretical and methodological traditions that Harry had developed as paradigms for further intellectual work.

It was in this context that some of the ideas for the present volume began to take shape. This volume of essays represents some of the work produced by Harry Triandis's colleagues, associates, and students—much of it using variants of his construct of subjective culture—and is meant to honor and celebrate his achievement in the field and at the same time reflect the current state of affairs in the social domain of cross-cultural psychology. The volume is not meant to be exhaustive in its breadth; many important and respected ideas and research programs in cross-cultural social psychology are not included. Rather, this book should be seen as a tribute to the scope and range of Triandis's 40-year love affair with a discipline that has ever so slowly come of age. It is to Harry C. Triandis that we dedicate this book with great affection.

ACKNOWLEDGMENTS

There are many individuals and institutions whose contributions were essential to the success of this project. Above all, we would like to thank Pola Triandis, whose enthusiasm and hard work made it all possible. The Psychology Department at the University of Illinois and its head, Ed Shoben, provided many resources, as did the Psychology Department at Grand Valley State University through its chair, Bob Hendersen. We would like to express our deep appreciation for the many and varied contributions of Walt Lonner, John Berry, Jim Nageotte of Sage, Christine Smith, and Niko Smith Adamopoulos, who arrived at the very start of this project and energized one of us in ways that he had never thought possible. Finally, we would like to thank the authors of the chapters included in this volume for their contributions, patience, and persistence. It is their work that is the real tribute to Harry Triandis.

— John Adamopoulos
—Yoshihisa Kashima

1

INTRODUCTION

Subjective Culture as a Research Tradition

John Adamopoulos
Grand Valley State University

Yoshihisa Kashima
La Trobe University

Harry Triandis's lifelong work constitutes the conceptual core of this volume. Over the past four decades, Triandis systematically and carefully explored the frontiers of culture and psychology. Arguably, his most significant conceptual contribution is the notion of subjective culture. Nearly two decades before psychology "discovered" socially shared cognition (Resnick, Levine, & Teasley, 1991), Triandis, in his 1972 book *The Analysis of Subjective Culture,* defined this notion as "a cultural group's characteristic way of perceiving the man-made [*sic*] part of its environment" (p. 4). More recently, Triandis (1994a) has suggested that subjective culture consists primarily of categories, attitudes, norms, roles, and values, and he has proposed various techniques for their measurement. In short, subjective culture is a conceptual-methodological package that points not only to the psychological concepts we need to emphasize but also to the methods by which we can investigate culture.

An example may help. Suppose we want to examine the subjective culture of U.S. college students. We would look at their beliefs and ideas about many aspects of their lives, like personal relationships, family, and politics. We would also want to know about what they consider appropriate behaviors in a variety of social situations—for example, dating, how to deal with professors, and how to behave toward their parents. In addition, we would want to know about their values, that is, what they consider to be important principles in their lives, such as individual freedom, world at peace, and concern about the natural environment.

One way to understand the notion of subjective culture is to think of categories, attitudes, norms, and values as *causes* of individual behavior. That is, the kinds of ideas people hold, obligations they feel, or values they espouse lead them to behave the way they do. However, it is important to realize that the elements of subjective culture are also phenomena that emerge from individual interactions with the social environment, social relationships, and group activity; in other words, subjective culture is also *caused by* individual behavior.

Honoring Harry Triandis's contribution, this book is founded on the notion of subjective culture. The authors of the chapters characterize it, extend it, and apply it to various problems in different domains of human experience in a variety of cultures. The majority of the chapters (Parts III to V) reflect this effort. Part III (*Elements of Subjective Culture*) shows how diverse elements of subjective culture can be approached, studied, and measured. Part IV (*Group and Interpersonal Processes*) extends this work to interpersonal, intragroup, and intergroup processes. Part V (*Applied Cross-Cultural Psychology*) describes some of the ways in which the analysis of subjective culture can benefit the solution of concrete human problems: training people for successful cross-cultural encounters, family planning, and organizational behavior.

To understand this body of work, it is important to think of it as a research tradition (Lakatos, 1970; Laudan, 1977) and to identify its core characteristics. By a *research tradition*, we mean a heterogeneous set of research activities that is characterized by common underlying theoretical assumptions and compatible methodological approaches. The typical, mainstream psychological approach can be characterized by a theoretical concern with the individual person—for instance, personality dispositions or individual cognitive processes such as memory and decision making. Methodologically, psychologists have developed research strategies that are compatible with this theoretical concern by putting the individual under a microscope. Social psychology has traditionally attempted to extend this theoretical orientation to include within its scope phenomena that involve both individuals and small groups in their social milieu. However, the methodological focus has remained on the individual.

In contrast, research in subjective culture has always had a clear theoretical concern with a large-scale collective or community that shares a culture and a methodological orientation of examining the psychological attributes of the individuals who constitute the collective. Thus, this research tradition expanded substantially the unit of theoretical concern in psychological research (i.e., from the individual or small group to a large collective sharing a common culture), without a corresponding expansion of the methodological focus. To put it simply, the research tradition of subjective culture can be characterized by conceptual collectivism and methodological individualism. We mean by *methodological individualism* the choice of the individual as the unit from which psychological data are collected. Although the same term is used to refer to a wider notion of a metatheoretical choice of the individual as a unit of analysis, our sense here is somewhat more restricted.

The emergence of this research tradition can be best understood from a historical perspective. Triandis and most of his early collaborators had their intellectual roots in the traditional psychological approach that considers the individual as the unit of analysis. In this way, they maximized the chance that they would be heard and have an impact on mainstream psychology by extending its approach to include large-scale collectives. In effect, the notion of subjective culture allowed researchers to describe and explain the collective phenomenon that is culture while maintaining a strong commitment to the individual as the center of theoretical construction in psychology.

Part I (*Reflections on Cross-Cultural Psychology*) represents this research tradition. The chapters, written by senior cross-cultural psychologists and colleagues of Triandis, reflect on culture's influence on individual behavior. Berry attempts to place much of his work on the ecocultural approach and Triandis's work on subjective culture within a unified framework. To the extent that this is possible, it may indicate their common intellectual roots, that is, conceptual collectivism and methodological individualism.

Both chapters in this section emphasize an important theme in cross-cultural psychology, namely, that there are universal attributes that bind all people or that there is unity in diversity. The focus of Berry's chapter is on the underlying conceptual unity that can be found in diverse psychocultural approaches. By contrast, Bond's chapter celebrates and explains the possibility of unity in heterogeneous societies.

The work described in Part I is based on a simple spatial metaphor of individual elements constituting the collective whole. In other words, the relationship between methodological individualism and conceptual collectivism can be thought of as the mapping of individual elements and processes onto a collective phenomenon, and the search for unity in diversity can be thought of as the mapping of the experiences of the many onto the experience of the unified whole.

The chapters of Part II (*Theoretical Orientations in Cross-Cultural Social Psychology*) add to this metaphor a temporal dimension. They represent an attempt to extend the core assumptions of the research tradition of subjective culture. As explained earlier, this tradition expanded the focus on the microprocesses of the individual to the macroprocesses of the collective. The chapters in this section add another important dimension to the research tradition by highlighting the temporality of the culture-mind relation. Feldman's chapter clearly focuses on short-term processes, whereas Adamopoulos's implies very long-term processes. The chapter by Kashima and Kashima reflects a concern with a range of time-dependent phenomena.

Yet another way in which some of the chapters in this section (by Adamopoulos and by Kashima and Kashima) attempt to extend the research tradition of subjective culture is by conceptualizing culture and individual psychology as mutually constitutive. As described earlier, subjective culture is conceptualized as both the cause and the effect of individual behavior. This implies that the individual is separable from culture, a causal agent who may influence or be influenced by culture. Instead, the work presented in these chapters takes the general view that culture and the individual are indistinguishable and constitutive of each other, and they should be studied not as distinct phenomena but as constructs with shared meaning.

The chapters in this volume can be thought of as variations on a theme inspired by the work of Harry Triandis. This theme, substantially expanded and modified over several decades, still constitutes a significant perspective in cross-cultural psychology and lies at the core of new research programs around the world that promise to make important contributions to the study of what it means to be human.

PART I

REFLECTIONS ON CROSS-CULTURAL PSYCHOLOGY

In the first chapter of this section, Berry presents a broad framework within which we can examine the current psychological research traditions on culture. His analysis not only reveals the diversity of the current field but also points to its underlying unity by showing that competing orientations can be understood within his framework.

Questions to keep in mind while reading Berry's chapter are as follows:

- What is Berry's framework?
- Are the three dimensions Berry outlines the most appropriate dimensions on which to classify various research traditions in culture and psychology?
- Berry's framework consists of continuous dimensions, as opposed to discrete categories. To what extent does this contribute to a more insightful analysis?

Bond's chapter advocates the significance of seeking to establish unity in a multi-cultural society. The diversity in multiculturalism is often considered to be a negative force that threatens to destroy the social fabric. However, he suggests that it is possible and desirable to find ways in which to improve social harmony.

Questions to keep in mind while reading Bond's chapter are as follows:

- Bond's chapter presents a very clear value orientation in studying the relationship between culture and psychology. Is the value-laden nature of his perspective a problem?
- What is the value orientation that he advocates? What are the strategies that he suggests we should employ?
- How effective do you think these strategies are in promoting a harmonious multicultural society?

2

ON THE UNITY OF THE FIELD
OF CULTURE AND PSYCHOLOGY

John W. Berry
Queen's University

This celebration of Harry Triandis's contributions to the field offers an opportunity to take stock of how the study of human behavior in cultural context has evolved over the past 30 years. Note that I have not given a name to "the field" but prefer to focus on the substance of what we are interested in ("behavior in cultural context"). Although not dismissing the name issue (see Dasen, 1993; Diaz-Guerrero, 1993; Krewer & Jahoda, 1993; Lonner, 1992; Poortinga & Van de Vijver, 1994; Segall, 1993), I believe that it may be more fruitful to explore the space between (and overlapping) psychology and anthropology with an "outlook that takes culture seriously" (Dasen & Jahoda, 1986, p. 143). Because I have previously used many and various names, I feel no need to be rigid: I began teaching a course called "cultural psychology" in 1970, gave my International Association for Cross-Cultural Psychology presidential address (Berry, 1985) on "cultural and ethnic psychology," and have participated in associations, textbooks, and handbooks all with the term "cross-cultural" attached to them.

My core position is that, in studying behavior, one has to be "cultural" before being "cross," but by remaining only "cultural," one loses out on the possibility of attaining generalizations about what is fundamentally (pan-) human. In my view, both of these approaches are necessary; neither is sufficient by itself.

In my first articulation of this position (Berry, 1969; Berry & Dasen, 1974), the field was seen as a sequenced set of steps: *imposed etic, emic,* and *derived etic.* These corresponded to the three goals of "transporting and testing" extant psychological knowledge (mainly from the West to other cultural groups), "exploring and discovering" psychological phenomena in these other cultures (essentially from the indigenous point of view), and finally "integrating and generating" findings and insights from the first two activities to achieve a psychology that is "universal" (see below).

Such a "universal" perspective, though currently being challenged by some scholars, has a long history not only in Western thought (Jahoda, 1992) but also in Chinese and Indian texts. In the *San Zi Jing* and the *Vedas*, the following couplets are fundamental:

> *Basic human nature is similar at birth;*
> *Different habits (customs) make us seem remote (different).*

> *Reality is one;*
> *But it is expressed in different forms.*

> *Truth is one;*
> *But scholars interpret it in diverse ways.*

It might be appropriate to note here that the *Vedas* also claims that "the genius lies in seeing the unity"!

The fundamental question for me, then, is not what little corners can we carve out and name but what are the overarching dimensions and unifying issues for "the field"? To take culture seriously into account when understanding human behavior is a value we all share; we diverge primarily with respect to *how* and *where* we do this. What follows is an attempt to define the culture-behavior space in which we all work, using three *dimensions* of variation in contemporary discussion of three underlying *issues*. The goal of this exercise is to exhibit our similarities, and the strategy is to be inclusive and eclectic.

ISSUES

Within and Across

Quite early on, it was evident that there are conceptual and methodological problems to be faced when studying human behavior across cultures (Berry, 1969; Frijda & Jahoda, 1966). A key issue lies in the common observation that general psychology is both "culture blind" and "culture bound." That is, general psychology had ignored culture as a possible influence on human behavior, and, furthermore, general psychology had taken little account of theories or data from cultures other than Euro-American. The solution to these problems was twofold: to conceptualize and study culture as an important context for human psychological development (a "cultural" approach) and to engage in comparative ("cross-cultural") studies of the influence of features of various cultures on human development and behavior.

The *emic-etic* distinction was prominent in these early writings. Although it too had a "naming" problem, the consensus was that *both* perspectives were necessary to the developing field. Local knowledge and interpretations (the *emic* approach) were essential, but more than one was required to relate variations in cultural context to variations in behavior (the *etic* approach); this joint perspective was advocated from the beginning by Pike (1967). These two notions became elaborated. First was the notion of *imposed etic* (Berry, 1969), which served as the starting point for comparative research, because it was obvious that all psychologists necessarily carry their own culturally based perspectives with them when studying other cultures; these perspectives were initial sources of bias (usually Euro-American), to be confronted and reduced as work progressed in the other culture(s). Second was the *emic* exploration of psychological phenomena and their understanding in local cultural terms; this provided the important indigenous culturally based meanings that were most likely missed when making the initial *imposed-etic* approach to psychological phenomena in various cultures. Third was the *derived-etic* approach, which might possibly be discerned following extensive use of *emic* approaches in a number of cultures; it was expected that some similarities in psychological phenomena might be derived by the comparative examination of behavior in various cultures. If so, then psychological universals (even a universal psychology) might emerge.

These three concepts, in turn, gave rise to three goals of cross-cultural psychology (Berry & Dasen, 1974): to *transport and test* current psychological knowledge and perspectives by using them in other cultures; to *explore and discover* new aspects of the phenomenon being studied in local cultural terms; and to *integrate* what has been learned from these first two approaches to generate a more nearly universal psychology, one that has pan-human validity. The existence of *universals* in other disciplines (e.g., biology, linguistics, sociology, and anthropology) provided some basis for the assumption that we would be able to work our way through to this third goal with some success.

Finally, these three goals have become identified with three theoretical orientations in cross-cultural psychology: *absolutism, relativism,* and *universalism* (Berry, Poortinga, Segall, & Dasen, 1992). The *absolutist* position is one that assumes that human phenomena are basically the same (qualitatively) in all cultures: "Honesty" is "honesty" and "depression" is "depression," no matter where one observes it. From the absolutist perspective, culture is thought to play little or no role in either the meaning or display of human characteristics. Assessments of such characteristics are made using standard instruments (perhaps with linguistic translation), and interpretations are made easily, without alternative culturally based views taken into account. This orientation resembles the *imposed-etic* approach. It was also characteristic of the early work that was undertaken by those who called themselves "cross-cultural" psychologists. Despite having moved beyond this initial orientation, cross-cultural psychology is still stereotyped and unfairly criticized for being in this earlier research mode.

In sharp contrast, the *relativist* approach assumes that all human behavior is culturally patterned. It seeks to avoid ethnocentrism by trying to understand people "in their own terms." Explanations of human diversity are sought in the cultural context in which people have developed. Assessments are typically carried out employing the values and meanings that a cultural group gives to a phenomenon. Comparisons are judged to be problematic and ethnocentric and are thus virtually never made. This orientation resembles the *emic* approach. It also resembles the approach currently espoused by those calling themselves "cultural" psychologists, although many do make comparisons (see Miller, 1997).

A third perspective, one that lies somewhere between the first two positions, is that of *universalism*. Universalism assumes that basic human characteristics are common to all members of the species (i.e., constituting a set of psychological givens) and that culture influences the development and display of them (i.e., culture brings about different variations on these underlying themes). Assessments are based on the presumed underlying process, but measures are developed in culturally meaningful versions. Comparisons are made cautiously, employing a wide variety of methodological principles and safeguards, whereas interpretations of similarities and differences are attempted that take alternative culturally based meanings into account (see Van de Vijver & Leung, 1997). This orientation resembles the *derived-etic* approach. It is characteristic of much of contemporary "cross-cultural" psychology, and it is also advocated by some "cultural" psychologists (e.g., Greenfield, 1997). It thus serves as a communal basis for convergence (see Lonner & Adamopoulos, 1997; Poortinga, 1997).

Different approaches can be distinguished according to their orientation to this issue. Though few today advocate a strictly absolutist/imposed-etic view, the relativist/emic position has given rise to numerous approaches: "ethnopsychology" (Diaz-Guerrero, 1975), "societal psychology" (Berry, 1983), "indigenous psychology" (Enriquez, 1990; Kim & Berry, 1993; Sinha, 1997), and, to some extent, "cultural psychology" (Shweder & Sullivan, 1993). And the derived-etic view has given rise to a "universalist psychology" (Berry et al., 1992). A mutual compatibility between the emic and derived-etic positions has been noted by many; for example, Berry et al. (1992, p. 384) and Berry and Kim (1993) have claimed that indigenous psychologies, while valuable in their own right, serve an equally important function as useful steps on the way to achieving a universal psychology.

To summarize this first issue, I believe that, from the beginning, there has been widespread acceptance by most cross-cultural psychologists of the necessity for *both* the *within* and *across* approaches to understanding relationships between cultural context and human experience and behavior. To rephrase my opening comment on this issue, it is not possible to be "cross-cultural" without first being "cultural," but to be only "cultural" (or to pretend that it is possible to be so) eliminates the attainment of general principles to which all sciences aspire.

Culture Contact

Equally early on, there was a recognition that studies in the general domain of culture and behavior had to take into account the fact that cultures are not static but change for a variety of reasons (Berry, 1980b). One reason is that when cultures come into contact with each other, the phenomenon of *acculturation* occurs. This process involves changes in both *group* or *collective* phenomena (e.g., language, politics, religion, work, schooling, and social relationships) and *psychological* phenomena (e.g., identity, beliefs, values, attitudes, and abilities). A good deal of early cross-cultural psychological work took place by comparing peoples who were not in contact with each other; indeed, this was a methodological necessity for comparisons requiring independence of cases. However, some early psychological work also took place in situations of intercultural encounters, often as a result of colonization, migration, or the continuation of culturally distinct communities living side by side in plural societies (e.g., Taft, 1977). This contact dimension was also identified by Taft (1974) as an essential part of the field.

Over the years, many cross-cultural psychologists have adopted the view that *both* kinds of work are legitimate and important ways of understanding human behavior as it is influenced by the cultural context in which it occurs (Berry, 1985). For example, in my own early work, samples were drawn from those that were relatively "traditional" cultural settings (minimally influenced by Euro-American culture) and from those that were "transitional" (in a process of change as a result of substantial Euro-American contact). Later, my "ecocultural framework" (Berry, 1976) explicitly included two major exogenous variables: *ecology* and *acculturation*. The former identified sources of cultural and psychological variation as a collective and individual adaptation to habitat; the latter sought such explanation for psychological variations in the historical and contemporary influences stemming from contact with other cultures. One major difference between these two lines of influence is that psychological phenomena during contact may be more difficult to understand and interpret than in noncontact situations because there are at least two sources of cultural influences; hence, *comparative* studies may be even more important here to tease out the relative cultural contributions to psychological phenomena (Berry, Kim, Minde, & Mok, 1987). A second major difference is that opportunities to create new cultural forms may be greater during the process of acculturation.

This interest in psychological phenomena resulting from culture contact has given rise to the suggestion that there could be an "ethnic psychology" or a "psychology of acculturation" concerned primarily with group and psychological acculturation phenomena (e.g., Berry, 1985; Berry & Annis, 1988). Another field to emerge has been that of "psychologie interculturelle," mainly in the French-language tradition (e.g., Clanet, 1990; Retschitzky, Bossel-Lagos, & Dasen, 1989). As intercultural contacts increase, this area of psychology will almost certainly grow in importance.

Culture as Given or Created

Alongside these changes in psychology has been a virtual revolution in anthropology's conception of "culture." Earlier conceptions of culture included the views that culture was "out there," to be studied, observed, and described; culture was a shared way of life of a group of socially interacting people; and culture was transmitted from generation to generation by the processes of enculturation and socialization. That is, culture was viewed as a "given" that preceded in time the life of any individual member (see Munroe & Munroe, 1997).

This long-standing view of culture has had a major influence on thinking in cross-cultural psychology. The main task was to understand how the established culture *influenced* the psychological development of individuals and *guided* their day-to-day behaviors. In recent years, along with the emergence of more cognitive approaches in many branches of psychology, individuals have come to be viewed not as mere pawns or victims of their cultures but as cognizers, appraisers, and interpreters of them. Thus, different individuals are now widely considered to experience different aspects of their culture, and in different ways. One example of this more cognitive orientation is in the framework for analyses of cultural contexts (Berry, 1980a) in which more subjective and individual "experiential" and "situational" contexts were distinguished from more objective and shared "ecological" and "cultural" contexts as factors influencing human behavior.

In sharp contrast to this established perspective on the nature of culture is one advanced by those adopting a "social construction" perspective (Misra & Gergen, 1993). From this perspective, culture is not something that is given but is being interpreted and created daily through interactions between individuals and their social surroundings. This view is one espoused by those identifying with "cultural psychology," which has been defined as "a designation for the comparative study of the way culture and psyche make up each other" (Shweder & Sullivan, 1993, p. 498).

This core idea, however, has been a part of the field for some time. There are numerous examples of interactions between context and person (e.g., feedback relationships in the ecocultural framework) and of reaction to contact (as one form of adaptation associated with acculturation) in the cross-cultural approach (e.g., Berry, 1976). This reciprocal relationship between person and culture, leading to the modification and creation of new cultural forms as a result of acculturation, has been of long-standing interest in the field and is not exclusive to those calling themselves "cultural" psychologists (Segall, 1993).

DIMENSIONS

Up until now in the literature, these three issues have been usually presented in polarized form: emic versus etic; traditional versus acculturated; culture as given versus culture as created. However, my description has tried to present them as points on underlying dimensions and as points that possess legitimacy. To me, it is evident that emic and etic approaches are part of a sequence, possibly a continuous circle of research activity (as it was for Pike, 1967). It is equally evident that no societies are untouched by acculturative influence, and none is so strongly acculturated that nothing is left of its original culture. Finally, it is clear to me that individuals are born into some extant set of social arrangements and they adopt most of them, but it is also clear to me that individuals are in constant interaction with their cultural surroundings, a process that results in both psychological and cultural changes.

POSITIONING

My firmly held view is that there can and should be a coherent and integrated approach to the study of relationships between human behavior and culture. I believe that there is a *common space* within which we all can work and that it really does not matter what this space is called. As outlined earlier, this space has three dimensions, based on the three issues. Different people, with somewhat different interests and at different times in their careers, explore, advocate, and emphasize different sectors of this space, but I contend that it is a unitary space.

During the course of this discussion, a number of names of approaches have been noted. Where might they be placed in this three-dimensional space? Figure 2.1 depicts this space, with the three issues defining the dimensions. The first dimension (comparative perspective) incorporates the sequence from absolutist/imposed-etic to relativist/emic to universalist/derived-etic variation; the second (acculturation) depicts the noncontact to contact variation; and the third shows the distinction between culture-as-given to the culture-as-created. Within this three-dimensional space are located the various approaches.

The absolutist/imposed-etic approach is rarely advocated now by researchers interested in the relationships between culture and behavior. However, it remains a dominant point of view in Western Academic Scientific Psychology (the "WASP" approach) and is also much in use among psychologists who work with cultural groups in plural populations (the "minority" approach); in both approaches, there is little interest in the culture of the groups involved. More commonly accepted in the field are the relativist/emic and universalist/derived-etic approaches. In the former are all those that emphasize the need to understand human behavior in local cultural context but not (at least initially) in comparison with others; these include the ethnopsychology, indigenous psychology, societal psychology, and cultural psychology approaches in noncontact situations and the ethnic psychology approach in culture-contact situations. At the derived-etic end of the dimension are the universal psychology approach in the noncontact area and the acculturation psychology and intercultural psychology approaches in the contact situation.

With respect to the third dimension, once again, conceptions of culture are irrelevant to the WASP and minority approaches. But for the relativist/emic and universalist/derived-etic positions, there are some important variations. Cultural psychology is most clearly advocating the view that culture is created rather than a given. Those concerned with psychological phenomena in contact situations are intermediate on the dimension (ethnic and acculturation psychologies) or more toward the created end (in the case of intercultural psychology). More toward the other end of the dimension (culture as given) are those that are rooted in, and advocate the importance of, a definable cultural tradition (ethnopsychology, societal psychology, and indigenous psychology) and that seek to explain psychological phenomena in terms of those traditions. Finally, universal psychology occupies a position closest to the culture-as-given end of the dimension. This placement is because a universal psychology operates at a fairly high level of abstraction and generalization, somewhat removed from the finer details of the day-to-day context of behavior.

CONCLUSIONS

Much has been made recently of relatively small differences in approaches to the study of relationships between culture and behavior. I believe that the main goal of the field is to convince general psychology that culture is an important contributor to the

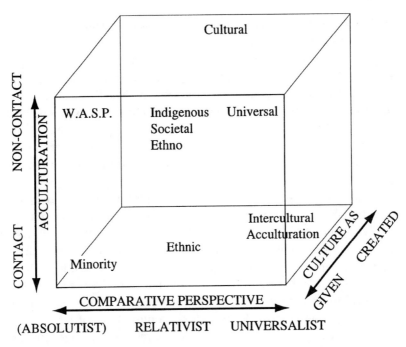

Figure 2.1. Common Space for Understanding Relationships Between Culture and Behavior

development of human behavior and is essential to our understanding and study of it. I also believe that our combined efforts should be directed toward achieving this goal, rather than toward establishing claims of the correctness of one particular orientation. I have tried to show that we all share common interests and that differences are matters of emphasis on common dimensions rather than matters of oppositions. There is much work to be done, both in the approaches that are already identified and in the sectors of the space that have so far been unclaimed. My fear is that if our internal relations are overly conflictual, our external relations (with a culture-blind psychology) will be neglected, and the role of culture will remain marginal to psychology as a whole.

Important steps toward achieving unity in the field have been undertaken by Harry Triandis, in both his leadership roles and his own scholarship. It is probably true to say that the editing of the first edition of the *Handbook of Cross-Cultural Psychology* (Triandis et al., 1980) was the most important factor in *consolidating* the field. Earlier activities, such as the founding of the International Association for Cross-Cultural Psychology (of which he was an inaugural member and early president) and of the *Journal of Cross-Cultural Psychology*, had served as *founding* activities, but the *Handbook* enterprise really established the field as a coherent body of knowledge.

In his research and writing, Harry Triandis has attended to all three dimensions of the field (as portrayed in Figure 2.1). In his development and use of the concept of *subjective culture* (Triandis, 1972), Harry has clearly distinguished between what is inside people's heads (the subjective representation of their culture) and what resides externally as part of social structures and cultural practices (objective culture). He has also clearly sought to establish relationships between subjective culture and features of the cultural context (Triandis, 1994a), using comparisons to gain access to variations in both sets of phenomena. These comparisons have made extensive use of both international and intranational cultural variation, representing both the noncontact and contact approaches to the field. And because he clearly thought of individuals as cognizers and interpreters of the day-to-day context in which they live, Harry can also be said to have partially bridged the culture-as-given/culture-as-created dimension. Such inclusive and generous perspectives are Harry's hallmark, and the field has been much enriched by it.

3

UNITY IN DIVERSITY

Orientations and Strategies for Building a Harmonious, Multicultural Society

Michael Harris Bond
Chinese University of Hong Kong

My objective is none other than the betterment of the world and the tranquility of its peoples. The well-being of mankind, its peace and security are unattainable unless and until its unity is firmly established.

—Baha'u'llah

In discussing the important emergence of global social change organizations, Cooperrider and Pasmore (1991) observed, "So much of what is being said and done in our journals is beside the point, unrelated to the crucial questions of human relationships in a global era of unprecedented change" (p. 771). The emergence of new political states and their assertions of a distinctive identity is one manifestation of this epochal ferment (Naisbitt & Aburdene, 1990, chap. 4). Many such states are young and enterprising enough to consider carefully the vision that will guide their nation building and channel their selection of institutions, laws, and norms accordingly.

AUTHOR'S NOTE: An earlier version of this chapter appeared in *Trames* (Estonia). It is reprinted here with permission of the publisher. I wish to express my appreciation to the following colleagues who provided thoughtful feedback on the earlier version of this chapter: Steven Burgess, Seena Fazel, James Liu, Walter Stephan, and Harry Triandis.

This chapter is offered in light of Cooperrider and Pasmore's (1991) challenge to be relevant, recent world developments, and the conviction that planned change is possible. I am a social psychologist. I have read widely in culture and cross-cultural interaction to help produce a recent text (Smith & Bond, 1998) and have long held a keen interest in humane forms of association. These two parts of my personal history have led me to ask how the yield from our discipline's labors can be used to design societies that are compatible with the pressures and opportunities provided by the 21st century.

In assuming this novel task, I will step outside my typical stance of purported objectivity and value-free analysis. I share what Cooperrider and Pasmore (1991) identified as "something of a 'hidden hunger' among social theorists from throughout the world to make their lives and their work count, and count affirmatively, as it relates to the questions of survival and human dignity in our time" (p. 779). Of course, many people share this hope for their labors in this life. Perhaps as social scientists, however, we are uniquely trained "to put idealism on empirical footing and to construct a science whose constructive mandate is to become a generative-theoretical partner with evolution itself, in the service of promoting the widest good and, ultimately, in the service of life" (Cooperrider & Pasmore, 1991, p. 780). Certainly, we can address questions about the probable consequences of the value stances and procedures, or what I have called "orientations and strategies," adopted by people, groups, organizations, and nations.

Awareness of these consequences can then be used to inform the consultation about what kind of social forms we wish to govern ourselves by as we structure our future. Our social scientific knowledge of persuasion techniques may even be used to ensure that awareness of these consequences figures in the consultation. Many other parties will be involved in this ongoing dialogue, and it would be naive and presumptuous to expect that the inputs of our professional community will be specially privileged. Nonetheless, these consultations, in whatever forms they occur, must take the psychological, social, institutional, and national consequences of changes into account. And in these areas of intellectual discourse, we are plying our trade.

In the following essay, I will try to articulate the considerations that I judge important to make in designing a harmonious, multicultural society. I will "render unto Caesar what is Caesar's" by specifying and defending the end state toward which I am hoping nations move and the procedures for attaining that end state, but I will "render unto God what is God's" by daring to specify and defend that end state in the first place.

A HUMANE HARMONY

So powerful is the light of unity that it can illuminate the whole world.

—Baha'u'llah

What is my vision of an ideal state, particularly now as our planet approaches the millennium? Other social scientists have undertaken the daunting task of answering this question (e.g., Naroll, 1983), and I claim no authority in the validity of my assertions beyond the fact that I have reached these conclusions in good faith and offer them up for consultation.

I would begin with the medical dictum *"Primum, non nocere."* For present purposes, that injunction implies that an ideal state is one in which any activity destructive to human life is minimized. At the individual level, injurious behaviors, ranging from taking hard drugs to committing suicide, are minimized; life expectancy is at a maximum. At the group level, norms are shared, ensuring that individual inputs to group life will be encouraged and attended to, even if not adopted; that process of adoption will not entail the exclusion of deviates. At the intergroup level, identifiable groups with different ideologies and agendas will be accommodated within the limits set by the laws necessary to preserve the fabric of society; systematic denial of access to resources will not be mandated or tolerated, nor will any form of genocide be practiced or racism be institutionalized. At the societal level, institutions such as the military and mechanisms such as international treaties and economic controls are in place and maintained to prevent the annexing of one nation by another.

My basic concern is that society not embed the individual within a dangerous social niche in which individual energies are fully deployed in preventing one's destruction and in merely surviving. One can readily think of contemporary societies in which a citizen's patrimony entails precisely such a consuming preoccupation. It is in this spirit that I would subscribe to the Russian adage that "a bad peace is better than a good war."

But my vision for the ideal state has an obverse, that is, a society that fosters and promotes distinctive, individual development while maintaining its own integrity and nurturing the conditions for social synergy. This broad mandate is best encapsulated in the concept of harmony. An essential component of any viable harmony is the integrity and distinctiveness of the constituent elements that compose the complex unit of which they are a part. Unification does not require homogenization or uniformity. Just as effective cooking preserves the distinctive flavors, textures, colors, and aromas of the ingredients used, so, too, the society I envision must remain responsive to the concerns, the needs, and the aspirations of its individual members, families, groups, and institutions.

I do not believe that such harmony presupposes or requires sameness in the citizens of a society:

> Where harmony is fecund, sameness is barren. Things accommodating each other on equal terms is called blending in harmony, and in so doing they are able to flourish and grow, and other things are drawn to them. But when same is added to same, once it is used up, there is no more. . . . There is no music in a single note, no decoration in a single item, no relish in a single taste. (*Discourses of the States*, China, 4th century B.C.)

We are each uniquely endowed, genetically and by socialization. We later distinguish ourselves further from one another by the acquisition of character and skills and knowledge. Society must then be ordered in such a way as to protect and use those differences to benefit both its members and itself. To attain such a harmony-engendering state of affairs, the resulting differences among citizens must be believed to arise from this fundamental logic surrounding individual abilities and opportunities:

An ideal unity in a state is all about equal life chances, about standardizing the life course to the point where people, despite their inescapable genetic and historical differences, perceive themselves as mastering the social order to the extent that resulting differences can be explained by individual choices or chance rather than attributed to external, social-structural causes. (Borneman, 1993, p. 315)

Each person will then be released to find his or her place within the ambient social order. A natural unity will thereby be fostered. "Indeed, it is precisely an inhering diversity that distinguishes unity from homogeneity or uniformity" (Baha'i International Community, 1995, p. 4). If this ordering is successfully achieved, I believe that unimagined human and social benefits will follow. For me, this vision of natural harmony and its shimmering promise is graphically illustrated in Escher's inspiring print *Verbum*.

Multiculturalism

Be anxiously concerned with the needs of the age ye live in, and center your deliberations on its exigencies and requirements.

—Baha'u'llah

Almost all contemporary nations are de facto multicultural. Indeed, this was probably the state of affairs historically for many countries as well. Economic, political, educational, and cultural migration, in both the past and the present, combined with arbitrary, geographic border drawing have made them so. However, the size, frequency, and visibility of contemporary migrant movements make the problems multiculturalism poses for host countries especially acute now (Weiner, 1995).

A concomitant development is the widespread interest in, and commitment to, multiculturalism. As defined by Fowers and Richardson (1996), "Multiculturalism is a social-intellectual movement that promotes the value of diversity as a core principle and insists that all cultural groups be treated with respect and as equals" (p. 609). These authors maintain that multiculturalism is, "at its core, a moral movement that is intended to enhance the dignity, rights, and recognized worth of marginalized groups" (p. 609). As such, they locate the movement squarely within "the moral and political traditions of Euro-American civilization" (p. 611).

Clearly, the proponents of multiculturalism are motivated by a liberal idealism that extends ideas "of individual uniqueness to cultural groups" (Fowers & Richardson, 1996, p. 612). This idealism is fueled by an empathetic response to the suffering of certain groups, an empathy that is sustained by a worldview espousing the ideology that "within the four seas, all men are brothers" (Confucius, *The Analects*).

There is no question in my mind that many groups, culturally and otherwise distinct, have been savagely mistreated. The Algerian and Rwandan and the Cambodian and Serbian situations come most recently to mind. The heart shivers before such atrocities. As Berger (1969) put it, "There are certain deeds that cry out to heaven. And it is this monstrosity that seems to compel even people normally or professionally given to such perspectives to suspend relativizations" (p. 85). These acts would be rejected almost universally, and they hardly require a Euro-American cultural legacy to do so; I do not believe that one must subscribe to Euro-American values to be a multiculturalist.

The cultural issue for multiculturalism is where a society positions itself on the universal value dimensions of conformity versus self-direction and hierarchy versus egalitarianism (Schwartz, 1992, 1994b). These outcomes are very much culturally shaped. Pressures for complete conformity will homogenize differences or lead to elimination of those who champion those differences; excessive self-direction undercuts the sociality necessary for a society to remain viable. The achievement of complete egalitarianism will eliminate group differences with respect to power but run counter to equity in resource distribution; rigid hierarchical structuring of society results in manifest injustices and cannot survive in a democratizing world.

Outside of these extremes, it seems to me that a harmonious multicultural society may be developed. But what kind of harmony? "God," Mozart is alleged to have asserted, "lives in the details." So, I next look at the key orientations and strategy issues whose addressing will play a key role in determining the viability of a society's solution to the multicultural challenge.

ORIENTATIONS AND STRATEGIES

It is incumbent upon every man of insight and understanding to strive to translate that which hath been written into reality and action.

—Baha'u'llah

I will approach this task as a social psychologist. This avenue gives me a narrow focus on the individual but, as we shall soon realize, must by necessity come to include the broad canvas of that individual's social world. The individual actor is the repository of the orientations I will discuss and the enactor of the strategies I will propose. However, "No man is an island, entire unto itself," to quote Donne. So, the ambient norms, traditions, and laws of the families, groups, organizations, and nation where that individual functions will potentate, sustain, and channel those orientations.

Orientations

Regard ye not one another as strangers.
Ye are the fruits of one tree and the leaves of one branch.

—Baha'u'llah

By orientations, I am referring to individual dispositions found in attitudes, stereotypes, emotions, beliefs, values, and features of personality. Certain of these orientations conduce toward the harmonious, multicultural society I described earlier; others counteract such a development.

One concern in making this selection is the problem of a criterion. Our goal is to predict those interpersonal behaviors that unite or divide persons and groups. Psychologists have generally been more adept at designing self-report measures of harmonizing or divisive orientations than they have been at validating them against the actual behaviors of interest. I will thus exercise my own judgment in selecting for discussion those few orientations, such as Altemeyer's (1981) right-wing authoritarianism, that have been validated against such outcomes and those, such as Leung and Bond's (1998) belief syndrome of social cynicism, that hold such promise.

Divisive Orientations

Any orientation that supports separation from and avoidance or isolation and suppression of others because of their ethnicity, national origin, language, color, or disability is divisive. So attitude complexes like ethnocentrism (Brewer & Campbell, 1976), most defensibly measured by Altemeyer's (1981) scale of right-wing authoritarianism, create such barriers (see, e.g., Peterson, Doty, & Winter, 1993). So, too, does nationalism, as opposed to patriotism (Feshbach, 1987).

Social dominance orientation (SDO; Sidanius, 1993) is an attitude syndrome that legitimizes the ranking of groups within a society and predicts higher degrees of ethnic prejudice in the national ethnic hierarchy in the United States (Pratto, Sidanius, Stallworth, & Malle, 1994) and in a number of cultures (Pratto, Liu, et al., 1996). SDO is also strongly correlated with nationalism across a number of American samples (Pratto et al., 1994).

Also divisive are stereotypes, packages of beliefs about out-groups and their members that characterize their personality as malevolent, especially when such negative evaluations are not counterbalanced by positive assessments on other dimensions, such as competence (see Gudykunst & Bond, 1997, pp. 129-131, for elaboration). Beliefs about the values held by members of other groups are also predictive of negative out-group sentiment (Schwartz, Struch, & Bilsky, 1990). Low presumed endorsement of Schwartz's (1992) value domains of universalism and benevolence seem especially important in this respect (Bond & Mak, 1996). In fact, stereotypes about out-group member values seem relatively more powerful than stereotypes about character in predicting negative prejudice (Esses, Haddock, & Zanna, 1993). This prejudice, though, is more likely to be translated into discriminatory actions by those high in right-wing authoritarianism (Haddock, Zanna, & Esses, 1993).

Specific stereotypic beliefs about particular out-groups may be decisive in generating prejudice toward them and their members. Beliefs that certain other groups are antagonistic to "our" group's way of life (the "symbolic beliefs" of Esses et al., 1993) are strong predictors of prejudice. So, too, I expect, are beliefs about historical episodes of unjust behavior by certain groups toward one's own group. These beliefs form important components of what Staub (1988) has identified as "ideologies of antagonism." These beliefs color attributions about current behavior, which then justify counterattack at the group level just as they do at the interpersonal level (Felson, 1978). Such beliefs are unlikely to arise out of personal experience but, instead, are transmitted through group lore, media portrayals, educational curricula, and other indirect means.

Emotions become associated with various out-groups as a result of historical alliances and hostilities, portrayals in educational curricula and the media, relative economic status, and personal experiences interacting with their members. When these emotions are negative, such as envy, fear, or anger, they predict negative prejudice (Dijker, 1987) over and above that predicted by stereotypic cognitions about the group (Stephan, Ageyev, Coates-Shrider, Stephan, & Abalakina, 1994). Fear, in particular, may drive the belief that out-groups are hostile toward one's own group, thereby promoting anticipatory aggression (Stephan & Stephan, 1985).

Beliefs are personal understandings about how the social, material, and spiritual worlds operate. For example, those who subscribe to a just world belief maintain that rewards are fairly distributed in this world. One consequence of such a general belief is that one assumes that those with unfortunate outcomes deserve what they receive (Lerner, 1980). Such a belief structure can readily function to support the status quo of a society's economic and political hierarchy or caste system (Staub, 1989). Similarly, Altemeyer (1988) asserts that a belief in humankind's genetic predisposition to violence promotes out-group hostility, because people so predisposed will be inclined to construe the intentions and actions of out-groups and their members as hostile (see also "Seville Statement on Violence," 1994).

Leung and Bond (1998) have collected a wealth of such beliefs operative in Chinese culture through interviews and surveys of literature, proverbs, and media reports. They combined these with those found in the psychological literature (e.g., Lerner's just-world belief scale) and administered them to a representative sample of Hong Kong persons. They grouped these beliefs into five dimensions through factor analysis. One of these groupings, reward for application, bears a striking resemblance to the just-world ideology mentioned above. Another, social cynicism, refers to beliefs that the powerful exploit the weak and that kindheartedness is socially ineffective. Both of these belief complexes appear to support social hierarchy and the status quo. So it is probable that these belief syndromes will be shown to legitimize group-based differences in access to material and social resources.

A person's values are yet another type of personal orientation that has been linked to prejudicial reactions toward members of other groups. Feather (1980) found that presumed overall value similarity between one's own group and another was associated with greater willingness to associate with out-group members. Bond (1988) identified a pan-cultural value factor from the Chinese Value Survey that contrasted the values of tolerance, harmony, and noncompetitiveness against respect for tradition and a sense of cultural superiority. Average individual scores on this dimension of social integration versus cultural inwardness varied across cultural groups and probably relate to stronger endorsements of prejudice and in-group favoritism. Stronger identifications with one's collective are linked to nationalism and in-group defensive reactions to criticism (Kowalski & Wolfe, 1994). This result seems consistent with findings that people who are strongly identified with their social group respond to threats to their group identity by derogating the out-group (e.g., Branscombe & Wann, 1994).

Finally, basic personality appears to be related to prejudice. If one accepts the Big Five as the fundamental dimensions of personality variation (Digman, 1990), then evidence shows that a person's endorsement of openness to experience is negatively and strongly linked to measures of prejudice, in particular, and political conservativism in general (Trapnell, 1994). Interestingly, the facet of openness most strongly linked to the measure of prejudice used, right-wing authoritarianism, was openness to values.

Personality considered at such a broad level as that of the Big Five may subsume some of the orientations mentioned above. So, the Big Five are related to the endorsement of certain value domains (e.g., Luk & Bond, 1993), although not apparently to the general belief complexes tapped by Leung and Bond (1998) in Hong Kong. As of yet, little work has been done by social psychologists to relate stereotyping of out-groups to personality dispositions. Integrative work of this sort would be most welcome, as prejudicial reactions may derive from common sources, variously labeled as attitudes, values, or beliefs.

One encouraging attempt at integration comes from Hagan, Rippl, Boehnke, and Merkens (1998). They argue that right-wing extremism arises from "near-term, group-linked interests of individuals in their own well-being, ascendancy or domination" (abstract). Focusing on the competitive logic of market-driven forces, they identify a constellation of four social-psychological factors—social comparison, individualism, preoccupation with material success, and the acceptance of social inequality. "These dimensions coalesce into a higher order, latent subterranean construct we call hierarchic self-interest" (abstract). These various personal orientations fuse in predisposed individuals to "accentuate, exaggerate, and dangerously distort the fundamental tenet of stratified market societies" (p. 3).

Hagan et al. (1998) show that hierarchic self-interest predicts the endorsement of extremist attitudes toward outsiders in both the former East and West Germanys, accounting for higher extremism both in males compared with females and in the former East Germany compared with the former West Germany. The value of this exemplary study lies in its integration of themes relating broadly to personality and driving the resurgence of political extremism.

Another integration uses the concept of threat, arguing that prejudice against other groups develops out of perceptions that these groups and their members pose a danger to oneself and one's group. "Integrated threat theory" (Stephan, Ybarra, & Bachman, 1998; Stephan, Ybarra, Martinez, Schwartzwald, & Tur-Kaspa, in press) identifies threat as arising from "symbolic threats based on value differences between groups, realistic threats to the power, resources and well-being of the in-group, anxiety concerning social interaction with outgroup members, and feelings of threat arising from negative stereotypes of the outgroup" (Stephan et al., in press). These four types of threats are conceptually distinct and empirically separate predictors of prejudice (Stephan et al., 1998). These authors believe that

the degree to which different threats are salient and therefore likely to be related to prejudice depends on such variables as the prior history of the relations between the groups, the relative status of the groups, the strength of identification with the in-group, and the amount and type of contact between the groups. (p. 15)

The process is complex, but its common focus on perceived threat synthesizes a considerable amount of literature and suggests strategies for intervention, to be discussed below.

Harmonizing Orientations

One could argue that harmonizing orientations are simply the bipolar opposite of divisive orientations. Berry and Kalin (1995) focus on the construct of tolerance, which they take to be the opposite of ethnocentrism. Likewise, Staub (1989) argues throughout his book *The Roots of Evil* that altruism counteracts the aggression that can be channeled toward out-groups and their members. An embracing universalism toward all others may well do so. However, social group boundaries are important qualifiers for many social behaviors, especially in more collective cultures (Triandis, 1995b), so a person's high level of in-group altruism may not extend to outsiders. Unfortunately, no measure of altruism specifically assesses one's humanity toward *all* varieties of different others, so we cannot yet test the relationship between altruism and prejudice. Similarly, the behaviors or strategies required to bring about harmony among groups may not simply be the opposite of those that foment disunity. At this stage, then, it makes sense to separate these two orientations. It is hoped that researchers will examine the empirical linkages among this congeries of divisive and harmonious orientations to clarify their relationships.

Much less work has been invested in exploring this positive side of the intergroup coin. The best known is that of Berry and his various colleagues in Canada on attitudes related to multiculturalism. One set of studies examined the attitude of ethnic tolerance, defined as "one's willingness to accept individuals or groups that are culturally or racially different from oneself" (Berry & Kalin, 1995, p. 306). Following a comprehensive survey of the various ethnic groups in the Canadian mosaic, Berry and Kalin concluded that "Tolerant individuals show little differential preference for various groups. Intolerant individuals on the other hand show relatively great positive preference for those groups that are generally preferred by the population, and great negative preference for groups least preferred" (p. 315). Individual tolerance flattens out the ethnic hierarchy; lack of tolerance sharpens it.

Another set of attitudes targets multiculturalism itself and is involved in Berry's (1990) two-dimensional typology of orientations toward ethnic acculturation. He distinguished attitudes toward the maintenance of own ethnic traditions from attitudes toward interethnic contact. The former sustain the sense of ethnic security required to maintain the ethnic mosaic; the latter support movement across group lines, creating the potential for positive intergroup relations. These attitude complexes have been instrumented and measured in immigrants, confirming hypothesized relations to their adaptation outcomes (Berry, Kim, Power, Young, & Bujaki, 1989).

What is needed is to extend these measurements to the host groups in a given society (Bourhis, Moise, Perreault, & Senecal, 1997). This needed extension will enable researchers to explore the attitudes and behaviors of the key groups toward members of other ethnic groups as well as toward the local norms and national policies surrounding their integration into the wider social fabric. These state integration policies will interact with group ideologies surrounding acculturation orientations to yield harmonious, problematic, or divisive outcomes (Bourhis et al., 1997).

Berry and Kalin (1995) explored the reactions of Canadians to their country's policy of multiculturalism by measuring three aspects of its implementation: attitudes toward the program, perceived consequences of multiculturalism, and multicultural ideology. They found that these three components cohere and together correlate with their measure of cultural and racial tolerance. So a disposition toward tolerance probably supports organizational and governmental policy initiatives aimed at promoting harmony in diversity.

Another constellation of attitudes that appears important for within-nation multiculturalism is internationalism or world-mindedness. Sampson and Smith (1957) were the first to explore this concept, defining it as "a frame of reference, or a value orientation favoring a world-view of the problem of humanity, with mankind, rather than the nationals of a particular country, as the primary reference group" (p. 105). This orientation showed a coherent clustering of attitudes on political, economic, social, and religious questions in their U.S. sample. Similar consistency has recently been confirmed with Hong Kong Chinese, using a similarly multifaceted scale of global culture developed by Walter Stephan (Fong, 1996; see also Der-Karabetian, 1992; Kosterman & Feshbach, 1989).

Logically, a person espousing internationalism would be less likely to endorse prejudicial attitudes toward people of any different ethnicity or race, be they within the country or outside. Sampson and Smith (1957) confirmed this deduction using an early measure of ethnocentrism. Internationalism may increase tolerance for other ethnic, racial, and national groups by weakening the strength of one's in-group identification or by embedding that in-group identification within a latticework of broader identifications.

Little work has been done on emotions and intergroup harmony, although a suggestive finding from Berry and Kalin (1995) was that higher levels of tolerance predicted feeling comfortable around members of various other groups.

It is difficult to link beliefs to tolerance empirically, because most contemporary "belief" scales, such as Rotter's (1966) I-E scale, are a pastiche of values and intentions along with assertions about what is true, that is, beliefs. Leung and Bond's (1998) study of "pure" beliefs identified "fatedness" as one of five such dimensions. Those high in fatedness beliefs assert that outcomes are determined; one may predict but not otherwise control these outcomes. We expect that people low on fatedness beliefs would struggle against the apparent givenness of intergroup divisions and hierarchy, a givenness that is sometimes justified by genetic or hereditary factors.

Personal values are related to integrative behavioral orientations. Sagiv and Schwartz (1995) found that readiness for out-group social contact was connected positively to the Schwartz value domains of universalism and self-direction but negatively to tradition, security, and conformity for the dominant Jewish group, but positively to the value domain of achievement for the subordinate Arab group in Israel. This finding suggests that the motives regulating out-group contact differ depending on the group's position in the social hierarchy.

Few studies have been done relating personality to integrative orientations across group lines. One suggestive finding comes from the work on attitudes toward global culture done by Fong (1996). He found that self-ratings on adjectival personality measures of openness and assertiveness positively predicted endorsements of this general constellation of attitudes, including the integrative facets of humanism, global welfare, and gender equality. Again, the important role of openness to experience found in the section on divisive orientations is underscored by its reappearance in this section.

People high on concern for others, in particular, and empathy, in general, show lower social dominance orientations, as do those high on Katz and Hass's (1988) humanitarian-egalitarian scale (Pratto et al., 1994). Lower SDO scores may be taken as a preference for lesser inequality among social groups, a probable unifying social feature in social groups (Wilkinson, 1996).

There is an absence of integrative approaches to studying harmonizing orientations. In this regard, it would be fascinating to examine the Baha'i commitment to the oneness of humankind, a cornerstone of that community's approach toward social relations (Baha'i International Community, 1995). Research has already shown that the people espousing this commitment have a distinctive value profile (Feather, Volkmer, & McKee, 1992). It is likely that they would also present a consistent set of beliefs about people and group life, of emotional responses to persons of difference, of personality dispositions like altruism (Heller & Mahmoudi, 1992), of group identifications, and of intergroup attitudes. All these characteristics may prove to be distinctive but interrelated manifestations of a commitment to the oneness of humankind.

From Personal Orientations to Social Action

All the above orientations are personality variables; in most research, they have been related to other personality variables, not to observed interpersonal behavior. Many psychologists are skeptical about our capacity to predict either divisive or harmonizing behaviors by reference to personality variations. Brown (1996) points out that personality variation fails to explain "the widespread *uniformity* of prejudice in certain societies or subgroups within societies" (p. 533). He also notes the historical specificity of prejudice: Its intense targeting of particular groups at particular time periods is not amenable to explanations requiring long-term socialization of members to become prejudiced. Instead, it appears that other social factors involving group identities and normative behaviors are more central in explaining prejudice and subsequent discrimination. The same could be said of harmonizing behavior.

Social psychologists have pointed out that interpersonal behavior that occurs across cultural lines may be construed by the actors along a continuum varying from interpersonal to intergroup (Brown & Turner, 1981; Tajfel, 1978). They argue that, under a variety of social conditions, behavior will shift from its more variable, personally shaped forms of the interpersonal mode to more uniform, normatively driven forms of the group mode. In this group mode, discriminatory behavior, be it divisive or harmonizing, is probably influenced much more by situational considerations than by personality orientations (Deutsch, 1994; Snyder & Ickes, 1985). A group's norms surrounding behavior between individuals of different groups should be especially decisive in such encounters.

These norms will shift depending on the construction of the relationship between the groups and the cultural ideology about group relations surrounding the interacting groups. When members of these groups perceive themselves as legitimately competing for the same fixed resource, such as land, jobs, food, and so on, interpersonal conflict across group lines is more likely and less tractable (see Deutsch, 1994; Tedeschi & Felson, 1994, on realistic group conflict). This conflict could be exacerbated by feelings of relative deprivation (see Walker & Pettigrew, 1984), feelings that would probably be greater in cultures characterized by an egalitarian ideology (Schwartz, 1994b).

Of course, in some cultural settings, it may be normative for members of one group to believe they are not entitled to compete against other groups either individually or corporately, as doing so may challenge accepted social hierarchies (see Hofstede, 1980, chap. 3, on power distance; Sidanius, 1993, on social dominance orientations). In other cultural settings, a history of violent intergroup hostilities may lead to widespread beliefs that *any* conflict will redound to the detriment of all parties. Such a "minus sum," as opposed to a "zero sum," expectation about the consequences of conflict (Bond, 1987) would stimulate the search for nondivisive modes of interaction.

Not all struggles are about material resources; respect and appreciation communicated across group lines are powerful bonding forces whose withholding or denial can generate intense conflict. Perceived denigration of a group's language, dialect, customs, religion, art, music, dress, and traditions can fuel intense defensive reactions and counterattack. Again, these feelings of unjust treatment are likely to be stronger in cultures with an egalitarian or individualist cultural tradition (Hofstede, 1980, chap. 5) in which human rights legislation (Humana, 1986) empowers groups as well as individuals. In this light, social norms promoting diversity and encouraging contact across group lines become countervailing forces against the drift toward group ethnocentrism. We need to begin the tasks of understanding the structure of these social norms (Moghaddam & Studer, 1997) and using information about these norms to predict intergroup behaviors in diverse societies.

Social Capital as Ballast and Momentum

What I am suggesting above is that divisive or harmonizing behaviors across group lines are socially controlled or potentiated. Even though these behaviors may involve only two persons, they are intergroup whenever the other may be categorized as an out-group member through cues of physiognomy, dialect, language, dress, or whatever. Even if the groups in question are not in conflict, interpersonal encounters across group lines will become increasingly construed in group terms as ethnic, religious, linguistic, and social class membership becomes politicized through democratization.

Intergroup encounters are channeled by each group's norms informing interpersonal encounters across group lines. These norms thus become a form of positive or negative social capital. " 'Social capital' refers to features of social organization, such as networks, norms of reciprocity, and social trust, that facilitate coordination and cooperation for mutual benefit" (Putnam, 1995, p. 67). "Coleman (1990) defines social capital as involving the creation of capabilities for action to achieve shared goals through socially structured relations between individuals in groups" (Hagan, Merkens, & Boehnke, 1995, p. 1018). Social capital may be nurtured in the family, schools, work organizations, and voluntary associations by building and sustaining strong social bonds of interdependence (Portes, 1998; Sampson & Laub, 1993). As Bourdieu (1986) asserts, "It is in fact impossible to account for the structure and functioning of the social world unless one re-introduces capital in all its forms and not solely in the one form recognized by economic theory" (p. 241). Social capital has been measured in various ways and at different levels of analysis (individual, province, nation); it is related to such important societal outcomes as rates of mortality, homicide, burglary, and assault (Wilkinson, Kawachi, & Kennedy, in press), and school delinquency and right-wing extremism among German youth (Hagan et al., 1995).

By extension, socially structured relations "that facilitate coordination and coopera-tion" may involve individuals interacting across group boundaries, not simply within group boundaries. Social capital in the intergroup sense would then be constituted by the harmonizing components of intergroup attitudes, stereotypes, emotions, and beliefs held by the participants from each of the groups; social liability would be constituted by the divisive components of the same types of orientation. And more. Intergroup social capital across individuals would be protected or augmented by the social norms (e.g., of political correctness), the laws (e.g., against racial discrimination), and the enforcement practices that structure relations across group lines in the wider society. Or restrained and undercut.

Such an amalgam of intergroup dispositions at the individual level of the different group members, combined with larger state policy, forms the building blocks of a recent theoretical model developed to explain consensual, problematic, or conflictual outcomes between immigrants and members of a host community (Bourhis et al., 1997). The logic of such approaches to understanding interpersonal outcomes is that a host of factors must be considered. A number of analytic levels are involved—the individual (orientations); the group, including the family (norms and attitudes toward intergroup contact); the organization (goals, intergroup policies and practices); and the nation-state (laws; multi-culturalism policies; group-targeted resource allocations; international memberships, relations, and treaties).

One could visualize a set of concentric circles surrounding the individual from the most proximal to the most distant influences combining to shape the individual orienta-tions that then direct interpersonal behavior across group lines. In this vein, Pratto et al. (1994) comment on the development of empathy with others, an individual orientation, by stating that "concern for others (particularly out-group members), is not just a fixed individual propensity, but instead seems likely to be influenced by social structures and policies" (p. 757). In trying to explicate the socialization of a social dominance orientation in particular, they assert that

> social structures and policies that prevent the formation of close personal relationships
> and empathy between high and low status persons (e.g., economically or legally enforced
> segregation, language barriers, publishing biases), would seem to discourage empathy
> between groups and the formation of a common identity. (p. 757)

Our task as social scientists is to identify, measure, and understand the orchestration of these forces. The model will be complex. Its development may be rendered more manageable, however, by conceptualizing its inputs in terms of intergroup social capital.

> For, the structure of the distribution of the different types of social capital at a given moment in time represents the immanent structure of the social world, i.e., the set of constraints, inscribed in the very reality of that world, which govern its functioning in a durable way, determining the chances of success for practices. (Bourdieu, 1986, p. 46)

I will use the concept of intergroup social capital to inform our discussion of strategies.

Strategies

Let not the means of order be made the cause of confusion and the instrument for union an occasion of discord.

—Baha'u'llah

There has been considerable recent work examining the impact of group diversity on group functioning (e.g., Earley, 1997; Jackson, 1991; Watson, Kumar, & Michaelsen, 1993). Contemporary researchers typically begin with a review of earlier studies and conclude with Maznevski and DiStefano (1996) that "diverse teams have the potential to create unique and innovative solutions to problems, but have great difficulty interacting to integrate their differences" (p. 5). These investigators note that the traditional paradigm for group process research assumed a narrow range of participant backgrounds and experiences. New organizational (and indeed national) contexts necessitate greater attention being deployed toward the integration of perspectives so that diverse teams (and nations) can avoid becoming mired in conflict and can harmonize their inputs to achieve success. Effective integration of differences will build social capital by the training of unit members to accommodate difference and by the bonding of members that arises out of success.

Maznevski and DiStefano (1996) have argued that successful integration requires three conditions: effective communication, collaborative conflict resolution, and constructive interaction. Developing measures for these interrelated constructs, they find that team success may be predicted by higher levels of these components and that it is the mastery of these issues that makes any team effective, be that team diverse or homogeneous. This outcome may help explain why Watson et al. (1993) found that their diverse groups eventually outperformed their homogeneous groups—part of their experimental procedure involved the experimenters meeting on a number of occasions with each group to consult about its performance problems. By forcing the diverse groups to confront their difficulties, it is probable that Watson et al. helped these groups to enhance the three components of successful integration identified by Maznevski and DiStefano.

This work trumpets a warning for any social unit striving to make its diversity a resource rather than a liability: Success will be the margin of good planning. A multicultural society is a fragile plant of potential beauty if astutely nurtured. I will propose some of the key issues that I believe need to be addressed in this planning.

Confronting Multiculturalism Openly

I accept the proposition of Hagan et al. (1995) that hatred toward out-groups is one kind of subterranean tradition, that is, a deviant attitude complex whose animus is not openly expressed in public discourse. Given the right mix of social and psychological conditions, however, virulent disdain of foreigners, immigrants, and other out-groups will be manifested in right-wing extremism, as Hagan et al. have demonstrated in Germany.

I propose that it is important to address this subterranean tradition explicitly and publicly, as a way of mobilizing controls around the animus. Such open discussion will be stimulated by the institutionalization of multiculturalism policies in nations, organizations, and groups. So, for example, in Canada there has been considerable debate about the merits of the country's 1988 Act for the Preservation and Enhancement of Multiculturalism in Canada. Heated exchange has centered around the economic value of Canada's immigration practices against the backdrop of its high unemployment, for example.

Recently, Berry (n.d.) has summarized the issues arising from the debate in Canada concerning the social psychological costs and benefits of having a policy of multiculturalism. He identified some of these benefits as morale and self-esteem for members of all groups arising from the knowledge that one's ethnocultural traditions are being considered; a sense of security arising from the knowledge that a primary prevention program is in place and enforced; a sense of collective esteem derived from being the citizen of a country that vigorously promotes human rights internationally; and the increased biculturalism or multiculturalism of many individuals within Canada.

Berry's (n.d.) assessment of the benefits is important but less important than the fact that they are being openly considered. The public airing and consideration of benefits in this and other forums is particularly important because they are rarely included in underground discourse about out-groups. The expression of these countervailing points of view balances the debate, generating greater support for out-groups than would be possible otherwise. This support arises because the issue of race and ethnicity has been openly discussed after being made institutionally explicit through leaders' speaking out or legislation being enacted. For this reason, I believe it is important for multiculturalism to become part of our public discourse.

Facilitating Contacts Across Group Lines

Berry and his coworkers have found that tolerance was associated with geographic mobility within Canada (Kalin & Berry, 1980) and with degree of ethnic mixing in a given area of Canada (Kalin & Berry, 1982). One way to explain these results is to assume that intergroup social capital increases as a result of nonhostile contact and exchanges across group lines. Recent work on this "contact hypothesis," however, makes it clear that only certain types of such contacts promote positive relations (Pettigrew, 1998). Hewstone and Brown (1986) concluded that the groups must be positively interdependent and enjoy "equal status" cooperation. Stephan et al. (1998) have summarized the conditions as optimal "when prior relations between groups have been amicable, the groups are relatively equal in status, the members do not strongly identify with the in-group, and contact has been extensive, voluntary, positive, individualized, and cooperative" (p. 15). These considerations may be used to frame the structuring of superordinate goals, considered next.

Creating Superordinate Goals

Social polarizations may be transcended through groups' and their members' uniting successfully around a common purpose or goal (Sherif, 1966). This might involve local tasks such as constructing community facilities. Community service projects, especially if involving younger students from various ethnic groups serving members of various other ethnic groups, may be especially effective in building trust and goodwill across group lines (see Holland & Andre, 1987; James, 1910/1970; Staub, 1989, chap. 18). National tasks, such as protecting the shared environment or, indeed, fighting off an invader, will accomplish the same unification. Social capital will then develop out of the experience of working together and subsequently out of shared pride in the ongoing benefit from the actual accomplishments themselves.

Ethnic diversity may be a particular resource here if each group has a distinctive contribution to make (Brown & Wade, 1987). This will be the case, for example, if increased tourism is being promoted as a national goal and ethnic groups can exploit their cultural legacy to develop tourist attractions. Internal tourism increases contacts across group lines; external tourism brings into the country wealth that diffuses across the constituent ethnic groups. Taxation and redistribution policies must ensure, however, that such diffusion occurs and is perceived by citizens to redound to the benefit of all.

Implementing Integrative Language Policies

Cooperative activities of any sort are facilitated by having a common script and spoken language available for joint use. When ethnic communities have different linguistic heritages, government educational policy must promote the acquisition of a common language by all citizens. Given the centrality of one's "mother tongue" to one's self-concept (Fishman, 1972), some care must be taken to avoid the policies themselves becoming a source of contention among ethnic communities. Promoting mutual bilingualism in the constituent languages of the country, as in Canada, or mastery of heritage languages plus a common language, as in Singapore, may be workable options to consider.

Promoting Cross-Cutting Social Ties

The potential divisiveness of group memberships may be moderated in two ways: First, a superordinate identity may be made salient, uniting members of oppositional groups under a common identity (Gaertner, Dovidio, Anastasio, Bachman, & Rust, 1993). This is the recategorization strategy adopted by political figures who appeal to the common citizenship of the people in a country. Nationalistic or patriotic rallying calls invoke this same dynamic.

Second, nonethnic associations may be encouraged when these associations have nonethnic membership criteria and can draw their members from various ethnic communities, such as professional societies, local parent-teacher groups, work organizations, labor unions, and so forth. Putnam (1995) has discussed the ways in which voluntary group memberships enhance social capital, and many researchers have operationalized their measure of social capital by indexing the extent of membership in such associations (see Putnam for examples). A given person may then have a number of competing loyalties whose balancing demands make any polarizing claims along ethnic lines harder to sustain (see Brown & Turner, 1979, on criss-cross categorization, or Dorai, 1993, on cross-cutting social ties). Associations that mix ethnic groups thereby increase the social opportunities for building intergroup social capital.

Avoiding Extremes of Wealth and Poverty

Wilkinson (1996) has documented the extensive evidence connecting relative economic inequality in nations and states within nations to a host of undesirable outcomes ranging from decreased longevity and poorer health to lower educational performance, higher accident rates, and increased crime. Hofstede (1980, chap. 3) had earlier shown a connection between inequality and the level of domestic political violence. Many of these effects, as in the case of homicide (see, e.g., Wilkinson, Kawachi, & Kennedy, 1998), persist even if the effects of average national or state wealth are held constant. Wilkinson et al. explain these socially undesirable outcomes as arising through a deterioration in the quality of social bonds, producing psychosocial stress for all, particularly those of lower status.

We know that norms of distributive justice vary across cultures, especially in the strictness with which equity principles are applied (Leung & Morris, 1996). Pratto, Tatar, and Conway-Lanz (1996) have found that those higher in SDO favored equity-based over need-based allocation of resources. This finding suggests that social and personal ideologies surrounding the distribution of resources may have to change in high-SDO cultures if greater egalitarianism across groups in society is to be promoted and greater economic democracy (Korten, 1993) achieved. In such societies, a sustained reorientation of value priorities will be required to support the lowered emphasis on material wealth and power that undergird a strict equity focus (Korten, 1993; Schwartz, 1994b).

Often, economic class divisions are confounded with ethnicity or racial differences. These divisions may have arisen historically through specialization by various groups in particular forms of subsistence activity, through immigrant status, or through systematic discrimination and denial of educational resources. Stereotypes will then coalesce around ethnic/racial group membership to legitimize these economic differences (Augoustinos & Walker, 1995). Economic cleavages across group lines seem particularly galling and incendiary because it then becomes easier to attribute one's low status to discrimination.

When these differences become sufficiently wide, ethnic/racial group membership can then be used to fuel and rally political and social agitation against the group status hierarchy. When a smaller ethnic group becomes notably wealthier, it often becomes the target of hostility from larger ethnic groups, especially when economic downturns occur (Mackie, 1976; Staub, 1989, chap. 8).

In contrast,

> Societies which are more egalitarian are not only healthier, but . . . are also more socially cohesive than others. . . . With reduced income inequality, people are connected in public life through a variety of social organizations, purposes and activities. Some sense of the moral collectivity and of social purpose remains important. (Wilkinson, 1996, p. 213)

Such societies have earned high levels of social capital. To achieve and expand this social capital, Wilkinson (1996) argues,

> Policies on education, employment, industrial structure, taxation, the management of the business cycle, must all be assessed in terms of their impact on social justice and social divisions. Economic management must have the explicit aim of increasing social cohesion and the social quality of life. (p. 223)

Special attention to such policy initiatives should be made in societies in which economic inequalities parallel ethnic, racial, or caste differences.

Enhancing Perceptions of Procedural Justice

Thibaut and Walker (1975) have demonstrated at the individual level that a person's reactions to an allocation decision are determined not only by the outcome received but also by the process that resulted in that outcome. Procedural justice focuses on the processes by which material and other resources are distributed in a social group (Lind & Tyler, 1988). A wide number of decision-making strategies, such as negotiation, third-party intervention, arbitration, and withdrawal, have been explored. Their use is determined in large part by the extent to which they are perceived to be fair to the participant.

The degree of fairness associated with a given strategy is jointly determined by properties of the decision-making process (procedural justice) and the quality of treatment received from the persons carrying out the procedures, that is, interactional justice (Tyler & Bies, 1990). Procedural considerations are the perceived control over the dispute process an approach gives the participant and the capacity of the approach to reduce animosity between the disputants.

A key feature of process control is the opportunity to express one's point of view (Folger, 1977). This granting of voice is often undertaken with some ambivalence because it opens the Pandora's box of possible disharmony and animosity in exchange for the process control it confers on the aggrieved party. Recently in the United States, for example, there has been considerable controversy arising from public debate in the media and in the courts. This debate centers on whether certain ethnic group practices, such as female clitorectomy, may continue to be performed even though they are at variance with mainstream American customs and even law (Shweder, Markus, Minow, & Kessel, 1997). Most multicultural societies will face such potential for conflict in accepted practices; the American model of multiculturalism grants voice to the ethnic groups involved. It appears to be a judgment call whether the increase in fairness judgments resulting from such conferment compensates for the struggle and possible social polarization that ensue.

Considerations about interactional justice include participants' assessments of decision makers as neutral, respectful, and benevolent. These assessments have been shown to exercise a stronger impact on fairness judgments than on perceived process control, and indeed they were even more important than outcome favorability (Lind, 1994). This relative emphasis on interactional fairness relative to outcomes is even more important to those in societies characterized by lower power distance (Tyler, Lind, & Huo, 1997).

Interactional unfairness seems to be particularly incendiary when it communicates disrespect toward the other. Tedeschi and Felson (1994) have integrated a body of literature to argue that violence follows the perception of unjustified attack, in particular, insults from the other (see also Wilkinson et al., 1998). This conclusion underscores the importance of decision makers' interpersonal behavior when processing disputes between parties to neutralize the potential for anger arising out of applying the procedures for conflict resolution themselves.

Procedural concerns thus seem to be fundamental to judgments of fairness. Lind and Tyler (1988) explain this power conferred by procedures using the group value model. It "is based on the notion that people are concerned about their standing in a group and infer their status from the treatment they receive from the group [or its representatives] in the procedures used to allocate social benefits and burdens" (Leung & Morris, 1996, p. 39). Unjust procedures belittle participants; it is this social communication and status outcome that seem so basic to the responses made by participants in allocation situations. This conclusion hearkens back to Wilkinson et al.'s (1998) explanation of how relative inequality leads to violence through the agency of felt disrespect.

Importantly, procedural considerations show no evidence of cultural variability. In their literature review, Leung and Morris (1996) draw two conclusions: "First, the available evidence suggests that the content of procedural and interactional justice is largely similar across cultures. . . . Second, the consequences of perceived procedural and interactional justice also seem to be similar across cultures" (pp. 40-41). What appears to vary culturally is the restraint of anger in the face of injustice. Higher power distance at the societal level (Gudykunst & Ting-Toomey, 1988) is associated with a muting of anger in response to perceived injustice. This finding is understandable in light of recent work on the appraisal theory of emotions (Ellsworth, 1994): Anger arises when situations are construed as controllable. In hierarchical societies, many interpersonal exchanges that lead to perceptions of interactional unfairness involve superiors and are hence less controllable by the subordinates (see, e.g., Bond, Wan, Leung, & Giacalone, 1985).

So the way that decision-making procedures are assessed for their fairness is culturally invariant; the expression of anger in response to that perceived unfairness is not. Again, it may be a social judgment call whether a group places a premium on the social debate that may arise when process control is promoted or on the apparent social order that appears in more hierarchical organizations.

Of course, all this research has been focused on the individual within a monocultural social encounter. An important question is how the key outcomes of perceived fairness and expressed anger will vary when the encounter shifts toward the intergroup end of the spectrum. Recently, Huo, Smith, Tyler, and Lind (1996) have examined the processing of interpersonal conflicts between bosses and workers across ethnic lines in U.S. organizations. They found that weak identification with the organization was associated with a worker emphasis on dispute outcome rather than with procedural concerns. Given that limited resources are available to distribute in any group, intergroup relations will be easier to manage by improving procedural (and interpersonal) considerations. What must be done is to enhance superordinate identification so that disputants' focus of concern shifts away from the less tractable outcome issues. Fortunately, as Huo et al. demonstrated, this superordinate identification need not occur at the expense of identification with the participant's own ethnic group (see also Berry's 1990 work discussed above).

Of course, we must appreciate that this research did not involve groups in a state of current or recent hostility. It also occurred in an organizational context in which participants have a basic level of commitment to the system. And finally, it was run in a nation that has a backdrop of legal and constitutional protections for minority groups. There is, in short, opportunity for voice throughout the whole social system, releasing minority group members from avoiding conflict by withdrawing. In many societies, the consequences of giving any voice to discontent may be too frightening to contemplate until such procedural mechanisms are instituted. Only after these are in place and are enacted in an interpersonally just way will a social system be able to reap the benefits that follow from perceptions of minimal fairness in treating group interests.

Without such publicly available mechanisms, the social specter of informal retribution will always be lurking across ethnic lines. Cultures of honor (e.g., Cohen, 1996; Peristiany, 1965) typically demand retaliation for injustices inflicted on one's group. These "blood feuds" (e.g., Dragoti, 1996) pass across generations, fostering an endless cycle of attack and counterattack. Available legal mechanisms and their enforcement are necessary to break this vicious cycle. A full range of social responses, including restitution, reconciliation (e.g., Moore, 1993), and other appeasement forms (Keltner, Young, & Buswell, 1997), needs to be explored so that this whole legal process not only satisfies demands for fairness but also restores (Consedine, 1995) intergroup social capital. This broadening of social responses should include a close assessment of the destructive costs of current legal processes in many nations characterized by the rule of law (Frankel, 1981).

Educational Provisions

There are many ways a society may decrease the divisive forces of intergroup disharmony through its educational provisions (Hollins, 1996). First, it can invest in open access to education based solely on considerations of pupil competence. Human resources will be enhanced generally, redounding to the benefit of the economy and stimulating associated benefits, such as improved health care. Also, the openness of educational training to all citizens will ensure that members of all ethnic groups in a society will gain access to trades and professions. Cross-cutting of social ties will thereby be promoted, embedding ethnic group membership in a wider latticework of associations.

Second, a part of standard school curricula should include a reorientation of spiritual priorities (Korten, 1993). Korten believes that a socialization for community and harmonious living must replace the contemporary focus on materialism if we are to enjoy a sustainable global future,

> as an act of collective survival, to recreate the political and economic structures of human society in ways that free our world from the grip of greed, waste, and exploitation . . . to re-establish the nurturing bonds of sharing on which human community and life itself depend. (p. 59)

This reorientation will help reduce the pressure on limited material resources arising from widespread acquisitive motivation and move society away from a status hierarchy based primarily on wealth (see also Hatcher, 1998; Schwartz, 1992, for the tradeoff between power motivations and values of benevolence).

One educational requirement that could be deployed toward "nurturing bonds of sharing" is community service (Holland & Andre, 1987; James, 1910/1970). Engaging students to assist other citizens outside the school setting would go some way toward achieving greater empathy from these future leaders of the nation, gratitude from the recipients of their contributions, and social capital generally. In addition, work at school could make greater use of cooperative learning tasks in which students interact to achieve a common goal (e.g., Sharan, Hare, Webb, & Hertz-Lazarowitz, 1980). Students learn to teach and help one another under these requirements. Both types of projects could be designed to span ethnic and racial boundaries. These opportunity structures would then help promote ethnic harmony within societies (Fishbein, 1996).

Another relevant educational module is the training of students for nonviolent forms of conflict resolution (Stevahn, Johnson, Johnson, & Real, 1996; Zhang, 1994). These skills would help reduce levels of ethnic disharmony within the school setting itself and also generalize to social settings outside school and later in life. Well-ingrained strategies for conflict resolution are a protection against escalation (Felson, 1978) and a vital form of social capital.

In addition, school curricula can be broadened so that a variety of skills—social, aesthetic, musical, athletic, and so forth—become nurtured and recognized (Gardner, 1993). Such an opening presupposes a wider definition of what it is to be fully human and provides alternative routes and rewards for self-development. An overemphasis on the professions ossifies and narrows the status hierarchy in a society and materially overcompensates the survivors of such a focused, competitive scramble. Also, the content of some of these additions to the curricula can be used to confront prejudice directly—for example, the songs from Time for Healing by the musical group Sounds of Blackness.

Third, liberal arts can be encouraged, both as major fields of study and as elective courses in the curricula. Altemeyer (1988) has found that lower levels of right-wing authoritarianism characterize students in the humanities and social sciences and that this level decreases over their course of study.

The content of history courses may be particularly important in promoting multi-culturalism; the inflammatory portrayal of ethnic group interactions in the past can fuel "ideologies of antagonism" (Staub, 1988) and divisive perceptions of history, affecting social identities (Liu, Wilson, McClure, & Higgins, 1997). Ethnically balanced reporting may be an antidote to possible in-group bias in historical representations in the school curricula. This balancing of content could also include a greater emphasis on peace building as a counterweight to the emphasis on war that currently dominates most people's perceptions of history (Liu, in press).

Fourth, culture as a topic of study should receive much more attention (e.g., Claydon, Knight, & Rado, 1977; Hoffman, 1996) to moderate students' attitudes toward race and other forms of difference (Banks, 1995). This exposure could include culture as the primary focus (e.g., Ladson-Billings, 1995) and with appropriate techniques (Pusch, 1979) or as a supplement to other social science or business courses in which cultural consid-erations are central to the validity of material presented (e.g., Smith & Bond's 1998 text on social psychology across cultures). By the identification of culture as a vital and worthy concern, ethnicities are legitimized and validated. Weight is given to cultural claims, and a sense of security is imparted to ethnic groups in the national mosaic.

THE INTERNATIONAL CONTEXT

The earth is but one country, and mankind its citizens.

—Baha'u'llah

This chapter has been focused on social-psychological recommendations for building harmonious, multicultural societies. The current context for undertaking these initiatives is dramatically different from what it was, say, at the end of World War II. As expressed by the Baha'i International Community (1995),

> History has thus far recorded principally the experience of tribes, cultures, classes, and nations. With the physical unification of the planet in this century and the acknowl-edgment of the interdependence of all who live on it, the history of humanity as one people is now beginning. (p. 18)

The novel, contemporary dynamic driving this change is the "porous border" (Rosenau, 1997), namely, the relative ease with which influences pass across national boundaries, placing enormous stress on those boundaries (Blake, 1998). These influences may be ecological, as with environmental pollution and resource depletion; financial, as with currency devaluations and huge, unregulated flows of capital; human, as with legal and illegal migrants; informational, as with the uncontrollable input available over the Internet; and ideological, as with the growing pressure for human rights and clean government. Added to this ferment is the unrelenting pressure on the ecosphere by continued population growth (Korten, 1993). The upshot of these developments is that all people on this fragile planet have become more interconnected and interdependent; the successful management of this relatedness has become a matter of our corporate survival. As Benjamin Franklin aptly put matters, "We must learn to hang together, or surely we shall all hang separately."

In forging this often-reluctant cooperation, we might pause to consider whether the same considerations will be needed to achieve unity at the international level as are needed at the national level. In thinking through this broader, global issue, the Baha'i International Community (1995) has written,

> Such rethinking will have to address practical matters of policy, resource utilization, planning procedures, implementation methodologies, and organization. As it proceeds, however, fundamental issues will quickly emerge, related to the long-term goals to be pursued, the social structures required, the implications for development of principles of justice, and the nature and role of knowledge in effecting enduring change. (p. 2)

I submit that this daunting agenda is exactly what we have been exploring in the main body of this chapter and that the possible solutions proposed here will be applicable internationally. As an important example, the emergence of global social change organizations (Cooperrider & Pasmore, 1991) is generating a growing body of social capital that transcends national borders and targets planetary concerns. This "international" social capital arises in part out of a belief in the oneness of humankind, and it adds to the momentum of this awareness and commitment through its investment in various projects. This "international" social capital will be augmented by practicing in relations across nations any of the harmonizing solutions discussed as applicable within nations. In all these ways, we will be better positioned to build a unified community of nations at the same time we are building more unified nations.

> *Mankind hath been created to carry forth an ever-advancing civilization.*
> —Baha'u'llah

PART II

THEORETICAL ORIENTATIONS IN CROSS-CULTURAL SOCIAL PSYCHOLOGY

Feldman's chapter is a thoughtful review of the principles often used in the current social cognitive approach to social behavior. Although cross-cultural researchers have not made very heavy use of social cognition, this has become a dominant approach in social psychology. Feldman extracts the most important concepts in this burgeoning literature and shows their potential uses in cross-cultural psychology, especially in considering the short-term processes that characterize individual interaction with the social environment.

Adamopoulos's chapter provides a potential extension of the social cognitive approach by describing how complex patterns of behavior can be traced to the emergence of different systems of meaning across cultures. Such emergence is subject to the existence of particular constraints that are basic to all human interaction, but the emphasis differs as a function of cultural experience. As a result, concepts like individualism and collectivism can be understood as reflecting certain underlying systems of meaning evolving over long periods of time.

Y. Kashima and E. Kashima's chapter is still another challenge to the contemporary social cognitive approach. They argue that, on the basis of the emerging connectionist conception of the mind, a connectionist approach can provide a dynamic approach to culture—that is, stability and change of culture over time. Although connectionism began to have an impact on social psychology only recently, its contribution in cognitive psychology and cognitive science is well established. Kashima and Kashima's chapter amounts to the assertion that the connectionist approach is more amenable to a social psychology that takes culture and time seriously.

- Feldman lists four major principles of social cognition. What are they? Do they exhaust all the important principles we need to consider in culture and psychology?
- Adamopoulos proposes a social exchange theory of culture. He suggests that important cultural syndromes like individualism and collectivism can be understood as emergent properties of fundamental principles of resource exchange. Is that a useful conceptualization?
- Kashima and Kashima assert that connectionism provides an alternative and powerful approach to cultural dynamics. In what ways does this add to the current understanding of cultural phenomena?
- How important is the temporal dimension in thinking about culture and psychology?
- The chapters in this section assume that culture and individual psychology are inseparable and mutually constitutive. In what ways are they different from the research tradition of subjective culture, as outlined in Chapter 1?

4

FOUR QUESTIONS ABOUT HUMAN SOCIAL BEHAVIOR

The Social Cognitive Approach to Culture and Psychology

Jack M. Feldman
Georgia Institute of Technology

The Passover holiday commemorates deliverance of the Jewish people from slavery and their receipt of the Commandments and the Torah. The seder, a ritual festive dinner, features the retelling of these events; the story is introduced by the youngest child's asking the "Four Questions" about Passover customs (e.g., "Why on this night do we eat only matzos?"). The leader of the seder recounts the events and comments on them; thus, four simple questions introduce a richly interrelated set of ideas, more detailed questions, and some tentative answers about the nature of faith and humans' relationship to the Creator.

This chapter has an infinitely more modest goal. I propose asking four questions about human behavior, whose purpose is to guide the way in which we tell and understand the many stories that make up human life. They are broad, multifaceted questions about the entire range of behavior, from individual judgment to group processes, from the effects of context on people's responses to simple questions to the influence of culture on perceptions, judgments, affect, and behavior. In raising these questions, I will retell some familiar stories, proposing general patterns to the origins of our actions.

The following are some fundamental assumptions:

1. People have limited attentional capacity (Kahneman, 1973). This principle is a cornerstone of theories of social judgment (e.g., Gilbert, 1989), motivation and self-regulation (e.g., Kanfer & Ackerman, 1989), attitude (e.g., Eagly & Chaiken, 1993), and other domains.

2. People do not maximize returns but, rather, aim for *satisfactory* outcomes. A principle of decision theory (see, e.g., Feldman & Lindell, 1990), "satisficing" is a natural consequence of limited capacity, explaining the use of stereotypes, heuristics, and other "shortcuts" in judgment and behavior (see Devine, 1989; Eagly & Chaiken, 1993; Fazio, 1990; Gilbert, 1989; Kahneman, Slovic, & Tversky, 1982). What is "satisfactory," however, depends on the current state, circumstances, and history of the individual.

3. People make up their lives as they go along. This constructionist principle (Feldman & Lynch, 1988; Murphy & Medin, 1985) holds that phenomenal experience at any moment reflects the output of processes that, although learned, are not always accessible to consciousness and not always volitionally engaged. Whereas some judgments, affective responses, and behaviors may be retrieved from memory and used reliably across contexts, others are constructed at the time. Furthermore, retrieval is not a completely reliable process, and reconstruction is always a possibility. (See, e.g., Bargh, 1994; Barsalou, 1987; Greenwald & Banaji, 1995; Jussim, 1991; Nisbett & Wilson, 1977.)

4. Perception, cognition, and affect at the individual level are the immediate, proximal causes of behavior. The history of the individual in a specific set of contexts (e.g., culture, unique individual history) and the immediate context in which the person behaves are considered distal causes, whose effect is mediated by processes internal to the individual and by specific (cognitive/affective) structures (schemata) developed by experience in these contexts. The nature of these structures is revealed by systematic patterns of perception, judgment, affect, and overt behavior *in interaction with* contexts (see, e.g., Mischel & Shoda, 1995). This view specifically integrates nomothetic and idiographic approaches (e.g., Pelham, 1993); "cultural," as opposed to "cross-cultural," psychology (Lonner & Adamopoulos, 1997; Miller, 1997); and recent views of situated or contextual cognition (Schliemann, Carraher, & Ceci, 1997).

The questions that follow are consistent with these assumptions. They are topics of inquiry that allow us to induce general principles from the variety of behavior exhibited by different individuals acting in different circumstances. I am adopting a natural science perspective: Any given cognitive structure, value system, specific motive, thought pattern, emotional response, and so on is assumed to be contingent and historically bound. It is the process by which these are generated that is assumed to be general.

The questions themselves are as follows:

1. *Accessibility.* What specific aspects of an individual's declarative and procedural knowledge and what affective responses are accessible at a given moment? Note that, to

study accessibility, one needs *detailed specification* of the nature of the concepts involved (e.g., motive, stereotype, etc.).

2. *Diagnosticity.* To what judgment or behavior is the accessible concept relevant? That is, what is the implication of one construct for another, in terms of the individual's cognitive structure? Knowledge of diagnosticity is required to study both accessibility and motivation.

3. *Motivation.* What specific motive is operating, and at what level of intensity? Motives have both directive and energizing properties (see, e.g., Kanfer, 1990; Kluger & DeNisi, 1996; Kruglanski & Webster, 1996; Kunda, 1990; Tetlock, 1992).

4. *Capacity.* What attentional resources are available to the individual at the moment of decision, judgment, or behavior? It should be noted that the concept of capacity is typically operationalized at the individual level through measures of skill and knowledge (e.g., IQ) and experimentally through the provision of distracting tasks. The former does not tap general capacity but, rather, *efficiency* of capacity use, as is produced via elaborated knowledge structures characteristic of experts or people with well-developed values (Alba & Hutchinson, 1987; Neisser et al., 1996). Thus, capacity refers to the total attentional resources available to a specific person in a specific situation.

I contend that focusing on these four interrelated questions will allow a principled explanation of human social behavior in any situation, culture, or time.

ACCESSIBILITY

Higgins (1989) defines accessibility as the "readiness of stored knowledge to be used" (p. 115). The import of this concept is that "momentarily activated cognitions [and affective responses] have disproportionate influence over judgments made about an object or on related behaviors performed shortly after their activation" (Feldman & Lynch, 1988, p. 421). "Judgments" include evaluations, sometimes intense; "behaviors" include those both impulsive and deliberate, sometimes far reaching in their implications. Objects of judgment and behavior may range from the trivial (e.g., bubble gum) to the profound (e.g., social justice).

Accessibility is inferred from the relative ease with which a given concept, procedure, affective response, and so on is used (other things equal) and thus is typically assessed by measures such as response time. As Higgins (1989, p. 115) also notes, however, other factors determine the *actual* use of an accessible construct. An important aspect of research, therefore, is determining the circumstances and stimuli likely to reveal accessibility effects. This activity, usually relegated to the pretest phase in studies of social cognition (e.g., determining stereotype content), is at the heart of substantive research in other domains; for instance, cross-cultural psychology focuses on the specifics of values, norms, and other "stuff" of daily life (see, e.g., Triandis, 1994a, 1995b). These two issues—the processes governing accessibility and its effects in the abstract and the specifics of the knowledge and affect structures that may be more or less accessible—are the substance of the first two questions: Exactly *what* is accessible to *whom* and under *what circumstances?*

Accessibility as Process

Several theories of the nature of accessibility exist; for the present purposes, we may regard them as equivalent. Two related types of construct accessibility have been discussed by Bargh (1994): temporary and chronic. *Temporary* accessibility is caused by relatively recent activation of a knowledge or affective structure; it is operationalized by manipulations such as priming (concept use in an apparently unrelated context) or the presentation of associated stimuli. Priming may be subliminal as well. Active motive states, processing goals, moods, salient stimuli, and so forth, may also influence the temporary accessibility of related knowledge, affective responses, evaluations, and the like (see Bargh, 1994; Bargh & Barndollar, 1996; Feldman, 1994; Fiske & Taylor, 1991; Higgins, 1996; Isen & Diamond, 1989; Kunda, 1990; Tetlock, 1992). Interestingly, increasing the relative accessibility of some constructs decreases that of others (Alba & Chattopadhyay, 1985; Hoch, 1984).

Chronic accessibility (Bargh, 1994) is readiness for use that is relatively high across contexts and states of the individual. It is associated with elaborated domains of knowledge and affect, such as expertise (Alba & Hutchinson, 1987), the self-concept (Markus, 1977), culture (Markus & Kitayama, 1991), or values (Fischhoff, Slovic, & Lichtenstein, 1980), and is thought to develop from frequent use of concepts or behaviors in a particular environment (e.g., Higgins, King, & Mavin, 1982). Temporary and chronic accessibility are additive (Bargh, Bond, Lombardi, & Tota, 1986), implying that a concept, procedure, or affective response made temporarily accessible might be used in preference to a more chronically accessible one. However, because there is no "accessibility metric," it is difficult to know how much temporary activation exists, or is sufficient, in a given case.

The above discussion begs the question of how accessibility effects occur. *Automaticity,* as discussed by Bargh (1994), is the key to the answer. Schneider and Shiffrin (1977) and Shiffrin and Schneider (1977) originally proposed that sufficient practice on tasks in which stimuli and responses were consistently mapped produces performance that is nonvolitional: under stimulus control; minimally or entirely undemanding of cognitive resources; autonomous, requiring no monitoring to completion; involuntary, in that they occur even when consciously unwanted (and require resource allocation to *suppress,* as in the Stroop task); and unconscious, in that only the results of their operation reach awareness. Automaticity is usually contrasted with controlled processing, which is deliberate, is capacity intensive, requires monitoring to completion, and is open to introspection. Aspects of controlled processing will be discussed subsequently.

Bargh (1994) has argued cogently that automaticity is not monolithic; each of its aspects may occur under different conditions. For instance, "preconscious" automaticity displays all the above criteria and describes fundamental perceptual experiences. It is associated with chronic accessibility, which in turn is a function of the unique history of the individual. In short, fundamental perceptual experiences are governed by cognitive structures and affective responses likely to be "momentarily accessible" because of their frequent use and elaboration. Examples are the influence of culture on the susceptibility to optical illusions (Segall, Campbell, & Herskovits, 1964); the effect of schematic personal constructs on self- and other perception (Fong & Markus, 1982; Markus, 1977); automatic stereotype and attitude activation (Devine, 1989; Fazio, 1990); the spontaneous attribution of dispositional causality (Gilbert, 1989; Newman & Uleman, 1989); and self-referent affect and belief associated with depression and other disorders (Higgins, 1996). In all these instances, highly elaborated conceptual, affective, and behavioral structures guide responding in a relatively effortless, nonvolitional manner. They determine the content of experience and may be overcome only with effort. They provide consistency in response across situations, but only as they have been practiced (see, e.g., Bettman & Sujan, 1987). It is important to remember that these processes are not conscious; what the individual *experiences* are their outcomes (Nisbett & Wilson, 1977). Likewise, behavior may often be governed by motives and scripts associated with elaborated cognitive and affective structures; what occurs to people to *do* may be automatic under many circumstances (see, e.g., Bargh & Barndollar, 1996; Cohen & Nisbett, 1994).

The influence of chronically accessible concepts is not limited to perceptual events (e.g., seeing a person as male or female or a physics problem as involving conservation of angular momentum). Preconscious automaticity may occur in the identification of behaviors as certain kinds of action (Kruglanski, 1980) as well as in the categories and other explanatory principles applied when one is consciously solving a problem (James, 1998).

Temporarily accessible constructs are linked to perception, inference, affect, and behavior via automatic processes as well, but automaticity in these cases has a different flavor. "Postconscious" automaticity is the result of conscious experience, for example, the use of a concept in a specific context, which then generalizes unintentionally to others. "Goal-dependent" and "intended" automaticity involve the elicitation of concepts or behaviors associated with goals (e.g., to form an impression of another, make a decision, satisfy a superior's wish), deliberate or not, or the intentional "triggering" of automatic processes to accomplish an activity (e.g., driving).

Priming effects (e.g., Srull & Wyer, 1989) exemplify the postconscious automaticity of temporarily accessible constructs, although priming does not *necessarily* involve conscious experience (Bargh, 1994). In these cases, primed concepts are preferentially used *without intention* in attributional problems and influence subsequent impressions and memory organization. Likewise, perceptual salience may evoke certain person categories, rendering them more likely to be used even without intention (Taylor & Fiske, 1978). Accountability to particular audiences, or the presence of specific goals, likewise influences the information that is retrieved and used to form a judgment (Eagly & Chaiken, 1993; Tetlock, 1992). Some framing effects in decision making may be attributed to the accessibility of particular concepts as a result of question wording (e.g., loss vs. gain; see Feldman & Lindell, 1990; Kahneman et al., 1982). Context and order effects in survey research may in some cases be traced to questions making a subset of beliefs or a specific response heuristic temporarily accessible (Feldman & Lynch, 1988). Wilson, Dunn, Kraft, and Lisle (1989) show how instructions influence the relative accessibility of cognitions and affect, which are used in the construction of attitude judgments under different circumstances. Higgins (1989) details how the priming of specific self-discrepancies may generate affective states such as anxiety and depression. Finally, temporary accessibility may influence perceptual experience, just as chronically accessible structures do (Goldstone, 1995; Moscovici, 1985, pp. 395-396).

Normative influences on behavior are similarly influenced by accessibility. Cialdini, Kallgren, and Reno's (1991) studies of littering demonstrate how salient environmental cues influence the accessibility of social norms as well as standards of judgment. De-individuation studies effectively reduce the accessibility of personal values as limits on behavior or increase the accessibility of immediate group norms at the expense of broader ethical standards (see, e.g., Krebs & Miller, 1985; Rodin, 1985). Of course, it must be realized that highly elaborated, chronically accessible standards of behavior reduce susceptibility to such influences (Blass, 1991; Bond & Smith, 1996).

In short, one's experience of the self and the world is a construction whose process is often inaccessible to consciousness and whose materials are those that both are minimally satisfactory and fall readily to hand. This position, however, begs a question: What is the blueprint? To what purposes are specific judgments, perceptions, and affective responses put? These are the questions of diagnosticity and motivation.

DIAGNOSTICITY

Following Feldman and Lynch (1988), diagnosticity may be defined as the degree to which one piece of information implies or determines one's response to a given question or other circumstance requiring a judgment or behavior. A "piece of information" may be a cognition, an affective response, or a prior behavior (or memory of the behavior).

For example, Leyens, Yzerbyt, and Corneille (1996) primed concepts differing in their explanatory applicability to specific behaviors (that is, the diagnosticity of the *behaviors* for the *concepts*). They found the fundamental attribution error to be determined by diagnosticity; when the primed concept did not permit the creation of a coherent story (Murphy & Medin, 1985; Read, 1987), subjects did not explain the observed behavior in terms of the accessible concept.

Schwarz's (1994) essay on conversational logic effects on interview and survey responses can also be interpreted in terms of diagnosticity. The implicit rules of conversation influence the interpretation of questions and thus the diagnosticity of given cognitions for their answers. For instance, respondents use their feelings of relationship satisfaction as input to judgments of life satisfaction if the "life" question is asked before the "relationship" question. The norm to avoid redundancy, however, leads people to exclude relationship judgments from life satisfaction ratings when the relationship question is first. Furthermore, the two questions are answered independently if they are placed in a distinct unit. In short, the use of even highly accessible information depends on its relevance to the judgment, which is itself a function of the schema used to conceptualize it (see also Edwards & Potter, 1993).

Diagnosticity is not always or even frequently determined by a controlled choice among clear alternatives. The individual may have accessible (via automatic *or* controlled processes) only one prior judgment, encoding of stimulus attributes, affective response, and so on in any given setting. If that cognition or affective response is sufficiently diagnostic for the subsequent behavior or judgment, no further search or response construction is motivated.

Because diagnosticity is an implicative relationship, it depends on prior knowledge. Both the organization of that knowledge—its structure—and the specifics of the knowledge matter. For example, a high degree of effort spent to achieve a given level of performance is diagnostic of low ability for children with "entity" or fixed-amount implicit theories of ability but of higher potential accomplishment for children with "incremental" or variable-amount theories (Dweck & Leggett, 1988).

The precise nature of cognitive structures or schemata (organized collections of declarative and procedural knowledge and affective responses) is a matter of debate (Smith, 1994). Schemata may be both flexible (Barsalou, 1987) and, with sufficient practice, automatic and invariant across contexts. Schemata such as categories seem to be organized internally and hierarchically (Rosch, 1977), and this organization is itself variable, responding to such contextual factors as mood (Murray, Sujan, Hirt, & Sujan, 1990). These attributes of cognitive/affective structures have important implications for diagnosticity.

In social behavior, a number of lines of research point to the same basic conceptualization. Mischel and Shoda (1995) represent personality as a system of cognitive/affective structures containing categories, interpretative procedures, links to affect, self-regulatory processes, and the like. These are developed through experience, in interaction with the person's inherent capabilities and response tendencies (e.g., neurological reactivity and processing speed; Neisser et al., 1996). Developmentally, experience produces structures that create behavioral consistency *in interaction with* situations. Thus, "personality" is defined by behavioral constancy *within a class of situations* that, ultimately, is defined by the person. The meaning of a "trait" such as conscientiousness is contained in specific *patterns* of behavioral variability. Thus, one person may be conscientious, meeting obligations or task demands, primarily in work situations, another in interpersonal settings. A third may show no such predictability, responding to momentarily salient environmental cues or to recently activated, temporarily accessible concepts or norms.

Mischel and Shoda's arguments recall Kelly's (1955) personal constructs theory and Markus's (1977) notions of schematicity. The central idea of all these is that individual differences cannot be adequately conceptualized in terms of points in a multidimensional space formed by universally applicable trait dimensions. Rather, each individual is in some ways unique; although a concept (e.g., extroversion, independence) may apply to certain individuals, the opposite of "extroversion," for example, is not "introversion." It is "does not apply." Furthermore, general concepts will *always* be of limited applicability to specific persons. To "know" a person requires appreciation of his or her unique pattern of cognitive, affective, and behavioral variance (e.g., Pelham, 1993).

Thus, the affective responses, concepts, and behaviors for which a particular piece of information is diagnostic depend entirely on the details of the structures operative at a given moment; the more elaborated, affect laden, and generalized these are, the more likely they will be accessible. But the degree to which behavior is predictable across persons based on general measures is *inherently* limited by the degree to which the details of the concepts overlap among individuals. Furthermore, the constructs themselves are variable in their operation because of circumstances and context.

What applies to personality also applies to culture. Mischel and Shoda (1995) call for research exploring the specifics of conceptual systems. Markus and Kitayama's (1991) discussion of the self-concept in individualist and collectivist (independent and interdependent) cultures may be seen as an effort in that direction. Triandis (1995b) discusses the physical and economic environments that give rise to one type of culture or another worldwide. Similar problems and opportunities seem to produce similar solutions regardless of time, place, or people (see also Anderson, 1991; Cohen & Nisbett, 1994). Briefly, the collectivist or interdependent person includes others in the concept of self. The person is *defined* in terms of relationships and reciprocal obligations rather than in terms of individual distinctions (e.g., abilities or attitudes). Though this is far from an all-or-none phenomenon and intraindividual variability exists within even the "tightest" cultures (Triandis, 1995b), enough similarity exists across specific cultures within a type to permit limited generalization. For the present purposes, the implication is that the basis for diagnosticity—especially in terms of preconsciously automatic linkages between objects or events and categorizations, evaluations, emotions, and behavior—does not differ quantitatively between cultures but *qualitatively*. Concepts and emotions centrally important to behavior in one culture may not exist in any real sense in another. Three examples will suffice.

Triandis (1972) discusses *philotimo*, an element of Greek implicit personality and self theory that roughly translates as "love of honor." It means meeting one's obligations to the in-group and connotes politeness, virtue, reliability, self-sacrifice, tact, respect, and gratitude. *Philotimo* is central to the Greek self-concept and their perception of others—it is "culturally schematic."

Similarly, in Japan, the concept of *amae*, the "desire to be loved or have social acceptance" (Kashima & Callan, 1994, p. 626), is central to the concept of interpersonal relations and the extensive network of reciprocal obligations they entail. Interpersonal relations form the core of the Japanese self-concept (see Markus & Kitayama, 1991).

Finally, "equity," the concept of fairness or distributive justice, is particularly important in the United States and has been proposed as the primary motive in social behavior (Berkowitz & Walster, 1976). But, as Homans (1976) observed, the concept has little meaning or emotional impact outside the American system of values. (See also related discussions of cognitive consistency in Eagly & Chaiken, 1993, pp. 505-539, and Markus & Kitayama, 1991.)

Thus, as in the case of personality traits, it is not reasonable to say that Americans are "low" on *philotimo* or *amae* or that Greeks and Japanese are "inequitable" any more than it is to say that people are "low" on the feature "wings" whereas birds are "high." The appropriate descriptor is "does not apply."

Markus and Kitayama (1991) also suggest that emotional experience may differ fundamentally between cultures. If emotions are labeled affective states, based on cognitive cues as well as attention to feelings and bodily sensations (Martin, Harlow, & Strack,

1992; Mesquita, Fridja, & Scherer, 1997), it is entirely possible that the nature of emotion shifts as a result of attentional focus and interpretation. For instance, a given degree of arousal under conditions of potential failure, requiring another's assistance, might be diagnostic of "performance anxiety" in an individualist culture and of a "feeling of indebtedness" in a collectivist culture, concepts with very different meanings. This argument has implications for recent debates about the cross-cultural generality of emotions and their identification. At the most general level of emotional experience, cross-cultural homogeneity in the origins of feeling and expression might be found and may well have physiological roots (e.g., Cacioppo, Crites, Gardner, & Berntson, 1994; Cacioppo et al., 1992; Osgood, May, & Miron, 1975). But given the complexity of learned patterns of association and evaluation, and their reciprocal relationship to physiology, it is hard *not* to imagine both cultural *and* individual specificity in the quality of experience (Higgins, 1996; Triandis, 1989).

The concepts of values and attitudes may be incorporated into the same framework. Values may be considered higher-order, schematic organizations of beliefs, evaluations, norms, and decision-making procedures. Value systems include implicative relationships, as assessed by, for instance, Triandis's "antecedent-consequent" method. Responses are elicited by this technique and a variety of others (e.g., response times to agreement and distribution of responses to scenarios permitting multiple interpretations) to construct a portrait of a given group's value system (Triandis, 1996). Methods such as James's (1998) conditional reasoning tasks may also be used to diagnose the degree to which given concepts chronically and automatically structure one's perceptions.

The lines between values, culturally mediated self-conceptions, and personality attributes are fuzzy and highly permeable. Consider the "culture of honor" said to characterize the southern male. Honor, a value, involves (in part) insisting on respectful treatment of one's self, family, and property; it engenders legitimate anger and violence when violated (Cohen & Nisbett, 1994, p. 552). Thus, certain behaviors on another's part are diagnostic of disrespect and of an aggressive reassertion of one's worth. Shame occurs if one fails to assert one's honor. To the extent that this value is highly elaborated, should it be regarded as a culture-common personality trait, a component of the self-concept (e.g., Higgins's, 1996, notion of the ideal self), or as a value?

Attitudes, defined as evaluative responses to some object of judgment (Eagly & Chaiken, 1993), are more circumscribed. Attitudes may be constructed from a variety of sources, including cognitions, affective responses, and memories of behavior and its circumstances; all may be diagnostic of an evaluative judgment. Even existing evaluations may be recomputed based on diagnostic information made accessible by context (Wilson et al., 1989; Woehr & Feldman, 1993). Attitudes themselves may be diagnostic of a variety of judgments and behaviors; they serve as heuristics, saving capacity especially in low-motivation or capacity-limited situations (Fazio, 1990; Fazio, Blascovich, & Driscoll, 1992).

It is important to note that attitudes may not exist for every object, and existing value systems may not provide input to their construction if values are not elaborated in the same domain. In such a case, *any* diagnostic input created by the momentary context may govern judgment formation. With sufficient rehearsal and elaboration, the newly formed attitude may then influence subsequent judgments and behavior (Fazio, 1989, 1990; Tesser, 1978).

The structure of attitudes—the relationships among beliefs, affective responses, and behavior—may be important for diagnosticity. For instance, issue involvement produces an expert-level knowledge structure in which evaluations of schematically related objects are consistent (Judd & Krosnick, 1989). Thus, one's evaluation of one object, say abortion, is diagnostic for that of another, say assisted suicide, via a hierarchically related value, such as "life" or "freedom." Attitudes may be associated with knowledge structures that are bipolar (containing pro or con beliefs), unipolar (containing only pro or con information), or even more complex (Eagly & Chaiken, 1993; Pratkanis, 1989). The diagnosticity of a specific attitude for a second judgment or behavior—for example, one's attitude toward hunting for a judgment about the desirability of gun control or a vegetarian diet—may well depend on details of the structure, as would the impact (diagnosticity) of persuasive arguments or affective stimuli on the attitude itself.

Furthermore, evaluative structure itself may be either unipolar or bipolar and may vary with circumstances (Cacioppo & Berntson, 1994). Thus, the diagnosticity of an attitude judgment for a given behavior may depend on which particular evaluative elements (positive, negative, or both) were accessible at the time of its construction and on their relationship to the behavior in question (Cacioppo & Berntson, 1994, pp. 408-409; see also the discussion of prejudice in Triandis, 1977a).

The Consequences of Variable Diagnosticity

If the diagnosticity of a given input to judgment or behavior varies across contexts, persons, and cultures, it suggests, first, that any attempt to characterize people in terms of a universal set of personality traits, values, or other nomothetic constructs is probably wrong. The cognitive/affective structures and processes that generate the responses whose covariance is used to infer such generality (see, e.g., Katigbak, Church, & Akmine, 1996, on personality dimensions; Schwartz, 1992, on values) vary in both their accessibility and elaboration, as well as in specifics of content. This implies that structures *already elaborated* in a form that matches the content and style of questioning will be well reflected by standard measures. But it also means that internally consistent patterns of responding may be *created by the act of questioning itself* so that sets of related questions may produce coherent response patterns where only the vaguest shared meaning existed before. Thus, Knowles (1988; Knowles et al., 1992) repeatedly finds that the internal consistency of standard personality measures increases within item subsets as a function of serial position, as do factor loadings; response times likewise decrease. The explanation for this phenomenon is that, *in the measurement context,* people can either retrieve responses to items or construct them. Those whose cognitive/affective structures in some way match the question structure ("schematics") reliably retrieve or construct answers using elaborated, context-independent heuristics and algorithms. "Aschematics" may respond using more generalized knowledge structures, initially adding random error to the overall item variance. However, as question meaning is narrowed by additional questions, answers to prior questions and the developing concept become not only highly accessible but *increasingly diagnostic* for subsequent responses. Thus, item covariation is increased, and (because of confounded processes) a "dimension" appears that seems to describe all respondents (Feldman & Lynch, 1988; Knowles & Byers, 1996; Panter, Tanaka, & Wellens, 1992).

Three consequences follow: First, prediction of behavior from such measures may be moderately good, because a subset of individuals *is* well described by the items, and the underlying schematic construct will guide behavior as it guides item responding. But the scatterplot relating test scores to behavior should be roughly triangular, as low scores should mean either low intensity of the construct or "does not apply," as in the case of a unipolar attitude organization.

Second, correlations between construct measures and behavior occurring immediately after construct assessment should be higher than those with later behavior (cf. Fishbein & Ajzen, 1975), because the construct created should be highly accessible and at least moderately diagnostic of the behavior. Predictability should decrease with time, however, and the consequences of one's immediate behavior should be regretted (Wilson et al., 1989; Wilson & Schooler, 1991).

Third, it is possible to create values, self-judgments, attitudes, and the like where none existed in a meaningful way by a process of questioning motivating elaboration and rehearsal in a particular direction. Note that McGuire's (1960) "Socratic effect" presumes just such a process, as does Tesser's (1978) theory and the elaboration/cognitive-response models of attitude (Eagly & Chaiken, 1993). Note, too, that chaos theory (e.g., Barton, 1994) suggests that a small impetus is sufficient to begin the process (and determine the direction) of self-organization. The moral of this story is clear: *There is no such thing as a "true score,"* in the generally accepted sense of the term, because specific concepts cannot be said to apply to each and every person. Rather, one may imagine constructs of greater or lesser generality, processing structures whose specifics overlap to some degree between individuals sharing similar environments and histories. This is what would be expected of fundamental processing mechanisms whose function is adaptation to a specific, *local* environment and whose guiding principle is satisficing, rather than maximizing (see, e.g., Anderson, 1991; Triandis, 1996).

This is not to say that there are no culturally general processes. People seem attuned to covariation in their environments and are able to aggregate instances and express generalizations, even if biased (e.g., Cheng & Novick, 1992; Fiedler, 1996). Causal reasoning, for instance, seems to be fundamentally human (White, 1988), as does evaluation (Osgood et al., 1975). But the *form* and *content* of such reasoning (or the evaluative process) are determined by the environment in which they occur, which makes some things easier to notice than others (Gilbert & Malone, 1995; Triandis, 1995b) and influences the local covariation of cues (LeVine & Campbell, 1972), yielding different operational theories (Morris & Peng, 1994). Furthermore, these theories operate in context, such that features of the immediate situation change the relative diagnosticity of one bit of information for a subsequent response (Hilton, 1995; Schwarz, 1994).

A second implication is that there is an inherent interaction between accessibility and diagnosticity. That is, inferences, affective responses, and behavior will be determined by the most accessible of the sufficiently diagnostic schemata, and the most diagnostic of the schemata equally accessible. Accessibility and diagnosticity are further correlated in the sense that extensive elaboration means that certain structures (e.g., scripts, values, expert knowledge) are easily, perhaps preconsciously, elicited and apply to a wide range of judgments, evaluations, and behavior. But, as shown by Trafimow, Triandis, and Goto (1991), increasing the accessibility of a less-elaborated schema will change judgments (relative to control conditions), provided only that sufficient diagnosticity exists.

Finally, it should be noted that *any* information may serve a diagnostic function if a response is necessary. Moods, for instance, may be inputs to certain judgments (Is my life happy? Is this person interesting? Do I approve of the government?), and, in fact, accessibility itself may serve as a diagnostic cue for relevant responses (Forgas, 1995; Schwarz et al., 1991; Wänke, Schwarz, & Bless, 1995).

This raises the issue of diagnostic sufficiency. That is, what determines the adequacy of retrieved knowledge, or affective responses, to guide judgment or behavior? This is the question of motivation.

MOTIVATION

Influences on the energy, direction, and persistence of behavior are studied under the label of motivation. In a sense, no behavior is "unmotivated"; all must be in some way energized, directed, and terminated. Interest is typically focused on either the general process by which these events occur or particular states or circumstances that might influence one or more of these functions. Research may examine individual differences, defining and measuring chronic motives, or circumstances creating motive states and their consequences. Both approaches have implications for affect, cognition, and behavior via accessibility and diagnosticity.

Energizing Behavior

A great deal of research concerns conditions promoting extensive information processing. That is, what makes people expend scarce resources on judgments, decisions, and behavior? One factor is uncertainty—that is, some ambiguity in the stimulus environment that precludes minimally confident categorization or evaluation of some stimulus object or the production or choice of behavior.

Srull and Wyer (1989) show, for example, that extra thought is given to cases in which affectively inconsistent information about a person is presented. Inconsistency is also thought to prompt controlled, algorithmic attributional processing—in this case, inconsistency between expectations based on a person category and observed behavior. Presumably, inconsistency engages a chronic motive to understand and control one's environment ("accuracy motivation"; Kunda, 1990).

The same phenomenon may be found in studies of group process and conformity (Allen, 1965, 1975; Isenberg, 1986; Laughlin, 1988; Moscovici, 1985; Wood, Lundgren, Ouellette, Busceme, & Blackstone, 1994). In classic conformity and obedience studies, the individual's attention is focused on discrepancies between expected and actual group behavior, energizing effortful search for behavioral guidance and attention to situational cues (e.g., of social support; Allen, 1975; see also Brown, 1986). In group-decision studies, disagreement engages effortful processing of the available cues, both heuristic (social comparison) and systematic (argument quality; Isenberg, 1986). Minority influence (Moscovici, 1985; Wood et al., 1994) seems to work similarly; consistent minorities whose views cannot be discounted via heuristic processing engage effortful, issue-relevant thought. The same processes emerge in group problem solving (Laughlin, 1988).

The more severe the possible consequences of misunderstanding, the more intense processing motives should be. Thus, although Gilbert (1989) finds that simply requesting an accurate judgment in laboratory circumstances is enough to prompt correction of spontaneous, automatic trait judgments (Newman & Uleman, 1989), the motive is typically aroused when some form of outcome dependence exists (Brewer, 1988; Fiske & Neuberg, 1990), causing personalized or individuated, rather than categorical, judgments. Feldman (1988) points out that individuated impressions may be formed of any object, provided there is sufficient motive intensity. It should also be noted that, in these cases, categorical information is not completely disregarded. Individuated processing is accomplished in the context of categorical information, producing (for instance) stereotype contrast and confirmation effects (Feldman & Hilterman, 1975; Kunda & Thagard, 1996).

Effortful processing may also be energized by external incentives. Tetlock (1992) discusses accountability produced by having to justify one's reasoning as one such motivating factor. Incentives define "issue involvement," in which an issue's personal outcome relevance produces more central, argument-based processing of persuasive messages. Intrinsic motivation, in the form of value or self-presentation relevance (see discussions in Eagly & Chaiken, 1993), likewise energizes central or systematic processing. Each type of involvement has directional effects as well, which will be discussed below.

Incentives and involvement influence more than judgments. Fazio (1990) argues that reasoned action, requiring the effortful construction and integration of "attitudes toward actions" and normative statements to produce explicit intentions, takes place only when there is no accessible, relevant (diagnostic) general attitude (or norm) or when the decision is sufficiently consequential to warrant effortful processing. Feldman and Lynch (1988) point out contextual factors that might also produce such reasoning.

Affective state likewise may energize processing strategies (Isen & Diamond, 1989; Schwarz, 1990) as well as provide informational input. Negative mood seems to promote more message elaboration and use of all diagnostic information in persuasion; positive mood, in contrast, is associated with the use of global judgments and heuristic cues. Presumably, because negative mood is associated with states requiring analysis to avoid or escape aversive events, it has become automatically linked to these procedures (Smith, 1994). Positive mood, in contrast, may signal states requiring no action (and, in fact, action may lessen the positive mood). Positive moods are found to relate to creativity and the creation of broad, novel categories; thus, the world may seem a different place to those in different moods because the construction of their experience is different.

Individual differences in motive structures play an important part in energizing cognitive effort. Need for cognition (Cacioppo, Petty, Feinstein, & Jarvis, 1996) is a very general disposition to seek and enjoy effortful reasoning and problem solving regardless of domain. Individuals to whom this disposition applies process message arguments centrally rather than relying on heuristic cues (e.g., credibility), and they typically develop more elaborated, consistent attitude, belief, and behavior systems.

Bargh and Barndollar (1996) present evidence that motives may operate automatically, as do other knowledge/affect structures; Kruglanski (1996) makes a similar argument for goals, and both recall Mischel and Shoda's (1995) arguments. Motive or goal structures may differ in elaboration, affective loading, and thus chronic accessibility and may be of many specific types. For instance, Higgins's (1996) discussion of ideal, ought, and actual self-discrepancies can be conceptualized in terms of chronically or temporarily accessible goals. Bargh and Barndollar (1996) demonstrate that active motives automatically energize (and direct, as discussed below) behavior for which they are diagnostic, presumably by influencing one's affective response to one's performance *and* by the concepts and behaviors that come to mind. This is another example of automatic inputs to conscious decision processes (Bargh, 1994).

Two issues should be addressed here. The first is to reiterate that there is no clear distinction between motives, goals, personality traits, values, and so on. We can impose a hierarchy on these, putting personality, for instance, at the top, subsuming values and general motives, which in turn subsume attitudes and specific goals, but this is an artificial distinction for *our* convenience, much as taxonomy is for the naturalist. From the point of view of the individual, *it is all the same.* Chronically or temporarily accessible motives, like categories, bring with them selective attention to cues, affective responses, and behavioral scripts. They motivate processing by changing the criterion for diagnostic sufficiency, itself an aspect of procedural knowledge associated with motives or other concepts (Cacioppo et al., 1996). Motives may be associated with quite general knowledge/affect structures, prompting (for instance) ruminative thought (Wegner, 1994; Wyer, 1996) as well as more effective self-regulation (Kuhl & Beckmann, 1994).

Second is Bargh and Barndollar's (1996) point that there is no necessary association between consciousness and decision/behavior quality. Automatic processes represent a summary of frequent, consistent experience in some (local) domain and thus an adaptation to it. Energizing thought or other effortful processes (rehearsing affect, for instance) may change judgments in ways that are unrepresentative of the person's habitual cognitive/affective pattern and, perhaps, of his or her typical environment (Feldman & Lynch, 1988; Wilson & Schooler, 1991). Formally "rational" judgments are not always adaptive (Feldman & Lindell, 1990).

Direction

If we accept the proposition that motives are variously elaborated knowledge and affect structures that may operate either automatically (in preconscious or postconscious modes) or deliberately (either in a goal-dependent automatic mode or as part of controlled processing), then it stands to reason that motive states act, as other schemata do, to make certain stimuli more salient and associated knowledge and affect more accessible. For instance, processing goals influence the likelihood that an impression will be formed, given equally accessible person information (Srull & Wyer, 1989; Woehr & Feldman, 1993). Chronically accessible concepts (traits and stereotypes) focus attention on certain features of persons and direct impression formation, unless overridden by other motives (e.g., values, self-presentation, accuracy motives) that engage alternative schemata (e.g., traits vs. stereotypes; Brewer, 1988; Fiske & Neuberg, 1990). Affective states have similar automatic effects on retrieval of episodic memories and procedural knowledge (Isen & Diamond, 1989; Schwarz et al., 1991). Such schematic effects have been found, for instance, in sexual cognition and behavior (Pryor & Stoller, 1994); cooperative versus competitive game behavior (Sattler & Kerr, 1991); and social anxiety (Pozo, Carver, Wellens, & Scheier, 1991).

Consciously operative goals, such as accountability to a biased audience, may motivate a directed search for information in memory or the environment. Kunda (1990) maintains that people balance two motives: the first, to arrive at whatever judgment, evaluation, or action satisfies the operative motive, and the second, to satisfy a (presumably automatic) standard of logical justification. Thus, the search focuses on constructing a logical rationale for the conclusion one wishes to draw. This position leads to some interesting predictions—for instance, that those high in need for cognition might be more biased in their reasoning than those low in need, depending on the strength of motives for biased processing. Another is that, in cultures in which collectivist norms of self-presentation and social interaction dominate motives for self-expression (Triandis, 1995b), selective retrieval and motivated processing following normatively consistent behavior would be reduced—simply because the response is motivated, not its justification. Normatively inconsistent behavior, however, would require substantial justification, resulting in increased accessibility of relevant knowledge structures (Trafimow et al., 1991).

The search process envisioned by Kunda (1990) is not necessarily conscious. A motive such as self-enhancement may operate preconsciously in accessing associated concepts. This is what would be expected of a highly overlearned skill.

As also noted by Bargh (1994), consciously held goals may have unanticipated consequences, especially when they involve performance of some sort. Kanfer and Ackerman (1989; Kanfer, 1996) discuss the ways in which external task performance goals may instigate self-regulatory and self-evaluative processes, interfering with learning and performance. One outcome of goal nonattainment is ruminative thought (Martin & Tesser, 1996), which may persist not despite but *because* of motivated attempts at suppression (Erber & Wegner, 1996; Wegner, 1994). Similar phenomena are seen in the domain of chronically accessible goal and affect structures (e.g., Elliot & Church, 1997; Higgins, 1996; James, in press). Motivational interventions like goal setting interact with accessible motive structures to determine the content and intensity of cognition and affect, as well as subsequent behavior (e.g., Harackiewicz & Elliot, 1993).

As noted earlier, the direction of processing depends on the specifics of the individual's schemata. Higgins's self-discrepancy manipulations, for instance, are individualized, whereas Schwarz et al.'s (1991) studies of context effects depend on highly specific analyses of reasoning processes and associative patterns. Thus, the particular thoughts, feelings, and behaviors observed when a specific motive (like self-evaluation) is aroused can vary greatly between cultures or between individuals who are "differently schematic."

Persistence

When does an individual divert energy from one goal to another? Naylor, Pritchard, and Ilgen (1980) have presented a resource allocation model that assumes a quasi-rational, cost-benefit allocation process similar to theories of reasoned action, but it is unlikely that the process is always (or even often) consciously regulated.

Assuming for the present that cognitive/affective processes do mediate behavioral persistence, what form might they take? Most current theories involve some goal or end-state representation, conscious or not (see Kanfer, 1990). Beach's (1990) image theory, for instance, postulates knowledge structures (images) representing desired end states and means of attaining them; the former are reminiscent of Higgins's (1996) "ideal" and "ought" standards. Beach postulates that behavioral options are first screened for compatibility with these images; a choice is then made among the remaining alternatives. Presumably, a motive may be said to be "satisfied" when a comparison of the current state with some representation of the goal state produces a sufficient match. Thus, any factor influencing the representation of the goal state, the similarity of the current state to the goal (or vice versa), the matching criterion, affective responses to goal attainment or nonattainment (e.g., Carver & Scheier, 1990), and so forth will influence the persistence of behavior.

The elaboration and affective saturation associated with schematic cognitive structures, whether these are called cultural values, personal values, motives, or personality traits, promote extensive and directed information processing when activated. Egalitarian values, for instance, prompt effortful individuated processing when the bigot would happily stereotype (Devine, 1989). Need for cognition engages effortful information processing as much for its own sake as for the importance of the decision or judgment. A complementary motive, "need for closure," is a desire for definite knowledge—that is, for "nonspecific closure" (Kruglanski & Webster, 1996). As need for cognition motivates more extensive processing, need for closure motivates rapid judgments and decisions as well as resistance to further processing. "State-oriented" individuals dwell extensively on long-term plans and goals but not on their implementation (Kuhl & Beckmann, 1994). Elaborated values, like schematic personality traits, prompt extensive message processing and argument retrieval when challenged (Eagly & Chaiken, 1993; Markus, 1977) but relatively simple processing when affirmed.

Externally imposed contingencies, such as outcome involvement or accountability for accuracy, may also promote extensive processing (Fazio, 1990; Petty & Cacioppo, 1990; Tetlock, 1992) or rapid closure (Kruglanski & Webster, 1996). The simplest explanation for this phenomenon is that the criterion of diagnostic sufficiency becomes more or less strict as either intrinsic or extrinsic outcomes of processing become more extreme or salient (Kruglanski & Webster, 1996, pp. 269-270). It may also be that a more or less detailed goal representation is generated, requiring different amounts of processing to achieve a satisfactory fit.

The nature of goal representations may vary with individuals and contexts, as well, increasing or decreasing required cognitive effort. Performance goals, whether chronic or imposed, may direct attention to an externally set, specific high goal level, whereas learning goals may direct attention to the slope of performance over time. Other goals, such as "getting by," may merely direct attention to some minimal performance standard (e.g., Elliot & Church, 1997). The amount of effort devoted to examining one's performance and the subsequent impact on self-assessments would be expected to differ in each case.

Comparing the outcome of judgment or behavioral processes with goal representations (whatever the nature of those representations) is a similarity judgment. Similarity judgments are highly labile and subject to contextual influences, though knowledge moderates these effects (Feldman, 1992; Medin, Goldstone, & Gentner, 1993). For instance, the degree of similarity between any two representations depends on which is more elaborated and on the direction of the comparison. The question "How similar is Canada to the United States?" would produce higher ratings, for instance, than "How similar is the United States to Canada?" (at least for U.S. citizens), because attention is directed to features of the subject of the comparison, and the more elaborated object contains more distinctive features. Thus, asking "How similar is my performance to the goal?" may produce a different answer than "How similar is the goal to my performance?" How people habitually frame such questions is undetermined (but see Catrambone, Beike, & Niedenthal, 1996).

It should not be assumed that the persistence of behavior reflects a conscious decision process. If, as Bargh and Barndollar (1996) argue, motives may be engaged preconsciously, it is reasonable to assume that associated regulatory processes may also be automatic. Thus, for instance, the relationship between emotional state or mood and elaborative processing (Forgas, 1995; Schwarz et al., 1991) probably operates by engaging highly practiced automatic procedures, which then determine the (consciously experienced) sufficiency of information for a particular purpose.

These automatic procedures may be largely responsible for the variety of relationships that can be observed between intensity, direction, and persistence of behavior. Low-involvement judgments or decisions, for instance, may lead to reliance on categorization and heuristic cues, but so may high-involvement, life-threatening ones. Extensive thought may lead to better or worse decisions; temporarily operative motives cause elaborative processing that supersedes automatic affective responses even when the latter are ecologically valid.

These considerations apply not only to individual judgments but also to group processes. Tendencies toward either heuristic or systematic processing, whether chronic or situationally aroused, would logically influence group processes, such as the success of minority influence attempts or conformity pressures (Kruglanski & Webster, 1996, pp. 272-273) and group polarization.

Of course, motivation does not operate in a vacuum. To process information effortfully, some attentional capacity must be available. How much capacity is present and how it is allocated are the final questions.

CAPACITY

It is impossible to discuss all the issues surrounding the concept of capacity, the total of the attentional resources available to the individual at a given time. Discussions of individual differences in capacity lead inevitably to discussions of ability and its assessment, one of the bitterest debates in psychology and one that I intend to avoid.

It *is* increasingly clear, however, that whatever one's inherent capacity may be, the capacity available to a given person in a given situation depends significantly on prior learning and the results of practice (Ericsson, Krampe, & Tesch-Römer, 1993; Neisser et al., 1996). Intense, long-term practice apparently creates "expert" knowledge structures that are automatically (perhaps preconsciously) engaged. These enable efficient organization of information in long-term memory in forms qualitatively as well as quantitatively different from those of novices. They also promote perceptual-level processing of familiar stimuli and problems as well as more extensive, high-level problem solving in novel situations (Alba & Hutchinson, 1987). Although these concepts have been most intensively investigated in the domain of physical and mental abilities, it is reasonable to assume that the same phenomena occur in the domain of values, motives, dispositions, and so forth; in these cases, "practice" and "feedback" would occur as a consequence of life in a particular social environment, producing the kinds of cognitive/affective structures discussed under "diagnosticity" (see Rogoff & Chavajay, 1995).

The implications of this viewpoint for capacity are twofold: One, within one's domain(s) of expertise, processing efficiency frees attentional capacity for extensive thought while other tasks are being performed, as when one ponders a difficult issue at work while driving a familiar route. Two, these capabilities are *highly* topic-specific; knowledge does not transfer automatically to unpracticed domains.

Individual differences have been largely overlooked in social cognitive research. In studies of stereotyping and impression formation, for instance, capacity has been manipulated by assigning an alternative task or processing goal (e.g., Devine, 1989; Gilbert, 1989; Srull & Wyer, 1989). In the domain of attitudes, similar manipulations (e.g., distraction) are sometimes used; although value differences are assessed, these are of interest because of their effect on processing direction, not efficiency (see Eagly & Chaiken, 1993).

Consideration of the nature of elaborated processing structures leads to some straightforward predictions. One is that people with higher levels of general verbal ability would be able to process narrative or message information better under conditions of diminished capacity, as a result of both greater procedural skill and more extensive knowledge. Thus, correcting attributional biases or responding to argument quality would be more likely when these individuals are motivated to do so. Those with less verbal ability would require more capacity to engage in "bottom-up" processing. This should apply to only general, culture-common domains (e.g., trait judgments), however. In domains requiring specialized knowledge, and in which accuracy rather than processing mechanics alone is an issue, specific knowledge and standards of judgment must be taken into account (see, e.g., Feldman, 1994, pp. 378-382).

Cultural differences in processing attributable to the more or less efficient use of capacity might also be observed. We can expect individuals from collectivist cultures to make spontaneous situational attributions much as individualists make spontaneous trait attributions; this implies that "correction" of inappropriate situational attributions requires capacity allocation. The same predictions apply in other domains—for instance, in the analysis and generation of behavior in superior-subordinate interactions or in situations in which attitudes and norms conflict, comparing cultures high or low in power distance or in "tightness versus looseness" (Triandis, 1995b).

At the individual level, the same kinds of predictions may be tested by comparing people differing on "tacit knowledge" of given domains (Sternberg, Wagner, Williams, & Horvath, 1995). As "IQ" represents the degree to which an individual has attained expertise in formal schoolwork skills, tacit-knowledge measures reflect expertise in other domains—organizational, social, and so forth. Such "practical intelligence" appears highly domain specific and in no way different from other aspects of skill and expertise (Alba & Hutchinson, 1987; Ericsson & Charness, 1994). The processing advantages conferred by tacit knowledge, however, need to be tested within relevant domains, such as in interpersonal relations. One might expect, for example, that people expert in a particular social context might require fewer resources to make judgments and decisions in that context but might require more available resources to adapt to new situations (e.g., in an unfamiliar culture).

In short, the question of capacity goes well beyond predicting when elaborative, bottom-up, systematic processing is possible. Research has established that, under some circumstances, attentional resources are necessary, and it has made the case for two interacting modes of cognition, affect and behavior generation (e.g., Epstein, 1994). Further progress depends on understanding the nature and limits of specific skills or response dispositions, whatever these are labeled.

SUMMING UP

This chapter presents at best a metatheory, in the spirit of Mischel and Shoda's (1995) and Triandis's (1996) call for the investigation of general processes within specific contexts. I have argued that we may pursue this strategy by asking four general questions about any problem of interest: accessibility, diagnosticity, motivation, and capacity. These questions apply equally well to correlational and experimental investigations across the domain of human behavior. Furthermore, and most important, they force one to adopt the perspective of the naturalist, who studies the smallest details of an organism's anatomy, physiology, and environment to understand its evolution, behavior, and ecological function. Each event, each person, each context, and each culture is unique and historically unrepeatable. What *are* general and repeatable are the processes that create these singular people, settings, groups, and societies and that make us all human.

5

THE EMERGENCE OF CULTURAL PATTERNS OF INTERPERSONAL BEHAVIOR

John Adamopoulos
Grand Valley State University

Recent approaches to the study of culture's influence on social behavior have emphasized cultural description on a number of distinct, if frequently correlated, dimensions that involve, among others, the notions of power, societal complexity, and role differentiation. The greatest amount of interest has focused on the cultural dimensions of individualism-collectivism (Hofstede, 1980; Triandis, 1989, 1995b) and its personality analogue, idio-centrism-allocentrism (Triandis, Leung, Villareal, & Clack, 1985).

An impressive amount of empirical evidence suggests that we can reliably distinguish cultures in which the individual derives the sense of self from, and is influenced primarily by, one or a few in-groups (collectivism) from cultures in which the individual conceives of the self and acts in a manner that may be relatively free of in-group influence (individualism). Triandis (1989, 1990) has provided exhaustive and clearly articulated reviews of this evidence. In fact, the empirical evidence for this distinction appears so strong that Triandis (1993) refers to these dimensions as "cultural syndromes."

However, despite the abundance of empirical descriptions for these cultural dimensions, there is no comprehensive theoretical system to account for the varied charac-

AUTHOR'S NOTE: I am extremely grateful to Christine Smith, who collaborated with me on an earlier project on which this chapter is based.

teristics of individualism and collectivism and to explain the origins of these patterns. As a result, a number of controversies have developed in this area, such as the relative frequency of prejudice and ethnocentrism in individualist and collectivist cultures, the relationship between competition and individualism, and, in an extreme case, the claim by at least one social scientist that, contrary to majority thinking, "practically all industrial nations of today are collectivist societies" (Beyer, 1968, p. 160).

The goal of this chapter is to propose a more integrated view of individualism and collectivism as behavioral patterns resulting from particular psychocultural processes. Specifically, the present analysis will focus on some basic components that define social exchange, such as the relationship between actor and recipient of action, and the type of resources that individuals exchange in different social contexts. Thus, this analysis is particularly informed by the resource exchange theory of Foa and Foa (1974), by assumptions about societal forces contributing to the emergence of individualism proposed by Triandis (1990), and by the behavior differentiation model formulated by Adamopoulos (1988, 1991b).

THEORETICAL ASSUMPTIONS

Most definitions of individualism and collectivism emphasize the interpersonal nature of these concepts and the relationship of the self to the collective (e.g., Triandis, 1989). Thus, the structural analysis of interpersonal behavior may offer significant insights into the composition of individualism and collectivism and into the relationships among their constituent parts.

Adamopoulos (1984, 1988, 1991b) has presented a framework for the analysis of interpersonal structure based on resource exchange principles proposed by Foa and Foa (1974, 1980). This framework assumes that the differentiation of fundamental components or constraints of social exchange over time results in the emergence of a number of (universal) dimensions of interpersonal behavior. Along similar lines, individualism and collectivism, in their variant forms, may be conceptualized as themes or prototypes of interpersonal relations that characterize different cultural contexts. These themes, or cultural patterns, result from the differentiation of basic components of social interaction in successive stages.

The analysis of interpersonal relations from a resource exchange perspective must involve at least three distinct features (facets): (a) the orientation or direction of the action involved in the exchange; (b) the orientation or relationship between actor and target(s); and (c) the type of resource exchanged. The first facet, action orientation, is of central concern to the study of individualism and collectivism because it involves the distinction between action oriented toward providing for the self and action oriented toward offering resources to others. Many investigators in this area assume, often implicitly, that this is the hallmark of the individualism-collectivism dichotomy (e.g., Triandis, 1988; see also Markus & Kitayama, 1991). For example, Verma (1986) has reported that normative considerations and concern with the social consequences of one's actions characterize behavior in a collectivist society (India), whereas affective or self-oriented concerns are relatively more important in an individualist society (the United States). Similar findings have been reported by Davidson, Jaccard, Triandis, Morales, and Diaz-Guerrero (1976) in a comparison of U.S. and Mexican decision making.

I assume that, culturally and historically, this is the first facet to be differentiated. Developmentally, the distinction between self- and other-directedness occurs as early as age 2 (Lewis & Brooks-Gunn, 1979). Furthermore, research on the development of self- and ethnic identities, and on the relationship between the two, suggests that children may develop a sense of their own race very early in life. Naturally, awareness of one's own racial identity also implies a differentiation of the self from others and the formation of corresponding attitudes (e.g., Devine, 1989). Historically, there is some evidence that awareness of the self as agent of action and dispositional (as opposed to situational) self-attributions were not prevalent in the earliest period of our recorded past (e.g., Adamopoulos, 1988; Jaynes, 1976; Sampson, 1988).

Once the self-other distinction is accomplished, the nature of the recipient in social exchange becomes paramount. Following earlier work (Adamopoulos, 1988), I assume that the "other's" (individual or group) relation to the self may be either specific or general. Specific others, involved in unique relationships with the self, cannot be easily substituted in the process of a particular social exchange without a great deal of difficulty and psychological discomfort. For example, in interpersonal expressions of love, the specific relationship between actor and target (e.g., lover, spouse, relative) is very important. Similarly, teachers perform their functions primarily in the presence of particular groups of people (students). The presence of a different person or group in these cases creates many difficulties and, indeed, may make the interaction impossible.

General others, however, are easily interchangeable. In this case, particular exchanges are not limited to specific relationships between the actor and one (or a few) individual or group. Rather, there is a good deal of overlap among different targets or recipients of action such that the same behavior can be performed with or toward a number of distinct individuals or groups. For example, most people presumably do not care which specific individual pays them for work done, as long as they receive appropriate payment. It may just as easily be a secretary, their employer, or a faceless entity called "personnel department." Along the same lines, in certain individual-to-group exchanges, the target is easily substituted. Many politicians with a particular agenda, for example, do not fundamentally alter their message when they present it to very different groups in their constituency. "No new taxes" or "no more crime" sounds equally attractive to most reasonable people, regardless of group affiliation.

This facet is a reconceptualization of current thinking in the analysis of individualism and collectivism. Hui (cited in Triandis, 1988) and Triandis (1988, 1995b), among others, have proposed that determining the number of groups that influence a person's behavior is central to understanding the two constructs. However, the idea of a particular distinguishing number of groups is rather awkward, for any such number is relative to specific cross-cultural comparisons and, therefore, arbitrary. In addition, it is not in-group influence alone that should be considered here but the spectrum of choices considered by the individual actor who will be the recipient of the exchange in a particular situational context.

The final facet in the framework concerns the nature of the resources exchanged. In the present context, following Foa and Foa (1974), resources are conceptualized as material or symbolic (abstract). The idea of resource exchange and sharing is considered important to the definition of collectivism (e.g., Hui & Triandis, 1986) and is, of course, central to the analysis of interpersonal structure. Historically, there is some speculation that the differentiation of concrete (material) and symbolic exchanges appeared fairly late in human evolution and marked the beginning of organized culture (Adamopoulos, 1988, 1991b). Finer discriminations of this facet are possible. For example, material resources may be broken down to goods, services, and so on, whereas symbolic resources may be understood as involving status or information. Future analyses may benefit from such discriminations.[1]

A STRUCTURAL MODEL
OF INDIVIDUALISM-COLLECTIVISM

The differentiation of the facets described above yields a number of prototypical patterns of behavior that may be conceptualized as predominant themes of interpersonal relations under different constraints. I must emphasize here that these themes are not conceptualized as exclusive or exhaustive descriptions of cultures but, rather, as indications of a few characteristic features of different cultures—similar to what Triandis (1993) identifies as cultural syndromes. It is expected that all themes may be present in any particular culture, because I assume that all facet components are present in most societies at this point in time. Thus, the core assumption here is that there are reliable and, therefore, predictable differences among cultures with regard to the degree to which particular themes are dominant in them. The major themes, or cultural patterns of behavior, are organized as a circumplex and are the results of the differentiation process outlined in Figure 5.1.

According to this model, the self-other distinction underlies the general dichotomy between individualism and collectivism. However, several easily identifiable and specific subtypes of each construct emerge as further differentiation takes place.

Ego-Sustaining Individualism

When the cultural context favors generalized relationships and the person is engaged primarily in the acquisition of material resources (goods, services) for the self, the concern is clearly with individual survival. This pattern may also be called protoindividualism, because it reflects a fundamental attempt to ensure individual well-being with little regard for the fate of the group or society. It is generally assumed that this pattern characterizes very simple, solitary hunting societies and may have begun to disappear with the emergence of social stratification and organized culture (Adamopoulos, 1982; Triandis, 1988). Alternatively, to the extent that individual survival is assured by modern society, this pattern may have been transformed over time to one emphasizing thrill seeking through the accumulation of material goods and experiences. Elsewhere in this

FACETS	COMPONENTS							
ACTION ORIENTATION	SELF				OTHER			
ACTOR-TARGET ORIENTATION	GENERAL		SPECIFIC		SPECIFIC		GENERAL	
RESOURCE EXCHANGE TYPE	MATERIAL	SYMBOLIC	SYMBOLIC	MATERIAL	MATERIAL	SYMBOLIC	SYMBOLIC	MATERIAL
PROTOTYPICAL BEHAVIOR PATTERNS	CONCERN WITH INDIVIDUAL SURVIVAL	NARCISSISM	CONCERN WITH SELF-ESTEEM & SELF-RELIANCE	COMPETITION	COOPERATION & CONCERN WITH PERSONAL RELATIONSHIPS	CONFORMITY & CONCERN WITH GROUP COHESIVENESS	CONCERN WITH SOCIETAL VALUES & ETHNOCENTRISM	PHILANTHROPY
INDIVIDUALISM-COLLECTIVISM TYPE	EGO-SUSTAINING	EGOCENTRIC	EGO-DEFENSIVE	ACQUISITIVE	INTER-PERSONAL	REFERENTIAL	IDEALISTIC	ALTRUISTIC
INDIVIDUALISM-COLLECTIVISM TYPOLOGY Triandis, 1995	HORIZONTAL INDIVIDUALISM		VERTICAL INDIVIDUALISM		VERTICAL COLLECTIVISM		HORIZONTAL COLLECTIVISM	
SOCIALITY MODEL Fiske, 1992	EQUALITY MATCHING		MARKET PRICING		AUTHORITY RANKING		COMMUNAL SHARING	

INDIVIDUALISM (spans SELF columns)   *COLLECTIVISM* (spans OTHER columns)

Figure 5.1. The Emergence of Various Types of Individualism and Collectivism

67

chapter I discuss a case (the Ik) in which this pattern may have appeared under extraordinary circumstances.

Egocentric Individualism

The emergence of culture probably coincides with the appearance of symbolic exchanges, such as exchanges of information about status and power. When the target is easily interchangeable, exchanges of this type involve the glorification of the self, with little concern for the interests of others.

This pattern can be documented in some of the earliest written records of human culture, dating back more than 3,000 years. Historians and literary critics have frequently argued about a fundamental difference in perspective found in the two Homeric epics, the *Iliad* and the *Odyssey* (e.g., Redfield, 1975). In the *Iliad*, which may reflect early humanity, people are judged by their relative position in society and by their influence on others rather than by their ability to develop an integrated and independent sense of self. In the *Odyssey*, there is a suggestion of the emergence of a different human being, concerned with a sense of personal worth and accomplishment. Indeed, examples of this transformation abound in the two documents. Adamopoulos (1988) has described the feud between Achilles, the hero, and Agamemnon, the supreme commander of the Greek forces during the Trojan War, as an essentially narcissistic one. Even relations among the gods follow this pattern. Consider Poseidon's anger with Zeus in the *Iliad*:

> This is outrageous! . . . Zeus may be powerful, but it is sheer bluster on his part to talk of forcing me, who enjoy the same prestige as he does, to bend my will to his. . . . So I am not going to let Zeus have his way with me. . . . And do not let him try to scare me with threats of violence, as though I were an arrant coward. (as cited in Rieu, 1950, p. 276)

In both these cases, the fact that the target (Agamemnon and Zeus) is an acknowledged leader is irrelevant to the exchange; it could just as easily have been a subordinate. The primary concern is with the unconditional celebration of the self, which we would consider today an extreme, even pathological, form of narcissism (Mazlish, 1982).

Ego-Defensive Individualism

As individuals begin to differentiate among recipients and, on that basis, select their interactions with appropriate persons, they shift to a much healthier—by modern standards—concern with developing and defending realistic self-esteem. Actions then become more responsive to situations, and expressions of self-esteem become dependent on context. Odysseus, the hero of the second Homeric epic, clearly exemplifies the emergence of this new man. Relations among the gods in the *Odyssey* also document this shift. Again, consider the following interactions between Poseidon and Zeus:

Then Zeus, who drives the storm cloud, answered, sighing: "God of horizons . . . why do you grumble so? The immortal gods show you no less esteem. . . . But if some mortal captain . . . cuts or defies you, are you not always free to take reprisal?" . . . Now said Poseidon . . . "Aye, god of the stormy sky, I should have taken vengeance . . . and on my own; but I respect, and would avoid, your anger." (as cited in Fitzgerald, 1963, p. 234)

This notion of properly situated self-reliance and self-esteem is thought to constitute one of the fundamental, culture-common components of individualism (Triandis, Bontempo, Betancourt, & Bond, 1986). I expect that Western expressions of the need for achievement are deeply rooted in this type of individualism.

Acquisitive Individualism

Concern with material gains for the self leads to the emergence of competition. Clearly, competitive interactions are target specific because they are dependent on situational context. Research on the development of social values suggests that children with different cultural backgrounds change from an essentially egocentric perspective to a competitive one, which involves a consideration of relative advantages in the specific situation, before moving on to cooperation (e.g., Kagan & Zahn, 1983; Knight, Kagan, & Buriel, 1981; McClintock, 1978). The label "acquisitive individualism" is intended to emphasize the primacy of individual effort in this type of social pattern.

Interpersonal Collectivism

Cooperation follows the development of competitive tendencies when the orientation of the action shifts from *self* to *other*. This transformation is necessary for the emergence of personal and intimate relationships, which are based on mutual cooperation and self-disclosure. Just as cooperation appears rather late in child development, intimacy—at least as we understand it today—may have appeared rather late in cultural evolution. Adamopoulos (1982, 1988) has reported some historical evidence supporting this hypothesis.

It is important to note here that, of course, intimacy does not belong exclusively to collectivist societies. The dimension of intimacy does not appear consistently, or in the same form, in modern cross-cultural studies of interpersonal structure (e.g., Lonner, 1980; see also Adamopoulos & Lonner, 1994). This suggests the possibility that intimacy is understood differently in individualist and collectivist cultures. Adamopoulos and Bontempo (1986) have defined intimacy as the exchange of target-specific and material resources. Thus, intimate interactions may characterize both acquisitive individualism and interpersonal collectivism. I propose, however, that somewhat different conceptions of intimacy are involved in the two cases.

Adamopoulos (1991a) has presented results of an investigation of the perception of personal relationships in an individualist culture (the United States) and a moderately collectivist culture (Greece) that indicate that Greeks report a relatively limited variety of such relationships (e.g., immediate family, close relatives and friends). Americans, on the other hand, report a wide variety of relationships that include elements of competition, status difference, and even conflict (e.g., client-therapist, pet owner). Greeks, in other words, emphasize the friendly and altruistic component of intimacy, whereas Americans consider the usefulness and hedonism derived from relationships.

Referential Collectivism

Other-directedness linked to symbolic exchanges with specific individuals or groups results in the formation of group bonds and the development of group cohesiveness. Norem, Ardyth, and Johnson (1981) have reported lower ego-defensiveness in individuals with cooperative, rather than competitive, orientations, which is probably because of the presence of more social reinforcers in interdependent relationships. Family cohesiveness and interdependence are major dimensions of collectivism identified in recent investigations (e.g., Feldman, Ah-Sam, McDonald, & Bechtel, 1980; Triandis et al., 1986).

The term *referential collectivism* emphasizes the significance of the reference group as a source of personal worth and esteem for the individual. A number of social psychological theories have articulated this process. For example, social identity theory (e.g., Tajfel, 1981) proposes that individuals consider their in-groups superior to out-groups because they are motivated by a need for high self-esteem. Indeed, the acquisition of social identity appears to be associated with improvement in self-esteem (Oakes & Turner, 1980). Research in collectivist societies (Korea, Japan, and China) indicates that, in contrast to the United States, personal accomplishment is gauged by its contribution to the family or in-group (De Vos, 1983; Yu, 1980).

Idealistic Collectivism

As the orientation of social exchange shifts to interchangeable "others," we would expect the appearance of cultural patterns of nationalism and ethnocentrism. Specific individuals and groups merge into a collective identity, which must be protected. The rise of ethnocentrism during periods of war may reflect such a process. Discrimination against out-group members that may occur in this case is qualitatively different from that which may occur, for example, in egocentric individualism: The former has a collectivity-protective function, whereas the latter may stem from a lack of concern for other people's interests because of an overwhelming emphasis on the celebration of the self.

This theoretical distinction of the functions of prejudice and discrimination in individualist and collectivist cultures leads to the following propositions: The group identification of the target is a more important determinant of prejudice in collectivist than in individualist cultures. In the latter, the target's lack of similarity to the individual, rather than his or her group identity, is the most significant determinant of prejudice. In individualist cultures, the essentially narcissistic patterns of interpersonal relations associated with egocentric individualism are encouraged by the affirmation of the self provided by similar others.

Cross-cultural research in in-group/out-group relations supports the above propositions. For example, Georgas (1986) has reported that Greeks (collectivists) define their in-group in terms of the extended family and all individuals with whom one may form interpersonal relations, whereas Americans (individualists) include in their in-group primarily similar others.

Examples of idealistic collectivism have been reported in China (Hofstede, 1980) and among individuals raised in the former USSR (Toren & Grifel, 1983).

Altruistic Collectivism

Like ego-sustaining individualism, this pattern is probably relatively rare in modern society and may occur only in periods of extreme crisis, when the very survival of the collective is threatened. Alternatively, it may appear in cases—all too rare—when there is an overabundance of resources and life is viewed as a non-zero-sum game.

THE EMERGENCE OF
INDIVIDUALISM AND COLLECTIVISM

Some critiques of the evolutionary approach to individualism-collectivism have focused on the criticism that most models in this approach imply a process of change from collectivist states to individualist ones (e.g., Kagitcibasi, 1990a). Such an implication is based on the untenable position that collectivist cultures are less "developed." However, there is no reason to assume that certain collectivist and individualist states cannot coexist in different behavioral domains at the same time.

So far in the present discussion I have implied an evolutionary process from the extreme cases of ego-sustaining individualism and altruistic collectivism toward acquisitive individualism and interpersonal collectivism. Triandis (1990) has proposed that the shift from collectivism to individualism is caused by societal affluence and complexity. In the present context, affluence may be conceptualized as resource availability. As resources increase (in relative terms), the actor-target orientation necessarily changes from general to specific because an increasing number of specialists (individuals or groups) must deal with the distribution of these new resources. Adamopoulos (1991b), for example, has described historical accounts of the rise of new classes and groups following the invention of the printing press. Increases in social or role differentiation inevitably result in greater cultural complexity (e.g., Doumanis, 1983). Thus, it is reasonable to assume that ego-defensive and acquisitive individualism and interpersonal and referential collectivism are recent forms of the two constructs.

When resources become less available, cultural complexity decreases, because many specific social roles and groups become nonfunctional and even redundant. In such cases, we would expect a shift toward altruistic collectivism and philanthropy. Examples of this are found during wars or natural disasters. However, in the extreme case in which resources become scarce, the circumplex presented in Figure 5.1 suggests that there is probably a shift toward ego-sustaining individualism. Such a change was reported as the result of the catastrophic circumstances that befell the Ik, the African hunters, who experienced almost complete cultural disintegration within a few generations after they lost most of their access to resources. The Ik, driven out of their traditional hunting grounds by a government decision to turn the grounds into a national game reserve, suffered an almost complete loss of material resources, goods, and territory. Within a few generations, most cultural institutions and traditions disappeared, including norms guiding family relations. The Ik became concerned almost exclusively with individual survival (Turnbull, 1972).

RELATIONSHIP OF THE STRUCTURAL MODEL
TO OTHER THEORETICAL FRAMEWORKS

The model outlined in this chapter implies a number of predictions about the structural relations among different components of individualism and collectivism. These predictions may be viewed primarily as guides for future research in the area. At the same time, these predictions make possible a broader conceptual analysis of the relationships that exist among several recent theoretical frameworks that propose to explain the structure of interpersonal relations. I will briefly outline such an analysis below. However, detailed contrasts among predictions stemming from these frameworks are clearly beyond the scope of the present chapter.

A Typology of Individualism and Collectivism

Triandis (1994a, 1995b) has proposed four distinct types of individualism and collectivism: (a) Horizontal individualism involves high individual freedom and equality; (b) vertical individualism emphasizes independence but also displays power and status differences among individuals; (c) horizontal collectivism involves interdependence and equality; and (d) vertical collectivism involves interdependence and significant power differences among individuals.

As shown in the lower half of Figure 5.1, horizontal individualism can be conceptualized as a pattern involving a self-focused action orientation and interpersonal exchanges in which the other's identity, status, and power are not significant components of the interaction. Vertical individualism, on the other hand, involves interactions in which the actor-target relationship (e.g., role and status differences) is important in the exchange.

Horizontal collectivism involves other-oriented, interdependent exchanges toward generalized others, with little emphasis on status differences. Finally, vertical collectivism involves other-oriented exchanges in which the particular actor-target relationship is typically of importance. Thus, role differences in power and status are likely to play a substantial role in determining the tone of the interaction in this case.

Elemental Forms of Social Relationships

Fiske (1990, 1992) has developed a model of the "elemental" forms of sociality in differing cultures that can also be understood within the present theoretical system. According to Fiske, interpersonal exchange is defined by individual participation in four basic types of social relationships: (a) equality matching (resource exchange among people of equal status); (b) market pricing (resource exchange involving profit seeking in the marketplace); (c) authority ranking (resource exchange based on the privileges of high-status individuals and on their responsibilities toward their subordinates); and (d) communal sharing (exchange among individuals who share resources from a communal pool).

Triandis (1994a, 1995b) has provided an interesting integration of Fiske's model with his typology of individualism and collectivism. As can be seen in the lower half of Figure 5.1, each of the four elemental forms of sociality can also easily be classified within the present theoretical system based on the extent to which it involves (a) exchanges that are self- versus other-oriented and (b) relationships characterized by status, power, and other role differences.

Both Triandis's typology and Fiske's model of sociality offer powerful descriptions of important cultural patterns of social behavior. The advantages of the system proposed in this chapter are that it offers (a) a richer set of potential cultural manifestations of individualism and collectivism and (b) a more comprehensive explanation of the origins of these cultural patterns.

The Universal Structure of Values

Following a different approach, Schwartz (1990, 1992) has derived a circumplex of culture-common values from ecological analyses of data obtained from a large number of samples across many cultures. This impressive research program has yielded an ordering of commonly held value types that is very much in line with the ordering of the individualism and collectivism types generated by the present model.

Schwartz (1992) has defined values as belief structures about goal states that guide behavior across social situations. He has proposed that specific values can be classified into broader motivational categories that reflect individual and group needs for inter-action and survival. The evolutionary assumptions underlying this reasoning are, of course, similar—in spirit, if not in substance—to the assumptions articulated earlier in the presentation of the proposed model. Furthermore, the notion that basic human needs may result in specific psychological structures with motivational properties is compatible with the proposal that the differentiation of fundamental human constraints results in the emergence of general themes about interpersonal dynamics.

The contrast of individual *and* group needs by Schwartz (1992) has yielded the classification of value types into those associated with individualist tendencies and those associated with a collectivist orientation. Following a somewhat different line of reasoning, a number of other psychocultural processes that result in the development of similar value structures are described here. Thus, the present model may be viewed as an alternative and useful explication of the emergence of interpersonal structures in differing cultural contexts.

Figure 5.2 presents a tentative mapping of the circumplex proposed by Schwartz, derived from cross-cultural data, onto the theoretical circumplex proposed here, which is derived from the sequential differentiation of culture-common facets of interpersonal exchange.

Clearly, a perfect fit cannot be expected between the two structures. After all, the values circumplex by definition precludes consideration of behavior patterns that are not socially desirable. The proposed model, however, includes a number of conditions that give rise both to pro-social and antisocial behavior. Consequently, it is not surprising that some value types appear to fit the model's individualism-collectivism types better than others. In addition, both structures involve continuous and overlapping regions, not discrete categories. Thus, the proper comparison of the two models should be focused on whether they map the same conceptual space rather than on whether there is a one-to-one correspondence between value and individualism-collectivism types. I have tried to indicate this by slightly rotating the two structures for a better conceptual fit.

It is fairly evident that the values in the upper half of the circumplex are generally associated with individualism, whereas those in the lower half of the circumplex are related to collectivism. In fact, Schwartz (1992) has also argued that universalism and security are points of transition between individualism and collectivism. This is very consistent with the proposed model, as acquisitive individualism and interpersonal collectivism share common features and are, structurally, neighboring regions. The same is true for ego-sustaining individualism and altruistic collectivism. The mapping of the two models presented in Figure 5.2 makes this structural correspondence clear.

On the individualism side, the order of values from self-direction to power is fairly similar to the order of the prototypical behavior patterns in the proposed model. Thus, for example, self-direction, which involves values such as "creativity" and "choosing own goals," may refer to the pattern of abilities and skills thought to be important—perhaps even necessary—for an individual's well-being or survival (as implied in ego-sustaining individualism). Stimulation (e.g., "daring," "exciting life") and hedonism (e.g., "plea-sure") can easily represent the narcissistic behavior patterns prevalent in egocentric in-dividualism. Achievement (e.g., "ambitious," "successful," "intelligent") clearly reflects a concern with self-esteem (ego-defensive individualism), and, finally, power (e.g., "social power," "wealth") is associated with competition and acquisitive individualism.

As we move toward the collectivist side, security is defined by values such as "family security," "reciprocation of favors," and "sense of belonging"—clearly reflections of a concern with personal relationships, a typical pattern of interpersonal collectivism. Conformity (e.g., "honor parents," "politeness," "obedience") fits neatly into referential collectivism, as has been shown already, and tradition (e.g., "respect for tradition") is related to the definition of idealistic collectivism. Finally, the values associated with benevolence (e.g., "helpful") and universalism (e.g., "social justice") are very strongly connected to the description of altruistic collectivism.[2]

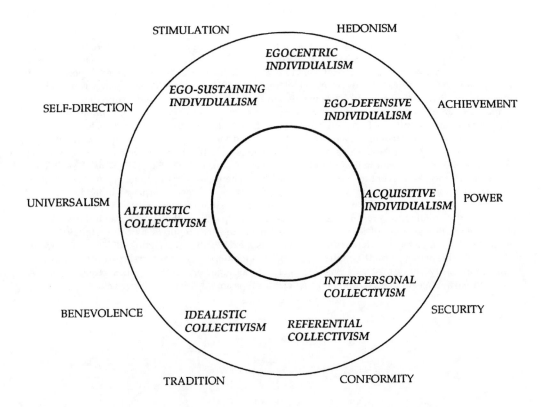

Figure 5.2. Mapping of the Culture-Common Value Structure (Schwartz, 1992) Onto the Proposed Individualism-Collectivism Model (Inner Circle)

Overall, considering that the two models were developed independently, the fit is impressive and suggests that the circumplex proposed here may provide a basis for the interpretation of obtained structural relations among values. Thus, this model integrates work on individualism-collectivism and on human values within the same general framework.

FINAL COMMENT

The model presented in this chapter makes explicit the notion that there may be just as many differences *among* collectivist or individualist cultures as there are *between* them. Consequently, the model may be useful in the interpretation of seemingly conflicting findings from different cultures assumed to belong to the same type. Furthermore, it proposes some "key" variables that must be measured to render interpretable results from cross-cultural studies on individualism-collectivism.

NOTES

1. The association of exchange rates of specific resource classes (e.g., love, status, information, money, goods, and services) with individualism versus collectivism is problematic for most current theories in this area. For example, Triandis (personal communication, September 28, 1990) considers it possible that collectivists exchange more of those resources that depend on a particular relationship between actor and target—such as love, status, and services—whereas individualists exchange more resources for which the specific actor-target relationship is not as important (money, goods, and information). This may be a result of the greater personalization of relationships in collectivist cultures. However, the reverse pattern may be just as prevalent in different behavioral domains. For instance, arranged marriages, which imply a depersonalization of close relationships, are more frequent in collectivist cultures. Such resource exchange differences may not be endemic to the individualism-collectivism dichotomy but, rather, may be a function of societal affluence. Whatever the case, the approach taken here considers all major types of exchange in both cultural contexts to develop an exhaustive typology of the major forms of individualism and collectivism. The idea that *some* forms of the two constructs appear much more frequently than other forms because of differential rates of resource exchange is quite compatible with the proposed framework.

2. The relative position of lower-order values in the research reported by Schwartz (1990, 1992) appears to vary somewhat in different samples, whereas the motivational categories of his framework are much more stable across cultural samples. The proposed model, which generates broad cultural themes, is thus more easily understood as a possible interpretive framework for Schwartz's general empirical structure than as a means of accounting for the relationships among the lower-order values.

6

CULTURE, CONNECTIONISM, AND THE SELF

Yoshihisa Kashima
La Trobe University

Emiko S. Kashima
Swinburne University of Technology

> *All things flow.*
> —Heraclitus (approx. 540 B.C.–480 B.C.)

> *Standing on a river-bank he said: it is what passes like that, indeed, not stopping day, night.*
> —Confucius (552/1 B.C.–479 B.C.)

At about the same time in human history, two of the fine minds in the East and the West were impressed by the never-ceasing flow of events that is the universe. Heraclitus, the pre-Socratic philosopher who was bitterly criticized by Plato and Aristotle, and Confucius, the quintessential wise man revered in the Chinese tradition, both commented on the perpetual flux of a river. The first opening quotation is a paraphrase from Plato's discussion of Heraclitus (Russell, 1945/1972). Perhaps developing the same theme, in

AUTHORS' NOTE: We thank M. Brewster Smith and Wolfgang Wargner for their constructive comments on an earlier draft of the chapter.

one fragment of what remains of Heraclitus's metaphysics, he said, "As they step into the same rivers, other and still other waters flow upon them" (translated by Kahn, 1979, 50). The second quotation, from Confucius, which was beautifully translated by Ezra Pound (1933, 16.1), was his exclamation at the sight of a flowing river.

The river is a metaphor for a conception of culture that we think is relevant for cross-cultural psychology. Our aim is to outline a dynamic conception of culture and psychology, which may shed new light on the relationship between culture and self. We try to do this in three steps. First, we briefly discuss two distinct images of culture that are present in psychology today. Second, we review major tenets of connectionism as an approach to psychological processes and examine how a dynamic conception of culture and a version of connectionism may be fruitfully integrated to provide a framework for conceptualizing the relationship between culture and psychology. Finally, this framework is applied to a particular question about the relationship between culture and self.

TWO IMAGES OF CULTURE

Culture is a central concept in social science. Yet its conceptualization has been extremely diverse. Not to mention Kroeber and Kluckhohn's attempt (1952) at enumerating its definitions, culture has been defined from many perspectives in the past. Despite the sometimes chaotic rush to embrace culture in psychology today, there are still some centers of gravity. As there are some explications of these differences (Lonner & Adamopoulos, 1997; Miller, 1997), we will instead provide a general description of two clusters of theoretical orientations, or images, that form fuzzy sets by family resemblance.

One of the images depicts culture as a relatively enduring system of meanings shared by a group of people in a certain geographic region during a certain period of time. To a well-known symbolic anthropologist, Geertz (1973), "the concept of culture . . . is essentially a semiotic one. [I believe] with Max Weber, that man [sic] is an animal suspended in webs of significance he himself has spun" (p. 5).

In social psychology, Triandis (1972) defined *subjective culture* as "a cultural group's characteristic way of perceiving the man-made part of its environment" (p. 4). Perhaps the most comprehensive delineation of culture in this vein was more recently proposed by Triandis (1994a):

> Culture is a set of human-made objective and subjective elements that in the past have increased the probability of survival and resulted in satisfactions for the participants in an ecological niche, and thus became shared among those who could communicate with each other because they had a common language and they lived in the same time and place. (p. 22)

In contrast, the alternative image characterizes culture as a dynamic process of production and reproduction of meanings in particular actors' activities in particular situations in time and space. Anthony Giddens (1976/1993) has suggested,

> Sociology is not concerned with a "pre-given" universe of objects, but with one which is constituted or produced by the active doings of subjects. . . . The production and reproduction of society thus has to be treated as a skilled performance on the part of its members. (p. 168)

Replacing "sociology" with "research on culture," we have a succinct statement about the dynamic conception of culture.

Another influential theorist, Bourdieu (1977), attempted to explain such dynamic regularities by equipping people not with rigid "habits" but with *habitus*, which he defined as "systems of durable, transposable dispositions . . . principles of the generation and structuring of practices and representations which can be objectively 'regulated' and 'regular' without in any way being the product of obedience to rules" (p. 72).

Some cultural psychologists (Greenfield, 1997; Miller, 1997) have endorsed a view of culture that treats it as a dynamic process. A similar image of culture has been espoused by some social constructionist critics of mainstream social psychology (e.g., Gergen, 1985; Shotter, 1993; for review, see Kashima, 1994). From a different perspective, Poortinga (1990) also presented a view that focuses on the effect of culture on a particular actor's particular behavior in a particular situation. Although his view emphasizes the constraining effect of culture on behaviors (just like Durkheim's "social facts"), rather than its enabling effect, Poortinga's emphasis on particularity in which culture interfaces with human action is a step in this direction.

The metaphor of culture as a river may make more concrete the dynamic conception of culture. Like a river, a culture is a continual flow of events. Like a river, culture has some enduring course and running streams. But, in one crucial respect, "river" may be a poor metaphor for culture. A river has a destination, always running into a sea or a lake; a culture, however, has no preset destination, we believe.

The two images of culture are complementary. The image of culture as a meaning system treats culture as a relatively stable *structure*; the image of culture as a dynamic process treats culture as a continual *structuring* (or structuration, as Giddens calls it). On the one hand, the systemic conception of culture enables us to *describe* a culture in comparison with others. On the other hand, the dynamic conception attempts to *explain* how a structure-like meaning system can be reproduced in particular actors' particular activities in time and space. The systemic approach gives us a descriptive strategy, whereas the dynamic approach may provide us with explanatory concepts.

As Poortinga (personal communication, August 1996) noted, the recent rift between cross-cultural and cultural psychologies fundamentally reflects a difference in conception of culture. Cross-cultural psychology, in its orientation to compare cultures, often treats culture as an enduring system, whereas cultural psychology, in its emphasis on cultural mediation of human action, typically treats culture as a dynamic process. Although the relationship between cultural and cross-cultural psychologies is often polemicized, we submit that they are complementary in the above sense.

CONNECTIONISM AND CULTURE

Connectionism is a label applied to a diverse range of conceptual models in cognitive science, which has recently come into popularity as a reaction to the serial computer metaphor of cognitive processes (e.g., Hinton & Anderson, 1981; Rumelhart, McClelland, & the PDP Research Group, 1986). Connectionism is often said to be "neurally inspired": It uses the brain as a main metaphor of the cognitive architecture. Information is processed not by the all-powerful central processing unit but by a collection of numerous simple processing units. The form of information processing is largely parallel, rather than sequential. Thus, a concept is represented by a pattern of activation over the processing units, and mental operations are carried out in parallel.[1] Y. Kashima and his colleagues (Kashima & Kerekes, 1994; Kashima, Woolcock, & King, 1998) recently began to use connectionism to model social psychological processes (for an overview, see Smith, 1996).

There are several advantages to the connectionist approach in conceptualizing the relationship between culture and psychology. First, connectionist models typically describe the learning of specific episodes and experiences in situ. This not only makes for the context sensitivity of these models but is also concordant with the episodic, particularistic conception of culture as a dynamic process. If culture is to be conceptualized as a flow of specific human actors' specific activities in time and space, the episodes of such specific activities must form the basis of the human actors' psychological processes. Connectionist models do this as a natural consequence of their architecture and processing assumptions.

Second, most connectionist models have the capacity to generalize "automatically," by virtue of their architecture. For instance, when a person learns to act in a certain manner in certain situations, the person can generate an action similar to the learned action in a situation similar to the situations in which the action was learned. This suggests that connectionist models can explain the reproduction of cultural practices, thereby suggesting an account of the stability of cultural systems.

Third, connectionist models can usually generate some action even if the models encounter a completely new situation that they have never encountered before. In other words, a person will not simply reproduce what he or she has learned before but will improvise. Such a generative property, or a capacity for "regulated improvisations," as Bourdieu (1977, p. 78) puts it, is again part and parcel of the connectionist-type architecture.

The compatibility of the connectionist approach and the dynamic conception of culture was noted by Quinn and Strauss (1993), acknowledging a similarity between connectionist models and Bourdieu's *habitus*. D'Andrade (1995) also suggested that cultural models that are shared by members of a culture may be realized in a connectionist-type architecture. From the perspective of situated cognition, Hutchins and Hazelhurst (1993) also used a connectionist model to examine how lexicons (arguably an element of a cultural model) may be generated from interacting dynamic systems. A connectionist approach as a dynamic model of the mind (see Port & Van Gelder, 1995; Vallacher & Nowak, 1994, for a general treatment of the dynamic approach) gives a natural counterpart to the dynamics of culture.

In sum, a dynamic conception of culture and a connectionist approach to psychological process may be fruitfully integrated. This framework treats both culture and psychology as dynamic processes: Just like sometimes converging and sometimes diverging streams, in the end, they form a seamless stream of human activities.

CULTURE AND SELF

The question about the relationship between culture and self is old. Ever since Herodotus, humans have been fascinated by how culture and people shape up each other. After the ill-fated culture and personality movement, the research interest in culture and self has been steadily growing in recent years (Kashima, 1995; Kashima et al., 1995).

One theoretical reason for this interest may be that self is conceived to mediate the influence of culture on psychological processes (e.g., Markus & Kitayama, 1991; Singelis & Brown, 1995; Triandis, 1989). Triandis (1989) argued that, although an individual possesses different types of self-representations, people tend to acquire some types of self-representations more than others depending on their cultural backgrounds. In individualist cultures, people tend to have more individualist (or independent) self-representations; in collectivist cultures, they have more collectivist (or interdependent) self-representations. Markus and Kitayama (1991) showed that different types of self-representations (or self-construals) are likely to lead to different types of cognitive, emotional, and mtivational consequences. Taken together, in this view, culture is an antecedent of psychological processes, in which self-representations act as a mediator of cultural influences on cognitive, affective, and motivational processes.

This view, however, presupposes a theoretical orientation that treats culture as an enduring system of meaning. To be sure, the introduction of self-representations at the interface of culture and psychology is a step toward a conception of culture that takes particular actors' particular activities seriously. Nonetheless, we wish to approach the topic from an even more dynamic viewpoint, using the approach we have discussed before. We will show that the dynamic approach may shed new light on the conception of culture as an enduring meaning system.

Self and First-Person Pronouns

To approach the nexus of culture and self in English-speaking cultures and Japan, we began with an examination of first-person pronouns, such as *I* in English and *watashi*, *boku*, and *ore* (and many more) in Japanese. An examination of first-person pronouns may enable us to trace the dynamic production and reproduction of the self in particular contexts. The use of first-person pronouns is a kind of deixis. Deixis is a linguistic phenomenon in which words (e.g., *I, you, here, there, now, then*) are used to refer to some features of the particular context of utterance; that is, words such as *I* and *you* do not have fixed referents but take on specific referents only in a particular utterance in a particular situation. As Lyons (1977) puts it, "Deixis, in general, sets limits upon the possibility of decontextualization; and person-deixis . . . introduces an ineradicable subjectivity into the semantic structure of natural languages" (p. 646).

Benveniste (1966/1971) made the strongest case for the function of deictic personal pronouns as a device for grounding a language to a particular context. According to him, *I* is a sign through which the speaker "takes over all the resources of language for his own behalf" (p. 220).

> [*I*] is linked to the *exercise* of language and announces the speaker as speaker. . . . Habit easily makes us unaware of this profound difference between language as a system of signs and language assumed into use by the individual. When the individual appropriates it, language is turned into instances of discourse, characterized by this system of internal references of which *I* is the key, and defining the individual by the particular linguistic construction he makes use of when he announces himself as the speaker. Thus the indicators *I* and *you* . . . exist only insofar as they are actualized in the instance of discourse, in which . . . they mark the process of appropriation by the speaker. (p. 220)

Benveniste's characterization of language as "a system of signs" may itself need to be reexamined from the present perspective, taking into account the "social laws of construction" (Bourdieu, 1991). That is, deictic personal pronouns enable the speaker not only to access the symbolic resources of language, but also to *construct* the symbolic representation of the self by virtue of the constructive function of symbols (e.g., Goodman, 1978). Deictic personal pronouns participate in the symbolic construction of the concrete persons in a particular situation.

Perhaps it is not a coincidence that more dynamically oriented inquirers of the self, such as William James (1890/1950; recall his "stream of consciousness") and George Mead (1934; a dynamic interplay of "symbolic gestures"), began their investigations by reflecting on the English first-person pronoun.

Self and Deictic Personal Pronouns in English and Japanese

We wish to focus on two major characteristics that differentiate English and Japanese deictic personal pronouns. The first is the number of first-person pronouns available as a language. This is a system characteristic of English and Japanese as a language (i.e., *langue* of Saussure, 1959). The second is more associated with the use of the first-person pronouns (i.e., *parole* of Saussure), which is the frequent drop of first-person pronouns in Japanese conversation. We also examined more empirical issues associated with deictic personal pronouns (Kashima & Kashima, 1997).

Japanese and English both provide deictic personal pronouns. However, as Kuroda (1992) pointed out, they present different sets of opportunities and requirements for their use. In English, there are only *I* and *you.* By contrast, Japanese has a multitude of first- and second-person pronouns: *watashi* and *anata, boku* and *kimi, ore* and *omae,* and so on. A particular first-person pronoun presupposes its counterpart, and a particular choice reflects the speaker's social relationship with the listener. To this extent, Japanese as a linguistic system appears to require that the speaker's symbolic construction of the self always be in relation to the listener. In contrast, English enables the speaker's symbolic construction of the self to be independent of the interpersonal relationship.

This systemic analysis of Japanese and English nevertheless needs to be qualified by their use. Of particular importance is the pervasiveness of ellipsis, or drop, of the subject of a sentence in Japanese conversation. According to the statistics of the Japanese National Language Research Institute (as cited in Martin, 1975), as high as 74% of the sentences in discourse do not explicitly state the subject. Ellipsis is often defined as "the omission of an element or several elements from the surface form of an utterance" (MacWhinney & Bates, 1978). However, recent linguistic research into Japanese ellipsis favors a view that it is more than just a syntactic issue of omitting what should be there. For the identification and recovery of elliptical slots requires contextual and sociocultural information, in addition to syntactic information (e.g., Hinds, 1982; Maynard, 1989).

Do these systemic and pragmatic differences in language use play a role in producing the cultural difference in self-representation? According to Markus and Kitayama (1991), *interdependent* Japanese selves contrast with *independent* American selves. They suggested that the self-representation of the Japanese tends to incorporate those of significant others, whereas that of the Americans tends to be separate from the representations of others. Consistent with their characterization, both Bond and Cheung (1983) and Cousins (1989) found that, in response to the question "Who am I?" the Japanese students described themselves using more social references than their American counterparts.

In addition, Cousins's (1989) research suggests that the Japanese self-descriptions are more contextualized than the American ones. When asked to describe themselves in specific contexts, the Japanese used clear personal attributes, whereas the Americans' self-descriptions were not as clearly defined (using modifiers such as "fairly," "more or less"). This was interpreted to mean that the Japanese self is more contextually defined than the American self.

Taken in combination, these findings are in line with Triandis's (1995b) analysis. According to him, collectivists (e.g., Japanese) show a closer interpersonal relationship with in-groups than do individualists (e.g., Americans, Australians) but a greater inter-personal distance with out-groups than do individualists. To put it simply, the Japanese interdependent self-representation should show a greater variability as a function of the in-group versus out-group context than should the American or Australian independent self-representation.

These findings may be restated in the connectionist framework in terms of the psychological similarity between self- and "other" representations. That is, the inde-pendent self implies that the self-representation is clearly separate from and dissimilar to the other representation; the interdependent self suggests a greater similarity between self- and other representations in some contexts but greater dissimilarity in others, showing a greater variability in self-representation.

We wish to show that the systemic and pragmatic aspects of the first-person pronouns in English and Japanese may be in part responsible for the difference in self-representation as described above. This is a kind of Whorfian hypothesis: Does the language use influence the way people think about themselves (Lee, 1950)? Although there is some evidence to support a weak thesis of the Whorfian hypothesis (e.g., see Hunt & Agnoli, 1991, for a recent review), we wish to go further and show that a connectionist model can provide an account of how the linguistic practice of deictic personal pronouns may affect the mental representation of the self.[2]

"Finding Structure in Time" by a Connectionist Network

In the article entitled "Finding Structure in Time," Elman (1990) proposed a connectionist model called the Simple Recurrent Network, which learns a sequence of events and reproduces that sequence. Unlike its predecessors in the connectionist tradition, the network does not explicitly encode the temporal sequence of events but, rather, "remembers" the sequence implicitly by encoding which event is followed by which event. In so doing, it can discover structure implicit in the temporal sequence. This architecture treats the temporal dynamics of an event sequence as its inherent and central aspect (Elman, 1995; Hanson & Hanson, 1996).

After describing Elman's research, we will show in the next section how this network architecture may be used to explicate the relationship between the use of personal pronouns and self-representations.

The architecture of the model is presented in Figure 6.1. The model consists of four sets of simple processing units (input, hidden, output, and context units). A unit can be activated at a level between 0 and 1 as a sigmoid (a nonlinear) function of the amount of activation it receives from other units. Initially, the connection weights between the units are set randomly. The network operates as follows:

1. The first event is represented by a pattern of activation over the input units and a random pattern of activation over the context units.
2. The activations spread forward to the hidden units as a function of the connection weights between the input and context units and the hidden units, and the hidden units are then activated as a function of the amount of activation they receive.
3. The hidden-unit activations again spread forward as a function of the connection weights between the hidden and output units, and the output units are activated as a function of the amount of activation they receive.
4. The activation pattern over the output units is then compared with the pattern of activation that represents the second event in the sequence. The amount of the mismatch is used to adjust the connection weights by the back-propagation algorithm (see Rumelhart, Hinton, & Williams, 1986).
5. In the next cycle, the pattern of activation over the output units, which represented the second event in the sequence in Step 4, is represented by the input

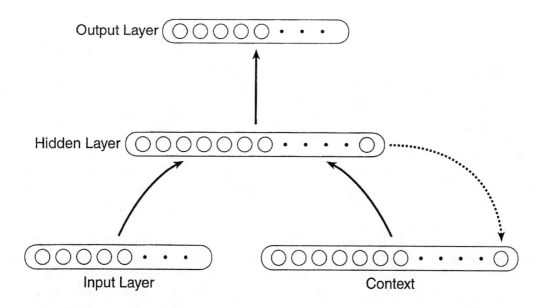

Figure 6.1. A Schematic Representation of the Simple Recurrent Network

units, and the pattern of activation over the hidden units for the first event (described in Step 2) is reproduced in the context units.

6. These activations spread forward to the hidden units as a function of the adjusted weights (Step 4), and the hidden units are activated as a function of the amount of activation they receive, as in Step 2.

7. The hidden-unit activations spread forward to the output units as in Step 3, and the output units are activated as a function of the adjusted connection weights. This pattern of activation is compared to the pattern that represents the third event in the sequence, and the amount of the mismatch is used to adjust the connection weights again.

The cycle of steps from 5 to 7 is repeated as long as the events in the sequence continue (for further detail, see Elman, 1990; for a program, see Freeman, 1994). This network architecture learns to predict successive events.

In one simulation study, Elman (1990) showed that his network can recover meaningful regularities from a stream of inputs even if the network had no prior information about the regularities that produced the inputs. Elman used a set of rules to generate 10,000 two- or three-word sentences using 29 different lexical items such as *man, cat, book, chase,* and *break.* The rules were designed to produce word sequences that roughly conform to the usual English grammar (e.g., the subject of a sentence is an animate object). This amounted to a sequence of 27,354 words without any punctuation between sentences. In other words, the input sequence consisted of a stream of events (or sentences) without any break.

The network consisted of 31 input and output units, as well as 150 hidden and context units. Each word was represented by a random pattern of activation over the 31 units. Therefore, the sequence of events to be learned was the series of 27,354 vectors with 31 elements in each. Elman then trained the network by feeding this sequence six times without a break. At this point, it is important to note that Elman's network had no information about the rule by which these inputs were generated.

After this training, Elman fed the same sequence of events through the network; however, this time without adjusting the connection weights. This allowed him to examine the activation pattern over the hidden units when a particular event (or word, in this case) was represented in the input units (Step 6). The pattern of activation over the hidden units is the internal representation of an input event developed by the network. This internal representation may simulate, and be analogous to, the mental representation of the input event developed by a human individual.

Elman conducted a hierarchical cluster analysis of the hidden-unit activations of the 29 lexical items and discovered that the word clusters can be meaningfully interpreted. The 29 words formed two large clusters: verbs and nouns. The verb cluster branched into words that obligatorily require a direct object and words for which a direct object is optional. The noun cluster split into two major groups: inanimates (e.g., cheese) and animates (e.g., boy). Animates were then divided into human and nonhuman objects (e.g., lion). To put it differently, the internal representations developed by the network contained the information about the meaning system embedded in the sequence of linguistic events.

Finding Self-Representations in Time

Just as Elman (1990) was able to discover lexical classes in the sequence of words, we may be able to "discover" self-representations from the use of deictic personal pronouns in simple language-like sentences. To explore this possibility, we conducted the following simulation. The simulator of the Simple Recurrent Network was written in *Mathematica* (Wolfram, 1991), based on Freeman's (1994) program.

The sequence to be learned was a series of vectors, which represented self, behavior, or target. To keep the simulation simple, we chose only two types of behaviors, positive and negative. Actor was always self, and target was always other, to which the self's behavior was directed. Thus, an example may be as follows: I-behaved-positively-to-you.

We constructed four types of sequences, involving a two-way factorial design. The first factor was whether the sequence had *systemic* characteristics similar to English or Japanese. In the English-like pattern, the sequence was actor-behavior-target, and there was only one "word" for self and one "word" for other. In the Japanese-like pattern, the sequence was actor-target-behavior, and there were three "words" for self and three "words" for other.[3] The second factor was whether the sentence-like sequence had a *pragmatic* characteristic analogous to English and Japanese, that is, whether it involved ellipsis, or dropping of the personal pronouns. In total, we had four stimulus conditions: an English-like sequence with and without ellipsis and a Japanese-like sequence with and without ellipsis. The detail of the simulation is reported in the appendix.

After a sequence of actor-behavior-target was fed through the Simple Recurrent Network, the hidden-unit representations for self, other, and behavior were examined using Elman's (1990) technique. For each "word" of self, other, and behavior, the pattern of activation over the hidden units was recorded, and the Euclidean distance between the vectors representing these patterns was computed. In the end, we produced four distance matrices, representing "word" configurations in the four conditions. Each distance matrix was then submitted to a multidimensional scaling analysis, using a Euclidean distance model.

Two dimensional models fit reasonably well to all four matrices (stress was from .01 to .18, R^2 was between .99 and .86). It is important to note that each "word" in a particular occurrence has a slightly different internal representation, although different occurrences of the same "word" are reasonably similar to each other. When the same matrix was used to conduct a hierarchical cluster analysis, the different occurrences of the same "word" formed a cluster. This observation is in line with the episodic and particularistic nature of connectionist models. The same "word" was represented differently in the hidden units because its context varied depending on which "word" preceded it. Therefore, one dot in the graphical presentation of the multidimensional solutions represents a particular occurrence of a "word."

Despite this general observation, the configurations in the four conditions show marked differences. First, compare the top panel and the bottom panel of Figures 6.2 and 6.3. We see that, when the first-person "words" are not dropped (top panels), there is a fairly tight clustering of self- and other representations, and the distance between the two clusters is fairly uniform. By contrast, in the conditions in which the first-person "words" are dropped (bottom panels), the self- and other representations are diffuse or quite variable, and the distance between self- and other representations varies markedly, sometimes much closer and other times much farther than in the no-ellipsis condition. Second, there appears to be some difference between the English-type and the Japanese-type systems (i.e., one vs. three first-person "words"). Comparing the two top panels, the English-type condition (Figure 6.2) seems to show even tighter clustering of self- and other representations than the Japanese-type condition (Figure 6.3). Again, a similar tendency appears when ellipsis occurs as well, though the contrast is less apparent.

Based on these simulations, the presence of ellipsis seems to be a primary factor that makes the self-representation more variable, though the systemic aspect such as the number of first-person pronouns appears to have some effect. To put it simplistically, those who often drop first-person pronouns tend to have more collectivist self-representations than those who do not. This insight gained by the simulation result was empirically borne out. Using Hofstede's (1991) data on individualism, a correlational analysis showed that country-level individualism can be significantly predicted by the presence or absence of ellipsis of first-person pronouns in the major language used in each country.

The simulation exemplifies the complementarity of the dynamic approach and the meaning system approach to culture. Cross-cultural research identified enduring cultural differences between English-speaking and Japanese cultures. A dynamic approach can then be deployed to interpret and explain these differences. Yet the present dynamic

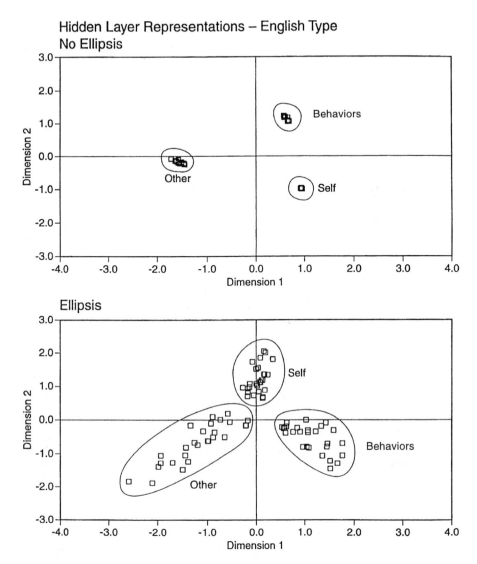

Figure 6.2. Multidimensional Solutions of the Hidden Layer Activation Patterns for the English-Type Language

approach revealed the possibility that some enduring self-representations may emerge from the dynamic flow of cultural practices and further prompted cross-cultural examinations of a relationship between personal pronoun use and cultural dimensions such as individualism and collectivism.

The simulation reported here is limited in scope. We need more extensive simulations to gain more detailed knowledge of the workings of the Simple Recurrent Network and to map out the learning of self-representations from a stream of language-like events. Nevertheless, it seems to give a promising lead in the direction of a dynamic conception of culture and psychology. Perhaps the most beneficial use of this type of simulation is to

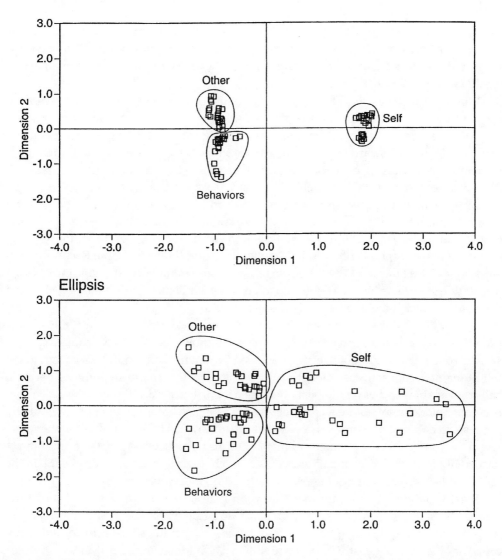

Figure 6.3. Multidimensional Solutions of the Hidden Layer Activation Patterns for the Japanese-Type Language

explicate specific hypotheses about a relationship between variables (e.g., relationship between aspects of language and self-representation) and to show that there exists *some* theoretical formulation that can explain the relationship.

CONCLUSIONS

The conception of culture as a relatively enduring meaning system shared by a group of people is strategically necessary in cross-cultural comparisons. However, when culture is conceptualized as a dynamic process, new perspectives may open up in theorizing the relationship between culture and psychology. Inspired by Heraclitus and Confucius, we suggested the river metaphor of culture, which is hoped to provide a concrete image of the dynamic process that is culture.

When culture is viewed as a dynamic stream of events, the psychological process too needs to be conceptualized in a like manner. We suggested that connectionism might provide a vehicle for bridging the domains of culture and psychology. Connectionism, with its orientation toward context-sensitive psychological processes and its strength in modeling the processing of particular event episodes in the world, invites the dynamic conception of the interplay between cultural and psychological processes.

An investigation into culture and self gives an example of this approach. Starting with a linguistic analysis of English and Japanese deictic personal pronouns, we suggested that both systemic and pragmatic aspects of the first-person pronoun use may shape the representations of the self. Simulations using Elman's Simple Recurrent Network suggest that the practice of dropping first-person pronouns may shape the self-representation to become more variable and interlinked with other representations, showing the characteristic of the interdependent self-construal.

The linking of connectionism and a dynamic conception of culture holds some promise. The framework can be used to explicate hypotheses. Just as we could hypothesize a strong negative link between first-person pronoun drop and individualism in the self-domain, a connectionist model could be devised to explore hypotheses between cultural variables and psychological phenomena. Furthermore, although any given connectionist model may not be a complete theory of a psychological phenomenon, it still suggests that there exist some processes that can give rise to the psychological phenomenon as a consequence of some specifiable cultural practices. We believe the Simple Recurrent Network shows that there exists a psychological process that can explain the relationship between first-person pronoun drop and individualism.

Finally, a connectionist approach may provide a new method for cross-cultural comparisons. Cross-cultural psychology has concentrated on comparisons between cultures by examining their symbolic representations (e.g., culturally specific or emic concepts) or by stipulating abstract etic concepts (e.g., individualism and collectivism), which are more abstract than existing cultural symbols and therefore may be called *super*symbolic. A connectionist approach provides an alternative: By examining the *sub*symbolic structure of representations in connectionist networks, we may be able to shed new light on cross-cultural differences.

Despite theoretical, methodological, and practical difficulties of approaching cultures dynamically, with constant innovations in all these fronts, we believe it is possible to investigate the dynamic flow and interplay of cultural and psychological processes. We attempted to provide an example of just such a possibility. If our attempt at approaching dynamically the phenomenon as complex as culture and self, albeit preliminarily, can be seen as charitable, other issues of culture and psychology may be approached dynamically as well. The dynamic approach to culture and psychology should be taken seriously.

APPENDIX

One "sentence" consisted of three "words": actor, behavior, and target. There were three "words" for actor, three "words" for target, and two "words" for behavior (positive and negative). There were six types of "sentences," as follows:

Actor	Behavior	Target
self (1)	behavior (+)	other (1)
self (2)	behavior (+)	other (2)
self (3)	behavior (+)	other (3)
self (1)	behavior (–)	other (1)
self (2)	behavior (–)	other (2)
self (3)	behavior (–)	other (3)

Note that a particular self "word" was used whenever its associated other "word" was used. This is in accordance with the Japanese language.

Each "word" was represented by an eight-element vector: There was one 1, and all other elements were 0. There was another vector with two elements, which were designated as the ellipsis indicators for self and other. Thus, if self is dropped, the indicator for self was off (0), but if it was explicitly mentioned, the indicator for self was on (1). The ellipsis indicator for target worked in the same manner. An 8-element vector and a 2-element vector were concatenated to form a 10-element vector.

In each of the four types of sequences, we constructed 27 "sentences" in which two thirds had behavior (+). For the English-like version without ellipsis, we used only self (1) and other (1), and all "sentences" were not ellipted. For the English-like version with ellipsis, we used self (1) and other (1), and two thirds of the "sentences" were ellipted. For the Japanese-like version without ellipsis, we used self (1) through self (3) and other (1) through other (3) with all the "sentences" being nonellipted. For the Japanese-like version with ellipsis, we used self (1) through self (3) and other (1) through other (3), with two thirds of the sentences ellipted. One random order of the 27 "sentences" was used for all conditions. This amounted to 81 ten-element vectors. The series of 81 vectors was fed through the Simple Recurrent Network three times without a break. Note that the number of units in the network was as follows: input = 10, output = 10, hidden = 50, and context = 50 units.

NOTES

1. This describes a "distributed," as opposed to "localist," connectionist representational system.

2. The relation between language and thought can be approached from the other direction as well. That is, people may use personal pronouns so that the language use is compatible with their self-conceptions. However, this link is not discussed at length here because of space limitation.

3. This was done to make the pattern of sequence analogous to English and Japanese. The word order is subject-verb-object in English, whereas it is subject-object-verb in Japanese. Furthermore, English has only one pair of words, *I* and *you,* for the first- and second-person pronouns, whereas Japanese has more than three pairs, as described before.

PART III

ELEMENTS OF
SUBJECTIVE CULTURE

The chapters of this section are key examples of recent research in the subjective culture tradition. Jaccard, Litardo, and Wan's chapter gives an overview of how subjective culture may be conceptualized now by incorporating the subsequent development of decision-making theories of social behavior, to which Triandis made an early and major contribution. They reframe subjective culture as a model of social behavior predicated on the premise that humans are social agents with the capacity to make conscious decisions who reflectively act on their social environment. The result is a universalist framework for approaching human agency. Whether one accepts it or criticizes it, the chapter points in one of the future directions of culturally sensitive social psychology.

Schwartz, Lehmann, and Roccas's contribution, a report in Schwartz's research program on human values—one of the central elements of Triandis's conception of subjective culture—displays methodological sensitivity and theoretical breadth. However, the authors not only preach the importance of a multimethod approach to culture and social behavior, but also carry out investigations of a contextualized measure of abstract values and an open-ended measure of self-construal (Twenty Statements Test). In doing so, they extend Schwartz's theoretical contribution to the area of self-construal.

The social psychological concepts that make up subjective culture are presumed to be universally applicable, etic concepts of human behavior. Yet a more culture-specific concept can provide a rich texture to the experience of a particular cultural group. Naidoo's chapter exemplifies this in her account of South Asian women's experience in the multicultural context of Canada. She suggests that the cultural concept of Shakti gives an insight into the dualistic coexistence of the traditional and the modern in South Asian women.

Marín's chapter is an excellent example of how subjective culture may be used productively in applied social psychology. The author summarizes his research on culturally sensitive interventions into health-related behaviors in California. Although currently prevalent intervention techniques show much sophistication, Marín points out that subjective culture can complement them and lead to results that are at once more theoretically defensible and practically effective.

Malpass, in his chapter, presents a subjective culture approach in the area of psychology and law. He illustrates some of the dramatic ways in which specific actions can be differentially sanctioned, socially or legally, in different cultures. This raises the issue of the validity of "cultural defense" or "social framework evidence" in the court of law. Malpass offers specific suggestions about the ways in which an analysis of subjective culture can contribute to the understanding of criminal cases.

- What role do the elements of subjective culture play in forming intentions and making decisions, according to Jaccard et al.?
- What is the value of measuring the elements of subjective culture using multiple methods, according to Schwartz?
- Naidoo suggests that many people in multicultural societies face the problem of dual, and sometimes opposing, subjective cultures. How do people cope with this problem? What conceptual role do culture-specific concepts play in the analysis of subjective culture?
- How does the analysis of subjective culture aid the process of social intervention, according to Marín? How does it help us understand the need for specific interventions and maximize their effectiveness?
- Based on Malpass's analysis, what do you think would be the effect of using "social framework evidence" in the legal system?

7

SUBJECTIVE CULTURE
AND SOCIAL BEHAVIOR

James Jaccard
Harold A. Litardo
Choi K. Wan
University at Albany, State University of New York

In an important book in cross-cultural psychology, Triandis (1972) developed the notion of subjective culture and specified general constructs that he believed could be used as explanatory mechanisms for behavior across diverse groups of individuals. Triandis argued that constructs such as beliefs, attitudes, norms, roles, expectancies, and affect, in the abstract, are variables that are potentially relevant for understanding the social behavior of individuals in any culture and, hence, are etic in character. To be sure, the ways in which these constructs manifest themselves may differ from one population to the next, and the relative importance of each in determining behavior may also be population specific. Nevertheless, Triandis (1972) has argued that there is a set of fundamental social psychological constructs that have widespread applicability and that social scientists can employ effectively to organize their thinking about why people in diverse cultural settings behave as they do.

The development of general theories of social behavior is not new to social or cultural psychology, and there are numerous examples of models that employ etic constructs for purposes of explaining the behavior of diverse groups. In social and health psychologies, some of the more popular models include social learning theory (Bandura, 1986, 1990), the Health Belief Model (Eisen, Zellman, & McAlister, 1992), Fishbein's theory of reasoned action (Ajzen & Fishbein, 1980), models of deviance (Benda & DiBlasio, 1994; Jessor, 1991), and Triandis's (1972) theory of subjective culture, to name a few. As an example, Fishbein's theory of reasoned action maintains that behavior is influenced by a person's intention to perform a behavior, which, in turn, is influenced by two variables, (a) the person's attitude toward performing the behavior and (b) the person's perceived pressure from important others to perform the behavior. A person's attitude toward performing the behavior is influenced by his or her perceptions of the advantages and disadvantages of performing the behavior. A given advantage or disadvantage has two components: (a) a belief component, which refers to the subjective probability that performing the behavior will lead to the advantage or disadvantage in question, and (b) an evaluative component, which refers to how positive the advantage is perceived as being or how negative the disadvantage is perceived as being. Fishbein provides a methodology for measuring all constructs within the model as well as a theoretical statement about how beliefs and expectancies combine to influence attitudes and, in turn, behavior. A range of detailed applications of the theory and specific measurement recommendations is presented in Ajzen and Fishbein (1980). The theory has been evaluated in hundreds of domains, including the analysis of such diverse behaviors as contraceptive use, eating habits, voting behavior, gun ownership, smoking behavior, drug use, alcohol use, blood donation behavior, and breast-feeding behavior. Typically, researchers in these applied domains use the constructs specified by the theory and then augment the analysis by including domain- or population-specific variables that may be predictive of behavior independent of the constructs emphasized by Fishbein.

The advantage of a general theory of social behavior is that it can serve as an organizing framework for research on any given behavior. In addition, as theoretical advances are made within the theory, these advances can be readily translated into the applied domain. The primary disadvantage of a general theory of behavior is that it may omit important domain- or population-specific variables that can explain behavior over and above the constructs within the theory. We believe that any analysis of social behavior benefits from the use of a general theory of behavior that evolves from sound social psychological research traditions, as long as such application is coupled with the analysis and integration of relevant domain-specific variables.

Models of social behavior often use explanatory variables that are relatively specific and directly tied to the behavior in question (e.g., the beliefs about the advantages and disadvantages of performing the behavior) or constructs that are more general and that serve as more distal behavioral determinants (e.g., age, gender, social class, personality). These latter, more broad-based determinants of behavior often work through or are mediated by the more immediate social psychological determinants of behavior that are tied directly to it. In the next section, we present a theoretical framework that synthesizes a wide range of cognitive, attitudinal, and social variables as the more immediate determinants of an individual's social behavior. We adopt the strategy of specifying etic constructs, as drawn from social psychological models of behavior, in the tradition of Triandis's (1972) model of subjective culture. We recognize that the theoretical statement does not include more broad-based explanatory constructs that may influence behavior through the specified constructs or even independent of the specified constructs. We also recognize that there may be a need to incorporate domain-specific or population-specific variables over and above those that we describe. Nevertheless, we believe that the framework represents a useful set of explanatory constructs that have widespread applicability, have been the subject of literally thousands of empirical studies across diverse populations, and have been shown time and again to have predictive utility.

A UNIFIED FRAMEWORK
FOR BEHAVIORAL ANALYSIS

The framework that we propose derives from applied decision theory and social psychology. People make many kinds of decisions in their lives. In general, decision theorists distinguish between three types of decisions. *Routine decisions* are those that are made on a routine basis, often out of habit and with little thought or consideration. These include such behaviors as tying one's shoes, opening a door, getting out of bed, and the like. *Impulsive decisions* are decisions that are made on the basis of one's first impulse and, again, are characterized by little thought about the different decision options. *Thoughtful decisions* are decisions that are reached after some thoughtful consideration of the different options at hand, including the different consequences of choosing a given option and the implications that follow from choosing that option. The present theory focuses on behaviors characterized by thoughtful decision making. Major life decisions that the individual deems important (e.g., career choices, purchase of major goods, divorce decisions) are usually of this character, as are many decisions that may be of lesser importance.

Another distinction made by decision theorists is between active and passive decision making. Active decision making focuses on the actual process of thinking about different courses of action and making a decision about which option to choose. Passive decision making refers to current behavior that is based on a decision that was actively reached on some prior occasion. For example, after careful consideration of the various types of birth control available, a woman may choose a diaphragm as her major method of choice. This decision then guides her subsequent use of the diaphragm relative to other methods of birth control. It is not necessary for her to rethink all the birth control options every time she has sex. The earlier decision dictates her current behavior. In this sense, the theory to be developed has applicability to a wide range of behavior, even if that behavior is "passively" driven.

In terms of thoughtful decision making, decision theorists typically analyze behavior in terms of a choice process. In any given situation, an individual must choose between alternative courses of action or behavioral options. At the simplest level, decisions are dichotomous, involving two behavioral options: to perform or not to perform a behavior (e.g., to use birth control or not to use birth control; to purchase a product or not purchase a product). At more complex levels, the individual is faced with choosing among many behavioral options, such as a case in which the individual must choose between a dozen or so contraceptive methods as her primary method of birth control. Decision theorists analyze the choice process in terms of seven activities that individuals may engage in (Jaccard, Radecki, Wilson, & Dittus, 1995). The first activity is problem recognition, in which an individual determines that a problem state exists and that a decision must be made. The second activity is goal identification, in which the individual considers those features of the scenario that he or she wants to optimize. For example, in the case of the contraceptive choice, goal identification would be analogous to specifying an idealized, optimal birth control method. This "ideal" method represents those features of a contraceptive method that an individual wants to optimize (e.g., high effectiveness at preventing unintended pregnancy, high effectiveness at preventing sexually transmitted disease, acceptable to one's partner, easy to use). The third activity is option generation, in which the individual identifies the behavioral options that are available. The fourth activity is information search, in which the individual seeks information about either what additional options might be available or the properties of one or more of the options under consideration. The fifth activity is the assessment of option information and choice, in which the individual considers the information he or she has about the different behavioral options, forms an overall evaluation of each option, and chooses one of the options for purposes of behavioral enactment. The sixth activity is behavioral translation, when the individual translates the decision into behavior. The final activity is postdecision evaluation, in which the individual reflects on the decision after the chosen option has been enacted and evaluates the decision process in light of the outcomes that have resulted. Not all these activities will be performed by an individual, and they need not be performed in the sequence described. However, they represent a comprehensive list of decision activities that individuals may engage in as they approach the choice process.

Most social psychological research has focused on the fifth activity within the sequence described above, namely, the kinds of information that people use and how they combine them for purposes of making a choice. The fifth process has been studied from the perspectives of diverse theoretical frameworks, the most popular of which are Fishbein's (Ajzen & Fishbein, 1980) theory of reasoned action (and a recent variant of it by Ajzen, called the theory of planned behavior, Madden, Ellen, & Ajzen, 1992); Bandura's (1986, 1990) social learning theory; various versions of the Health Belief Model; and Triandis's (1972) theory of subjective culture. Recently, the National Institute of Mental Health sponsored a workshop in which the primary architects of each theory (Fishbein, Bandura, Becker, and Triandis) were asked to meet for intensive interactions over the course of a week to develop a common theoretical framework that integrated the core constructs of each theory (Fishbein et al., 1993; personal communication, 1995). Although they did not come to complete agreement, a general framework emerged that is summarized here, including our own modifications.

The variables of the model are organized into two sequences. The first sequence focuses on the immediate determinants of behavior, as illustrated in Figure 7.1. Behavior is influenced by four core variables. First, an individual must be motivated to perform the behavior. Unless the individual intends to perform the behavior, it is unlikely he or she will attempt to initiate it. Second, the individual must have the requisite knowledge and skills to enact the behavior. Even if motivation is high, if the individual does not possess the ability and skills to perform the behavior, then behavioral performance will not result. Third, there must be no environmental constraints that render behavioral performance impossible. For example, in the area of contraceptive behavior, a woman

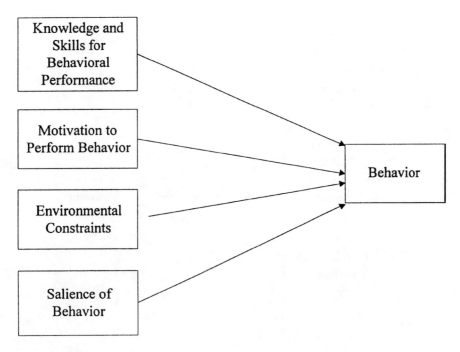

Figure 7.1. Determinants of Behavior

might be highly motivated to obtain and use Norplant, but if it is not available, then it is not possible to do so. Fourth, the behavior must be salient to the individual. Numerous studies have found that individuals fail to perform a behavior simply because they forget to do so (i.e., the behavior is not salient to them; see Jaccard, 1975; Pomazal & Jaccard, 1976). This can occur even when motivation for behavioral performance is strong, environmental constraints are minimal, and the individual possesses the skills and knowledge for behavioral performance. These four variables combine in a multiplicative fashion to influence behavior such that if any one is suboptimal, behavior will not result. Stated another way, favorable conditions on a given component (i.e., high motivation, high behavioral skills, low environmental constraints, and high behavioral salience) are a necessary but not sufficient condition for behavioral performance.[1]

The second aspect of the theoretical framework focuses on the determinants of an individual's motivation to perform the behavior or his or her decision to perform the behavior. There are six major factors that serve as the immediate psychological determinants of one's motivation to perform a behavior, as illustrated in Figure 7.2. The construct of attitude comes from Fishbein's (Ajzen & Fishbein, 1980) theory of reasoned action and the Triandis (1972) model of subjective culture. It refers to how favorable or unfavorable the individual feels about performing the behavior. The more favorable an individual feels about performing the behavior, the more likely he or she will be motivated to do so, everything else being equal. Normative influences derive from the theory of reasoned action and are also represented in Triandis's model. They reflect the idea that the more normative pressures an individual feels to perform a behavior, the more likely it is that

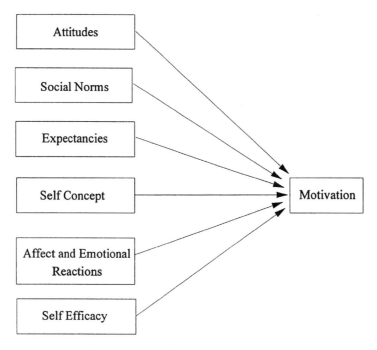

Figure 7.2. Determinants of Motivation to Perform Behavior

he or she will be motivated to perform the behavior. Expectancies derive from all the theoretical frameworks and refer to an individual's perceived advantages and disadvantages of performing or not performing the behavior. Fishbein and Triandis rely heavily on the expectancy value formulations of expectancies described earlier. In general, individuals are more motivated to perform behaviors that lead to positive outcomes and that minimize negative outcomes. Self-concept refers to an individual's conception of the self and whether performing the behavior is consistent with that self-image. In general, individuals who perceive behavioral performance as being counter to their self-image will not be motivated to perform the behavior. Affect refers to fundamental affect and emotional reactions to behavioral performance. It derives from Triandis's model. Whereas most of the previous variables are cognitive based, this variable emphasizes affective reactions to behavioral performance. In general, individuals who have an overall negative emotional reaction to a behavior will be less motivated to perform it. Self-efficacy derives from Bandura's (1986, 1990) social learning theory and refers to one's perceived confidence that he or she can perform the behavior. In general, if an individual does not believe he or she can effectively perform a behavior, then he or she will not be motivated to try. Note that the core constructs of the Health Belief Model (perceived susceptibility, perceived effectiveness, perceived severity, and perceived benefits) are not directly in the model but are subsumed within the different variable categories. For example, perceived benefits, barriers, and severity all fall within the expectancy construct.

We must emphasize that the theorists disagree about many aspects of the model as represented above. For example, Fishbein (Fishbein & Ajzen, 1975) contends that expectancies are a major determinant of attitudes and influence the motivation to perform a behavior only through their impact on attitudes. Triandis (1972), on the other hand, argues that expectancies can have an independent influence on the motivation to perform a behavior, over and above attitudes. There is also disagreement about whether certain classes of variables combine in an additive or multiplicative fashion to influence motivation. Despite this, the variables represent broad classes of constructs that make intuitive sense and that have a rich empirical and theoretical history within the behavioral sciences. A focus on these variables will undoubtedly yield large returns in terms of explaining variation in behaviors that are of social significance in society.

Two features of the unified framework should be emphasized. First, the six core predictor variables are presumed to be the primary determinants of one's decision to perform a behavior. More distal constructs, such as personality variables, demographic variables, and biological variables, may influence behavior, but they do so through their influence on these primary variables. For example, in the area of adolescent contraceptive behavior, there may be age differences in the use of a given birth control method. According to our formulation, these differences exist because older versus younger adolescents differ on one or more primary determinants of behavior. For example, the self-concept of older adolescents may be more consistent with using a particular form of birth control than is the self-concept of younger adolescents. Or the perceived advantages and disadvantages of using a given method might be different for younger as opposed to older adolescents. Using the theory in conjunction with more distal demographic, personality, and contextual variables has the advantage of providing insights into the mechanisms by which these distal variables influence behavior.

Second, the framework maintains that the relative importance of the constructs in influencing behavior can differ from population to population. For some individuals, normative influences may be the primary determinant of the motivation to perform a behavior, whereas for other individuals, self-concept may be of primary importance. This has implications for the design of interventions because one must first identify the relative weights of the core predictors in determining behavior to identify the appropriate emphasis of the intervention. A program that targets self-concept for change will be ineffective if self-concept is not a primary determinant of behavior. The notion of differential weighting also accommodates often observed across-study inconsistencies in the correlations between social psychological variables and behavior. Such "inconsistencies" occur because the relative importance of a given predictor can change from one study population to another. The theoretical framework remains silent about *why* differential weights occur from one population to another, and it does not permit one to predict a priori about when such differential weighting will occur. Such predictions require theoretical supplementation from the substantive domain of interest.

Thousands of studies have supported the utility of the main constructs of the unified framework we have presented. Although many theoretical issues remain to be addressed within the model, we believe that the core constructs and general theoretical structure are a sound basis for analyzing a wide range of behaviors. Despite these strengths, it is also evident that the framework addresses only a subset of the major decision activities identified by decision theorists. For example, the model offers little guidance on the analysis of how people generate options for inclusion in a choice set or how they seek out information about those options. The framework could be adapted to study some of these other features of the decision process. For example, one could study the behavior of "obtaining information about birth control from a health clinic" using the core variables within the model, thereby formally applying the model to the analysis of information search. Nevertheless, research on the full range of decision activities is needed, whereas, to date, research emphasis has clearly been on the choice process per se.

A central aspect of decision theory is the importance of studying all the behavioral options within a choice set. One cannot understand the choice process by studying how individuals evaluate a single decision option. As an example, consider two women who each feel moderately positive toward using an oral contraceptive. Suppose that one of the women feels very negative about all other forms of birth control, whereas the other woman feels very favorable about using a diaphragm. Even though these women have identical attitudes toward oral contraceptives, their behavior will most certainly differ, with the first woman using oral contraceptives and the second woman not using them (and instead using the diaphragm). Unless the attitudes toward each option in the choice set are explored and modeled, the predictive utility of the attitude construct will be underestimated (see Jaccard, 1981; Jaccard & Becker, 1985, for elaborations of this point in the contraceptive choice situation).

The conceptual approach developed above does not emphasize the importance of behavioral alternatives within a choice set, an omission that we believe is unfortunate. However, the framework can be readily modified to incorporate this focus. For each option in a choice set (e.g., choosing between Norplant, birth control pills, the diaphragm, etc.), one can measure the attitude toward choosing that option, the normative pressure toward choosing the option, the expectancies about the advantages and disadvantages of choosing the option, the extent to which choosing the option is consistent with one's self-image, the affective and emotional reaction toward choosing the option, and one's perceived efficacy about being able to perform the option. The choice of a given option is then a function of these variables.

Our own theoretical predilection is to give precedence to the construct of attitude and then to use this construct in accord with classic decision theory. This version of the unified framework is as follows: An attitude is the extent to which an individual feels favorable or unfavorable toward performing the behavioral option in question. For a set of n choice options, an individual will have n attitudes, which we refer to as a preference structure. The individual's choice of a behavioral option will be a function of this preference structure. The most likely function is based on what decision theorists call an optimizing principle: The individual will choose that option toward which he or she feels most positive. However, there are exceptions to this principle, as evidenced by satisficing-based decision rules (see Jaccard et al., 1995). Abundant empirical evidence indicates that preference structures are indeed predictive of choice across a wide range of behaviors and, thus represent a useful formulation within the unified framework (e.g., Jaccard, 1981; Jaccard & Becker, 1985; Jaccard & Wood, 1986).

A person's attitude toward a given option is influenced by the core constructs of the unified framework we have presented. That is, a person will feel favorably or unfavorably toward performing a behavior depending on the kinds of social pressure he or she perceives to perform the behavior, the perceived advantages and disadvantages of performing the behavior, the extent to which the behavior is consistent with his or her self-concept, the affect and emotional reactions associated with performance of the behavioral option, and the perceived self-efficacy about being able to perform the behavioral option. As discussed earlier, there will be individual differences in the relative weights of these constructs in determining a given attitude, and these must be addressed in empirical applications. A more general discussion of this version of the theory, how it contrasts with other formulations, and its psychometric foundations is provided in Jaccard (1995).

A recent literature in attitude theory also merits consideration. This research focuses on the concept of attitude strength. An attitude is traditionally viewed as how favorable or unfavorable an individual feels about performing a behavior. It is possible for individuals to have identical attitudes toward performing a behavior but for the attitudes to differ in their strength. Attitude strength has three dimensions. The first dimension is the *salience* of the attitude, or how accessible the attitude is from memory. A large body of research suggests that attitudes that are salient are more likely to influence behavior than are attitudes that are not salient (e.g., Petty & Krosnick, 1995). The second dimension is the *confidence* with which an attitude is held. Two individuals may hold the same attitude (i.e., feel equally favorable toward performing a behavior) but may differ in how confident they are in their attitude (e.g., how confident they are that their overall evaluation of a given method of birth control is correct). Research indicates that individuals who are confident in their attitudes are more likely to behave in accord with those attitudes and are more resistant to attitude change attempts than are individuals who are less confident in their attitudes (e.g., Petty & Krosnick, 1995). The third dimension is attitude *relevance*, or importance, and refers to how central the attitude is to the person and his or her current life circumstances. For example, the issue of birth control is more relevant to individuals who are sexually active than to individuals who are not sexually active, and this, in turn, can have implications for how an attitude influences behavior (e.g., Petty & Krosnick, 1995). The framework for behavioral analysis described above fails to include the construct of attitude strength, even though research suggests it may have a key role in influencing behavior. We recommend that such constructs be included in the framework. In our version, this would mean measuring attitude salience, confidence, and importance for each behavioral option and then taking these variables into account when predicting choice from the preference structure. It may be, for example, that an individual will choose an option that is not the most favorable one (e.g., the second most favorable option) if the individual has more confidence in the attitude toward that option as compared with other options. Or an individual may be more likely to choose an option that is less favorable than another if the attitude toward the former is more salient than that toward the latter.

In sum, the framework we have presented is a conceptual tool for integrating a range of psychological constructs that have a rich tradition in applied research. All the variables within the model have been extensively studied in the research literature. The constructs have a detailed psychometric history that lends itself well to empirical research. Given the history of the constructs, it is hard to imagine scenarios in which the model will not explain substantial variation in behaviors of interest to social scientists. This will be especially true if the theoretical analysis includes a focus on a complete set of behavioral options rather than a single behavioral option and the theoretical analysis includes the construct of attitude strength.

INTEGRATION WITH
BROAD-BASED EXPLANATORY VARIABLES

As noted, the primary variables in our framework represent relatively immediate determinants of behavior. This should not be taken to mean that more distal variables are irrelevant. Rather, they are assumed to influence behavior through the social psychological mediators we have identified. In this section, we briefly comment on some of the broad classes of distal variables that researchers should consider when analyzing behavior.

Contextual Analysis

Recently, a number of researchers have pursued contextual analyses of social behavior (e.g., Brewster, Billy, & Grady, 1993; Ku, Sonenstein, & Pleck, 1993). These analyses examine the impact of school-, community-, tract-, county-, and even cultural-level variables on individual behavior. For example, Brewster et al. argue that community-level variables may influence behavior by defining a local opportunity structure that channels and constrains the behavior of community members. In addition, community characteristics may dictate a normative climate that then engenders actions in accord with those norms. Traditional research adopting a contextual perspective has tended to focus on local social and economic conditions. For example, Brewster et al. found that female divorce and separation rates in communities were negatively related to contraceptive use at first intercourse for adolescents and that female labor force opportunities were positively associated with contraceptive use at first intercourse. We believe that contextual analyses of this type are important and, when coupled with individual-level models, are extremely powerful for understanding social behavior. Although much contextual research has tended to focus on traditional demographic, community, and cultural variables for defining "context," it is possible to define contextual variables using all the explanatory categories in Figure 7.2. For example, one could characterize communities in terms of their mean scores and variances on any of the variables within the unified framework and then use these community-level attributes to conduct contextual-based analyses of behavior using random coefficient regression modeling of the form characterized by Bryk and Raudenbush (1992). Thus, communities might differ in the mean normative pressures experienced by members of the community to perform a behavior, in the mean affect associated with behavioral performance, in the mean self-efficacy for behavioral performance, and so on. These psychologically defined community-level "norms" may be useful predictors of across-community variations in behavior.

Social and Familial Variables

In the context of our framework, many of the social variables studied in the social psychological literature serve as distal variables that influence behavior through the core constructs of the model. For example, people often form expectancies about the advantages and disadvantages of performing a behavior based on their interactions with their peers. One's self-concept and how this pertains to behavioral performance may be shaped by peer interactions. The kinds of support networks that a person has may alter that person's perceived self-efficacy. Familial variables also operate as distal determinants of behavior. For example, interactions with parents can shape the expectancies that adolescents form about the advantages and disadvantages of performing certain behaviors. The family structure and family environment can influence self-concept, self-efficacy, and the impact that peers have on adolescents, all in complex ways. For further discussion of these issues, see Brinberg and Jaccard (1989).

Personality Variables

A wide range of personality variables pertaining to influencing the behavior of individuals has been studied by social psychologists. Such variables are assumed to have their influence on behavior through the core mediators identified in our theoretical framework. For example, the behavior of individuals may differ depending on their sex role identity and how "masculine" or "feminine" they are. These behavioral differences, as a function of personality, presumably result because individuals with differing sex role orientations have different expectancies, attitudes, affect, self-concept, and/or normative pressures with respect to engaging in a behavior.

Demographic Variables

There have been many studies of demographic correlates of social behavior, with most attention given to ethnic, class, religious, gender, marital, and educational differences. In general, demographic researchers have been remiss about empirically identifying the mechanisms by which differences in behavior as a function of demographic variables manifest themselves. To be sure, there are studies that *speculate* about underlying mechanisms or empirically evaluate a limited number of possible mediating factors. But there are too few studies in the demographic literature that adopt a theoretically compelling, multivariable framework of mediating variables in conjunction with demographic analyses. The framework that we have presented could be used effectively in this regard.

In addition to these classes of distal determinants, others may also be relevant, such as media influences, biological influences, genetic influences, and cultural influences, to name a few. It is our belief that the exploration of these variables in conjunction with a general theory of the more immediate determinants of behavior (such as the one we have presented) using etic constructs operationalized in culturally appropriate emic ways will be fruitful for the analysis of a wide range of human behaviors.

CONCLUDING COMMENTS

In conclusion, theorists such as Triandis have had a major influence on the analysis of social behavior by developing a general theory of behavior based on his analysis of subjective culture. The constructs within his model are etic in character and have widespread applicability to many behavioral domains. The present chapter has furthered this theoretical orientation by specifying a general framework that builds on this approach by integrating additional perspectives from other behavioral theories, research on attitude theory, and research on decision making.

NOTE

1. Our representation of determinants in Figure 7.1, as well as in Figure 7.2, should not be interpreted as a traditional path diagram (which would imply main effects but not interactions between the explanatory variables). The figures indicate only the variables involved and the general causal direction.

8

MULTIMETHOD PROBES
OF BASIC HUMAN VALUES

Shalom H. Schwartz
Arielle Lehmann
Sonia Roccas
Hebrew University of Jerusalem

A major theme running through the work of Harry Triandis is an emphasis on the importance of "multimethod probes" of our central constructs, especially in cross-cultural work (e.g., Triandis, 1994b; Triandis, McCusker, & Hui, 1990). Triandis draws approvingly on Campbell (1986) and Fiske (1986), who argue that findings from single methods often fail to replicate and that multiple methods, including both "hard" and "soft" approaches, should be coordinated. In this spirit, this chapter reports research in the domain of basic human values (Schwartz, 1992, 1994a). We address two questions: (a) Can the key postulates of the theory of individual values, validated thus far with a single instrument, be validated with a new, alternative instrument? (b) Is the distinct content of 10 motivational types of human values specified by the theory also expressed in spontaneous self-construals?

AUTHORS' NOTE: The research reported here was supported by Grant 187/92 from the Basic Research Foundation (Israel Academy of Sciences and Humanities); by Grant 94-00063 from the United States-Israel Binational Science Foundation (BSF), Jerusalem, Israel; and by the Leon and Clara Sznajderman Chair of Psychology. We are grateful to Anat Bardi, Marina Barnea, Gila Melech, Ariel Knafo, Lilach Sagiv, Naomi Struch, and Noga Sverdlik for their comments on earlier versions of this chapter.

The multitrait-multimethod approach advocated by Campbell and Fiske (1959) seeks to resolve the issue of how well operations (measurements) match the concepts they are intended to measure. This approach requires a clear, unequivocal definition of each concept, and it assumes that a particular operation or set of operations is intended to measure the criterial attribute(s) of that concept. This is the approach taken in the first study reported below. We measure the central constructs in the theory of basic human values with two different "hard" methods and compare the findings. In so doing, this study presents, for the first time, an alternative instrument designed to measure value priorities among children and adults for whom the previously available instrument was too abstract.

The second study reported below follows Triandis's recommendation and example by employing "soft" as well as "hard" methods of measurement. It examines predicted correlates of value constructs as a method for validating the distinctiveness of the 10 value types. This study tests the hypothesis that people express their values in their self-conceptions. It explores relations between the priorities people attribute to the motivational types of values and their own self-construals. Specifically, we test the hypothesis that the more importance people attribute to particular types of values, the more likely they are to describe themselves spontaneously by using terms that reflect these values.

OVERVIEW OF THE VALUES THEORY

The theory of basic human values has two core components (see Schwartz, 1992, 1994a, for a fuller elaboration). First, it specifies 10 motivationally distinct types of values that are postulated to be recognized by members of most societies and to be comprehensive of the different types of values that guide them. Second, the theory specifies how these 10 types of values relate dynamically to one another. That is, it specifies which types of values are compatible and mutually supportive and which types are opposed and likely to conflict with one another. The theory defines values as desirable, transsituational goals, varying in importance, that serve as guiding principles in people's lives. The crucial content aspect that distinguishes among values is the type of motivational goals they express. Table 8.1 lists the 10 value types, each defined in terms of its central goal.

The dynamic relations among the value types arise because actions taken in pursuit of each type of value have psychological, practical, and social consequences that may conflict with or may be compatible with the pursuit of other value types. The total pattern of relations of conflict and compatibility among value types postulated by the theory is portrayed graphically by the circular structure in Figure 8.1. Competing value types emanate in opposing directions from the center; complementary types are in close proximity going around the circle.

The nature of the compatibilities among value types is clarified by noting the shared motivational orientations of the adjacent value types. Viewed in terms of these shared orientations, the adjacent types form a motivational continuum within the circular structure of Figure 8.1: Power and achievement both emphasize social superiority and esteem, for example, and achievement and hedonism both express self-centeredness. In

TABLE 8.1 Definitions of Motivational Types of Values in Terms of Their Goals

POWER: Social status and prestige; control or dominance over people and resources.

ACHIEVEMENT: Personal success through demonstrating competence according to social standards.

HEDONISM: Pleasure and sensuous gratification for oneself.

STIMULATION: Excitement, novelty, and challenge in life.

SELF-DIRECTION: Independent thought and action, choosing, creating, and exploring.

UNIVERSALISM: Understanding, appreciation, tolerance, and protection for the welfare of all people and for nature.

BENEVOLENCE: Preservation and enhancement of the welfare of people with whom one is in frequent personal contact.

TRADITION: Respect, commitment, and acceptance of the customs and ideas that traditional culture or religion provides.

CONFORMITY: Restraint of actions, inclinations, and impulses likely to upset or harm others and violate social expectations or norms.

SECURITY: Safety, harmony, and stability of society, of relationships, and of self.

SOURCE: Adapted from Schwartz (1994a, p. 22).

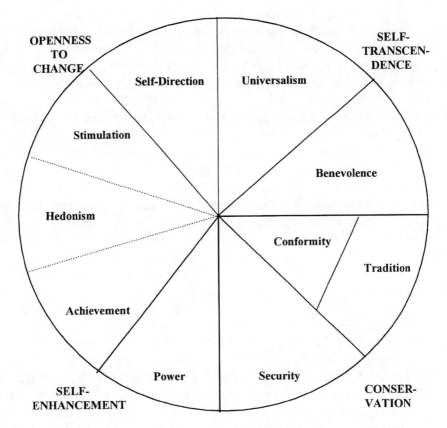

Figure 8.1. Theoretical Model of Relations Among Motivational Types of Values
SOURCE: Adapted from Schwartz (1992), p. 45.

contrast, the motivational goals of the value types in opposing positions within the circle cannot easily be pursued at the same time. For example, the pursuit of achievement values may conflict with the pursuit of benevolence values: Seeking personal success for oneself is likely to obstruct actions aimed at enhancing the welfare of others who need one's help. And the pursuit of novelty and change (stimulation) is likely to undermine preservation of time-honored customs (tradition).

STUDY 1: MULTITRAIT-MULTIMETHOD ANALYSIS: THE SVS AND THE PORTRAITS QUESTIONNAIRE

Past research on the theory of basic human values has employed the Schwartz Value Survey (SVS).[1] In the SVS, respondents rate the importance of 56 (recently 57) single values, each followed by an explanatory phrase in parentheses—for example, creativity (uniqueness, imagination)—"as a guiding principle in my life." The following rating scale is employed: *of supreme importance* (7), *very important* (6), (unlabeled; 5, 4), *important* (3), (unlabeled; 2, 1), *not important* (0), *opposed to my values* (–1). Specific values were selected a priori to represent each of the 10 motivationally distinct value types. During the past decade, some 65,000 people from 65 nations around the world have completed the SVS. Multidimensional structural analyses of the relations among the single values, in different cultures, support the distinctiveness of the 10 value types as well as the circular structure of relations among them (Fontaine & Schwartz, 1996; also references in Note 1). Based on results of these analyses, indexes were developed for measuring the importance of each value type.

Past research provides substantial support for the values theory, but this support is based on using a single measurement instrument. Moreover, this instrument is largely limited to use with literate adults. The multitrait-multimethod analysis of Study 1 tested the key postulates of the values theory by asking whether the SVS and an alternative method of measurement (a) distinguish the same 10 motivationally distinct types of values and (b) yield the same circular structure of relations among the value types. In developing the alternative method of measurement, called the Portraits Questionnaire, we set ourselves the goal of finding a way to measure value priorities that can be used with early adolescents and with adults who have minimal schooling and find the SVS too abstract.

The Portraits Questionnaire (PQ) presents descriptions of 28 different people. Each portrait consists of two sentences that characterize the person's goals, aspirations, and wishes, all expressive of a single value type. For example, "Thinking up new ideas and being creative is important to him. He likes to do things in his own original way" (self-direction). "She looks for adventures and likes to take risks. She wants to have an exciting life" (stimulation). By emphasizing what is important to the person—the goals and wishes he or she pursues—the portraits describe the person's values rather than his or her behavior or traits. The number of portraits prepared for each value type reflects the conceptual complexity of the type revealed in earlier studies: two each for stimulation, hedonism, and power; three each for self-direction, achievement, security, conformity, tradition, and benevolence; and four for universalism. Table 8.2 provides an

TABLE 8.2 Exemplary Items Representing the 10 Value Types From the SVS[a] and the Portraits Questionnaire (Male and Female Versions Mixed)

Value Type	Items From the SVS	Items From the Portraits Questionnaire
Power (PO)	social power; wealth	He likes to be in charge and tell others what to do. He wants people to do what he says.
Security (SE)	clean; national security	It is important to her that everything is clean and in order. She really doesn't want things to be a mess.
Conformity (CO)	politeness; obedient	It is important to him to be polite to other people all the time. He believes he should always show respect to his parents and to older people.
Tradition (TR)	devout; humble	She thinks it is important to do things the way she learned from her family. She wants to follow their customs and traditions.
Benevolence (BE)	helpful; honest	He always wants to help people who are close to him. It's very important to him to care for the people he knows and likes.
Universalism (UN)	a world of beauty; broad-minded	It is important to her to listen to people who are different from her. Even when she disagrees with them, she still wants to understand them and to get along with them.
Self-Direction (SD)	creativity; choosing own goals	He thinks it's important to be interested in things. He is curious and tries to understand everything.
Stimulation (ST)	daring; a varied life	She likes surprises and is always looking for new things to do. She thinks it is important to do lots of different things in life.
Hedonism (HE)	enjoying life; pleasure	He looks for every chance he can to have fun. It is important to him to do things that give him pleasure.
Achievement (AC)	successful; ambitious	It's very important to her to show her abilities. She wants people to admire what she does.

a. SVS = Schwartz Value Survey

exemplary portrait for each value type as well as examples of single values used in the SVS for that type.

Respondents indicate "How much like you is this person" by checking one of six boxes labeled as follows: "very much like me," "like me," "somewhat like me," "a little like me," "not like me," and "not like me at all." The similarity judgment task of the PQ requires respondents to compare the portrait to the self rather than the self to the portrait. This is important because studies reveal that similarity judgments are influenced by the direction of the comparison: A less salient stimulus (e.g., another person) is perceived as more similar to a salient stimulus (e.g., the self) than vice versa (Holyoak & Gordon, 1983; Srull & Gaelick, 1983; Tversky, 1977). Thus, when respondents focus on the values of the person in the portrait and compare them to the values of self, they are likely to notice any overlap that exists and recognize some similarity. However, if respondents focus on the many characteristics of self with which they are familiar and then compare themselves to the person in the portrait, they will find that many of these characteristics are absent in the portrait and they may not attend to any value similarity.[2]

The PQ was developed in decentered Hebrew and English versions, with modifications made until it was suitable for 11-year-olds in Uganda, Canada, and Israel.[3] Separate male and female wordings were prepared. Portraits were ordered randomly with the constraint that those intended to represent the same value type be separated by at least three other portraits.

The goals, aspirations, and wishes included in the portraits were selected in three ways: (a) We used phrases from the SVS that had demonstrated substantial equivalence of meaning across cultures to make them less abstract. For example, the SVS hedonism value "enjoying life" was used here in "She really wants to enjoy life." (b) We paraphrased items from the SVS. For example, the universalism value "protecting the environment" was paraphrased as "He strongly believes that people should care for nature." (c) Portraits were built directly from the conceptual definitions of the value types (see Table 8.1), using terms not included in the SVS. For example, the following portrait drew on the definition of the achievement value type: "It's very important to her to show her abilities. She wants people to admire what she does."

There are several notable differences between the SVS and PQ methods for measuring individual value priorities. First, the SVS asks for ratings of the importance of values as guiding principles in one's life, whereas the PQ obtains judgments of the similarity of another person to the self. Second, the stimuli in the SVS are a set of abstract, context-free values, whereas the stimuli in the PQ are persons, portrayed in terms of their goals, aspirations, and wishes. Third, the SVS uses a nine-point numerical response scale with both labeled and unlabeled scale points, whereas the PQ asks respondents to check one of six labeled boxes. Most generally, the SVS elicits direct, self-conscious reports of one's values, whereas the PQ measures values only indirectly. Respondents to the SVS typically describe the experience as requiring serious deliberation on the relative importance of their values. Respondents to the PQ answer quickly (about 8 to 10 minutes) and mention no difficulty in reaching their judgments.

Procedure and Analyses

A sample of 105 Israeli adults, ages 18 to 60, completed the SVS and the PQ, in counterbalanced order. To assess whether the 10 value types were distinguished and whether their interrelations corresponded to the hypothesized circular structure, responses to the SVS and the PQ were analyzed separately using smallest space analysis (SSA; Guttman, 1968; cf. Canter, 1985). This nonmetric multidimensional scaling technique represents items as points in a multidimensional space such that the distances between the points reflect the intercorrelations among the items. To test the postulates of the values theory, we examined whether the items intended to measure each value type formed separate regions in the space and whether these regions were located relative to one another in a way that fits the hypothesized relations of conflict and compatibility among the value types, as shown in Figure 8.1. This is a "configurational verification" approach (Davison, 1983; Dillon & Goldstein, 1984; cf. Schwartz, 1992).

Results

SVS

The two-dimensional projection of the SSA of the 57 values from the SVS yielded a circular structure similar to the theoretical prototype in Figure 8.1, with two deviations: (a) The three adjacent value types of self-direction, stimulation, and hedonism formed a single intermixed region rather than three distinct regions, and (b) the tradition value type formed a region behind the conformity region but stretched behind the adjacent benevolence region as well. As discussed in Schwartz and Sagiv (1995), this degree of deviation may easily be attributed to measurement error, especially with a sample size of fewer than 200 respondents. The spatial locations of all the values included in the standard SVS indexes to measure the importance of each value type justified the use of these indexes in the current research.

PQ

As shown in Figure 8.2, the two-dimensional projection of the SSA of the 28 portraits in the PQ yielded a circular structure identical to the theoretical prototype in Figure 8.1. One conformity item was located somewhat farther from the center than expected, and one benevolence item was located slightly lower in the figure than expected. Such variation is certainly within chance levels. Given these results, indexes of the importance of each value type were constructed. The similarity judgments (coded 1 through 6) of the portrait items constructed a priori to measure each type were summed and divided by the number of items.

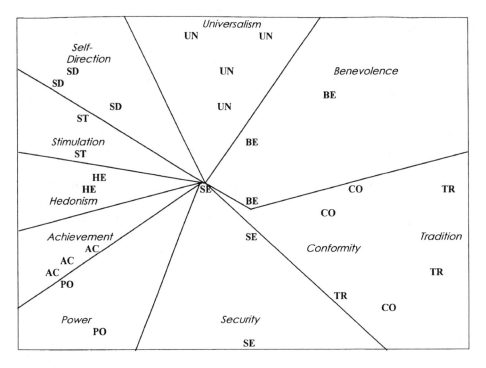

Figure 8.2. Smallest Space Analysis of Portraits Questionnaire
NOTE: Coefficient of alienation = .19.

Multitrait-Multimethod Analysis

Using the 10 value-priority scores of individual respondents from each instrument, a multitrait-multimethod correlation matrix was computed. Such a matrix presents the correlations among a number of constructs or "traits" (here, the 10 different value types) as measured using different methods (here, the SVS and the PQ). If the same traits are measured by each method, the single-trait/multimethod correlations should be more positive than the multitrait-multimethod correlations. For example, the correlation between hedonism measured using the PQ and hedonism measured using the SVS should be higher than the correlation between hedonism measured using the PQ and any other value type measured using the SVS.

In addition, if the various traits are conceptually different, the single-trait/multimethod correlations should be more positive than the single-method/multitrait correlations. For example, the correlation between hedonism measured using the PQ and the SVS methods should be more positive than the correlation between hedonism measured using the PQ and power measured using the PQ. We expect this condition to hold for value types that are at some distance from one another within the motivational circle of values but not necessarily for value types that are adjacent in the circle. This is because adjacent value types overlap conceptually in the motivation they express (e.g., tradition and conformity). The combination of conceptual overlap and a shared method of measurement may yield multitrait/single-method correlations among adjacent value types that are more positive than some single-trait/multimethod correlations.

Table 8.3 presents the matrix. The correlations between the same value type measured using the two different instruments (that is, the single-trait/multimethod correlations) are found on the diagonal. Above and below the diagonal are the multitrait-multimethod correlations (the correlations between a value type measured by one method and a different value type measured by the other method). The means of the index for each value type, as well as the standard deviations and alpha reliabilities, are also shown.

For 7 of the 10 value types, the single-trait/multimethod correlation (on the diagonal) is greater than any of the other 18 correlations in each value's column or row, and for one (benevolence), it is greater than all but one other correlation (which is tied). For tradition, there are two exceptions: Both multitrait-multimethod correlations with conformity are higher than the single-trait/multimethod correlation. In addition, the single-trait/ multimethod correlation for achievement is weaker than the multitrait-multimethod correlation between achievement measured by the PQ and power measured by the SVS. Not shown are the 90 correlations between different value types measured by the same method (multitrait/single-method rectangle). As expected, 76 of these correlations are less positive than those on the diagonal. Of the remaining 14 correlations, 11 are between conceptually overlapping, adjacent value types and 3 are between nearly adjacent types (e.g., benevolence and security). Overall, these results suggest that the latent priority given to the value types has a stronger impact on responses than does the method of measurement.

Discussion

The data collected with the Portraits Questionnaire replicated the support for the circular structure of 10 value types previously found with the SVS. Value types postulated to be compatible were located in adjacent positions in the structure, whereas types postulated to be incompatible were located in opposing positions. This finding, with a new and quite different method of measurement, constitutes an important validation of the key content and structure postulates of the theory of basic human values.

Results of the multitrait-multimethod analysis also support the conclusion that the alternative instruments for measuring the 10 value types both measure similar under-lying constructs.[4] The few exceptions to the pattern of correlations expected on the basis of theory should be assessed in light of the structure of relations among value types postulated by the theory of basic human values. Recall that, according to the theory, adjacent value types are compatible, conceptually related, and, therefore, expected to correlate positively. Achievement and power, which yielded a higher than expected correlation in the PQ, are adjacent value types. Tradition and conformity are especially close conceptually, according to theory, because of their shared motivation to submit to external expectations (Schwartz, 1992), so their high intercorrelations are also not surpris-ing. However, the unusual weakness of the single-trait/multimethod correlation for tradition suggests a problem with the measurement of this value type. A possible explanation for this weak correlation is the fact that the tradition items include explicit

TABLE 8.3 Multitrait-Multimethod Matrix of Correlations Among 10 Value Types Using the Schwartz Value Survey (SVS) and the Portraits Questionnaire

Survey

	PO	SE	CO	TR	BE	UN	SD	ST	HE	AC	Mean SD Alpha
PO	**.62**	.23	.01	.02	−.03	−.17	−.02	.26	.07	.38	2.26 1.19 .56
SE	.38	**.65**	.36	.25	.14	.01	−.08	.14	.19	.24	3.27 1.07 .58
CO	.16	.43	**.61**	.42	.36	.05	−.16	−.10	−.03	−.01	1.97 .91 .58
TR	−.22	.23	.31	**.26**	.14	−.02	−.25	−.27	−.01	−.31	1.70 .89 .50
BE	.14	.42	.36	.10	**.42**	.22	−.02	.06	.03	.14	3.82 .81 .58
UN	−.04	.16	.18	.03	.37	**.55**	.22	.25	.14	.06	3.27 .95 .70
SD	.08	.07	.00	−.04	.13	.42	**.64**	.51	.16	.27	3.61 .95 .71
ST	.27	.17	.04	−.03	.16	.25	.42	**.72**	.23	.33	2.70 1.39 .86
HE	.29	.23	.00	.05	.16	.08	.24	.52	**.57**	.20	3.12 1.20 .85
AC	.52	.19	.17	.05	.17	−.02	.15	.31	.19	**.43**	3.11 1.08 .76
Mean SD Alpha	2.98 1.39 .73	4.24 1.06 .61	3.55 1.20 .69	2.51 1,20 .58	4.65 0.99 .74	4.07 1.02 .71	4.98 0.87 .59	3.78 1.33 .70	4.17 1.16 .67	4.59 1.07 .74	

Portraits

NOTE: Single-trait/multimethod correlations are on the diagonal; multitrait-multimethod correlations are above and below the diagonal; and multitrait/single-method correlations are not shown. For value-type abbreviations, see Table 8.2.

religious content in the SVS but not in the PQ. In a recent refinement, such content has been added to the PQ.

Additional research must be conducted with the PQ before it is widely adopted to measure values. We are currently revising it to improve the measurement of tradition, benevolence, and achievement values. It is yet to be shown that value priorities measured by the PQ relate to attitudes, behavior, and background variables in meaningful ways, as found with the SVS. It is also not known whether the PQ is suited for cross-cultural research. The language of the PQ is no more complex, and often simpler, than that of the SVS, so translation of nuances should be no more problematic. But the greater concreteness and context-boundedness that are produced by describing people may pose other problems when moving across cultures. Also, though people in most cultures undoubtedly make similarity judgments, the outcomes of such judgments may be affected by differences in the ways that people perceive the boundaries between self and other (Kim, 1994; Schwartz & Ros, 1995; Triandis, 1990).

As noted above, the PQ was designed for use with preadolescents and with populations with low levels of education. Should further research substantiate the validity of this instrument, it will open up possibilities for studying value development among young people as well as value priorities in groups whose literacy level made them inaccessible to studies with the SVS.

STUDY 2:
VALUE PRIORITIES AND SELF-CONSTRUALS

Study 2 addressed the question, Is the distinct content of 10 motivational types of human values specified by the theory also expressed in spontaneous self-construals? If values are a central aspect of the self-concept, as Rokeach (1973) has argued, they should find expression in the way people think about and describe themselves. Hence, self-construals should correlate with individual differences in value priorities and provide an indirect avenue for probing them.

Self-concepts are people's mental representations of their own personalities, social roles, past experiences, future goals, and so on. Representations of self are similar to representations of other concepts, but representations of self are more complex, varied, and rich (Fiske & Taylor, 1991). When asked to describe themselves, individuals apparently select a subset of their many attributes, most likely choosing attributes that are particularly salient to them (McGuire & McGuire, 1988). For example, a person might describe herself with the attributes "a woman, a student, a part-time worker in a restaurant, friendly, ambitious, and overweight." Attribute salience depends on both the situational context and the stable structure of an individual's identity (Deaux & Major, 1987). Higgins and King (1981) make a similar distinction between the acute (situational) accessibility of an attribute and its chronic (stable) accessibility.

Attribute distinctiveness and cultural background are the two main influences on the accessibility of self-attributes that have been studied. Certain attributes of self distinguish individuals from those around them in the current context (e.g., one woman among many men) or have distinguished individuals during their past socialization (e.g., dark-haired people in a country of blonds). Such distinctive attributes tend to be more salient and are mentioned more frequently in self-descriptions (McGuire & McGuire, 1988). Cultural variation in conceptions of self apparently affects self-descriptions as well. For example, Cousins (1989) reported that Japanese students mention more attributes concerning social roles and fewer concerning personal qualities than Americans do. And Triandis et al. (1990) reported that students from Chinese cultures use attributes related to social groups in their self-descriptions more frequently than do students from the United States and Greece.

In the present research, we focus on the chronic accessibility of self-attributes. We assume that values are part of the stable structure of individuals' identities. We therefore postulate that values influence the chronic accessibility of self-attributes. Triandis et al. (1990) provide some support for this view in data from the People's Republic of China. Those who emphasized a cluster of values sampled from the benevolence, conformity, and security types mentioned group-related attributes more often in their self-descriptions. And emphasizing a cluster of values sampled from the hedonism, achievement, and self-direction types correlated negatively with mentioning group-related attributes.

The hypothesis tested in Study 2 assumes that the importance of the 10 different motivational types of values influences the attributes that are mentioned in self-descriptions. Of course, situational and personality factors also affect the attributes mentioned. Consequently, individuals may mention attributes unrelated to important personal values and overlook attributes that are related to their values. We postulate, however, that people tend to view the attributes that relate to their important values as more central to their self-identity than those unrelated to their personal values. This follows from Rokeach's (1973) claim that a major function of personal values is to maintain and enhance the total conception of self. Phrased differently, people tend to construe the self as possessing qualities that are congruent with and instrumental to the attainment and maintenance of their cherished goals (i.e., values).

In this study, we examined the correlations between self-descriptions on an open-ended questionnaire and value priorities measured with the SVS. We hypothesized that the importance attributed to each of the 10 value types in the SVS (e.g., benevolence or stimulation) correlates positively with the importance attributed to spontaneously mentioned self-attributes that are relevant to each of these value types (e.g., kind or thrill seeking).

Methods

A sample of 122 social science students at the Hebrew University completed two questionnaires in fixed order. First, to measure spontaneous self-construals, they responded to the "Who Am I?" questionnaire (Kuhn & McPartland, 1954), using the following instructions:

> In the spaces provided below, please give twenty different statements in answer to the question, "Who am I?" Give these answers as if you were giving them to yourself, not to

somebody else. Try to give responses as they occur to you, without trying to organize or explain them. Write fairly rapidly, for time is limited.

These instructions were followed by 20 numbered lines on the right half of the page. The left half of the page was covered by a strip of paper that respondents were asked to remove when they finished writing. On doing so, they found an additional set of instructions:

Carefully read over the statements you have written. Which statement is most important for your self-identity? Which statement is least important to your self-identity? Now, try to evaluate each statement according to its importance to your identity.

A response scale from 1 (*not important at all*) to 7 (*very important*) was printed to the left of each numbered line.

Next, to measure their value priorities, respondents completed the SVS.

Results and Discussion

Most respondents listed 20 self-attributes (M = 16.45; SD = 4.41). Two coders, trained in the conceptual definitions of the 10 value types and aided by the list of SVS value items, coded each Who Am I protocol. They sought to assign each listed statement to one of the 10 value types, if possible. An assignment was made if the attribute indicated the pursuit of a particular type of value (often one of the values in the SVS itself, e.g., ambitious, intelligent) or suggested a motivation expressive of one of the value types (e.g., "nice" interpreted as relevant to benevolence). Of the 2,007 statements listed, coders were able to assign 617 (31%). The remaining statements (e.g., lonely, overweight) were not clearly relevant to any specific value type. The two coders agreed on 98% of their assignments of attributes. Disagreements were resolved by discussion.

Attributes relevant to benevolence values were the most commonly listed (n = 220; e.g., kind). Almost all respondents mentioned at least one. Attributes relevant to achievement (n = 104; e.g., ambitious) and self-direction (n = 73; e.g., curious) values were also listed frequently. These results are congruent with the known tendency of people to perceive the self as both benevolent and effective (Greenwald & Pratkanis, 1984). Ordered from next-most to least-frequently mentioned were attributes relevant to universalism (n = 58; e.g., broad-minded), tradition (n = 39; e.g., conservative), hedonism (n = 36; e.g., pleasure loving), conformity (n = 32; e.g., polite), security (n = 30; e.g., orderly), stimulation (n = 18; e.g., adventuresome), and power (n = 7; e.g., authoritative) values. The infrequent mention of power and stimulation values is congruent with their relatively low importance in samples across the world (Schwartz, 1994a).

The relatively infrequent mention of attributes related to security, conformity, and tradition values also deserves comment. These three motivational types of values constitute a higher-order conservation value type. They share an emphasis on commitment to the social order and maintenance of certainty in relationships with close others, institutions, and traditions. The shared motivation inherent in these values may be expressed in a tendency to look for similarity between self and others rather than to focus on unique characteristics of self. Hence, people who give high rather than low priority to conservation values tend to describe themselves on the "Who Am I?" questionnaire more in terms of their shared memberships and identities (e.g., student, Israeli) and less in terms of personal characteristics that are value relevant (Roccas, 1997).

To explore the associations between self-construals and personal value priorities, we noted the attributes relevant to each value type that appeared in the "Who Am I?" descriptions of each respondent. We then summed the importance given to these attributes by the respondent. In this way, each respondent received a score that reflected the importance he or she gave to attributes relevant to each value type in his or her self-construal (zero, if no relevant attributes were mentioned).[5]

Finally, we correlated the scores from the self-descriptions with the importance of the value types as measured by the respondents' SVS. We tested the hypothesis that individuals' scores for the attributes relevant to a specific value type in their self-descriptions correlate positively with the importance they give to the corresponding value type. The correlations that test this hypothesis are printed in bold in Table 8.4.

A complementary set of expectations can also be derived from the structural postulate of the theory of basic values. Individuals who give much importance to a value type should deemphasize attributes relevant to the structurally opposed value types in their self-descriptions. For example, those for whom power and achievement values are especially important should rarely mention attributes relevant to benevolence and universalism values in their self-descriptions. We also examine evidence for this derivation in Table 8.4.

Openness to Change

For stimulation and self-direction, the two types that form the openness to change higher-order value type, there were significant positive correlations between responses on the SVS and responses on the "Who Am I?" (.33 and .28, respectively), as hypothesized. As shown in Table 8.4, the derivation from the structural postulate of the values theory also received support. The correlations between responses reflecting stimulation and self-direction on the "Who Am I?" correlated negatively with responses on the SVS for the opposing conservation value types—tradition, conformity, and, weakly, security values.

Self-Enhancement

For power, achievement, and hedonism, the three types that form the self-enhancement higher-order value type,[6] responses on the SVS also correlated positively and significantly with responses on the "Who Am I?" (.15, .28, and .16, respectively). Moreover, those who attributed much importance to values from the self-transcendence higher-order value type that opposes self-enhancement did not emphasize self-enhancing attributes in their self-construals. Self-descriptions as a self-enhancing person correlated negatively with ratings of universalism and benevolence as important values on the SVS, although some correlations were weak.

TABLE 8.4 Correlations[a] of Value Priorities (SVS)[b] with Value-Relevant Attributes Mentioned in the "Who Am I?" Self-Descriptions

Attributes in the "Who Am I?"	Value Priorities in SVS									
	ST	SD	PO	AC	HE	UN	BE	TR	CO	SE
Openness to Change										
Stimulation (ST)	**33**	2	18	19	1	08	–6	–26	–23	–10
Self-Direction (SD)	6	**28**	–6	3	9	12	–3	–29	–21	–9
Self-Enhancement										
Power (PO)	13	–9	**15**	11	14	–8	–5	–9	2	5
Achievement (AC)	22	15	22	**28**	17	–12	–23	–22	–11	–2
Hedonism (HE)	4	0	5	14	**16**	–10	–23	–22	–11	–2
Self-Transcendence										
Universalism (UN)	17	11	–8	–14	–3	**22**	15	–9	–14	–21
Benevolence (BE)	3	–11	–8	10	0	2	**16**	–3	2	13
Conservation										
Tradition (TR)	–18	–15	–4	–20	–25	2	15	**25**	17	15
Conformity (CO)	9	4	9	5	9	–6	2	–10	**10**	13
Security (SE)	11	6	2	2	6	–3	10	–9	7	**–7**

a. Multiplied by 100 to eliminate decimals. Correlations equal to or greater than 15 are significant, $p < .05$.
b. SVS = Schwartz Value Survey.

Self-Transcendence

For universalism and benevolence, the two self-transcendence value types, responses on the SVS also correlated positively and significantly with responses on the "Who Am I?" (.22 and .16, respectively). Self-descriptions as a self-transcending person correlated negatively with four of six ratings of power, achievement, and hedonism as important values on the SVS, with one correlation at zero. All six correlations were quite weak, however.

Conservation

Of the three conservation value types, only tradition yielded results in line with the hypothesis. There was a significant positive correlation between responses on the SVS and the "Who Am I?" questionnaire (.25) and significant negative correlations between self-descriptions as a tradition-oriented person and ratings of stimulation and self-direction as important values on the SVS. Results for conformity were inconsistent and weak, and results for security were reversed and weak.

In sum, 9 of the 10 correlations that tested the hypothesized positive association between spontaneous self-construals and the importance of the relevant values were in the predicted direction, and 8 of these correlations were significant. These results provide considerable support for the hypothesis. Moreover, 18 of the 24 correlations between spontaneous self-construals relevant to a particular value type and the SVS importance ratings of values representative of the structurally opposed value types were negative, and none was significantly positive. These results support the discriminant validity of the value constructs. They suggest that people tend to construe the self as possessing qualities that are congruent with and instrumental to attaining and maintaining their cherished goals. People's perceptions of their actual attributes are far from identical to their values, however, as indicated by the relative weakness of the correlations.

Almost all the data that do not support the hypothesis involved self-construals related to conformity and security values. How do these value types differ from the others? We noted above that inherent in conformity, security, and tradition values is a shared motivation to look for similarity between self and others rather than to focus on unique attributes of self. People who give high priority to these values express this priority by describing themselves in terms of common social categories to which they belong (Roccas, 1997). Mentioning social categories in self-descriptions may substitute for mentioning attributes relevant to these value types. This would explain the failure to support the hypotheses for conformity and security. But why, then, was the hypothesis for tradition values supported? Those who gave high priority to tradition values were mainly religious students. Many of them expressed this social identity by describing themselves as "religious," codable as relevant to tradition values. This yielded the hypothesized correlation.

GENERAL CONCLUSION

We have reported studies involving two very different probes relevant to individual values. Results of both studies increase our confidence in the key postulates of the basic values theory and in the SVS instrument as a measure of basic value priorities. The two indirect approaches for probing values provide additional evidence for the distinctiveness of the 10 value types and for the structure of relations of compatibility and opposition among these value types that are postulated in the values theory.

The two approaches differ substantially in their methodology. The PQ is closed-ended, whereas the "Who Am I?" obtains "soft," spontaneous self-reports. The approaches also differ in their theoretical significance. The PQ is intended to provide a new, alternative method for appraising value priorities. That is, it is intended to shed light on the same constructs measured by the SVS and to provide an independent test of the validity of the content and structure claims of the values theory. Results of the multitrait-multimethod analysis of the PQ and the SVS suggest that, pending further refinement and construct validation, the PQ may provide an alternative method for measuring value priorities, especially useful with groups for whom the SVS is too abstract.

The self-descriptions in the "Who Am I?" were viewed theoretically as correlates of value priorities rather than as alternative measures of these constructs. They were linked to value priorities by theorizing about causal relations among values and self-conceptions. The observed associations between self-descriptions and value priorities extend the nomological net in which values are embedded. They strengthen claims about the significance of values for understanding the self.

This research employed multiple probes for two purposes: to explore the nature and components of one set of constructs with different methods (PQ and SVS) and to explore theorized correlates of these constructs ("Who Am I?" and SVS). These purposes could be distinguished because we specified the criterial attributes of the constructs (i.e., the value types). In this, our approach differs from Triandis's (1994b) use of multiple probes to study individualism and collectivism, which he views as broad cultural syndromes of "beliefs, attitudes, norms, roles, values and behaviors" (p. 50).

Triandis designates certain attributes as typical of each syndrome, but he defines no particular attributes as criterial. For example, emotional detachment from the in-group typically characterizes individualist cultures, and an emphasis on family integrity typically characterizes collectivist cultures. Yet the presence or absence of these attributes does not decisively determine that a culture is individualist or collectivist. He provides no unequivocal definition of these cultural syndromes, arguing that individualism and collectivism can "take very different forms in different parts of the world" (Triandis et al., 1990, p. 1018). In our view, specifying the criterial attributes of individualism and collectivism would be beneficial. Doing so would make it possible to distinguish whether probes of these two cultural syndromes inform us about their nature and components, on the one hand, or about their correlates, on the other.

NOTES

1. For detailed descriptions of development, procedures, statistical properties, cross-cultural validation, and so on, see Schmitt, Schwartz, Steyer, and Schmitt (1993), Schwartz (1992, 1994a), Schwartz and Sagiv (1995), and Schwartz, Verkasalo, Antonovsky, and Sagiv (1997).

2. Greater accessibility of self-knowledge, as compared with knowledge of others, may characterize people of Western but not of Eastern cultural backgrounds (Markus & Kitayama, 1991). Hence, the direction of comparison may matter less or even have a reverse effect when applying the PQ methodology in Eastern cultures.

3. We thank Vicki Owens (Uganda) and Meg Rohan (Canada) for their help.

4. Because of the small number of items included in the indexes for each value type, their reliabilities were only moderate. Correcting the correlations for attenuation raised five of them over .9, and the remainder ranged from .48 (tradition) to .78 (universalism), further supporting the idea that the instruments measure similar constructs.

5. It has been suggested that the order in which attributes are listed reflects their relative importance to the self (e.g., Gordon, 1968). There is little support for this idea, however, and it was not supported in the current study.

6. Hedonism shares elements of both openness to change and self-enhancement, according to theory (Schwartz, 1992). In the current data, it is more aligned with self-enhancement.

9

THE EXPERIENCE OF CONTRASTING SUBJECTIVE CULTURES

The Case of South Asian Women in Canada

Josephine C. Naidoo
Wilfrid Laurier University

HISTORICAL PERSPECTIVE

My ancestral heritage has its roots in the traditional collectivism of India and the philosophical orientation of Hinduism. This was tempered by at least a century of familial contact with "Western" European Christianity and British culture. My weltanschauung, therefore, was a complex interaction of both collectivist and individualist values, vertical but often also horizontal in orientation. Thus, dutiful deference to parental authority (vertical collectivism) within an extended family bonded by interdependence and sharing of resources (horizontal collectivism) was the accepted norm in our Asian Indian community. Interwoven with this collectivist lifestyle was a competitive achievement orientation (vertical individualism) reinforced by rewards for high academic performance. Academic excellence won unique respect from family and community; the usual distinctions by age, status, gender, and socioeconomic differences were "blurred"; relationships were equalized (horizontal individualism). The formulation of the structure of such a worldview has best been explored by Harry C. Triandis over a 20-year study of the nature of these constructs.

125

Canada became my chosen country in 1964. It was a period of "open door" immigration policy initiated by the federal liberal government of Pierre Trudeau in the mid-1960s. Canada reversed its traditional closed attitude to peoples of non-Western origins. For the period from 1967 to 1974, large numbers of South Asians, with ancestry in the Indian subcontinent, came to Canada in response to the Canadian need for professionals in universities, medicine, and engineering. However, by the mid-1970s, immigration policy became more restricted; the Immigration Act of 1976 defined specific linkages between immigration and domestic manpower needs.

In the early 1970s, this same government had responded to the *Report of the Royal Commission on Bilingualism and Biculturalism* ("Cultural Contribution," 1969) that the contributions of Canada's diverse ethnic groups to the cultural enrichment of their adopted home be recognized. A policy of multiculturalism (1971) within an English-French bilingual framework was introduced; Canada officially sanctioned a policy that encouraged the retention of traditional cultural identities. Protection of equal rights and benefits and of heritage and language rights for all Canadians were entrenched within Section 15 and Section 27, respectively, of the 1982 Canadian Charter of Rights and Freedoms. The 1988 Canadian Multiculturalism Act reinforced the aspiration that multiculturalism is part of what it means to be a Canadian.

The *Report of the Royal Commission on the Status of Women in Canada* (1970) expressed the perspective that cross-cultural data contribute to our conceptualization of the place of men and women in the natural order. The commission recognized that the psychological characteristics of either sex may be derived not from nature but, rather, from cultural habits.

Naidoo's studies emerged from this political zeitgeist. The motivation for her research involved understanding the "subjective culture" (Triandis, 1972) underpinnings of South Asian behavioral expression. In Triandis's conceptualization, such an analysis involves probing the target group's characteristic way of perceiving its social environment, identifying the attributes of its cognitive structure in response to social settings. Naidoo focused on three areas of interest: negatively perceived behaviors, integration within a pluralistic society, and achievement orientation of South Asian women.

Negatively Perceived Behaviors

Historically, Canada has not welcomed people different by race, culture, religion, or values. During the 1900s, white fear of an "invasion" of Asians into British Columbia (B.C.) determined Canada's exclusionary immigration policy. The hostile Komagatu Maru incident of 1914, barring prospective Punjabi immigrants from entering B.C., remains a blot on Canada's reputation for racial tolerance. The entry of South Asians into the country in the early 1970s was marred by reports of violence, overt racism, verbal abuse, and hate literature (Naidoo, 1980b). An early study of white perceptions of South Asian women (Naidoo, 1980a) indicated rejection of traditional dress (the sari), the dot on Hindu women's foreheads (the *tikka*), "jewels" on the face (nose ring), and perceived subservience of the women to their spouses.

Integration Within a Pluralistic Society

In 1971, Prime Minister Pierre Trudeau stated, "Cultural group freedom from discrimination must be founded in one's own individual identity; out of this can grow respect for that of others and a willingness to share ideas, attitudes, and assumptions" (as cited in Berry, Kalin, & Taylor, 1977, p. 224). Contrary to this view, Naidoo's (1980a, 1980b) finding indicated that official multicultural policy in fact fostered the emergence of South Asian and Anglo-Saxon "solitudes." To questions about informal interactions between the two groups, 77% of white Canadians and 64% of South Asians responded that such interactions were confined to their respective in-groups. To achieve "unity in diversity," education and communication at all levels of Canadian society was imperative.

Achievement Orientation of South Asian Women

In general, studies of North American women reveal a significant correlation between "traditional" socialization and low achievement and between "contemporary" socialization and high achievement (Lipman-Blumen, 1972). The literature indicates that these trends may derive from the historical-cultural dichotomization of the nature of female-ness-maleness that existed in Western culture until relatively recently (Naidoo, 1980c). One theoretical focus was to examine the nature of the relationship between socialization and achievement aspirations in middle-class South Asian women. Some support exists for the assertion that a complementary view of the nature of femaleness-maleness prevails in South Asian Hindu culture rooted in ancient Vedic teachings (Cormack, 1961). The prediction from this assertion is that South Asian women are perhaps freer than their Western counterparts to model themselves on behaviors that traditionally have been categorized as either "female" or "male" in Western culture. Thus, it may be expected that, though South Asian women experience and retain traditionally feminine behaviors, this traditionalism will not necessarily extend to achievement orientation—that is, traditional socialization and achievement may be independent dimensions in South Asian culture rather than correlated dimensions as in Western culture (Naidoo, 1980c).

SOUTH ASIAN DEMOGRAPHIC PROFILE

The South Asian presence in Canada and official attitudes toward this minority fall into three key categories: (a) broadly discriminatory at the turn of the century, with voting rights won only in 1947; (b) liberalization of immigration policy in the mid-1960s and general receptive official attitudes until the mid-1980s; and (c) tightening of immigration policy, especially "family reunification," and shift toward preference for "entrepreneurs" in the late 1980s.

The 1991 census for Canada (Statistics Canada, 1991) places the South Asian population at 420,295, including people with origins in India (54.3%), Pakistan, Bangladesh, and Sri Lanka. South Asians make up 1.6% of the total Canadian population; the heaviest proportion of these (57.7%) has settled in the province of Ontario. South Asians make up 2.3% of the population of Ontario and 4.9% of metropolitan Toronto. Gender distribution is approximately 50% at the national, provincial, and city levels. The largest South Asian religious group is the Hindus. The statistics for the Hindu population are Canada, 37.4%; Ontario, 46.1%; and Toronto, 47.3%. Other major religious representations include the Sikhs, Muslims, Buddhists, and small groups of Jains, Zoroastrians, and Christians.

By far, the most frequently listed language for South Asians, male and female, is English. A surprising 40.6% of the South Asian population listed "English" under groupings of "mother tongue" in the 1991 census. For South Asian women across the country, 41.4% identified English as at least one "mother tongue"; 49.4% listed English in Ontario, and 49.1% in Toronto. For both genders, other language preferences follow this order: Punjabi, Gujarati, Hindi, Urdu, and Tamil. Triandis (1972) notes the importance of linguistic factors on subjective culture. The shift toward a shared language by this acculturating group has important implications for transformations in its culture-cognitive "maps."

Both male and female South Asians are relatively young; the populations for girls and boys peak at 5 to 14 years and for adult females at 25 to 30 years and 40 to 54 years. A high 66.5% of women over 15 years old are in the labor force, employed mostly as clerical workers, in sales and services, and as semiskilled manual workers at one end of the scale and as professionals, middle management, and semiprofessionals/technicians at the other end. Markedly low are both women and men in senior management positions. South Asian women earn consistently less than South Asian men in any education category, but women with higher university education fare best. In general, the women are quite well educated: 31.1% have some university or bachelor of arts background, and only 13.1% have less than a Grade 9 education.

SOUTH ASIAN WOMEN IN CANADA:
LITERATURE REVIEW

In 1977, Norman Buchignani, well-known scholar of South Asians in Canada, published an extensive bibliography in the *Journal of Canadian Ethnic Studies* on the South Asian presence in Canada. Of some 300 citations, not a single title referred to South Asian women.

Research involving women with ancestral roots in the countries of South Asia has gathered momentum in the past two decades. In a recent review of the literature, Naidoo (1994) identifies some 200 studies exploring issues pertaining to the cultural adaptation of these women drawn from empirical and clinical research in psychology, sociology, anthropology, and psychiatry.

The early studies of South Asian women, published in the 1970s and mainly conducted in the western provinces and British Columbia, explored a wide range of scattered research interests, including family relationships, marriage, religious practices, identity and self-perceptions, prejudice and discrimination, adjustment, and day-to-day problems. Naidoo reports on and assesses these studies in a 1987 essay on the topic. Overall, the studies reviewed emphasize that South Asian women welcome modernization, but they do not want Westernization. Reporting on a survey of South Asians in Toronto in 1983, the respected *Toronto Star* chose to highlight this comment made by one interviewee: "Our unique backgrounds are too ancient to disappear in one melting pot: One never loses one's roots" ("South Asians," pp. C1, C4).

Naidoo's several comparative studies of South Asian and Anglo-Celtic women, conducted in the 1980s in metropolitan Toronto and cities of southern Ontario, identified a more complex adaptation pattern (Naidoo1980a, 1980b, 1980c). Her studies revealed a duality in the nature of the South Asian women's life orientation with both "traditional" and "contemporary" attitudes and values. The former related to family, religion, and marriage; the latter, to education, achievement, and success. Furthermore, her study of acculturation and adaptation to the host setting (Naidoo, 1980c, 1985b) revealed a clearly selective approach in the women's emulation of aspects of Canadian culture. South Asian women adapt to many forms of behavioral expression in Western host societies, Naidoo reports, but some forms of expression are considered integral parts of cultural identity, and these remain firmly anchored in the women's psyche (Naidoo & Davis, 1988).

Several studies published in the '80s and early '90s lend support to Naidoo's contentions. Thus, findings indicate that the Indian idealization of women as wives/mothers is viewed as compatible with goals of high education achievement (Agnew, 1986). The women show a conscious desire to maintain cultural identity but adopt new (host) patterns deemed advantageous to them (Ghosh, 1983). Although the woman's self is grounded in loyalty to family, there is a shift toward embracing contemporary values of the larger Canadian society (Khosla, 1982) and toward the suggestion that the *pativratya* ideology (deference to spouse) weakens as the women acquire resources and experience more equal gender relationships (Dhruvarajan, 1988). Though young, educated South Asians want their own personal spousal choices, they also seek parental consent (Vaidyanathan & Naidoo, 1990). Furthermore, Indian concepts of love, marriage, and religious ritual were preferred over concepts of dating and romance in the host country (Filteau, 1980).

DEFINITION OF TERMS

Naidoo has defined the terms *traditional* and *contemporary* in both a broad and narrower sense (Naidoo & Davis, 1988). In the broad sense, the word *traditional* describes the general sociocultural perspectives of South Asian women pertaining to values, beliefs, and customs handed down from generation to generation, firmly adhered to, and less subject to forces of acculturation as migratory groups come in contact with other cultures. The term *contemporary*, implying modern and characteristic of the present, is used to designate those values, beliefs, and customs prevailing in the host culture to which migratory groups have been or are being acculturated (Burchfield, 1972, p. 619). Persons who are "modern" are characteristically open to new experiences, they shift allegiance from traditional figures of authority (parents, priests), and they abandon passivity and fatalism. They have high ambitions for themselves and their children to achieve high educational and occupational goals (Frank, 1981, p. 186).

In the narrower sense, the terms *traditional* and *contemporary* are used specifically regarding beliefs about women's responsibilities to home and family versus freedom to pursue education and work outside the home, respectively (Lipman-Blumen, 1972).

Triandis (1993) more pointedly defines concepts inherent in Naidoo's definitions, but clearly there are parallels in the two authors' conceptualizations. Thus, Triandis views the cultural syndrome of collectivism as the organization of elements of subjective culture (attitudes, beliefs, values) around family, tribe, work or consumer group, state, and ethnic or religious group; by contrast, he views the organizing themes central in the cultural syndrome of individualism to be autonomy, independence, self-focus, freedom, and egalitarianism (Triandis, 1991, 1995b). Collectivists are basically traditional, motivated by the norms and duties imposed by the in-group collective entity; individualists are attuned basically to "contemporary," "modernistic," current values prevailing in the society, motivated by their own personal preferences and needs.

RESEARCH OVERVIEW:
A DUALISTIC WORLDVIEW

The focus of the present analysis is an in-depth study of the emic characteristics (Triandis, 1972) of the worldview of South Asian women located within the indigenous concepts of Hinduism. Hindu Asian Indians compose the largest proportion of people originating in South Asia. Naidoo's major study conducted in metropolitan Toronto in the early 1980s accurately reflected this demographic characteristic. Furthermore, a rigorous sampling design was employed to minimize potential sampling error for this very diverse population. For comparative purposes, a corresponding "Anglo-Celtic" sample with ancestry in the British Isles matched by residential location was used (Naidoo, 1986; Naidoo & Davis, 1988).

Multiple methods and multiple measures (Triandis, 1972) across psychology, sociology, and anthropology were used to probe the rich, complex inner life of these particular women. Careful attention was given to the control of variables such as response sets and social desirability; tests were conducted to establish the cultural rather than gender basis for the study findings (Naidoo & Davis, 1988). Ethical considerations were viewed from a gender-cultural perspective (Naidoo, 1996a). The findings of this major study are corroborated by results from several other studies of South Asian women conducted by Naidoo in southern Ontario over a 10-year period.

The worldview of educated, middle-class Indian women with reasonable family incomes parallels Triandis's contentions of coexisting collectivist-individualist cognitive systems. Naidoo's studies augment the meager data on how women process changes in cognitive structure necessitated by their migration to achieve their own unique collectivist-individualist "balance" (Triandis, 1995b). The data reveal that the women are clearly entrenched in the traditional collectivist values of their heritage culture, but they exhibit a willingness to selectively adapt to certain Western forms of behavioral expression characteristic of their contemporary/individualist host society. This basic dualistic pattern persists regardless of the respondents' marital status, age, education, social class, income, length of stay in Canada, and amount of intercultural contact (Naidoo, 1996a). The empirical determination of the relative importance of cultural values composing the traditional/contemporary dimensions at the individual and group levels awaits future research, as does the generality of this dualistic worldview in Asian Indian immigrant populations in other countries.

THE HINDU IDEOLOGY OF FEMALE DUALITY

Naidoo speculates that the South Asian women's dualistic worldview is rooted in the Hindu ideology that "femaleness" makes up an essential duality. Anthropological writings on women in Hindu tradition (Wadley, 1977) offer insight. Figure 9.1 illustrates this conceptualization in simplified form.

In Hindu cosmology, all life emerges from a unity between matter (*prakrti,* or the female, nature, undifferentiated component) and spirit (*purusa,* or the male, symbolically culture, differentiated component).

At biological conception, all human beings partake of matter and spirit. However, because the female component is equated with nature, earth, soil into which man places his seed (*Laws of Manu,* A.D. 200), women partake more of nature.

Significantly, the female component comprises a further crucial duality: On the one hand, it is composed of the nature-matter-earth-nurturant (*prakrti*) component; on the other, it is composed of an active-energizing-potentially aggressive component, *sakti* (also known as Shakti). Shakti is conceptualized as the energizing principle of the universe. It underlies both creation and divinity and is female; all human beings have their share of Shakti (endowed at birth but increased or decreased through later actions). Shakti, therefore, is embodied in the woman and is the original energy of the universe. Naidoo (1980c, 1988) argues that the existence in Hindu cosmology of a concept of duality in female nature—a duality making up a powerful, active "Shakti Power" element, albeit ideally submerged—is a "plus" for South Asian women. Inherent in this active/power element, symbolized ubiquitously in the forehead *tikka* of Hindu women, is the potential for self-determination, ego strength, belief in self, and action orientation.

RESEARCH FINDINGS:
TRADITIONAL AND CONTEMPORARY DIMENSIONS

Commenting on Naidoo's studies, Canadian anthropologists Buchignani and Indra (1985) state, "South Asian women seem to want the best of both worlds . . . they desire a greater range of freedom outside the home . . . but they continue to ground their identity in the family" (p. 157). Triandis's insights (1995b) regarding culture-specific influences in people's worldview and the meanings attached to life events bear special relevance for understanding the dynamics of acculturation in South Asian women.

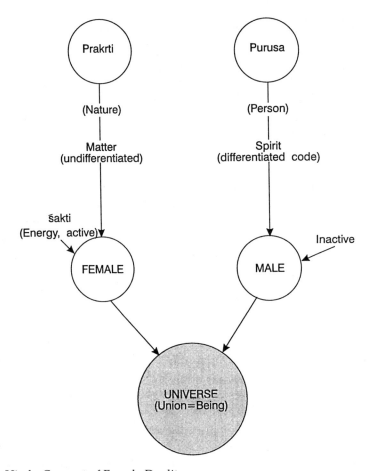

Figure 9.1. Hindu Concept of Female Duality
SOURCE: "Women and the Hindu Tradition," by S. S. Wadley, *Signs*, 1977, 3(1), 115. Copyright 1977, University of Chicago. Used with permission.

South Asian women share, broadly, a geographic, historic, linguistic, and cultural vertical collectivism, but within this commonality they also experience unique allocentric freedoms. Moreover, most middle-class South Asian women immigrants to Canada have moved beyond the closed in-group collective, speaking English and familiar with Western (British) customs and traditions.

Naidoo's studies for South Asian samples reveal a consistent dualistic, complementary characteristic, both traditional/collectivist and contemporary/ individualist. This author has asserted elsewhere that the basis of the South Asian dualistic self-orientation should be sought in Hindu culture (Naidoo, 1980a, 1980b, 1980c). By contrast, the Anglo-Celtic samples tested emerge as basically "contemporary" (individualist). The pattern of their self-perceptions, aspirations outside the home, and achievement orientation parallel findings for other mainstream North American female populations (Horner, 1970; Lipman-Blumen, 1972).

RELIGIOUS, PHILOSOPHICAL, AND
ACHIEVEMENT VALUES

For South Asian women, "subjective" culture is clearly embedded in the religious norms and spiritual and philosophical values of their respective adherence to Hinduism, Sikhism, Islam, and, to a lesser degree, Buddhism, Jainism, Zoroastrianism, and Christianity. They indicate significantly higher levels for both importance of religious beliefs and practice of teachings emanating from these religious beliefs than do their Christian (Protestant) Anglo-Saxon counterparts (Naidoo, 1996b). Thus, they report the significant importance in their lives of the basic teachings of their faiths; beliefs in a Supreme Creator; God as a guiding spirit and as creator of the universe; imitation of prophets and deities; and brotherhood as a path to God, paradise, and nirvana. To enhance meaningfulness of spiritual concepts, these were probed from the women's particular religious perspective. Thus, the Creator was expressed as "Brahman" (Hindus), "Allah" (Muslims), "the True Name" (Sikhs), and "Ahura Mazda," which means wise lord (Zoroastrians).

The South Asian women also endorsed significantly "stronger practice" on items such as doing one's duty according to rules of religion ("Dharma"), family obligations, spiritual development through prayer and meditation, following Scripture teachings and rules of fasting/penance, celebrating religious aspects of traditional festivals, supporting development of religious affiliation in Canada, and making pilgrimages to holy places. Again, spiritual practice was probed from the women's unique perspectives. Thus, for example, to a question about Scriptures, the women were asked to focus on sacred books in their particular lives, Upanishads/Bhagavad Gita (Hindus), the Koran (Muslims), the Guru Granth Sahib (Sikhs), the Tripitaka (Buddhists), and Avesta teachings (Zoroastrians).

In contrast to Muslims, Hindus and Sikhs believe there is no one true and only religion, but all three groups believe good actions in this life determine their afterlife (for Hindus and Sikhs, "karma"; for Muslims, "paradise"). All groups also feel strongly about keeping holy books and shrines in the home for prayers or offerings. Purification and religious rules of diet are also important.

In general, the women have not changed their religious attitudes since their teens, and most expect their children to continue practicing traditional religions, albeit more liberal versions. Though they clearly do not want the religious values of the host country, they do not experience undue stress as a result of the fear of losing religious identity or of practicing their religion in a Christian country with different religious-based holidays such as Christmas and Easter.

In her study of the functions of religious activities for South Asian women, Ralston (1992) contends that the migration experience has increased the saliency of religion in "sacralizing" identity for these women.

In Triandis's thinking, these women basically are vertical collectivists, tightly pursuing the teachings of their particular religions and obedient to the dictates of such, yet they have some horizontal collectivism in that they extend love to all in their strong feelings about "brotherhood."

The women's traditionalism, however, seemingly does not extend to inquiries about personal achievement, careers outside the home, experience of fear of success, and aspirations for the most promising daughter.

As reported elsewhere (Naidoo, 1980c; Naidoo & Davis, 1988), the underlying motivation themes to their stories on the Matina Horner (1970) scenario "After first term finals, Anne finds herself at the top of her medical school class" are clearly positive. Respondents quickly projected their own life experiences into the contrived scenario. The consequences of "success" were personal and family happiness, pride, a career, and contribution to society. There was no hint of fear of losing friends, not finding a marriage partner, or social rejection, or of anxiety about the future. The all-too-familiar "fear of success" theme, describing the responses of young U.S. college women to the Horner storytelling situation, today is reported widely in social psychology texts. Horner's findings have taken on the status of a universal etic characteristic of female achievement behavior. Triandis challenges such generalizations. Naidoo's several studies provide consistent empirical data of the high-achievement orientation of South Asian women, unfettered by fears and anxieties that academic, educational, or career success will bring social rejection. Naidoo argues that "fear of success" should be viewed as a culture-specific "emic" variable (Triandis, 1995b) pending further research on women outside Euro-American cultures.

As compared with Anglo-Celtic women, the Asians also reported experiencing significantly higher levels of respect for learning and education in their homes during adolescence (Naidoo, 1980c). Indeed, the goddess Saraswati, symbol of learning and fine arts education, is glorified by many. For the Asian respondents, in general, the belief that "knowledge and learning leads to God" is significantly highly endorsed (Naidoo, 1996b). The women assert they were encouraged to model their behavior on the best-educated people in the family; parents had higher achievement expectations of girls than of boys, and they promoted high school performance through rewards. A consistent finding is that fathers shared the girls' intellectual interests more frequently than mothers, but both parents valued higher education for women.

Now in Canada, the women express high aspirations for the "most promising" daughter in the family; a medical career is highly favored, with the expectation of "active involvement" by parents (Naidoo & Davis, 1988). The most admired and wanted cultural values of the host country are "careers for women," "educational aspirations," and "opportunity for all" (Naidoo, 1986). There is a generally favorable attitude toward women's liberation movements. The most striking change is the increased usage of the English language in Canada. There is, however, a concern about retention of heritage language(s) as the harbinger of culture. They exhibit considerable ego strength in their belief in the self and their own capabilities and a determination to succeed in a new country (Naidoo, 1985b, 1992b).

These findings of allo- and idiocentric values expand Triandis's contentions to an understanding of sense of self for women in transition from ancestral to host culture. As indicated earlier, findings for the South Asians contrast sharply with related data for North American female samples.

IDEAS ABOUT FAMILY,
RELATIONSHIPS, AND MARRIAGE

With regard to the Hindu family, sociologist Ross (1961) says, "Women are the main media through which the traditional love of the family and society is passed on to the next generation" (p. 292). Naidoo's studies (1985a) indicate that women remain the core of family strength. They dislike and do not want from the host culture ideas about family relationships, marriage, and children, preferring to keep such values from the home culture. People-related values are viewed of primary importance. The values the women model for their children are, for example, respect, tolerance, sharing, giving, and helping. There is awareness that these interpersonal values guided by principles of dharma (doing one's duty) and harmonious living are possibly at variance with those fostered in the larger, more aggressive and competitive individualist society.

As discussed by Naidoo (1980c), in the traditional Indian social system, there is no dating; girls are carefully protected; and most women marry, usually by full or partial parental arrangement. Marriage is regarded as cementing families and ensuring family continuity, and it is considered an essential phase in the human life cycle; hence, parents play a role in selecting spouses for all their children. Clearly, the women want to keep ideas about marriage from the home culture; they dislike and do not want host values on marriage (Naidoo, 1986). Moreover, they report "feelings of disturbance" about Canadian free-choice marriage based on romantic love and adolescent boy-girl dating customs (Naidoo, 1985b). They do assign high importance to the value "sexuality," understood as a holistic concept of life, sexual function, and continuity of life as envisioned in Hindu thought. Indeed, sexual being is vividly portrayed in Hindu art and temple architecture (Naidoo, 1985a).

A study on the arranged marriage (Vaidyanathan & Naidoo, 1990) does, however, reveal shifts in traditional marital thinking that lend support to Triandis's contentions (Triandis, 1995b). As noted by Triandis, as well as sociologists in Canada studying the place of love in marriage, in traditional Eastern thinking, one loves the woman or man one marries, as contrasted with the Western romantic belief that one marries the woman or man one loves. The Vaidyanathan and Naidoo study of two generations of Hindus and Sikhs in southern Ontario indicates clear differences in priorities for desirable marital—demographic, personal, and family—attributes. Parents (first generation) stressed religion and caste quite strongly; they also stressed good character and good family and individual attributes as important in a prospective bride or groom; and they were willing to accept dating only in a committed relationship. By contrast, their children (second generation) of marriageable age viewed religion and caste as negligible, stressed partner attractiveness and individual attributes, and felt dating was a healthy, desirable practice. However, both generations viewed premarital sexual relations as "unacceptable" in Indian culture, and both generations in this well-educated sample endorsed individual-choice marriages with parental consent.

SELF-IDENTITY, ROLE PERCEPTIONS,
AND SALIENT VALUES

Several sources of data from the Naidoo studies (1980a, 1980c, 1985a; Naidoo & Davis, 1988) identify a stable duality in the women's outlook on life as they seek adaptive "balance" between the cultural forces originating in their ancestral countries and those of the host society (Triandis, 1995b).

Insight into the women's sense of self was gleaned from a series of measures administered to comparable samples of South Asian and Anglo-Celtic women. Thus, to a "Who Am I?" test probed by cue phrases "I have," "I am," "I want," "My goals are," and "I would like to be," there emerges the family-oriented versus self-improvement themes in the content analysis of the South Asian responses. As symbolized in the figure of Sita, devoted and loyal wife of Lord Rama, hero of the Hindu religious epic the *Ramayana*, the woman's sense of self is rooted in being a "wife," a "mother," and a "woman." On the other hand, these women clearly want to realize their own potential, further their own education, and pursue careers. In general, there was more focus on the self, personal growth, recognition, and justice for women in the responses of the Anglo-Celtic sample. On a role perception test, the complementary nature of the South Asian self-perceptions reappears. Simultaneously, strongly expressed collectivist and tradition-based feelings, such as "the child's natural mother is always the best person to raise the child" and "women want foremost to be men's companions and mothers," were balanced by equally strong individualist and contemporary feelings related to potential personal self-actualization regarding equal opportunity with men to attend college/university, strive for personal growth and recognition, and access professional and career training. As predicted, Anglo-Celtic women emerged as significantly more "contemporary" than their South Asian counterparts. In a study of salient values in life, two clear conceptual categories of responses were identified in a χ^2 test analysis for the two cultural groups. The Asian traditional focus has both a vertical and horizontal collectivist character in the women's endorsement of such values as respect for elders, doing one's duty, obedience to authority, first loyalty to family, and cooperation. By contrast, the "contemporary" individualist and more autonomous cognitive structure emerges in their significant endorsement of the values self-confidence, intellectual ability, and self-development (Naidoo, 1992a).

Sociologist Lipman-Blumen (1972) defines three levels of mode of achievement outside the home adopted by graduate student wives in a study conducted in the Boston area: (a) direct through one's own efforts, (b) balanced through own and husband's efforts, and (c) vicarious through the accomplishments of the husband. Naidoo's studies of this characteristic over a 10-year period in the 1980s revealed a pronounced shift from "vicarious" to "balanced" in the achievement-seeking aspirations of these women outside the home. Indeed, there was some shift toward the direct contemporaneous position of the Anglo-Celtic women. Explanations for shifts in women's life perspectives over time may be sought in historical, legal, and societal structural changes; improvements in socioeconomic circumstances; and control over environmental forces. In this regard,

Triandis's contention that once people become more affluent, with better material resources, their cognitive value systems move toward individualism warrants attention.

CONCLUSION:
THE PERSPECTIVE OF INDIGENOUS CULTURE

Triandis presents impressive empirical evidence that the collectivist and individualist constructs are cultural syndromes comprising elements of subjective culture that identify people sharing commonalities of language, history, and geography. Naidoo asserts that her consistent findings of a dualistic traditional-contemporary self-image for South Asian women are rooted in Hindu culture. The writings of anthropologists (Wadley, 1977) and religious historians (Pearson, 1996) on women in Hindu tradition offer a more rounded understanding of the women's cognitive values. Thus, a powerful tradition-bound (collectivist) outlook pervades much of the culture—for example, the constraints on women's autonomy imposed by the Code of Manu, the important symbol of loyal and virtuous Sita as the ideal woman, the ideology of *pativratya*, and the postulate of a nurturant (*prakrti*) component underlying female nature. At the same time, many aspects of the culture influence it in a "modern" (individualist) direction—for instance, the existence of a complementary, rather than dichotomized, view of female-maleness that dates back to Vedic writings, the profound respect for learning symbolized in the figure of the goddess Saraswati, and the postulate of a component of strength and action (Shakti) in female nature.

One consequence of Canada's selective immigration policy has been that South Asian women who have come to Canada have brought with them a rich philosophic and religious heritage deriving from their collectivist culture: Many are well versed in both Eastern and Western cultures, and they generally have a good command of the English language. Originating in a culture that abounds with beliefs, myths, symbols, and devotional ritual, the concept of "Shakti Power" should provide these women with the cognitive and psychological resources to meet the challenges of the host country. Indeed, the multicultural climate of Canada should foster their cultural self-determination and unique culture-based creativity. The women's potential contribution to their adopted individualist home country holds exciting promise.

10

SUBJECTIVE CULTURE
IN HEALTH INTERVENTIONS

Gerardo Marín
University of San Francisco

A substantial number of recent publications in the area of mental and physical health promotion in the United States have argued for the need to develop prevention efforts that appropriately reflect the cultural characteristics of the targeted ethnic or cultural group (e.g., Cross, Bazron, Dennis, & Isaacs, 1989; Davis & Voegtle, 1994; Marín, 1993; Marín et al., 1995; Marín, Amaro, Eisenberg, & Opava-Stitzer, 1993; Orlandi, 1992; Roberts, 1990). This emphasis on identifying and applying the basic characteristics of a culture in health-promotion activities is probably due in part to the importance assigned to social marketing principles in public health and community change programs (e.g., Andreasen, 1995). The increased awareness of the needs and of the numerical importance of ethnic minority groups in the United States also may have contributed to the attention being given to a group's basic cultural characteristics in the development of health-promotion materials and interventions. During the 1990 census, the major ethnic groups in the United States (African Americans, American Indians, Asian Americans, and Hispanics) accounted for well over 24% of the total population of the country. That proportion is expected to increase at a fast pace over the next few years so that by the year 2050, the Bureau of the Census estimates that those four ethnic groups will account for the majority of the population of the country. Those figures obviously require that special

AUTHOR'S NOTE: Portions of this chapter were presented at the 26th Interamerican Congress of Psychology, São Paulo, Brazil, July 1997.

attention be given to the needs of ethnic groups in the United States by developing interventions that properly recognize their cultural characteristics.

This chapter briefly summarizes the role of a subjective culture analysis in the development of culturally appropriate interventions, with particular attention being given to the promotion of health, although the principles apply equally well to fields such as community change, education, and marketing. The relevance of such an analysis within the framework of cultural appropriateness is examined first, followed by examples derived from major prevention efforts carried out among Hispanics in the United States in the areas of cigarette smoking and alcoholic beverage consumption.

DEFINING CULTURALLY
APPROPRIATE INTERVENTIONS

As mentioned above, various recent publications have argued for the need to develop health-promotion interventions that take into consideration the basic characteristics of the individuals being targeted (e.g., Catalano et al., 1993; Cross et al., 1989; Fisher & Fisher, 1992; Marín, 1993; Marín et al., 1995; Marín, Amaro, et al., 1993; Muninjaya & Widarsa, 1993-1994; Orlandi, 1992; Weissberg & Elias, 1993; Winkleby, Flora, & Kraemer, 1994). These arguments often have been based on the need to take into consideration the cultural characteristics of the various ethnic groups that are part of multicultural societies such as the United States.

As could be expected from authors writing about an evolving concept, different labels have been used. Some have argued for *culturally sensitive* interventions (e.g., Bayer, 1994) or *culturally tailored* programs (Ramirez, MacKellar, & Gallion, 1988), whereas others have suggested the need for *culturally competent* interventions (e.g., Cross et al., 1989; Orlandi, 1992; Roberts, 1990) or *culturally informed* etiological and preventive models (Weiss & Kleinman, 1988). In this chapter, the term *culturally appropriate* is preferred over its homologous terms because it can be perceived as being more comprehensive and more closely related to the development of community and behavior-change interventions. For example, *culturally appropriate* can be described as involving more than being sensitive to cultural differences and nuances, as could be implied in the use of the label *culturally sensitive*. Furthermore, the term *culturally competent* is reserved for individuals or interveners who are culturally sensitive and culturally informed and who may be in charge of developing or implementing culturally appropriate interventions. Indeed, as suggested by various authors (e.g., Cross et al., 1989; Davis & Voegtle, 1994; Orlandi, 1992; Roberts, 1990), culturally competent individuals should be expected to have a number of special abilities that are different from the properties expected of the interventions they have developed or are implementing, such as awareness and feelings of comfortableness with cultural differences, consciousness of the parameters of intercultural dynamics, and having the necessary skills to promote personal adaptation to cultural diversity.

Although a number of authors have acknowledged the need for culturally appropriate interventions (including primary through tertiary prevention efforts), little has been written to describe systematically what is implied in developing such interventions (e.g.,

Marín, 1993; Nobles & Goddard, 1993). In general, the need for developing culturally appropriate interventions has been based on three basic premises. First is the acknowledgment on the part of researchers and interveners of the fact that culture does indeed influence behavior and that there are important examples of cultural diversity around the world and within nations. This is, of course, an assumption too familiar to cross-cultural psychologists and to the readers of this book. Nevertheless, this realization seems to have escaped numerous researchers in other fields.

A second important premise in the definition of culturally appropriate interventions is the assumption derived in part from social marketing (Andreasen, 1995; Rogers, 1983) that suggests that whenever interventions are specifically designed for a given group (culturally appropriate in the case of ethnic groups), they will be not only more easily accepted by members of the group but also more effective (Marín, 1993; Rogers, 1983; Uba, 1992; Varela, 1971; Vega, 1992; Winett, 1995). Evidence has begun to accumulate showing that, indeed, culturally appropriate interventions are producing significant changes in behavior among the individuals being targeted (e.g., Marín & Pérez-Stable, 1995; Pérez-Stable, VanOss Marín, & Marín, 1993; VanOss Marín, Marín, Pérez-Stable, & Hauck, 1994).

The third premise is the belief that the development of culturally appropriate interventions must go beyond the adaptation and/or translation of interventions previously developed for members of other ethnic groups (Bayer, 1994; Marín, 1993). This premise does not imply that "mainstream" interventions will not be effective with members of defined cultural groups. Studies have shown, for example, that well-developed "mainstream" prevention interventions are also effective with members of specific ethnic groups (e.g., Sussman et al., 1993) and that certain adapted or modified "mainstream" interventions also can produce some of the desired effects (e.g., Bohon, Santos, Sanchez-Sosa, & Singer, 1994; Botvin, Schinke, Epstein, & Diaz, 1994; Botvin, Schinke, Epstein, Diaz, & Botvin, 1995). Rather, this assumption argues that the level of acceptability and effectiveness of a prevention intervention may be higher when the intervention is designed to meet the characteristics and guidelines of a culturally appropriate intervention that are mentioned below. As a matter of fact, certain authors (e.g., Reid, Killoran, McNeill, & Chambers, 1992) have argued that acceptability of an intervention should be one of the central criteria when choosing health-promotion interventions.

One recent effort at defining the components of culturally appropriate interventions (Marín, 1993) has been heavily influenced by the work of Harry Triandis and indeed incorporates a limited analysis of the subjective culture of a group as part of the process. This approach to developing culturally appropriate interventions suggests incorporating three basic components: (a) the basic cultural values or cultural dimensions of the targeted group, (b) certain behavior-specific aspects of the subjective culture of the group (e.g., attitudes, expectancies, situational antecedents, and perceived norms), and (c) group-specific preferences for intervention modalities (e.g., preferred sources and/or channels of information, valued behavioral activities, etc.). As mentioned above, one basic assumption of this model for culturally appropriate interventions is the belief that there are important differences across cultures and ethnic groups to warrant the development of group-specific interventions.

BASIC COMPONENTS OF A
CULTURALLY APPROPRIATE INTERVENTION

The paragraphs that follow describe what is meant by each of the components of a culturally appropriate intervention (Marín, 1993) and provide examples derived from our work with Hispanics to illustrate not only cultural differences but also how each component helps to shape a culturally appropriate intervention in terms of its content and strategies.

Group-Specific Cultural Dimensions or Syndromes

The model for developing culturally appropriate interventions proposed by Marín (1993) suggests that the intervention needs to be informed by the basic cultural dimensions or cultural syndromes that characterize individuals of the targeted group. In the case of Hispanics and Latin Americans, there is substantial research providing support for the existence of culture-specific cultural dimensions and scripts. For example, work by Triandis and colleagues (Marín & Triandis, 1985; Triandis, 1990; Triandis, Marín, Lisansky, & Betancourt, 1984) has shown the significance of a collectivist orientation among Hispanics that supports the influence of members of the collective in shaping an individual's behavior as well as the importance of the role of family members as behavioral and attitudinal referents and providers of emotional, economic, and other types of support (Sabogal, Marín, Otero-Sabogal, VanOss Marín, & Pérez-Stable, 1987). Indeed, cultural dimensions, when supported by empirical evidence, can serve an important role in the development of culturally appropriate interventions by directing interveners in choosing the overall orientation of the intervention, identifying the role of particular normative members of the community, describing the way in which attitudes and behaviors are changed, and pointing out those beliefs that are central to a group's worldview.

Earlier research in the social sciences had shown the existence of various cultural dimensions among Hispanics, including an orientation toward subjugation to nature, with the inherent sense of powerlessness of human beings toward the forces of nature and toward God's will (Heller, 1966; Kluckhohn & Strodtbeck, 1961). Nevertheless, some of these early cultural dimensions have received little empirical support probably because they were not well-defined or because they may represent the experiences of rural Hispanics, who no longer represent the majority of Hispanics in the United States. For example, the preference for a subjugation-to-nature perspective has been supported by empirical studies with relatively small samples (Sjostrom, 1988; Szapocznik, Kurtines, & Hanna, 1979; Szapocznik, Scopetta, Aranalde, & Kurtines, 1978), whereas other studies have found the opposite (Grebler, Moore, & Guzman, 1970).

Other cultural dimensions and associated scripts or behavioral patterns that are commonly assigned to Hispanics seem to have found stronger support in the literature. For example, the cultural syndrome of collectivism has, thanks to the pioneering work of Harry Triandis (1990, 1995b, 1996; Kim, Triandis, Kagitcibasi, Choi, & Yoon, 1994), surfaced as a central cultural dimension of Hispanics. Applications of collectivism in the development of culturally appropriate interventions have been based on shaping an intervention that recognizes, supports, enriches, and makes use of important characteristics of collectivist individuals such as the greater valuing of the views and needs of the members of the in-group, the willingness to share resources without concern for individual utilitarian considerations, the acceptance of the group's norms, and personal values such as intrdependence, cooperation, and sociability (Hofstede, 1980; Hui & Triandis, 1986; Triandis, 1990, 1994a, 1996).

The early work of anthropologists suggested a preference for a being orientation among Hispanics (Heller, 1966; Kluckhohn & Strodtbeck, 1961) that has received some empirical support and has been of importance in the development of culturally appropriate interventions. This being orientation is primarily based on the importance assigned to the individual and to personal experiences of reality and the generalized concern for human values and the spirit (Bañuelas, 1995; Fitzpatrick, 1971; Goizueta, 1995; Isasi-Díaz & Tarango, 1992; Magaffey & Barnett, 1962). This orientation may have been influenced by the Spanish traditions of courteous and congenial demeanor (De Miguel, 1990; Gillin, 1965; Gilmore, 1987; Hooper, 1986; Wagley, 1968; Wolf, 1956) or by the French sense of *politesse,* or civilized courteous politeness (Montandon, 1995; Picard, 1995). This dimension is seen by various researchers as a possible source of such social scripts as *Simpatía* (Triandis, Marín, Lisansky, & Betancourt, 1984), *Personalismo,* and *Respeto* that have been central to the design of culturally appropriate interventions targeting Hispanics.

Together with some cultural dimensions, a number of cultural scripts also have been identified as central to Hispanic culture and of importance in the design of culturally appropriate interventions. For example, familialism (also labeled familism by some authors) has been suggested as central to understanding Hispanic culture because it places the family as the main institution in the social world of Hispanics with obligations including solidarity, reciprocity, commitment, nurturance, and loyalty (Kagan, 1977; Triandis, Marín, Hui, Lisansky, & Ottati, 1984). The familialism script also makes it possible for individuals to benefit from their participation in the familial relationship, including receiving emotional and financial support (Keefe & Padilla, 1987; Mannino & Shore, 1976; Murillo, 1976) and protection from physical and emotional stressors (De la Rosa, 1988; Grebler et al., 1970; Markides, Costley, & Rodriguez, 1981; Markides & Krause, 1985).

Other important Hispanic cultural scripts that have received empirical support and that can be of importance in the design of culturally appropriate interventions include *Simpatía,* with its expectation of harmony, loyalty, dignity, friendliness, politeness, affection, respect, and positivity in interpersonal relations (Triandis, Marín, Lisansky, & Betancourt, 1984), and *Personalismo,* with its emphasis on individualized and deferential personal interactions (Fitzpatrick, 1971; Padilla, 1964; Wagenheim, 1972).

The model for developing culturally appropriate interventions proposed by Marín (1993) requires not only that interveners and intervention designers need to be aware of those cultural dimensions that show promise in characterizing a cultural group—Hispanics in this case—but also that the interventions incorporate components that are in agreement with the dimensions and scripts. For example, and as mentioned below, the cultural dimension of collectivism was useful in shaping a self-help smoking-cessation campaign directed at Hispanics (Marín & Pérez-Stable, 1995; Pérez-Stable et al., 1993). In this intervention, the opinions of community members were used to support each of the various behavior changes promoted by the program, through the use of pictorial vignettes and sidebars with printed testimonials included in a self-help manual as well as through radio and television programming. Likewise, our research has shown that familialism and the associated heightened concern and sense of responsibility for the welfare of family members have been of particular importance among Hispanics in curtailing cigarette smoking and the consumption of alcoholic beverages (e.g., Marín, in press-b; Marín, VanOss Marín, Otero-Sabogal, Sabogal, & Pérez-Stable, 1989; VanOss Marín, Marín, Pérez-Stable, Otero-Sabogal, & Sabogal, 1990; VanOss Marín, Pérez-Stable, Marín, Sabogal, & Otero-Sabogal, 1990).

An Analysis of a Group's Subjective Culture

A second characteristic of a culturally appropriate intervention according to the model developed by Marín (1993) is the inclusion of the results of an analysis of the subjective culture of a specific group regarding the targeted behavior. This aspect of developing a culturally appropriate intervention involves identifying all or most of the components of a group's subjective culture (e.g., values, norms, attitudes, expectancies) to properly shape the actual content of the intervention materials. In this sense, if research shows that members of a given ethnic group (e.g., Hispanics in the United States) have attitudes toward a targeted behavior (e.g., cigarette smoking) that are different from those held by members of another group (e.g., non-Hispanic whites), then the intervention needs to be shaped so that the attitudes of the targeted group are reflected in the contents of the intervention materials. This is a situation that is particularly important in multi-cultural societies in which interventions may be shaped by members of one ethnic group (usually those in the numerical majority) and therefore reflect the attitudes of a group that may bear little resemblance to those of the targeted group.

The need for this component of a culturally appropriate intervention is based on the fact that research has shown that members of ethnic and cultural groups share some group-specific attitudes, norms, expectancies, and values related to certain behaviors, which in turn are different from those held by other cultural groups or by members of the numerical majority in multicultural societies. For example, our research (as detailed below) has identified a number of group-specific components of the subjective culture of Hispanics in the United States regarding tobacco smoking (Marín et al., 1989; Marín, VanOss Marín, Pérez-Stable, Sabogal, & Otero-Sabogal, 1990b; VanOss Marín, Marín, et al., 1990) and the drinking of alcoholic beverages (Marín, in press-b; Marín, Posner, & Kinyon, 1993), which are significantly different from those held by non-Hispanic whites also residing in the United States. These differences in attitudes, expectancies, norms, and values imply that a culturally appropriate intervention for Hispanics that incorporates the group-specific components of a subjective culture will necessarily be better received and more effective than an intervention that has been developed by non-Hispanic whites reflecting non-Hispanic white attitudes, norms, values, and expectancies.

Indeed, research outside the cross-cultural environment has shown that, when the content of a message is shaped to match the values and needs of the audience, its effectiveness is enhanced (Clary, Snyder, Ridge, Miene, & Haugen, 1994). In addition, researchers (e.g., Catalano et al., 1993) have argued for the need to tailor prevention messages to address group-specific risk behaviors. For example, Catalano et al. (1993) suggest the need to develop drug-abuse-prevention programs for African American youth that take into consideration such risk factors as aggressiveness (which is a prominent risk factor primarily among African Americans) as well as those risk factors that seem to be common to African American and non-Hispanic white youth (e.g., access to marijuana, presence of friends who drink, and lack of out-of-school involvement opportunities).

As mentioned above, evidence has begun to accumulate that supports the notion that there are group-specific attitudes, norms, values, and expectancies for a number of behaviors. Our recent research has shown that Hispanics in the United States have a number of expectancies toward various behaviors that differentiate them from those held by non-Hispanic whites. For example, one of our studies on the expectancies held by Hispanics regarding the consumption of alcoholic beverages (Marín, Posner, & Kinyon, 1993) showed that Hispanics were more likely to agree with most of the possible expectancies for the consumption of alcoholic beverages (e.g., laughing more, becoming more talkative and more aggressive, being careless, feeling happier, becoming sleepy, and feeling romantic) than were non-Hispanic whites. A more recent study (Marín, in press-b) with large random samples of Mexican Americans in California and Texas again showed that Mexican Americans hold different cognitions than those held by non-Hispanic whites. In this last study, Mexican Americans were more likely to hold a number of negative expectations such as drinking producing fights, violence and aggressiveness, losing self-control, showing a bad example to children, having problems at work and at home, and becoming depressed and careless. In addition, Mexican Americans felt that drinking would make a person more independent and more romantic.

Some of our earlier research has shown that Hispanics also share expectancies regarding cigarette smoking that are quite different from those held by non-Hispanic whites. For example, a series of studies showed that Hispanic smokers are more concerned than non-Hispanic white smokers that, by smoking, they provide a bad example to their children and that they are threatening the good health of children by exposing them to environmental tobacco smoke (Marín et al., 1989; Marín et al., 1990b; VanOss Marín, Marín, et al., 1990). Our research also showed that there were a number of consequent expectancies that more readily discriminated Hispanic from non-Hispanic white smokers. For example, an analysis of expectations about the consequences of cigarette smoking showed the significant concern on the part of Hispanic smokers for damaging the health of children by exposing them to environmental cigarette smoke, whereas non-Hispanic whites were more concerned about the lack of personal control implied in cigarette smoking (Marín et al., 1990b). Hispanic smokers were more readily willing to consider quitting to provide a good example to their children, to improve relationships with their relatives, to breathe more easily, and to have a better taste in their mouths. On the other hand, non-Hispanic white smokers felt that an important consequent expectancy of quitting smoking was the ability to accomplish something difficult (Marín et al., 1990b).

As could be expected, there are expectancies held by Hispanics for behaviors such as the drinking of alcoholic beverages or cigarette smoking that are similar to those held by non-Hispanic whites. Likewise, certain demographic variables (e.g., gender, acculturation) and the actual experience with the behavior (e.g., frequency, intensity) also affect the type of expectancies held by Hispanics and non-Hispanic whites (Cervantes, Gilbert, Snyder, & Padilla, 1990-1991; Marín, in press-b; Marín, Posner, & Kinyon, 1993; Marín et al., 1989; Marín et al., 1990b). For example, the Marín, Posner, and Kinyon (1993) study found differences due to drinking status (with abstainers being more likely to expect impairment), and the same was true of the study with Mexican Americans (Marín, in press-b). An analysis of antecedent expectations to cigarette smoking showed that Hispanics considered their cigarette smoking as less frequently motivated by events related to relaxation at home or while enjoying a meal than did non-Hispanic whites, whereas both groups considered emotional and social events as important antecedents to smoking (Marín et al., 1990b). Nevertheless, research seems to be fairly consistent in supporting the notion of the existence of group-specific attitudes, norms, expectancies, and values. These differences as well as the similarities across ethnic and cultural groups need to be incorporated into the design of culturally appropriate interventions.

As an example of this integration of subjective culture components with the contents of an intervention, consider the previously mentioned result of our studies in which Hispanic smokers were found to consider the protection of a child's health as a good reason for quitting smoking (e.g., VanOss Marín, Marín, et al., 1990). Likewise, our subjective culture studies showed that preventing the exhibition of a bad example to children was also an important motivator to quit. Our culturally appropriate community intervention directed at Hispanic smokers (Marín & Pérez-Stable, 1995; Pérez-Stable et al., 1993) made use of those group-specific attitudes (which could also be perceived as reflecting the cultural script of familialism) in a number of ways. Smokers were frequently told in our self-help manual as well as in other media that by quitting smoking they would be protecting the health of their children and not providing a bad example for minors. For example, the first page in the self-help manual (Institutos Nacionales de la Salud, 1993) dealt with answers to the question "Why should I quit smoking?" Four areas (identified as part of the subjective culture study) were covered: (a) to protect the health and welfare of my family; (b) to improve my health; (c) to avoid serious health problems in the future; and (d) to improve my physical appearance. Among the specific reasons mentioned under the first area (protecting the health and welfare of the family), smokers were told that by quitting smoking they would provide a good example to children, prevent illnesses such as emphysema and colds in their children, improve their relationships with relatives, save money, and live many more years to enjoy their children and grandchildren. These expectancies were precisely the ones that had been found to be important to Hispanic smokers during a subjective culture study, and many of them were found to be more important to Hispanic than to non-Hispanic white smokers (Marín et al., 1989, 1990b; VanOss Marín, Marín, et al., 1990).

The same themes related to familialism and the concern for children were carried out in pictures, posters, billboards, and other media that were part of our culturally appropriate smoking-cessation intervention (Marín & Pérez-Stable, 1995; Pérez-Stable et al., 1993). For example, a poster showed a young child facing a large floor mirror while dressed in his father's clothes and holding a cigarette in his hand. Billboards often proclaimed *"Deje de fumar por usted y por su familia"* (Quit smoking for you and for your family). The state of California, in its smoking-cessation campaign targeting Hispanics, also made use of these subjective culture findings by producing billboards depicting a burning cigarette on an ashtray placed in front of the portrait of a young girl with the caption *"Si tu fumas, ella fuma"* (If you smoke, she smokes).

What these examples show is that the results of the subjective culture study of a specific cultural group regarding a behavior can be effectively used to develop the messages that make up the intervention. In many cases, the basic motivation or orienting principles of the intervention will differ significantly from those developed for other groups given the differences in attitudes, expectancies, values, and norms identified in the subjective culture study. As mentioned above, our smoking-cessation intervention with Hispanics had as a primary motivator the protection of children (a value concordant with collectivism and with familialism). This is a principle fairly different from smoking-cessation programs developed by and oriented toward non-Hispanic whites in which gaining personal control over one's life (an individualist concern) seems to be a central motivation for quitting smoking.

Group-Specific Preferences for Intervention Modalities

The third component of the model of a culturally appropriate intervention as suggested by Marín (1993) is the identification and use of group-specific preferences for intervention modalities. This suggestion is based on the assumption that cultures may have specific preferences (based on perceived usefulness, credibility, trustworthiness, motivating power, etc.) for certain behavior-change modalities (e.g., individualized counseling vs. group-based approaches and information disseminated through electronic media vs. printed media). Likewise, within a given choice of behavior-change modality, the assumption can be made that cultures differ in their evaluation (again based on characteristics such as perceived credibility, trustworthiness, and motivating power) of various sources of information (e.g., physicians, priests, peers, teachers, actors, and entertainers) as well as of various channels for the dissemination of information (e.g., television, radio, books, newspapers, and magazines).

The model for developing a culturally appropriate intervention that we have suggested (Marín, 1993) proposes that an evaluation needs to be made of these cultural preferences and that only those with marked positive characteristics should be used. Indeed, communication theoreticians have often argued for the use of appropriate sources and channels of information in developing effective messages and interventions (Bettinghaus, 1986), and evidence exists that shows culture- or group-specific differences in the evaluations of various intervention strategies (Marín, 1996; Marín & VanOss Marín, 1990) and in the patterns of use of various information dissemination channels (Alcalay et al., 1987-1988; Marín, in press-a; Marín & Gamba, in press).

Currently, there is evidence showing that members of certain cultural or ethnic groups have little interest or show high dropout rates or low participation rates in some intervention strategies that may not fit their needs or that may conflict with cherished cultural beliefs. This has been shown for self-help groups in which participation is low and dropout rates are fairly high (Ahluwalia & McNagny, 1993; Pérez-Stable et al., 1993). An increasing body of knowledge also shows culture-specific patterns of use of certain media. For example, Hispanics prefer certain approaches or types of media in proportions that are different from those of non-Hispanic whites or of other ethnic groups in the United States. Some of our research (Alcalay et al., 1987-1988) showed that Hispanics in San Francisco spend approximately the same amount of time per day watching television (approximately 3 hours) as they spend listening to the radio, although a greater propor-tion watch Spanish-language television (72%) than listen to Spanish-language radio (47%). This same survey showed that relatively few respondents (60%) read newspapers on a weekly basis. National data indeed show a strong preference by Hispanics of electronic media over printed media. For example, a 1992 survey of Hispanic households (cited in Reddy, 1995) showed that a larger proportion mentioned exposure to television (95%) and to radio (84%) than to newspapers (66%) and magazines (40%). Though these figures may reflect actual availability of certain media in a given market, they need to be considered in deciding the specific channel to be used in developing an intervention. In the case of Hispanics, the above-mentioned data would suggest that special attention needs to be given to the use of electronic media (radio and television).

A few recent studies have analyzed the evaluation made by Hispanics of various channels of information (Marín, 1996; Marín & VanOss Marín, 1990). In our earlier study, we found that Hispanics rated an AIDS hotline as the most credible source of information about AIDS or HIV infection, followed by printed channels (e.g., books, pamphlets, and newspaper articles) and television and radio commercials (Marín & VanOss Marín, 1990). More recent studies analyzed various channels of information for tobacco and alcohol information in terms of their credibility and motivating power among large random samples of Hispanics and non-Hispanic whites in California and Texas. In those studies (Marín, 1996), we found that printed channels (books and newspaper and magazine articles) and television news programs were evaluated as the most credible and motivat-ing by Hispanics and non-Hispanic whites alike. Television and radio commercials were generally next in credibility, followed by display media such as posters, billboards, and bus signs. The least-credible channels were serialized soaps on radio or television. In general, Hispanics tended to assign greater credibility to the various channels than did non-Hispanic whites. The more-acculturated Hispanics were also found to rate the various channels in a way more similar to that of non-Hispanic whites than to that of the less-acculturated Hispanics.

The data on channel characteristics tend to suggest that attention should be given to electronic media in developing community interventions, given the high esteem in which they are held by Hispanics and non-Hispanic whites alike. This is therefore an area in which cultural differences are of less importance than in other areas of the model for culturally appropriate interventions developed by Marín (1993). Nevertheless, the data are also useful in suggesting that certain channels that have been considered to be "culturally relevant" for Hispanics (such as serialized soaps—*telenovelas* and *fotonovelas*) because of their saliency in Latin America may owe their popularity to their entertainment value, but they are perceived as having low (although not insignificant) value as sources of information about health.

Various health-promotion programs and interventions have emphasized the involvement of individuals perceived as highly credible and expert. For example, health care providers, and particularly physicians, have been proposed as effective sources of information because of their credibility, trustworthiness, and perceived expertise (Reid et al., 1992); other programs have suggested the use of priests and pastors because of their central role in shaping norms among certain ethnic and cultural groups (Stillman, Bone, Rand, Levine, & Becker, 1993). This is an area in which empirical information needs to be obtained to use those sources of information who are perceived by members of the targeted group as experts, highly credible, trustworthy, and motivating. Data from our studies on alcohol and tobacco (Marín, 1996) information dissemination are instructive here.

Our surveys (Marín, 1996) with large random samples of Hispanics and non-Hispanic whites in California and Texas showed important differences in the ways in which various sources of information are perceived across cultural groups. In general, Hispanics perceived the following sources as most credible for transmitting tobacco- or alcohol-related information: physicians, cancer patients or former alcoholics, peers, friends, and priests. Non-Hispanic whites reported similar sources as the most credible, except that teachers replaced priests as one of the five most credible sources. The data showed that Hispanics tended to rate most sources in a more positive fashion than did non-Hispanic whites in terms of credibility, expertise, and trustworthiness. Likewise, these studies showed important differences among Hispanics as a result of their level of acculturation. The most highly acculturated respondents tended to rate the various sources of information in a fashion more similar to that of non-Hispanic whites than to that of the less-acculturated Hispanics.

The data on the evaluation of sources of information provide support for certain levels of generalizability across the two ethnic groups included in our studies while at the same time point to the particularly high possible impact of priests as disseminators of health information among Hispanics. What these data also show is that individuals evaluated sources and channels of information differentially and that a properly targeted culturally appropriate intervention needs to identify and use those sources and channels of information that are rated most highly by members of the group or groups in question. Interventions can be expected to be better received and more effective when they make use of highly credible and trusted sources and channels of information. Indeed, that has been our experience with the smoking-cessation community intervention that targeted Hispanics (Marín & Pérez-Stable, 1995; Pérez-Stable et al., 1993). Physicians and individuals who could be construed to be members of the community were used in the self-help manual and in television and radio commercials as sources of information on reasons for quitting smoking; they shared their experiences of successfully quitting smoking as well.

CONCLUDING REMARKS

The model for a culturally appropriate intervention proposed by Marín (1993) was derived from our experiences developing and evaluating a smoking-cessation community program for Hispanics in San Francisco, California, for approximately 6 years. The intervention is described in a number of publications (Marín & Pérez-Stable, 1995; Marín, VanOss Marín, Pérez-Stable, Sabogal, & Otero-Sabogal, 1990a; Pérez-Stable et al., 1993; VanOss Marín et al., 1994) and included wide distribution of the self-help manual mentioned above (more than 70,000 copies were distributed); the production of television and radio commercials and talk shows; the provision of individualized counseling over the telephone on approaches to quitting cigarette smoking; the implementation of a communitywide raffle for those quitting smoking within a given period of time; and the printing and distribution of informational fliers, posters, bumper stickers, and bus signs.

Evaluations of the smoking-cessation community intervention (Marín et al., 1990a; Marín & Pérez-Stable, 1995; Pérez-Stable et al., 1993; VanOss Marín et al., 1994) as well as of the self-help manual (Pérez-Stable, Sabogal, Marín, VanOss Marín, & Otero-Sabogal, 1991) showed that the shaping of an intervention using the group-specific characteristics (norms, expectancies, attitudes, etc.) identified through a subjective culture study produced important cognitive and behavioral changes. Our data showed that, after approximately 6 years of implementation of the culturally appropriate intervention, Hispanics in San Francisco (the targeted group) reported great acceptance of the intervention and its messages, including an increased awareness of the intervention's components, increased levels of information about the effects of cigarette smoking, a decrease in the number of cigarettes smoked, and an increase in the number of attempts at quitting.

As mentioned at the beginning, this chapter was designed to describe the role of culture and its analysis in the design of culturally appropriate interventions. As societies become more multicultural, the need for such interventions will necessarily increase as we try to develop optimally effective and efficient interventions to promote health as well as to introduce other much-needed changes in society. The psychological study of culture and its determinants will necessarily help interveners, social agents, and community activists to design better and more appropriate interventions. The techniques and approaches used by cross-cultural researchers, many of them pioneered by Harry Triandis, will significantly contribute not only to the development of better interventions but also to the enhancement of our understanding of human behavior and to the improvement of the human condition—certainly, a noteworthy contribution.

11

SUBJECTIVE CULTURE AND THE LAW

Roy S. Malpass
University of Texas at El Paso

A man from Juarez, Mexico, was arrested at the United States–Mexico border in El Paso and charged with smuggling drugs. He had attempted to carry a small package across the border that was discovered by customs officials to contain drugs. He claimed he did not know what was in the package and that he had carried it across the border at the request of his brother-in-law. He claimed he was to deliver it to an address he was given. He said he did not ask his brother-in-law what the package contained. He thought this was not an unusual request—and he also thought it would not have been correct to ask for an explanation.

Defense attorneys saw the possibility of a difference between the cultural conventions in force for the cultural context of the law and the cultural context of their client. In the "source culture" of U.S. law, persons are individuals and have individual responsibility for their actions. Citizens are supposed to be aware of the consequences of their actions and place obeying the law ahead of family and personal considerations. But what if these priorities are weakened by cultural conventions? What if the cultural standards of another nation (in this case, Mexico) routinely require that duty to family receive a very high priority? Could a cultural convention in conflict with the suppositions behind a nation's laws become the grounds for a defense in court?

There are two vantage points from which we can view and grapple with this little vignette. The first is to analyze the event from the point of view of an expert called to testify on behalf of the court (more likely on behalf of the defendant). The second is to analyze the event from the point of view of cross-cultural psychology, to examine whether this behavior is in fact normative, which seems to be the man's claim.

SOCIAL FRAMEWORK TESTIMONY

A recent development in psychology and law has been the infusion of behavioral science research findings into legal decision making. An early and prominent example is *Brown v. Board of Education of Topeka* (1954). But today there are many examples, from product liability suits to competence hearings to civil and criminal actions resulting from "recovered" memories (Loftus, 1993) to evidence concerning "rape trauma syndrome" (Vidmar & Schuller, 1989) and expert testimony regarding eyewitness memory, cross-race deficits in facial identification (Chance & Goldstein, 1996), and many other matters. Collectively, these areas of contribution to legal decision making have been called social framework testimony. The term *social framework evidence* was introduced by Monahan and Walker (1988) in part in response to the discrepancy between the understanding of the finders of fact—judges or juries—and scientific knowledge. Usually, the focus is on facts that are contested and about which the judge or jury will have to decide. Here are some cross-cultural examples.

Conceptions of Property

An interesting area of cultural difference concerns conceptions of property, especially intellectual property (e.g., music, folklore, and their commercial exploitation) among indigenous peoples.

The Ami Singers

An interesting example concerns the Ami rice farmers of Taiwan. In 1987, a group of Ami singers performed in France and were recorded—without their knowledge—by the French government for a limited-release academic CD. A group of German pop musicians named Enigma heard the recording and obtained rights from the French government to use part of one song in a pop tune, but no one asked the Ami. "Return to Innocence" sold more than 5 million copies and stayed on the pop charts for 6 months, but the Ami received no compensation ("All Things Considered," 1996).

Salamanca, New York

The people of Salamanca, New York, live with an interesting and perhaps unique system of land ownership. As a result of a long-standing treaty with the U.S. government and events that ignored the terms of the treaty, the Seneca Nation has come to assert exclusive ownership of the land on which Salamanca was built. "Own" in this case takes on the sense of contemporary U.S. concepts of property ownership, because it is "owned" under U.S. law. Usual concepts of property are strained in this unusual case. The land ownership and transfer system imported to North America by Europeans sits on top of an indigenous system of ownership and concept of property. Anyone, including the conventional real estate marketing system, can "buy and sell" land and buildings in Salamanca. But at base, the land is Seneca, and those "Europeans" who "own" it have it only on lease. To many Native Americans and other indigenous people around the world, it is preposterous to think that land can actually be "sold," as if you are buying it off the shelf. This difference led to many difficulties as the Europeans invaded North America. And a major part of the difference of conceptions of land ownership was this: For Europeans, the central core of the concept of "ownership" is the exclusion of others from the land. The concept of exclusion was not part of the indigenous property concepts in many North American groups.

Culture and Sexual Practices

I was recently told by a Romanian psychologist that in some areas of Romania it is culturally acceptable for adult family members to touch the genitals of young children as they speak with them. This behavior is inappropriate with children over 4 or 5 years old and inappropriate for adults outside the family. The sex of the child or the adult does not seem to matter. This behavior would certainly be considered inappropriate—perhaps even deviant—in the communities I know in the United States, and in some others, this would be considered criminal.

This issue came to the attention of the public in Dallas, Texas, in 1989 in the case of Sadri Krasniqi, an Albanian Muslim. Krasniqi attended his son's karate tournament with his 4-year-old daughter and was allegedly observed to fondle her under her dress. Physicians testified that they found no evidence of abuse. Experts testified that Krasniqi's actions were appropriate in Albanian culture. Even though he was found "not guilty," Child Protective Services took custody of his children and brought them to a family that forced them to eat pork, wear crosses, and convert to Christianity (Muslim Public Affairs Council, 1996; "Muslims in Dallas," 1995).

There is earlier case law on a related question from 1974. In the state of New York, a Nigerian man admitted using excessive corporal punishment with his 7-year-old son. He struck the child with his hands, a belt, and his feet. At a hearing over removal of the child from the home, he argued that he and his family were Nigerian, that the family was still in touch with Nigeria and its culture, and that these were appropriate techniques of discipline for his culture. The appellate court did not allow the family's cultural background to supersede existing enforcement practices with regard to child abuse and discipline.

This creates an interesting set of problems. In complex multicultural societies, can we hold that it is acceptable to stroke the genitals of small children in one's family if one is from Albania or Romania, whereas others would be carted off to jail? This is not merely an academic question. The *Country Walk* case in the United States—one of our celebrated satanic ritual child sexual abuse cases—began with a child's report that a young Honduran woman at the day care center "kisses all the babies' bodies" (Ceci & Bruck, 1995; Nathan & Snedeker, 1995). It is common, and culturally appropriate, for Honduran mothers to kiss the bodies—indeed the genitals—of small children until they are about 3 to 4 years old (Nathan & Snedeker, 1995). Disregarding the questions of whether this is sexual abuse and whether this harms the child or pleasures the mother, people are going to jail for what might seem like a clash of cultures.

South African Murder Trials:
SARHWU and the Queenstown Six

The South African courts employed the "doctrine of common purpose" to expand prosecution of persons associated with murders associated with crowd behavior. I'll describe two examples, drawn from Colman (1991a, 1991b).

The case of *Sibisi and Others* (1989) involved the murder of four black men who had refused to join others in a strike. The strike was a particularly bitter one by members of the South African Railway and Harbor Workers Unions (SARHWU) against the railway over the unjustified firing of one of their members. Large numbers of people gathered at the union headquarters in subsequent days, and finally the police shot dead six of the strikers. On the following payday, strikers found that they had also been fired. The five nonstrikers were kidnapped from their work sites by an angry group of fired strikers. Many people were involved. One of the five escaped, but the others were killed by a mob. Eight people were charged with the murder, although only three or four had participated in the actual killings. The others were convicted on grounds of the common purpose doctrine. Four were sentenced to death, although this sentence was later lifted on the basis of psychological evidence given in extenuation.

The case of *Gqeba and Others* (1990)—the Queenstown Six—followed a conflict between Xhosa-speaking African National Congress supporters who had sponsored a boycott of merchants in Queenstown and police units loyal to the Zulu Inkatha leader Chief Buthelezi. During the conflict, Inkatha police had killed 11 people among a large number who were gathered at a church to discuss the boycott. On the day following the funeral, a group of young activists sought to punish a young woman who was accused of being an informant and of sleeping with an Inkatha policeman. After a flogging, the mob grew to more than 200 people. The young woman was taken to a central area of the township, where a car tire was placed around her neck, doused with gasoline, and set alight. The mob sang and danced while she burned to death. Six members of the mob were convicted of the murder through the doctrine of common purpose. Apparently, none of them had taken part in the actual killing. Five of these men were sentenced to death, but due to technical issues, the trial was set aside. These same persons were later retried and sentenced to 60 months in prison, with 40 months suspended. The difference was the introduction of social psychological evidence in the second trial.

Psychological evidence—social framework evidence—was offered in the extenuation phase of these trials. It was based on an interrelated set of social psychological principles, including deindividuation and related processes (Diener, 1980), conformity and obedience (Asch, 1956; Milgram, 1974; Tanford & Penrod, 1984), and bystander apathy, among other social psychological concepts and findings. Colman (1991a, 1991b) argued that the conditions of crowding, and the continuous singing and dancing, contributed to deindividuation and enhanced obedience and conformity pressures. The court was warned to not underestimate the importance of external, situational pressures and overestimate the importance of internal motives—the fundamental attribution error (Ross, 1977).

Preferences for Conflict Resolution

In collectivist communities, the ongoing relationships among persons are important (Triandis & Gelfand, 1998). Even when there are disputes, it is important to maintain relationships. So we would expect that collectivists would be more reluctant to pursue conflict with members of their own group, compared with individualists. This strategy of conflict resolution is to avoid embarrassment and to promote group harmony and solidarity over time (Bond, Leung, & Wan, 1982). These basic predictions were confirmed for comparisons between the more collectivist Hong Kong and the more individualist United States. Kwok Leung, Michael Bond, and their colleagues in Hong Kong have been pursuing research in this area for more than 15 years, and they have published some of the first work in this area (Leung, 1987, 1988a, 1988b; Leung & Bond, 1984, 1989; Leung, Chiu, & Au, 1993; Leung & Iwawaki, 1988; Leung & Li, 1990; Leung & Lind, 1986; Leung & Park, 1986). Leung (1987) reviews the somewhat inconsistent literature on preference for procedural models for conflict resolution. He points out that what appears to be a general preference for adversarial (rather than inquisitorial) procedures may be restricted as appealing to Western societies but not to more traditional societies. The cultural dimension of individualism-collectivism is important in determining preferences for dispute resolution. The defense argument on behalf of the "Mexican mule" depends on the premise that, in a relatively collectivist society like Mexico, actions will be undertaken to maintain harmonious relationships in the family. But Leung's work raises even more fundamental questions about the "fit" between the U.S. legal system's mode of resolving disputes through adversarial procedures and the sense of justice indigenous to other cultures that live within the nation and are thus subject to its legal processes. It is not surprising, then, that members of many immigrating groups prefer to solve their problems within their ethnic communities according to traditional standards of justice.

LAW AND
CULTURALLY DIVERSE SOCIETIES

It is highly likely that, in modern nations, public understanding of law and its supporting rationales is unevenly and imperfectly distributed. The degree to which the scientific study of behavior is represented in law and the degree to which legal professionals and laypeople understand behavioral issues in law are also unevenly and imperfectly distributed. This is well documented in the field of eyewitness identification (Deffenbacher & Loftus, 1982; Kassin, Ellsworth, & Smith, 1989). As the scientific understanding of behavioral issues in law becomes more fully developed, more contributions to legal decision making will come from this domain of understanding and from expert witnesses who interpret scientific findings for the court. A widening range of behavioral phenomena is being explained to legal decision makers on the basis of scientific research. Some of these are based on matters of cultural phenomena and cultural difference. Others derive from differences between common understanding in an ethnic minority community and the formal understanding of the dominant culture, as reflected in law. These are similar—but in some ways quite distinct—phenomena.

Many nations in the world have legal systems that are developed out of historical cultural populations. Presently, these nations are inhabited by many other populations as well, and questions arise from many sources about the domains in which (and the extent to which) the rules and customs of a historical culture ought to govern the actions of culturally different populations making up larger nations. This is a worldwide phenomenon. China recognizes more than 70 minority cultural groups and modifies its school exams to take this into account for nearly 70 million minority test-takers every year. For some nations (e.g., Germany, the United States, the United Kingdom, and Canada), minority populations have been imported, and in others, the current inhabitants have taken over the land and the law and dominate the remnants of the indigenous populations (most of the Americas and much of Pacific Oceania). For still others, indigenous populations have established political—and thus legal—control (Africa, in general, and South Africa, in particular).

In any case, an important part of their task is to administer public life in the face of important customary differences on a wide range of issues. Because law is in many important ways based on the behavioral assumptions of the homogeneous historical population from which it emerged, some of these do not "fit" when applied to different cultures.

The examples given above involve providing a general context or framework for decision making by judges or juries—hence the term *social framework testimony.* Generally, it is only in clinical areas—forensic psychology—in which specific expert testimony is given concerning the facts of the particular case. For example, judgments about a defendant's competence to stand trial may be made by expert witnesses or judgments about dangerousness and other characteristics may be offered. Experts in eyewitness identification sometimes make case-specific judgments, although they rarely (if ever) examine the witnesses or defendants in cases at trial. However, experimental psychologists serving as expert witnesses have offered judgments about the amount of light present in a particular place at a particular time and its sufficiency for observing a person at a certain distance, and evaluations of the process and materials used for eyewitness identification in specific cases have been made. It is not a very large step, then, to consider the status of certain specific actions and the behavioral environment in which they occurred in the cultural context of particular persons.

Let us assume for the moment that U.S. courts (or U.S. juries) will be open to the idea that, for some categories of ethnic populations, local practices that conflict with codified law in the relevant jurisdiction may not lead to a criminal prosecution or a finding of criminal guilt. Moving past the specific mechanisms that might be put into place to achieve such a result, let's consider the information on which a claim to exception from existing law (or interpretation of law) might be based. The process in general seems very straightforward. Assuming a defense perspective, we begin with two requirements: (a) to show that there is a cultural difference in the acceptability of the acts in question between the culture of the law and the culture of the defendant and (b) to show that, in his or her own cultural milieu, the defendant's actions would be, first, acceptable and, second, not illegal.

It would be a stronger case to show that the actions involved are not just acceptable but are normative. The second of these is for lawyers to deal with. The first is for us. The immediate need would be to find procedures with which to determine what actions are thought of as being closely related to one culture and not to another.

Those who attempt to apply the knowledge base of their field often find that no data precisely fit the situation at hand. One must almost always interpret existing knowledge, make generalizations, express caveats, and so on. But in cases in which the specifics of an event can be scrutinized—such as a police identification process—very focused and specific information can be sought. So for the purposes of the cultural defense under discussion, the normative data of previous ethnographic investigations might not be sufficient. A careful and close study of the specific behavioral events and categories under discussion of the case at hand may well not have been the explicit object of scrutiny by psychologists and ethnographers in the scholarly literature. Almost inevitably, the more general knowledge about the cultural contexts of behavior obtained by these professionals will not have focused on the specific issues of a particular case in court. The task of gathering general scientific knowledge is quite different from that of addressing the specific questions surrounding a particular and concrete set of events.

The conceptual groundwork needed for this task is provided in Triandis's (1972) work on subjective culture. In general, work on subjective culture begins with large primitive categories such as *community, persons* or *roles, acts* or *behaviors,* and *situation* or *context.* In broad outline, the process begins with these primitive categories and fills them in with local (to the culture under investigation) concepts and lists of subtypes. So the roles to be studied might come from a study in which the investigator first identifies roles by querying informants about specific persons in the physical/social environment and their relations to others. Some of these are known in advance because of their universality: Kinship roles are relatively easy to identify, as are other caretaker roles, religious roles, healing roles, and so forth. It is not necessarily easy to know the exact nature of those roles with respect to the categories of behavior that are appropriately (and inappropriately) exchanged between two role incumbents. Take, for example, the role pairs of physician to patient and patient to physician in the United States. The physician appropriately offers advice, gives medicines, and asks very personal questions of the patient, but the patient does not do these things in return. The patient gives money and social greetings to the physician. Offering sexual relations is inappropriate in either direction of this relationship, and, most often, when examinations are sexual in nature, a third person (a health professional such as a nurse) is generally present. This differentiates the physician-patient interaction concerning sexual organs from other sexual interactions either physician or patient may have.

To identify the categories of behavior and the specific actions appropriately exchanged between role incumbents, one would implement a study in which these are elicited from informants given a pair of roles (e.g., father-son, merchant-customer).

Alternatively, behavioral categories and actions can be derived from any source and informants queried about their appropriateness in various role pairs.

The application before us is slightly different, however. Here we are interested not as much in general knowledge of a culture as in the appropriateness (indeed, normativeness) of specific actions between particular role incumbents in particular contexts. The roles, acts, and contexts would have to be specified carefully to fit the facts of the case at hand.

To understand such a cultural analysis, it would probably also be required that certain comparisons are made. One might be to show that a comparable person in the cultural context from which the law was derived would act as the law presupposes, whereas the defendant and his or her people would act as the defendant did. A second comparison might be to show that there is not a total disconnection between the two cultures and that, at some other level of importance in the same category of the act, the two cultures are similar in their judgments of appropriateness.

Here is a suggestion of how we might generally proceed, with notes about the application to the example with which we began: the case of the Mexican mule.

1. *Specify empirically and specifically the cultural community in which the focal person lives and with which he or she identifies.* The purpose of the investigations we propose are necessarily closely targeted to the conditions of the particular case in consideration. The samples on which further research will be carried out need to have a high degree of similarity to the defendant to be relevant to the case at hand. So it will have to be discovered what the political and social dimensions of the community are, the degree to which these are marginal versus mainstream representatives of the community, and how the target person or family is situated in the social nexus of the community.

2. *Specify empirically and specifically a cultural community that can serve as a standard for the source culture.* There is a question as to whether this cultural community ought to be standard in some sense of typicality or whether it should be the community in which the prosecution is brought. The former, for the United States, would be the social science equivalent of identifying the "all-American community," one that typifies the American values and behavioral norms implicit in the law of the nation. It is possible, of course, that no such community exists—but trying to find it would be an interesting enterprise. No doubt, our colleagues in anthropology, cultural geography, political science, and sociology could be of assistance. In any case, an appropriate comparison group must be identified, against which the data on norms and expectations from the defendant's community would be compared. To specify this community empirically would require developing a case for its typicality or representativeness.

For our Mexican mule, we would not want to take our comparison group from one of the many Mexican American communities in Texas because we might well find the same contrast with the law and custom of the source population that might be present across the border. The comparison community should reflect the culture of the law and its presuppositions.

3. *In both communities, identify empirically the particular social/cultural situation or context in which the events of interest occur.* Again, we have to draw on our theoretical knowledge to form some dimensions of behavioral contexts. Was the action under study public or private, within or outside of a family structure, done with or without the observational knowledge of persons besides the actor and whatever other persons were involved? Was there a status difference between the two parties, and, if so, what kind of status difference was this?

In the example case, the context was a request by a relative (sister's husband). So the immediate context was of relationships within the family.

4. *In both communities, identify the domain of behaviors or actions of interest.* Was this explicitly an exchange relationship, and, if so, what was the nature of the exchange? Was the act an obligation? Did it involve service? Did it involve harm or benefit to others? Was it collaborative?

In the example case, the act appears not to have involved an explicit exchange, was possibly an act of obligation, and did not do apparent harm to others. What is particularly interesting in this context, however, reminds me of the Sherlock Holmes story in which the significant event was that the dog did *not* bark. The actor—the defendant—claims that he did not ask what was in the package and did not ask why he was being asked to deliver it. In an important way, it is this lack of action that forms an important focus for investigation. Do Anglo individualists readily perform favors for brothers-in-law while asking no questions about the objects, persons, or actions involved? Is it normative for Mexican brothers-in-law to do so?

The questions that Triandis's subjective culture process would have us ask concern reports on the appropriateness of the request of one brother-in-law to another and the appropriateness of questioning the request. At least these two questions are important. Also important, perhaps, is the estimate of the expectation that a brother-in-law would ask one to do an illegal act or an act that would do harm to the person complying with the request. Empirically, the questions can be framed as a behavioral differential (Triandis, 1972).

5. *Identify and specify the persons or roles of interest—as actors or as recipients of actions.* Was this an act involving only one person? Was it an interaction between a person and an object(s)? Was the actor acting as an agent for another person? What was the relationship? Once the roles are established, they can be framed for empirical analysis as role differential items.

6. *Identify the relations among persons and actions that are of interest in the specified environments and frame questions designed to elicit these relations, to quantify them, and/or to confirm them.* Was the action a matter of family obligation, employment, exchange of service for money?

When quantitative comparisons are made of the answers to the resulting questions, from suitably sized samples of respondents, an investigator will be able to respond to the question of whether there is a cultural difference in the appropriateness of the actions in question between the culture of the law and the culture of the accused. What can be made of this information in the legal culture is a very interesting question.

We have just scratched the surface of techniques that can be used to identify cultural differences in the appropriateness of actions in contrasting cultural communities. To observers with varying personal, philosophical, and political views, those coming into a nation ought to be held to the standard of the law in some areas and not in others. An important question concerns the stance a nation takes on these issues and the breadth with which it is applied. Surely, immigrant groups that come to nations and settle as communities, rather than dispersed throughout the "native"[1] population, have regulated their own affairs, even in the face of great differences between their standards of governance and those of the host society.

NOTES

1. It is difficult for me to think of any citizen of North America of European origin as a native, but I suppose it is just a matter of terminology.

PART IV

GROUP AND INTERPERSONAL PROCESSES

This section contains chapters on group and interpersonal processes—what Triandis understood to be a central focus of social psychology. Georgas focuses on family as a neglected topic in the social psychology of culture. In particular, together with an informative survey of the multidisciplinary literature on family—including his own research on the Greek family—he highlights some cross-cultural and theoretical limitations and inadequacies of the nuclear family as a model of family process and makes a persuasive case for further explorations of family functioning as a major determinant of social psychological processes.

Leung and Chan's contribution examines the impact of culture on one of the integral and inevitable parts of social life: conflict. The authors argue that, at both the interpersonal and intergroup levels, culture is intertwined with the ways in which a conflict may arise and its resolution may be explored. In particular, the authors present a general framework in which to analyze intercultural conflict and examine a specific case of conflict in the culturally diverse organizational environment.

E. Kashima and Y. Kashima's chapter highlights one of the neglected aspects of interpersonal processes, that is, the use of language. They briefly review the literature on language and culture within the tradition of cross-cultural psychology and call for further research in the area. In particular, their focus is on the relationship between language use and individualism.

- According to Georgas, what is the relationship between cultural models of family structure and psychological functioning?
- In what ways, according to Leung and Chan, can a cultural analysis aid in explaining the emergence of interpersonal and intergroup conflict and its resolution?
- What is the role of language in assessing cultural patterns of behavior such as individualism and collectivism, according to Kashima and Kashima?

12

FAMILY IN CROSS-CULTURAL PSYCHOLOGY

James Georgas
University of Athens, Greece

Most psychologists would probably agree that, historically, psychology's primary concern has been the study of the individual, or more specifically, psychological processes such as cognition, personality, motivation, and so on, and how they interact with the environment. Three fields of psychology—social psychology, developmental psychology, and clinical psychology—have been interested in studying interaction processes between dyads or within small groups. However, psychology has had little interest, with a few exceptions, in studying how the family influences psychological functioning. The exceptions are few. Within clinical psychology, family therapy is employed as a psychotherapeutic technique. This has led to the formulation of theories related to the structure of the family, different types of pathological families, and their effects on the pathology of the client-member of the family (Touliatos, Perlmutter, & Straus, 1990). Learning theory has studied interactions among members of the family—for example, how the behavioral exchanges between aggressive children and their parents lead to mutual reinforcements of their behaviors (Patterson, McNeal, Hawkins, & Phelps, 1967)—without, however, an attempt to explain these phenomena in terms of a theory of family. Both Bandura (1977) and Rotter (1954) have studied the interaction between behavior and environmental factors looking at the role of the family, but again, without a specific theory of family interaction. Developmental psychology from the 1920s until the 1940s was interested in the study of interaction between family members through direct observation (Touliatos et al., 1990). However, only after the interest in the study of infant-mother interaction in the 1960s (Bell, 1968) did developmental psychology look more closely at the role of the family, again, without specific theories of family interaction. Levine and Moreland (1992) suggest that an explanation for social psychology's lack of interest in studying the family, although it has clearly been interested in small group dynamics, is perhaps the dominance of the laboratory experiment as its research paradigm.

This chapter argues that psychology should study how the structure and function of the family affects psychological variables. It further argues that (a) the study of the individual should employ an ecological approach in which psychological variables are studied as embedded within the context of the family structure, the immediate community, the social context, and the physical environment (Berry, 1976, 1979; Bronfenbrenner, 1979, 1986; Cowan, Field, Hansen, Skolnick, & Swanson, 1993; Georgas, 1988, 1989, 1991a, 1993; Kagitcibasi, 1990b, 1996; Triandis, 1980); and (b) the study of different family structures and different types of functioning within these structures can be accomplished with cross-cultural theory and methodology (Georgas & Berry, 1995; Kagitcibasi, 1996; Triandis, 1995b; Triandis & Vassiliou, 1972).

PERSPECTIVES IN THE STUDY OF THE FAMILY

The description of the structure and function of the family is approached here from different perspectives: sociology, social anthropology, clinical psychology and psychiatry, and cross-cultural psychology. A brief sketch of the signal characteristics of each approach follows.

Sociology of the Family

The first scientific analysis of the role of the family in society was conducted by sociologists. Christensen (1964) described three stages in the study of marriage and the family. In the first stage, prior to 1850, most ideas regarding the family were based on traditional beliefs, religious pronouncements, moralistic exhortations, poetic fantasies, and philosophical speculations.

The second stage, which began in the second half of the 19th century, can be described as a period that spawned three influential sociological theories of the family. One model was a form of Social Darwinism in which the structure of the family and its function was considered to be part of the process of biological adaptation of this social organism to the environment (Hofstadter, 1955). A second major theory of the family was influenced by Marxism. In contrast to the explanatory power of biological determinism in Social Darwinism, Marxist theory employed the concept of economic determinism to explain how economic resources determined social power, which in turn determined class struggle. The Marxist model explained authority and power among the father and mother and the children in the family. A historical analysis of economic development during the industrial revolution also explained the evolution of the nuclear family in urban centers (Engels, 1884/1948). The third model during this period was *functionalism*, and its proponent was Durkheim (1888, 1892/1921). Functionalism explained the existence and the changes in family structure and function in terms of the family's functional role in the preservation of society. Functionalism analyzed the role of family as part of a greater whole, in which other units combined to establish an equilibrium. Also, changes in one part of the system reverberated to other parts. Causation, therefore, could have multiple causes, in contrast with the monocausal biological or economic determinism of Social Darwinism and Marxist theory, respectively.

The third stage of family sociology began early in the 20th century, during the rise of socialism. During this stage, sociologists undertook an empirical orientation, with one goal being the direct study of the effects of deleterious economic and social changes on the family.

Burgess (1926) published a seminal paper in family sociology that introduced to the study of the family the concept of *symbolic interactionism*, that is, the relationship between individuals and society and their impact on socialization and personality organization. An approach toward the systematic observation of group interaction processes that led to the differentiation of *instrumental* and *expressive* roles was made by Bales and Slater (1955). Another approach studied *power* in family roles, defined as the "legitimate authority" of husbands and fathers to exercise control over wives and children (Blood & Wolfe, 1960; Safilios-Rothschild, 1970; Shehan & Lee, 1960). Herbst (1952, 1954) constructed formal theoretical models of family power based on Lewin's field theory.

Talcott Parsons and the Nuclear Family

Perhaps the most influential theoretician, who during the postwar years profoundly shaped the thinking about the structure of the family, particularly the nuclear family, is Talcott Parsons (1943, 1949, 1965). Parsons employs a structural-functional perspective in which society is viewed as an organism that strives to resist change and to maintain itself in a state of equilibrium (Broderick, 1993; Smith, 1995). The family has two types of functions: *instrumental*, which are related to survival, and *expressive*, related to the maintenance of morale and cooperation. According to Parsons, the adaptation of the family unit to the industrial revolution required a nuclear family structure, which could carry out societal functions and could satisfy the physical and psychological needs of family members. Parsons argued that the nuclear family is fragmented from its kinship network, which leads to psychological isolation. Its reduction in size results in loss of its productive, political, and religious functions. The nuclear family becomes primarily a unit of residence and consumption. Its financial and educative functions are dependent on the state, and its major remaining function is to provide for the socialization of the children and the psychological equilibrium of the parents. The nuclear family parents, who have chosen each other freely based on love—in contradistinction to the extended family system in which marriage choices are based on family interests and not romantic love—are isolated from their kin and share rational and pragmatic values. Social mobility, particularly in the highly mobile U.S. culture, was made possible by the breaking of family ties.

As will be discussed later, Parsons's theory of the structure and function of the family has become an ideology. One of the purposes of this chapter was to examine the evidence regarding the functional aspects of the nuclear family. It can be stated here that both historians of the family and anthropologists have diametrically opposed views from both Parsons's historical analysis and this description of the family, and, furthermore, the evidence from social support and other studies essentially destroys this "myth of the nuclear family . . . as structurally nuclear but functionally atomistic" (Uzoka, 1979, p. 1096).

Cultural Anthropology and the Family

Perhaps the most enduring and still accepted definition of the family is that of Murdock (1949):

> The family is a social group characterized by common residence, economic cooperation, and reproduction. It includes adults of both sexes, at least two of whom maintain a socially approved sexual relationship, and one or more children, own or adopted, of the sexually cohabiting adults. (p. 1)

The anthropological approach to the study of the family is too broad to be analyzed here. We can point to only a few approaches. The holocultural methodology of social anthropology has demonstrated the variety of family types and functions and the functional relationships in relation to cultural variables (Levinson & Malone, 1980). We can perhaps particularly point to the work of Whiting, Child, and their associates for their exemplary study of the relationship of culture, family types, and psychological variables (Minturn & Lambert, 1964; Whiting & Child, 1953; Whiting & Whiting, 1975).

Clinical Psychology and Psychiatry

Clinical psychology and psychiatry both employ family therapy as a psychotherapeutic technique. This has resulted in the construction of models of family functioning and techniques of psychotherapy directed toward the family (Ackerman, 1938; Mittelman, 1944). It must be emphasized that psychiatry and clinical psychology employ populations that present specific problems of adjustment or psychopathology. Thus, there is always an epistemological question of the generalization of findings based on families with psychological problems to theories of families in the general population. Bateson, Jackson, Haley, and Weakland's *double-bind* hypothesis (1956) was a quantum leap from the focus on unconscious processes that characterized psychoanalysis to interactions among family members and communication theory. The focus on miscommunications in the families of schizophrenics inevitably led to the study of the social context of the family (Touliatos et al., 1990).

Family therapy is based on models of the family, and *family systems theory* views the family as an organic system striving to maintain equilibrium during the process of confronting external pressures (Hill & Rodgers, 1964). This model, based on general systems theory (Smith, 1995), views the family as a system that strives to maintain equilibrium and to adapt to changes, both internal and environmental, through communication and information exchange. General systems theory requires relating the family to other systems, such as family networks, the neighborhood, school, the workplace, the community, and so forth. The human ecology theory of Bronfenbrenner (1979, 1986) is basically a family systems model.

Cross-Cultural Psychology

A perusal of the literature indicates that cross-cultural psychology has not been very concerned with the effects across cultures of family structure and function on psychological variables. Triandis was one of the first to analyze the Greek family (Triandis & Vassiliou, 1972) in a study that would be classified today as cultural psychology. However, looking through the subject indexes of the six volumes of Triandis's (1980) *Handbook of Cross-Cultural Psychology,* the subject *family* is found only in a few of these volumes, and the topic is only tangentially discussed. In two more recent publications by Triandis (1994a, 1995b), studies regarding the family are referred to but without a systematic analysis of how its structure or function affects psychological variables. In two recent excellent and comprehensive textbooks in cross-cultural psychology (Berry, Poortinga, Segall, & Dasen, 1992; Segall, Dasen, Berry, & Poortinga, 1990), only six pages are listed for *family* in the subject index in the former, and none are listed in the latter.

On the other hand, there have been some efforts in this direction, such as D. Sinha (Sinha, 1988; Sinha & Bharat, 1985) and J. B. P. Sinha and Verma (1987) in India. Individualism and collectivism have engendered interest in the role of the family as a context variable. This issue has also been discussed by Triandis (1994a, 1995b) and by Fijneman, Willemsen, and Poortinga (1996).

Kagitcibasi (1990b, 1994, 1996) has presented a model of family change that she describes as a *contextual-developmental-functional* approach with the goal of having cross-cultural relevance. Three contextual patterns of family—*interdependence, independence,* and *emotional interdependence*—are described as prototypes of family systems and function in different socioeconomic cultural context models. These patterns are differentiated according to two dimensions: emotional and material.

The pattern of *interdependence* is the classic model of the extended family found in rural and agrarian traditional societies, with close family relations and patrilineal structures. Although households may be nuclear, the members of the extended family cooperate in production (economic), consumption, and child care. Kagitcibasi characterizes the culture of the family at the interpersonal level as *dependent-interdependent* (with *overlapping personal boundaries),* the latter referring to a construal of the *interdependent self* of Markus and Kitayama (1991) and what Triandis (1989) has termed the *collective self.*

The pattern *independence* refers to the nuclear family, characteristic of Western, industrial cultures and urban or suburban middle-class society. The family culture is described as *separateness* of both the family from other families and its members from one another. Kagitcibasi equates separateness with individualism and describes this concept as similar to that of the *independent self* of Markus and Kitayama (1991). It is also similar to Triandis's (1989) concept of the *private self.* Kagitcibasi claims that, although the model of independence and the nuclear family is more an ideal or abstraction than reality, and perhaps not all families in the Western cultures fit this mold, this is the prototype and the norm of these societies.

The third pattern, *emotional interdependence,* is claimed to be found in the more developed areas of the Majority World with cultures of collectiveness in which social structural and economic changes are prevalent and cultural continuity is an important value. In this pattern, the individual manifests *interdependence* in the emotional realm at both family and individual levels but manifests *independence* at both levels in the material realm.

TYPES OF FAMILIES

I previously referred to the definition of the family by Murdock (1949). Family sociologists suggest that there are many definitions of *family* (Smith, 1995), which often reflect a particular theoretical perspective (Doherty, Boss, LaRossa, Schumm, & Steinmetz, 1993).

There are also different taxonomies of family types. Levinson and Malone (1980) employ five types. The *nuclear* family consists of husband/father, wife/mother, and their children. The *matrifocal* family consists of mother and her children. The *polygynous* family is composed of husband/father, two or more wives/mothers, and their children. The *polyandrous* family consists of one wife/mother, her children, and two or more husband/fathers. The *extended* family is composed of individuals recognized as both husband/father and son/brother or wife/mother and sister/daughter at the same time.

Stanton (1995) employs a taxonomy with the *nuclear* family, the *extended* family, *single* families, and *divorced* families. Stanton's definition of the *extended family* contains some important concepts relevant to its relationship to the nuclear family type:

> The extended family is a corporate economic and political unit, as well as a kinship-based group. The extended family is an ongoing body with a geographical base and it transcends the lifetime of its members. The composition of the extended family with its nuclear families and independent single adults changes constantly, but the extended family itself continues with new leaders and new members as individuals depart or as the generations pass away. (p. 100)

There are other taxonomies of family types that are not presented here (Laslett & Wall, 1972; Nimkoff & Middleton, 1960; Spiro, 1965) that make other finer differentiations, but the primary family types refer to the nuclear family, the various subtypes of the extended family, and the various types of one-person families.

Structure and Function

Two further concepts are important at this point, *structure* and *function. Structure* refers to the "number of members of the family and to the designation of familial positions such as parent, spouse, child, other kin," and so on, whereas *function* refers to manners "in which families satisfy member's physical and psychological needs and . . . meet survival and maintenance needs" (Smith, 1995, p. 9).

Determinants of Family Types

The issue of how family types are related to the type of society, simple or complex, or type of economic activity has been studied by a number of anthropologists and sociologists. Levinson and Malone (1980, p. 86) refer to "determinants of family types," emphasizing the social conditions, including economic activity, that may "determine" a family type and may influence changes in family type. Blumberg and Winch (1972), in what is named the *curvilinear hypothesis,* found that the small independent or nuclear family is typical in small hunting and gathering societies and in urban areas in industrial societies, and the extended family is found in settled, agricultural societies. Nimkoff and Middleton (1960) found evidence, in addition to evidence in agreement with the curvilinear hypothesis, that highly differentiated social stratification is found in extended families, as compared with less stratification in nuclear families.

THE NUCLEAR FAMILY

The nuclear family is the key to studying how family structure is related to function, how it affects psychological differentiation, and how family type is related to economic base and culture.

Defining the Nuclear Family

The definition of the nuclear family appears to be very clear-cut: mother, father, and children in a single household. The problem, however, which is the main point of this chapter, is that the above definition refers to only the *structural* aspects of the concept and to common residence in a single household. The major problems of definition, and, particularly, of measurement of the nuclear family, have resulted from researchers' ignoring the *functional* aspects of the nuclear family.

It would be informative to present Levinson and Malone's (1980, pp. 87-88) viewpoint regarding Murdock's controversial conclusion of the universality of the nuclear family. Murdock (1949) analyzed 250 societies and concluded that

> the nuclear family is a universal human social grouping. Either as the sole prevailing form of the family or as the basic unit from which more complex familial forms are compounded, it exists as a distinct and strongly functional group in every known society. (p. 2)

Anthropologists attempted to challenge this statement, looking for societies that did not have a nuclear family system. Levinson and Malone explain that Murdock's claim of the universality could not be disproved because what he really meant was that "the nuclear family is the *basic form* from which more complex familial forms are compounded . . . a distinct and strongly functional group in every known society" (Levinson & Malone, 1980, p. 88).

Most definitions of the family agree with Murdock (1949) that its functions include *common residence, economic cooperation,* and *reproduction.* Let us look more closely at "common residence." The critical question, which is methodological, is how does one define or measure "common residence"? In an early epidemiological study of the Greek family, Vassiliou (1966) reported that approximately 65% of Athenian families were nuclear in structure. Hindsight would tell us that questions were omitted regarding the residence of the relatives and the frequency of contacts with relatives. In recent studies in Athens in which we attempted to measure the patterns of residence of relatives of the members of the nuclear family, together with frequency of actual contact and telephone contact, a completely different picture of the nuclear family in Athens was obtained (Georgas, 1991b; Georgas et al., 1997). The pattern indicated that close relatives (mothers, parents, in-laws, sisters, uncles, aunts, and grandparents) lived in either the same apartment building or a nearby apartment building or in the neighborhood, with very frequent contacts and communications, both personal and telephone. Thus, if one attempts to define the nuclear family in terms of only its structural elements within a specific home, the functional aspects of the family vital to the analysis of the nuclear family–extended family system differentiation are omitted. This example suggests that if the functional aspects are not included in the study of the nuclear family, the results can be misleading.

The Diachronic Dimension

By the diachronic dimension, I refer to two aspects of family. The first concerns the predictable sequences of family life-cycle changes precipitated by family members' biological, social, and psychological needs development (Smith, 1995). The different stages of family development—beginning with marriage, the birth of the first child, maturity of the children, until death—underline the continual changes of the structure and function of the family. This issue is directly relevant to the issue of the differentiation of the extended family from the nuclear family. The classic extended family, for example, as defined by Stanton (1995) as a body with structure and continuity, undergoes a crisis of leadership when the patriarch of the family dies: "The composition of the extended family with its nuclear families and independent single adults changes constantly, but the extended family itself continues with new leaders and new members as individuals depart or as the generations pass away" (p. 100). In the joint family, the father's death leads to the temporary dominance of the elder brother, until each of them eventually begins his own extended family. Thus, it becomes obvious that even the classic extended family, composed of the patriarch, his married sons/fathers, and their children, probably has a lifetime of perhaps 20 or 30 years; after the death of the patriarch, the cycle begins again, but now with a small group of nuclear families. Segalen (1986) reports that "all domestic groups are in transition. . . . [I]n France . . . well-to-do-farmers had their children living with them for a few years before leaving to settle independently on another farm" (p. 27). There are two points to be made. The first is that even the extended family system in its ideal form has a brief life span. The second is that what might appear to be a nuclear family, if one focuses only on the numbers of its members or its structure, might be an extended family system. Once again, the argument is that one must also study the functional aspects of the family, in conjunction with its structural aspects.

Historical Development of the Nuclear Family

A second diachronic aspect concerns the study of the development of the nuclear family within the social and historical context and the ecological conditions of cultures (Rodgers & White, 1993).

As discussed above, many sociologists, anthropologists, historians, and psychologists hold that Parsons's theory of the structure and function of the nuclear family has become an ideology. Parsons emphasized that adaptation of the family unit to the industrial revolution required a nuclear family structure; this resulted in its isolation from its traditional extended family and kinship network and, most important, led to psychological isolation and anomie.

The psychologist Uzoka (1979) refers to a number of studies, most conducted in the United States, that have shown that the nuclear family is embedded in a network of extended kin who provide social support. Others (Gubrium & Holstein, 1990; Smith, 1995; Stacey, 1990) suggest that sociologists have not yet understood variations in family structure, function, and interaction because families are viewed in comparison with a white middle-class nuclear family model, rather than on their own terms and within a particular sociohistorical context.

On the other hand, Kagitcibasi (1996) refers to historical evidence indicating that the nuclear family and individualism predated industrialization in Western Europe, particularly England, by several centuries. She also refers to Razí (1993), who claims that the typical British family was nuclear rather than extended; the bond between family and land was weak; wider ties of kinship were also weak, so villagers relied on institutional support rather than on the assistance of kin; rural society was highly mobile; and children were often left home in their teens and spent a few years as live-in servants in other families. Also, some historians believe that the nuclear family and individualist patterns of behavior can be traced to the Middle Ages in Britain, so Western individualism was not an outcome of industrialization.

Apparently, there are different interpretations of the history of the nuclear family in Western cultures, as well as Parsons's model of the nuclear family. Segalen's (1986) book *Historical Anthropology of the Family* argues that recent historical and anthropological research has debunked a number of myths about the prevalence of the nuclear family in European societies from the 15th century till recently and that many sociologists' ideas that kinship relations were overstretched by the effects of incipient industrialization were exaggerated. Indeed, she argues that kinship relations were in fact maintained and certain forms were even strengthened as a defense to threats of wars, epidemics, and even industrialization. She presents evidence that parish records from the 16th, 17th, and 18th centuries in England indicated that the size of the domestic group in England was close to that of the present day, which would indicate the presence of nuclear family structure.

However, Segalen points out that analysis of the structure and function of these "nuclear family" groups indicates "a certain form of organization governing the transmission of practices, values, family and work, family and power, family and possessions and also the degree of intimate social relations among members of the kinship group" (p. 22).

Anderson's (1971) analysis of the 1851 census in Preston, Lancashire, England, proposes that the urban industrial revolution led to the *increase* in the numbers of parents and married children living together because of

> the economic constraints arising from industrial work, such as shortage of housing, need for the mother to work and the difficulty of minding the children. Since there was no real social provision for illness or poverty, all the individual could do in such cases was to turn to his nearest relatives and set up wider domestic groups within which mutual help was possible. General models of the structure of American households in the 19th century also show that, for the same structural reasons, between 12 and 15 per cent included distant relatives and between 23 and 30 per cent boarders and lodgers. (as cited in Segalen, 1986, p. 30)

Segalen (1986) concludes that the dominant ideology of the postwar years, as exemplified by Parsons's analysis of the nuclear family, was that of individualism and freedom. "This has meant that each family cell tended to be seen as unique and independent of cultural influences of economic and historical contingencies" (p. 3). She maintains that many sociologists studying present-day families have an a priori assumption that the domestic group is shrinking and that kinship has almost disappeared as a basis of relationships.

In concluding this section, I would argue that the issue of whether the nuclear family was historically characteristic of England or was a result of the industrial revolution and the development of urban society is not as important as the evidence that the Parsonian model of the nuclear family as independent, autarkic, and isolated from kin is a myth. It did not exist in this isolated form historically and, as we shall see, where it exists in present-day urban Western society is the exception rather than the rule.

NETWORK THEORY AND SOCIAL SUPPORT

The research on social support, those external copying resources made available through the larger social network in which the individual is embedded (Ruble, Costanzo, & Oliveri, 1992), played a major role in identifying the members of the immediate family, kin, and friends and associates who ameliorate the deleterious psychological and somatic effects of stress. Two recent reviews report the most recent conclusions of research over the past 35 years (Adler, 1994; Kessler, Price, & Wortman, 1985) regarding the important relationships of social support to stress. The findings are many, but all converge on the relationship of social ties to pathology. For example, the absence of adequate social ties or the disruption of social networks leads to greater stress, and the social networks of psychotics are smaller and kin-based, whereas those of neurotics are looser and sparser (Kessler et al., 1985). The degree of social connection—that is, social isolation—and the number of individuals in the social network are also related to pathology (Adler, 1994).

Segalen (1986) reports a number of studies that show the existence of active kin networks and social support in urban areas in France and Britain. Michel (1970) studied urban families in Paris and Bordeaux regarding help received by young couples with regard to housing, child care, and financial aid and found parental aid either in terms of financial aid or services such as caring for the children. Roussel (1976) studied young couples and couples old enough to have been parents with a national survey in France and found that 75% of married children lived less than 20 kilometers from their parents. Gokalp (1978), again in France, found that 63% of people with both living parents and married children lived less than 20 kilometers from their parents, 60% lived less than 20 kilometers from their parents-in-law, and 51% less than 20 kilometers from their married children. When they lived in close proximity or shared a home, 90% saw daughter, 86% saw mother, 83% saw son, and 82% saw mother-in-law at least once a week. Cribier (1979) studied retired Parisians and found more frequent contacts between married children and their parents after retirement. The children often aided their retired parents to keep up a network of friends. In Bethnal Green, a working-class area of London, a majority of couples lived near the wife's parents, and there was a high daily level of the exchange of contacts, visits, services, and advice between mother and married daughter (Young & Wilmott, 1968). Rosser and Harris (1968) reported a strong mother-daughter link in Swansea, an industrial Welsh city.

Marks and McLanahan (1993) analyzed giving and receiving social support in traditional two-parent families and in nontraditional two-parent or single-parent families based on national survey data ($n = 5,686$). Kin, especially parents, were often found to be an important source of support for single parents. In social support relationships, there was little evidence that mothers in nontraditional two-parent families were less likely to be involved in social support relationships with kin, especially with parents. The only exception was mothers with a cohabiting partner who had reduced contact with parents. Besides parents and siblings, however, it appears that friends, and not other kin, were the most significant members of the social support networks of nontraditional families. Levitt, Weber, and Guacci (1993) also reported that younger persons included fewer family members and more friends in their networks, and they received more support from friends.

Finally, in a study focusing on African American families, Jayakody, Chatters, and Taylor (1993) concluded that the social and economic functions and responsibilities of black families are managed by extended rather than nuclear family units. African American single mothers do not live and function in isolation but in extended family situations that are composed of kin and fictive kin, and they use social and economic resources of the extended family unit to offset the absence of the father. The majority of single mothers lived in close proximity to their families, had daily contact with kin, and reported feelings of closeness to and satisfaction with their families.

THE CROSS-CULTURAL STUDY OF THE EFFECTS OF FAMILY STRUCTURE AND FUNCTION ON PSYCHOLOGICAL VARIABLES

The purpose of this chapter is to argue that cross-cultural psychology should study how family structure and function affect psychological variables. It should employ an ecological approach in which psychological variables are studied as embedded within the context of the family structure, the immediate community, the social context, and the physical environment. Kagitcibasi (1996) strongly emphasizes the contextual-developmental-functional approach in the study of family dynamics and family socialization.

Georgas (1988, 1991b, 1993) has presented an ecosocial model of the impact of family on the psychological differentiation of the individual under a contextual approach. The model contains three basic concepts: ecological factors, social institutions, and group interactions. The ecological factors consist of features of the physical environment and the human-made physical environment and are based on Berry's ecocultural model (1975, 1976, 1979). The organization and institutions of society make up the economic system, the political and judicial system, the educational system, religion, and means of mass communication. The bonds with groups in the immediate community include the degree and quality of contact with significant groups within the immediate community such as costudents, neighbors, shopkeepers, and so forth (Christakopoulou, 1995; Georgas & Christakopoulou, 1993). The ecological and cultural model has been employed to delineate the context variables within which to analyze psychological variables (Georgas & Berry, 1995).

According to the model, family is the primary source of influence in the psychological differentiation of the individual, but it is also affected by societal and ecological factors. The structure and function of the Greek family within these context variables and an analysis of how they have affected family values have been presented from the perspective of indigenous psychology (Georgas, 1988, 1993, 1994).

Georgas et al. (1997) employed a contextual approach in exploring the relationship of family bonds to family structure and function across five cultures: Greece, Cyprus, the Netherlands, Britain, and Germany. The overall findings indicated systematic differences in measures of family structure and function between societies of north Western Europe (Britain, Germany, the Netherlands) and Mediterranean societies (Cyprus, Greece). Two types of family structure were investigated: the nuclear family, composed of members of the nuclear family, and the extended family, represented by grandparents, cousins, uncles, and aunts. No systematic differences were found in emotional closeness, frequency of meetings, or telephone contact with members of the nuclear family across the five cultures. It is with the members of the extended family that functional differences between the individualist and collectivist cultures were found. In Greek and Greek-Cypriot societies, the family functions extended to a larger kinship network, with grandparents, uncles, aunts, and cousins, in terms of frequency of meetings and contact by phone. In contrast, in the three societies in north Western Europe, the family structure was more limited to intergenerational networks. These studies are being extended to non-European cultures.

Fijneman et al. (1996) conducted a cross-cultural study of the relationship of family functions and institutional functions with individualist and collectivist cultures. They also reported that the pattern of emotional closeness to members of the nuclear family was quite similar across the cultural groups.

CONCLUSIONS AND PROPOSALS

At this point, the evidence appears to lead to some conclusions. One conclusion appears to be that one cannot define and study the family, nuclear or extended or other types, by looking only at its structure—that is, the number of its members and their roles—and dwelling in a single household. This leads to erroneous interpretations of the data, which essentially view the nuclear family from an a priori perspective of isolation from its kin.

A second conclusion is that, in studying either the nuclear family or other family types, one has to take into account its kinship networks and social support networks of friends.

A third conclusion is that the Parsonian model of the nuclear family—that is, fragmented from its kin, independent and autarkic, with psychological isolation—has been challenged by anthropologists, historians, and sociologists, and from a great deal of data coming from social support studies. The same concerns the historical interpretation of the development of the nuclear family as a response to the industrial revolution.

A fourth conclusion is that it appears to be fruitless to try to argue that the Western societies have a model of the nuclear family whereas the other cultures in the world have a model of the extended family. It appears to be very probable that nuclear families appear in almost all cultures, but in Western industrial cultures, the proportion of nuclear families is probably higher than that in other cultures. However, if one ignores the kinship and supportive friend network, and also other functional variables such as residence patterns, then these measures of structure may lead to misleading conclusions. For example, in urban areas of Western cultures, such as New York and London, because of economic reasons, an adult son or daughter can afford to rent or buy a flat and live separately from his or her parents. In New Delhi or Cairo, for example, this may not be possible for economic reasons. The critical question, however, is to what degree do the son and daughter maintain communication with their parents, contribute economically to the family, accept economic aid, and so on, in New York and New Delhi? It is these *functional* aspects, related to residence, economic cooperation, communication, and social support from their networks, and how they might affect psychological variables that should be the objects of study of possible differences between *families* in Western and other cultures, and not a priori categories such as "nuclear" or "extended" family.

A further conclusion is that variations of family and structure within a single culture cannot be as illuminating to the full range of interplay between the family and psychological variables as can those provided by cross-cultural comparisons. This chapter also argues that family can be employed as a context variable within the ecocultural framework of a society, together with social variables and environmental variables, to study cross-culturally the effect of family type on psychological variables.

13

CONFLICT MANAGEMENT
ACROSS CULTURES

Kwok Leung
Darius K.-S. Chan
Chinese University of Hong Kong

As the world is becoming a truly global village, it is common for people from different cultural backgrounds to come into contact with each other. Ethnic diversity is prevalent in many societies, such as the United States and Malaysia. Globalization of businesses has created many multicultural work groups. Cross-cultural negotiation has also become an essential practice in international business and political activities.

In view of the fact that not much has been written on the topic of intercultural conflict management, we attempt to provide some insights by integrating the results of recent studies in conflict research. In this chapter, we will first outline a conceptual framework that systematically examines factors affecting intercultural conflict management. Specifically, our framework summarizes the large amount of cross-cultural conflict studies and identifies barriers to effective conflict management across cultural lines. Then we will proceed to discuss how part of this general framework can be used to understand conflict resolution in culturally diverse workplaces—one type of intercultural conflict management that has become increasingly important in organizational psychology.

Before we begin our discussion, we should note that much of our thinking is shaped by the groundbreaking theoretical work on culture and social behavior by Harry Triandis.

AUTHORS' NOTE: The preparation of this chapter was supported by a research grant (CUHK 151/96H) provided by the Research Grants Council, Hong Kong.

Although Triandis's work is primarily basic in nature, he is always concerned about applications and has written extensively on such applied issues as cultural training and economic development. Our work is a continuation of Triandis's effort in addressing practical issues with solid basic research.

A FRAMEWORK FOR UNDERSTANDING
INTERCULTURAL CONFLICT MANAGEMENT

It is well-known that productive conflict management is difficult in and of itself (e.g., Pruitt & Carnevale, 1993). In intercultural conflict management, the situation is even more complex because cultural issues enter into the picture and often create additional difficulties. To analyze the effects of culture on conflict management across cultural lines, we propose a simple framework to classify the barriers to productive conflict management (Leung, in press). A number of theoretical frameworks have been proposed for understanding cross-cultural differences in human behavior (for a review, see Jahoda, 1980). These frameworks are by nature broad-brush, and three major domains are identifiable in these frameworks, namely, motivational, cognitive, and normative. We follow this scheme in analyzing barriers in intercultural conflict management. In the motivational domain, we argue that intercultural contact leads to motivational processes that may hinder conflict resolution. In the cognitive domain, intercultural contact may trigger cognitive processes that are counterproductive to conflict resolution. In the normative domain, normative differences across cultures may produce difficulties in resolving intercultural conflict effectively.

Motivational Domain

Intercultural Anxiety

Stephan and Stephan (1985) have argued that when two cultural groups are in contact, a certain level of anxiety, which they term *intergroup anxiety*, may be produced. Three sets of factors are hypothesized to influence the level of intergroup anxiety experienced. First, if prior intergroup relationship is favorable, intergroup anxiety would be low (e.g., Islam & Hewstone, 1993; Stephan & Stephan, 1989). Second, if one is knowledgeable and holds positive views about the other group, intergroup anxiety would be low. Third, if the context is well-defined, the relationship is interdependent, the in-group outnumbers the out-group, or the status of the in-group is high, intergroup anxiety would be low.

Intercultural anxiety may constitute a major barrier to effective conflict management in culturally diverse groups. Intergroup anxiety may lead to avoidance of contact (Pancer, McMullen, Kabatoff, Johnson, & Pond, 1979; Stephan & Stephan, 1985). It is well-known that productive conflict management relies on joint problem solving, and avoidance is usually a suboptimal strategy. Intercultural anxiety may also result in schematic processing, which leads to the reliance on stereotypes and the occurrence of self-fulfilling prophecies (Stephan & Stephan, 1985). Because in intercultural contact, out-groups may be viewed in a negative light, stereotypes and self-fulfilling prophecies will create a vicious cycle. Snyder and Swann (1978) reported that aggression may be triggered by the fear of hostility of the other party. Negative stereotypes may lead to preemptive actions that result in retaliation, thus fueling a cycle of conflict escalation. Intergroup anxiety may also lead to ego-defensive reactions and suppression of innovative thinking (Stephan & Stephan, 1985). Obviously, these reactions hinder effective problem solving that is fundamental to the identification of win-win solutions.

Power Equalization

In multicultural situations, it is rare that resources are divided equally among all groups. Typically, some groups are in a more advantaged position and enjoy a larger share of the resources. A wide array of empirical evidence has shown that disadvantaged groups are more likely than advantaged groups to see injustice in the allocation of resources across groups. For instance, Azzi (1992) found that, in both the United States and South Africa, participants who assumed the identity of a minority group member were more likely to endorse the equality principle in allocating political power across groups than were those who assumed the identity of a majority group member. The use of an equality principle would give the minority group more political power despite its smaller size. In a different experiment, Azzi (1993) reported that minority group members were more likely to choose a procedure that would give them veto power when they were sensitized to the possibility of intergroup conflict. Minority group members also rated such a procedure as fairer than did majority group members.

Studies conducted with actual members of majority and minority groups yielded results consistent with those reported by Azzi. In the United States, Arthur, Doverspike, and Fuentes (1992) examined the fairness perception of two selection procedures under affirmative action to give minority group members better employment opportunities. In one condition, two job applicants were described as equally employable, but the job applicant with a minority status was given the job. In another condition, the minority applicant was described as not as capable as the majority job applicant but was given the job anyway. The reactions of three groups of participants were contrasted: majority, minority, and foreign nationals from Latin America and East Asia. The minority participants and the foreign nationals regarded both procedures as less unfair than the majority participants did. In the United Kingdom, Branthwaite and Jones (1975) reported that Welsh college students, the minority group, showed a stronger in-group bias than English college students, the majority group, in allocating a reward across these two ethnic groups.

Because the disadvantaged group tends to demand a larger share of a resource to attain a more balanced distribution of power and resources, it is difficult for two groups that differ in power and resources to arrive at an arrangement to both parties' satisfaction.

Instrumental Concerns

Recently, on the basis of the group value model of justice, Tyler and his associates (Huo, Smith, Tyler, & Lind, 1996; Tyler, Boeckmann, Smith, & Huo, 1997) have argued that the social categorization process affects how groups make fairness judgments. If two groups see each other as out-groups, instrumental concerns become more salient and individuals are more likely to be dissatisfied if their outcome is low. In contrast, if two groups identify with each other, the fairness of interpersonal treatment becomes more salient and plays a more important role in justice judgments.

In intercultural contexts, it is typical that ethnic or cultural groups are often disconnected from or even uncooperative toward each other. The analysis of Tyler and his associates suggests that, in these situations, groups tend to focus on maximizing their outcomes in the intercultural interaction, making intercultural collaboration difficult to achieve.

Cognitive Domain

There is a growing literature on how cognitive biases lead to suboptimal conflict resolution (e.g., Bazerman & Neale, 1992). In intercultural conflict, additional biases may occur that hinder effective conflict resolution.

Ethnocentric Fairness Bias

In-group favoritism is probably one of the most robust findings in intergroup research. People tend to favor their in-group and derogate the out-groups (e.g., Pettigrew, 1979; Tajfel, 1982). In allocating resources, people were found to allocate a larger share to in-group than to out-group members (e.g., Ng, 1984; Tajfel, 1978). People also tend to regard their in-group as morally superior and more trustworthy than out-groups (Brewer, 1986). This bias also operates in intercultural allocation. In Belgium, van Avermaet and McClintock (1988) reported that Dutch-speaking schoolchildren allocated a larger reward to a Dutch-speaking group than to a French-speaking group.

According to social identity theory, this in-group bias reflects people's desire to maintain a positive, group-based social identity (Tajfel & Turner, 1979). Social identity theory suggests that, in an intercultural context, cultural groups tend to inflate their deservedness and demand that their share of a resource be larger than what other cultural groups are willing to give them. Thus, in-group favoritism typically leads groups to expect a larger share than what they actually get, and, as a result, it is likely to generate a sense of injustice in resource allocation across cultural lines.

In a different line of work, people were found to recall more fair acts and fewer unfair acts performed by themselves than by others; this tendency is labeled the egocentric fairness bias (e.g., Liebrand, Messick, & Wolters, 1986; Messick, Bloom, Boldizar, & Samuelson, 1985). Subsequent work shows that this fairness bias also operates across gender groups (Boldizar & Messick, 1988). Although we know of no empirical work that extends this result to an interethnic or intercultural context, a similar bias should be expected, which may be termed an *ethnocentric fairness bias.* That is, people may have a similar tendency to perceive the actions of their in-group as fairer than the actions of the out-group and to be able to recall more fair acts performed by in-group members than by out-group members. Some indirect support for this argument comes from a study comparing the just-world belief of British and white South African students (Furnham, 1985). South African students showed a stronger belief in the just world, and Furnham (1985) argued that this difference can be interpreted as a mechanism for whites in South Africa to justify the negative treatment of the victims of apartheid.

Similarity Bias

It is well-known that people are attracted to others who are similar to themselves (Byrne, 1971). In resource allocation across cultural groups, it is possible that a similarity bias is in operation, which may lead to intercultural conflict. In a multicultural situation, this reasoning suggests that the dominant group may reward members of subordinate groups who are more similar to themselves. Leong (1996) has reported some results that are consistent with this reasoning. Both studies are concerned with the occupational outcomes of Asian Americans. In the first study, it was found that more-acculturated participants reported a higher level of job satisfaction. Acculturation here refers to the adoption of the values and practices of the mainstream American culture. The second study found that Asian Americans who were more acculturated were given higher performance ratings by their supervisors. These two sets of results suggest that members of minority groups who are more acculturated and hence more similar to their superiors from the majority group are likely to enjoy better job outcomes. Minority group members who are less acculturated are likely to see their lower outcomes as a manifestation of the bias of their superiors against them, and conflict may result.

Attributional Differences

In a series of studies, Morris and Peng (1994) reported that attributions are channeled to the individual actor's internal, stable predispositions in the United States, whereas attributions are channeled to the actor's embeddedness in a social context in China. Similarly, Miller (1984) found that Indians were less likely to make dispositional attributions than were Americans. Cha and Nam (1985) found that Koreans were less likely to make internal attributions than were Americans. Al-Zahrani and Kaplowitz (1993) found that, compared with Americans, Saudis made more external attributions for others' behavior. Consistent also is the argument that Japanese expected less consistency between attitudes and behaviors than did Australians (Kashima, Siegal, Tanaka, & Kashima, 1992).

Because members of different cultural groups may perceive the cause of an event differently, the way they approach a problem may be very different. For instance, Hamilton and Sanders (1988) reported that, because Japanese are more likely to adopt a social explanation of deviant behavior, they tend to view a transgression as reflecting the failure of society to socialize and guide the individual properly. Accordingly, their goal in punishing a transgression is to redress this inadequate socialization, and the function of sanctions is for restoring the relationship between actor and victim and providing restitution for the victim. In contrast, Americans are more likely to attribute misbehavior to individual predispositions and, as a result, are more likely to suggest sanctions to isolate the individual to avoid the expression of such dispositions again. Consistent with this argument, Na and Loftus (1996) reported that Korean respondents showed more favorable attitudes toward lenient treatment of criminals than did their American counterparts. The leniency of Koreans is probably based on their belief that society is partly responsible for an individual's misbehavior.

Misattribution

In a cross-cultural situation, culture is a very salient factor and may easily be invoked as a cause of the behavior of members from a different cultural group. In misattribution, people erroneously attribute the cause of an individual's behavior to his or her cultural background. It is well documented that stereotypes affect individuals' behavior toward others who are from a different cultural group and are likely to lead to self-fulfilling prophecies (e.g., Hamilton, Sherman, & Ruvolo, 1990). Misattribution based on negative stereotypes may divert attention from the real cause of the conflict and thus creates unnecessary animosity among members of different cultural groups.

Normative Domain

Norms for Resource Allocation

Cultural groups may differ in norms and practices, and such differences are often the cause of perceived injustice and conflict in intercultural contact. Leung and Stephan (in press) have provided a review of the literature, and the following is largely based on their discussion. One important issue concerning intercultural contact is the allocation of resources across cultural groups. Distributive justice is achieved if all cultural groups regard their share of a resource as fair. To avoid a sense of distributive injustice, participants must agree on the allocation norms used and on the way the norms are to be applied. However, cross-cultural research has clearly shown that cultural groups may have diverse views on these two issues. Cultural groups may regard different inputs as important. For instance, Japanese organizations place a greater weight on seniority than do U.S. organizations (e.g., Ouchi & Jaeger, 1978). If Japanese and Americans are to decide on bonus payments jointly, conflict is likely to arise because these two groups cannot agree on the weight assigned to seniority.

Cultures may also differ in what they regard as desirable outcomes or in the level of importance attached to different types of outcomes. For instance, American negotiators often regard the outcome of a negotiation as very important, whereas many cultural groups, including Chinese, Malaysians, and Japanese, regard establishing a cordial relationship between the negotiators as very important (for a review, see Leung & Wu, 1990). Tinsley and Brett (1997) have proposed to use the concept of a "relational bargaining frame" to describe the interpersonal orientation in bargaining by Chinese.

Perceptions of injustice often arise when cultural groups regard different allocation rules as fair. The influence of culture on the preference for allocation norms has been widely studied (for reviews, see James, 1993; Leung, 1988b, in press). For instance, the equality norm is more likely to be adopted in collectivist than in individualist cultures (Leung, 1988b). Cultural differences in perceived fairness of justice norms make it difficult to arrive at allocations that are regarded as fair by all cultural groups, and conflict is likely to occur.

Procedural Norms

When disputes arise, some sort of procedure is often chosen to resolve the dispute, and such a choice is typically guided by procedural norms. In studies of procedural justice, the focus is on the procedures and processes used in decision making. Again, different cultural groups may regard different procedures as fair. For instance, Leung (1987) found that Chinese participants showed a stronger preference for mediation and negotiation than did Americans, and these cultural differences were due to the Chinese participants' perception that these two procedures were more likely to lead to animosity reduction. Bierbrauer (1994) reported that Kurds and Lebanese who were asylum seekers in Germany were less willing to use state law to resolve a conflict with family members or acquaintances than were Germans. The Kurds and Lebanese also regarded the norms of religion and tradition as more legitimate, and state law as less legitimate, for conflict resolution than did Germans.

In addition to different preferences for the procedures to be used in resolving conflicts, people in different cultures may also differ in their styles of conflict resolution. Preferences for styles of conflict resolution are probably strongly influenced by individualism and collectivism. For instance, people from collectivist cultures (e.g., Brazil, Mexico, Hong Kong, Japan) show a greater preference for accommodation than do people from individualist cultures, such as the United States or Britain (e.g., Gabrielidis, Stephan, Ybarra, Pearson, & Villareal, 1997; Kirkbride, Tang, & Westwood, 1991; Ohbuchi & Takahashi, 1994; Pearson & Stephan, in press).

If members of different cultural groups prefer different procedures to handle a conflict, or if they have different conflict-resolution styles, it is unlikely that they can agree on a particular mode of conflict resolution, which results in an escalation of the conflict.

Norms of Interpersonal Treatment

It is widely documented that interactional norms may vary considerably across cultures. Misattributions and misinterpretations of the actions of members of other cultural groups may generate unnecessary conflict. From their own cultural standpoint, people may interpret the behavior of an individual from a different cultural group as being rude and condescending, but this behavior may be perfectly acceptable in the other culture (for a review, see Gudykunst & Bond, 1997). For instance, Foster (1992) suggested that, in Mexico, bargaining is unstructured, many people may speak simultaneously, and turn taking is usually ignored. Such behavior would be regarded as very rude by

American negotiators. Misinterpretation of the behavior of the other party may lead to negative feelings such as dissatisfaction and anger, making the resolution of disputes more difficult.

Norms for Hierarchical Relationships

In high-power-distance societies, the intervention of a high-status third party in a dispute will probably be regarded as more legitimate than in low-power-distance societies. Consistent with this argument, in high-power-distance countries such as Japan, it has been documented that court litigants look to the judge to provide facts about the case and ultimate justice, whereas in low-power-distance countries such as the United States, litigants are more inclined to rely on their own efforts to argue for their case (Benjamin, 1975; Tanabe, 1963). In a culture-level study of 23 national groups, Smith, Peterson, Leung, and Dugan (in press) found that participants from low-power-distance countries were more likely to rely on their peers or their subordinates to resolve a disagreement in the workplace than were participants from high-power-distance countries. Tse, Francis, and Walls (1994) found that, compared with Canadian executives, executives from China were more likely to consult their superiors in a conflict. In light of the above differences, if disputants are from cultures that differ in power distance, it is likely that they have different expectations about the role of a third party in a conflict, and this difference will affect their receptivity of the intervention of the third party. Thus, the effectiveness of a third party will depend not only on his or her skills but on the match between the third party's intervention strategies and the disputants' expectations based on their cultural backgrounds.

In the next section, we focus our discussion on conflict resolution in culturally diverse workplaces, one type of intercultural conflict management that is becoming more and more important in organizational psychology. In addition, cultural diversity in the workplace also provides an excellent context for illustrating how the conceptual framework discussed above can be applied to understand practical issues in organizations.

CONFLICT RESOLUTION
IN CULTURALLY DIVERSE WORKPLACES

Background

Managing cultural diversity has received considerable recent attention in the organizational literature because culturally diverse work groups are now prevalent (see, e.g., Chemers, Oskamp, & Costanzo, 1995; Cox, 1993; Henderson, 1994; Jackson & Associates, 1992; Jackson & Ruderman, 1995). Many scholars have proposed theoretical models for understanding or managing diversity. For instance, Triandis, Kurowski, and Gelfand (1994) proposed one of the most comprehensive frameworks, which posits specific relations among 18 variables that have been found to affect intercultural interactions. The key variables included are cultural distance, perceived similarity, sense of control, and culture shock. Although tests of the complete model are not yet available, empirical examination of some parts of it has yielded supporting findings (Goto, 1996). Others have developed conceptual frameworks for managing workforce diversity (e.g., Bartz, Hillman, Lehrer, & Mayhugh, 1990; Sue, 1991; Thomas, 1992) or instruments for measuring various types of diversity in the workplace (Hegarty & Dalton, 1995).

Although the literature on workplace diversity is mushrooming (e.g., Milliken & Martins, 1996), relatively few empirical studies have looked into one important area of diversity, namely, managing conflict in a culturally diverse workplace. Although a number of scholars have provided conceptual analyses of conflict in culturally diverse organizations (e.g., Donnellon & Kolb, 1994; Horowitz & Boardman, 1994), these papers deal mainly with policy recommendations and implications for resolving conflicts arising from diversity. In this section, we build on our conceptual framework and focus on some of the particularly important but largely unexplored variables that may affect how employees approach and resolve conflicts in culturally diverse workplaces.

Factors Affecting Diversity Dispute Resolution in Organizations

Intergroup Stereotypes

Perhaps one of the most neglected variables in diversity research is intergroup stereotypes. As Cox (1993) pointed out, many conflicts in diverse organizations can be analyzed from an intergroup perspective. Specifically, many interpersonal conflicts in culturally diverse workplaces may in fact be a manifestation of group-identity-related conflict. When members of different racial or cultural origins work together, needs to assert one's own cultural identity become salient (e.g., what kind of language is considered acceptable). In many occasions, such assertions can cause misunderstanding and conflict.

According to conflict research, perception of the opponent's characteristics (e.g., tough or soft strategies used, personality, or needs) can affect one's resolution styles (see, e.g., Druckman, 1994, for a review of opponents' strategies on negotiation behavior). Within the context of diversity disputes in the workplace, such a perception is likely to be affected by intergroup attitudes in general and intergroup stereotypes in particular. As mentioned earlier, intergroup stereotypes are one of the fundamental problems in intergroup relations because they can easily lead to misattribution (e.g., Stephan, 1985). It is conceivable that intergroup stereotypes, or intergroup attitudes in general, also play an important role in conflict resolution for diversity disputes. For instance, if a Korean who is in conflict with an American colleague has a stereotype that "Americans are extremely competitive," he or she is not likely to negotiate with this colleague in order to avoid any direct confrontation. Instead, he or she may opt for third-party intervention such as mediation or arbitration. However, very little research has been conducted to examine how intergroup stereotypes (or intergroup attitudes in general) affect resolution styles in diversity disputes in the workplace.

Influences of Individualism-Collectivism

General Conflict-Resolution Styles

As mentioned earlier, findings from cross-cultural comparisons of procedural norms reveal systematic differences between individualists and collectivists. Tinsley and Brett (1997) proposed that such differences in conflict styles may be a result of the different conflict frames that individualists and collectivists adopt when approaching a conflict. By comparing the negotiation styles of Americans and Hong Kong Chinese, they argued that Americans tend to use an "integrating interests" perspective (i.e., focus on the interests of both parties by more direct sharing and bringing in multiple issues to create a solution that is best for both parties involved), whereas Hong Kong Chinese negotiate from a "relational bargaining" perspective (i.e., more sensitive to the collective and the concerns of high-status third parties and more likely to involve upper management). This difference in conflict frames can create problems for conflict resolution when disputants from the two cultures are involved, such as in Chinese-U.S. joint ventures. Others have also mentioned problems in managing such relationships (e.g., Davidson, 1987; Ding, 1996; Weldon, Jehn, Chen, & Wang, 1996).

When a workplace dispute involves members from the two types of cultures who do not have sufficient knowledge of the other culture, problems can arise because the individualist may try to resolve the conflict by open discussion and direct confrontation, acts that are perceived as pushy and inappropriate from the collectivist's perspective. Likewise, the collectivist may try to avoid any direct discussion related to the conflict, a stance that is perceived as detrimental from an individualist's perspective. In either case, an unintended result of conflict escalation is likely to follow.

Intra- Versus Intercultural Conflict Resolution

In addition to the above cultural differences in procedural norms, studies on intercultural conflict resolution suggest that disputants tend to behave differently in intercultural and intracultural conflicts (e.g., Adler & Graham, 1989; Weldon et al., 1996). Adler and Graham reported interesting changes in negotiators' behavior when they engage in intercultural negotiations. Specifically, Japanese negotiators achieved lower levels of payoff in negotiations with Americans than with fellow Japanese. Anglophone Canadians achieved lower levels of payoff when negotiating with Francophone Canadians, despite the fact that the Francophones were more cooperative when negotiating interculturally.

Weldon et al. (1996) asked managers working in a U.S.-People's Republic of China joint venture to list and rate various resolution procedures they would use when involved in intercultural versus intracultural conflict. Using a multidimensional scaling procedure, the authors found that both the U.S. and Chinese participants used strategies in intercultural conflict different from those they used in intracultural conflict. Specifically, when handling intercultural conflict, Chinese tend to use indirect actions (e.g., go to the boss, raise the issue in a meeting) to solve the conflict, whereas Americans are more likely to interact directly with the different-culture colleague. Contrary to the notion that Chinese are more collectivist and prefer more harmonious ways of conflict resolution (e.g., Kirkbride, Tang, & Westwood, 1991; Westwood, Tang, & Kirkbride, 1992), Chinese managers also suggested several direct, vindictive responses expected to intensify the conflict, whereas the Americans were more concerned with maintaining good relations with colleagues from different cultures.

These results echo the notion that collectivists, such as Chinese, are more sensitive to the in-group/out-group distinction (see, e.g., Chan, Triandis, Carnevale, Tam, & Bond, 1997; Leung & Wu, 1990; Triandis, 1995b); in this case, they might have treated the U.S. managers as out-group members and thus were more confrontational than when they were interacting with in-group members. Given these findings, it seems particularly important to conduct more research on intercultural conflict because disputants may behave differently in intercultural conflict than they do in intracultural conflict.

Power Distance: Norms for Hierarchical Relationships

Cultural differences in power distance are likely to influence conflict resolution in workplace disputes that involve disputants who are of different ranks. This cultural difference in the norms for hierarchical relationships has several implications for diversity disputes in organizations.

Subordinates' Likelihood of Pursuing a Conflict

When involved in a conflict with one's superior, members from high-power-distance cultures are less likely to pursue the conflict than those from low-power-distance cultures, especially when the superior belongs to the majority culture (e.g., a Japanese subordinate involved in a dispute with an American supervisor in an American firm). Results from Bochner and Hesketh (1994) provide indirect evidence for this speculation. Specifically, these authors examined employees in a multicultural organization in Australia and found that those from high-power-distance cultures (e.g., Hong Kong, Philippines) were less open with their superiors than were employees from low-power-distance cultures (e.g., Finland, Britain). For instance, employees from high-power-distance cultures were less inclined to argue against their superiors' decisions and were more cautious about discussing work problems with a superior from a different ethnic background than were those from low-power-distance cultures. It is conceivable that such a difference will also be manifested in the way they handle conflict with a superior.

Superiors' Likelihood of Pursuing a Conflict

When involved in a conflict with one's subordinate, members from high-power-distance cultures may exploit the status imbalance and foster a particular resolution because it may be the quickest way to resolve the conflict (Ury, Brett, & Goldberg, 1988). On the contrary, members from low-power-distance cultures may be more willing to accept the challenge and discuss the issue directly with their subordinates. Results of two cross-cultural organizational studies illustrate this point. Kozan (1989) found that Turkish managers, who were found to belong to a high-power-distance culture (Hofstede, 1980), were more likely to use power tactics (e.g., forcing) for conflicts with subordinates than with superiors; no such differences were observed for their U.S. counterparts, a relatively low-power-distance culture. Similarly, James, Chen, and Cropanzano (1996) reported that Taiwanese workers, another high-power-distance culture in Hofstede's study, were more likely to endorse coercive power as a legitimate leadership strategy than were their U.S. counterparts.

Third-Party Intervention

According to the norms for hierarchical relationships, it is expected that when involved in a conflict with a peer from a different culture, members from high-power-distance cultures are more likely to go to their superior and ask for a resolution than are those from low-power-distance cultures. Empirical evidence from cross-cultural comparisons of high- versus low-power-distance cultures has lent support to this speculation (Tse et al., 1994). Specifically, these studies reveal that subordinates from high-power-distance cultures are more likely to rely on their superiors to resolve a conflict.

Although this review of conflict resolution in culturally diverse workplaces is by no means exhaustive, it generates a number of hypotheses that are worth pursuing. To reiterate, there is very little empirical work in this area. According to Milliken and Martins's (1996) comprehensive review of the effects of diversity in work groups, negative affect and low organizational commitment among the minority group members have consistently been found to be some of the outcomes of cultural diversity in the United States. To improve organizational effectiveness, examining conflict resolution in culturally diverse workplaces thus becomes a particularly important issue.

CONCLUSION

As the world is becoming smaller, intercultural contact is becoming an integral part of our daily life. Effective conflict management across cultural or ethnic lines is pivotal to racial or ethnic harmony, one thing that Harry Triandis cares about deeply. Unfortunately, our knowledge in this area lags behind its practical importance. In his career spanning over four decades, Triandis has paved the way for us to tackle such pressing and important problems in a globalizing world. Through his significant contributions to our understanding of culture, exemplified by such works as *The Analysis of Subjective Culture* (1972) and *Individualism and Collectivism* (1995b), we are now in a stage when we can develop and test well-defined theoretical statements about conflict management across cultures. We hope our chapter will bring this topic to the spotlight and stimulate more research in the search for racial and ethnic harmony.

14

NEGOTIATION OF THE SELF IN INTERPERSONAL INTERACTION

Japan-Australia Comparison

Emiko S. Kashima
Swinburne University of Technology

Yoshihisa Kashima
La Trobe University

Language is central to cultural process. Yet it has not been a major focus of inquiry in cross-cultural psychology. Granted, language has played an important methodological role. Language has been used as a primary tool for measurement, or a medium of instruction, in virtually all cross-cultural studies. To be sure, a great deal has been said about translation and cross-cultural equivalence (Lonner & Berry, 1986). All the same, cross-cultural psychology has not examined a more fundamental theoretical question about the role of language in cultural process.

A quick search of Psyc Lit confirms this impression. Of the 1,512 journal articles from January 1990 to June 1996 identified by the keyword *cross-cultural* in the Psyc Lit database, only 40 (less than 3%) were relevant to the issue of culture and language. The majority fell into three general categories: 10 studies looked at language as a barrier in intercultural interaction, 25 treated language as an indicator of cultural differences in cognitive/

AUTHORS' NOTE: We would like to thank Michael Bond and Cindy Gallois for their comments on an earlier draft of the chapter.

meaning systems and communication style, and only 3 examined language as an agent of socialization or cultural learning. Our main objective is to argue for the importance of the last category that includes three studies (less than .2%), calling for a systematic investigation of what seems to be a critical issue in cross-cultural psychology, that is, the role of language in the transmission of culture.

However obvious this suggestion may seem, the relation between culture and language requires much explication in contemporary social science. Traditionally, the relation between culture and language has been dominated by two competing views. On the one hand, one school of thought suggests the primacy of thought over language. Fodor's (1975) is probably the most articulate form of this argument. According to this view, humans have an innate language of thought. An individual must learn a natural language to express this language of thought; however, the natural language has a minimum effect on the thought process per se. As Pinker (1990) put it, language is just "grafted on" thought, from this perspective. Clearly in a similar vein is Piaget's (e.g., 1955) theory of language development and Chomsky's (1980) theory of linguistic competence. Basically, this viewpoint *assumes* the universality of human thought; culture is a nonissue.

On the other hand, if cultural diversity is to be taken seriously, there is the Sapir-Whorf hypothesis (Whorf, 1956, for the original theses; for review, see Brown, 1976; Hardin & Banaji, 1993; Hunt & Agnoli, 1991), which opposes the language of thought hypothesis. Its stronger form claims that language *determines* culture, or a cultural group's characteristic worldview. Or, in a weaker version, it is suggested that language *influences* culture. The hypothesis has attracted numerous studies in the past 40 years (for empirical tests of the hypothesis, see Brown & Lenneberg, 1954; Cole & Scribner, 1974; Gerrig & Banaji, 1994). Despite a recent resurgence of research interest in the culture-language relationship (Gumperz & Levinson, 1991; Hardin & Banaji, 1993; Hill & Mannheim, 1992; Hunt & Banaji, 1986; Lucy, 1992; Lucy & Wertsch, 1987; Rosch, 1988; Sherzer, 1987), the Sapir-Whorf hypothesis remains controversial.[1]

To put it simply, in the traditional framing of the culture-language relation, both culture and language are relatively stable systems; the question is whether the system of language engraves the linguistic community's view of the world (i.e., a significant aspect of a culture). This framing of the question presumes that there exists an abstract language (*langue*, as Saussure, 1959, put it) and a culture that are separable from the concrete actors' social activities, including speech (*parol*, as Saussure called it). Instead of trying to answer this traditional question, our aim here is to argue for an alternative framing of the question about the culture-language relationship (e.g., Sherzer, 1987) in which the focus is on concrete speech rather than on abstract language. That is, we argue that culture is transmitted in part through concrete uses of language.

In this chapter, we first show how cross-cultural psychology's treatment of language failed to address the dynamic process by which language is involved in the transmission of culture through particular interpersonal activities in particular social context. We then briefly review theoretical frameworks and well-known research programs related to language in cross-cultural psychology. While acknowledging the important contribution each approach made, we point to their shortcomings as a guiding principle in an inquiry into the role of language in the transmission of culture. In the second section, we review a broad theoretical orientation that takes the situated uses of language seriously. This orientation regards cultural practices in particular situations as fundamental to cultural transmission. Finally, we summarize some of our own research, which incorporates the practice-oriented perspective within a research program about individualism and collectivism.

LANGUAGE IN
CROSS-CULTURAL SOCIAL PSYCHOLOGY

Despite the controversial nature of the concept of culture, all theorists agree that culture is transmitted from people to people, from one generation to the next, by symbolic means, most notably, through language. Triandis (1994a), for instance, takes communication by language to be a central aspect of his definition of culture:

> Culture is a set of human-made objective and subjective elements that in the past have increased the probability of survival and resulted in satisfactions for the participants in an ecological niche, and thus became *shared among those who could communicate with each other because they had a common language* and they lived in the same time and place. (p. 22 [italics added])

As Segall, Dasen, Berry, and Poortinga (1990) put it, cross-cultural psychology is "the study of human behavior and its *transmission*, taking into account the ways in which behaviors are shaped and influenced by social and cultural forces" (p. 1 [italics added]). How, then, is culture transmitted? As does Triandis, we suggest language plays a major role.

The importance of language in culture is a central premise of contemporary cognitive anthropology, which is mainly concerned with how people in various cultures describe, categorize, and organize their knowledge about their world. Its central concept is often called "cultural models." As suggested in D'Andrade's (1990) definition of culture, the cognitive anthropological approach generally emphasizes natural language: "Culture consists of learned and shared systems of meaning and understanding, communicated primarily by means of natural language" (p. 67).

The role of language in the transmission of culture has been acknowledged by cross-cultural psychologists in the past. As we will see, both Triandis's (1972) model of subjective culture and Berry's ecocultural model (1974; Berry, Poortinga, Segall, & Dasen, 1992) point to the importance of language in cultural learning and transmission. We will also briefly discuss other research topics in cross-cultural social psychology that dealt with language. Despite the concerns and interests, we will argue, these early efforts failed to examine the role of language in the process of cultural learning and transmission at the level of personal and interpersonal activities.

Triandis's Subjective Culture

Triandis (1972) regarded a cognitive category to be the building block of subjective culture. According to Triandis, humans use cognitive categories at various levels of abstraction. At the most concrete level, any stimuli that are perceptually discriminable form elementary categories, such as phonemes (e.g., the *v* of *vintage*). At the next level, these elementary categories are combined to form meaning categories, such as morphemes (e.g., the *vin* of *vintage*). At the next abstract level are concepts that are expressible by words. Elemental cognitive structures, including tasks, expectations, roles, norms, and stereotypes (e.g., "Connoisseurs appreciate vintage wine"), are located at a level more abstract. This theoretical framework clearly acknowledges the intimate involvement of language in the process by which individuals categorize and interact with their world. It also underscores that each language system has its unique contribution to the associated cultural worldview. For instance, a host of knowledge connected to the concept of *vintage* and experiences linked to it are shared within cultures in which wine is consumed, and they constitute a unique part of these cultures. In cultures in which wine-drinking customs do not exist, the concept and experiences that involve *vintage* would also be absent. In Triandis's own words, "Different language-culture communities will provide different opportunities for the categorization of experience" (p. 12).

Although Triandis clearly pointed to the fundamental role of language in the makeup of subjective culture, language in this framework was maintained as a stable system rather than as having dynamic uses that change their shapes and functions in the context of social actions. In his subsequent development of research on culture and social behavior, Triandis (1977a, 1994a) generally moved away from language, leaving it at the beginning stages of subjective culture.

Berry's Ecocultural Model

Berry's model (1974) of cultural influences on behavior emphasizes the importance of ecology in the development of particular cultural patterns. In an early version of the ecocultural model, Berry theorized that ecology has an impact on individuals both directly and indirectly, mediated by four classes of factors: (a) culture (group's aids for individual adaptation to recurrent ecological pressures), (b) socialization (a part of culture that shapes human behavior), (c) nutrition and disease (e.g., protein availability and parasites), and (d) gene pool. The first class, cultural aids, included language. Language specifically was considered to assist in the development of the cognitive skills required to cope with ecological demand.

To test the proposition that language functions as an aid for adaptation via enhancing cognitive ability, Berry compared the availability of geometrical spatial terms that are believed to have different degrees of adaptive values in different ecological groups. Supporting this expectation, in comparison with Temne agriculturists, Inuits, who relied more on their geometrical spatial perception for hunting food, were found to have more geometrical spatial terms. In a more recent version of the ecocultural model (Segall et al., 1990), psychological variables are influenced by sociopolitical context as well as ecological context. The two types of contexts exert their influences on behaviors, traits, motives, abilities, and attitudes through biological and cultural transmission processes. The framework provides a functional analysis of language in the context of human adaptation to ecology.

Other Language-Related Topics
in Cross-Cultural Social Psychology

In an early part of the history of cross-cultural psychology, language was a central concern in major research areas such as translation and affective meaning. These concerns reflected cross-cultural psychology's approach to language (Wagatsuma, 1977). First, in the research on translation, language was regarded as a major methodological barrier in cross-cultural comparison, and to conquer this problem, researchers developed and evaluated methods of translation that can establish a cross-cultural equivalence of test materials used in research (e.g., Brislin, 1976; Seleskovitch, 1976). Alternative methods that avoid translation were also proposed (e.g., Triandis, 1976). All in all, language was a burden, something that one had to reckon with to identify cross-cultural comparability and equivalence.

At a more substantive level, research by Osgood and his colleagues on connotative meaning (Osgood, Suci, & Tannenbaum, 1957) was centrally concerned with language in comparing cultural meaning systems. The research suggested that, despite the major differences among languages in syntax, semantics, and pragmatics, connotative meaning can be characterized by three basic dimensions: evaluation, potency, and activity. This research gave a strong impetus to many areas of cross-cultural social psychology, including a method of attitude measurement by semantic differential scales and cross-cultural comparisons of affective meanings of various social concepts. This research program, ironically, *looked through*, rather than looked at, language. No doubt, given Osgood's psycholinguistic research program, he was centrally concerned with the psychological meaning of concepts. It is curious, however, that Osgood's basic view to language was that it was "a barrier" in cross-linguistic research, as might be reflected in his statement "If [the psycholinguistic relativity] were literally true, then cross-linguistic comparisons of subjective culture would be impossible in principle" (Osgood, 1971, p. 20).

Thus, both methodologically and substantively, language was generally a nuisance to a cross-cultural comparison. Somewhat different from these, Edward Hall's (1966, 1973, 1976) approach was to explore unconscious assumptions of one's worldview, or hidden dimensions of culture (e.g., perceptions of time, space, formality, and directness) that are embedded in each different language and influence communication behaviors (see also, Singelis & Brown, 1995). This approach to language and culture stimulated subsequent research in the area of cross-cultural communication (e.g., Blum-Kulka, House, & Kasper, 1988; Gudykunst, Ting-Toomey, & Chua, 1988; Wiseman, 1995) as well as research into differences in social behaviors and judgments often exhibited by bilinguals in different linguistic situations (Ervin-Tripp, 1964; Gallois & Markel, 1975; Marín, Triandis, Betancourt, & Kashima, 1983; Pierson & Bond, 1982). Nevertheless, the aspect of cultural transmission was not a major concern for these traditions either.

Summary

Major theoretical frameworks and empirical research programs acknowledged the importance of language in cross-cultural psychology. However, the early work in cross-cultural psychology did not examine the role of language in *the process of cultural transmission at the level of personal and interpersonal activities*. On the one hand, although the theoretical frameworks pointed to the role of language in cultural transmission, they fell short of actually examining this process. It was simply assumed that culture and language are intricately interrelated. On the other hand, research programs such as translation equivalence and affective meaning treated language as a barrier to cross-cultural comparisons, again failing to direct attention to the microprocess of cultural transmission and the role of language in it.

AN ALTERNATIVE PERSPECTIVE ON THE CULTURE-LANGUAGE RELATIONSHIP

An alternative perspective on the culture-language relationship is emerging in various neighboring areas. Broadly speaking, this perspective focuses on the concrete linguistic activities through which culture is transmitted. There are several common characteristics to what may be called the *practice-oriented* perspective. First, language use, rather than the language system, is a main focus of inquiry. To put it somewhat differently, pragmatics and, to a lesser extent, semantics take on a theoretical significance that has not been accorded in the traditional Chomskian linguistics, whose central program consisted of the explication of universal syntax (e.g., see Clark, 1985). Second, the "situatedness" of language use is taken seriously. That is, it is centrally recognized that linguistic activities take place among concrete actors in concrete situations in time and space. Third, culture and language are so intricately bound up together in everyday discourse that it is difficult, if not impossible, to separate the two. The acquisition of one is that of the other. Fourth, the culture-language interplay is inherently dynamic. That is, time is centrally involved in the process of cultural transmission. This shifts one's attention to ontogenetic development and the stability and change in culture and language.

Vygotsky's Influence

One significant intellectual source of the situated practice perspective is Vygotsky, especially his later writings (1978). Vygotsky emphasized the role of language in the acquisition of cognitive skills and knowledge. To him, language, or more generally, any external sign, is a "tool" by which children acquire higher-order psychological functions such as planning and reasoning (Wertsch, 1991). This is perhaps most apparent in his theory of internalization. Internalization refers to a process in which "an interpersonal process is transformed into an intrapersonal one" (Vygotsky, 1978, p. 57). Basically, an adult's instruction to a child while working on a task together will be remembered and later serve as a self-regulative guide for the child (Wertsch & Hickmann, 1987). Thus, Vygotsky (1978) argued,

> The specifically human capacity for language enables children to provide for auxiliary tools in the solution of difficult tasks, to overcome impulsive action, to plan a solution to a problem prior to its execution, and to master their own behavior. Signs and words serve children first and foremost as a means of social contact with other people. The cognitive and communicative functions of language then become the basis of a new and superior form of activity in children. (pp. 28-29)

And, therefore, "the use of signs leads humans to a specific structure of behavior that breaks away from biological development and creates new forms of a culturally-based psychological process" (p. 40).

In Vygotsky's view, language assumes an important role in the development of the child's cognitive and behavioral repertoire. Language enables the adult to construct a representation of the task or the event and permits this construction to be transmitted and stored for a later use by the child. Language is a medium of cultural acquisition and transmission.

Vygotsky's influence is visible in theoretical developments of many related areas. For example, in the contemporary theories of cognitive development and language acquisition, there is a growing consensus that language and cognition influence each other, rather than one predominantly determining the other (e.g., Gelman & Byrnes, 1991). This brief summary does not do justice to Vygotsky's fertile ideas; for much fuller explications of Vygotsky, see Ratner (1991), Valsiner (1988), and Wertsch (1991).

Linguistic Socialization Approach

Linguistic socialization consists of the dual process of acquiring linguistic *and* cultural competence. Schieffelin and Ochs called this "socialization through language and socialization to use language" (Ochs, 1986, p. 2). Central to this approach is the notion that language and culture are practiced together in the process of personal development and cultural transmission, bringing in changes to both communicative competence and other psychological aspects (i.e., attitude, evaluation, social representations, and emotions) of the newcomer to the culture (Habermann, 1996).

Ochs (1986) considers the cultural transmission process to take place through an acquisition of the uses of various verbal and discourse features, including morpho-syntactic construction, lexicon, speech-act style, conversational sequencing, turn taking, and so forth. For instance, conveying relative statuses of the interactants may be particularly important in some sociocultural situations, and this may be practiced using certain linguistic elements such as terms of address, tense/aspect, ellipsis, sequences, and prosody (e.g., Wierzbicka, 1991). The learning of the appropriate uses of these linguistic features will enable the speaker to participate in the ongoing social interaction. Thus, becoming a linguistically competent speaker entails becoming culturally competent at the same time.

Linguistic socialization does not involve an acquisition of correct speech acts only in mechanical ways. Miller and Hoogstra (1992) pointed out the importance of acquiring "a map to the social terrain" that speech acts provide across social context. In essence, speech covaries with social context; speech that takes place in a situation involving particular roles, statuses, and events differs in systematic ways from speech that takes place in a different situation involving different roles, statuses, or events. Hence, choices of linguistic options are connected to and indicate different categories of social situations. Linguistic socialization involves an acquisition of competence to appropriately define different social situations according to the cues provided by others' speech practices and to participate in the ongoing social activity by using those speech practices appropriately to the situation.

In sum, linguistic socialization makes possible a reproduction of the social order in the social situation. It prepares the learners for a reproduction of fundamental cultural beliefs about the way people are (Clancy, 1986) and for internalization of cultural knowledge or cultural models (D'Andrade, 1990) sustained by language use.

Other Allied Approaches

Whereas the linguistic socialization approach focuses on verbal practices, Lave and her colleagues (e.g., Lave & Wenger, 1994; Rogoff, 1990) approach the process of socialization from a more global perspective of situated practice. Lave contrasts two broad perspectives on learning. The traditional view conceptualizes learning as a change in abstract cognitive processes or conceptual structures separate from the context. In contrast, according to the situated practice view, learning occurs through participation in the practice associated with task performance and event activities. Transmitted are knowledge and skills, as well as values and beliefs, that are presupposed in the practice. Proof of learning is not in the understanding of the ideas in abstraction; learning is demonstrated in ongoing interaction. Through repeated participation as an "apprentice" in situated practice, an individual gradually becomes a full practitioner in the "community of practice."

A concrete example of this general approach is provided by Jordan (1989), who describes the situated learning of midwifery by a Maya girl in Yucatan as an apprenticeship that happens in daily life. Maya girls who eventually become midwives usually come from families of midwives. In the process of growing up, girls in such families absorb the essence of midwifery practice and specific knowledge about many procedures through exposures to numerous situations in which their mothers administer their practice. Furthermore, narrative stories of various cases are told to transmit their knowledge. Eventually, after numerous occasions of apprenticeship and verbal narration, when a girl has had a child herself, she might have her first opportunity to practice the task. Here, cultural skills and knowledge are acquired through participation in social activities in situ. Language plays a central role in this type of learning according to this perspective.

More recently, Tomasello, Kruger, and Ratner (1993) proposed a theory of cultural learning. They argued that cultural learning is possible because of humans' unique social cognitive abilities to take multiple perspectives on events and objects. At the most developed stage, achieved around 6 years of age, the child can understand other people not only in terms of their intention ("He is showing me this picture") and intersubjectivity ("He knows I don't know this picture"), but also in terms of the child's own reflective thoughts and beliefs ("I know teacher thought Jack didn't like the picture"). Tomasello et al. argued that these social cognitive capabilities are essential for children to learn behaviors and information through imitation, instruction, and collaborative problem solving. This theoretical view points to the crucial importance of language, cognitive system, and the copresence of the interactants in a situation as necessary conditions for the process of cultural learning to take place.

Despite the diversity in research focuses and programs, these perspectives share the view that culture and language have interrelated functions in the context of cultural learning and transmission. Instead of regarding culture as an enduring system of meanings, which in turn cause behaviors, culture is taken as the continuous flow of social activities, in which both verbal and nonverbal actions in particular social situations are learned by individuals to be reproduced and at times modified in other social situations. In these recurrent patterns of practices, both culture and language appear as abstract theoretical constructions.

INDIVIDUALISM-COLLECTIVISM AND LANGUAGE USE ACROSS CULTURES

How does the preceding discussion bear on the research in cross-cultural psychology? Our ongoing research program on culture and language use may serve as an example. We attempted to approach the topic of individualism and collectivism (Hofstede, 1980, 1991; Triandis, 1995b), one of the most prominent topics in cross-cultural psychology today, from the practice-oriented perspective. Two main objectives guided the research. First, we attempt to identify cultural practices that are widely different across cultures but to some extent similar within groups of cultures (i.e., individualist or collectivist cultures). Once such cultural practices are identified, some practices may be more or less related with one another and may reflect a coherent theme. Our second objective then is to describe and explain the linkage among the cultural practices.

As a preliminary point, it is important to emphasize that cultural practices should be identified in terms of both specific social *acts* that are performed in daily life (e.g., greeting, swearing, teaching, and explaining) and the *context* in which they take place (e.g., over the shop counter, in the schoolyard). The unit of analysis, then, becomes a meaningful action-in-context. To see the significance of this point, note that greeting, swearing, and so forth occur as social acts in virtually all cultures; however, these acts may occur primarily in some contexts in some cultures, whereas they may occur in other contexts in other cultures. When taken as action-in-context, these cultural practices may reveal significant cultural differences (for a related point, see Kroonenberg & Kashima, 1997).

To identify cultural practices in individualist and collectivist cultures, we observed conversations of Japanese and Australian monocultural dyads under comparable, controlled conditions (Kashima & Kashima, 1997). Participants, who were all female, participated with either a "friend" or a "new acquaintance" and were similar in age and social background. The language used was their native language. The task was to "reach a joint decision" on some opinion issues (e.g., support or reject euthanasia, like or dislike Hillary Clinton).

When the conversations were transcribed and analyzed, two aspects were identified whereby Japanese and Australians differed in manners in which they expressed themselves in relation to their conversational partner and the context of the task. We called these *self-practices*. The first class of self-practice had to do with *coproduction* of sentences, in which two participants jointly constructed a sentence, such as the following:

1. *A:*   *Sore ga juu-nen*   *ka dou-ka/*
   it   *S ten-years Q*   *whether-Q*
   'Whether it is 10 years or not'

2. *B:*   *wa/ wakaranai*   *desu kedo/*
   T   *understand-NEG*   *BE*   *though*
   'is not clear, though.'

Overall, the Japanese participants coproduced sentences more frequently than did the Australians. However, this overall cultural difference was qualified by the relationship between the participants. The Japanese friends coproduced more often than did the Japanese with a new acquaintance, whereas the Australian participants did not show a difference as a function of the type of conversation partner (see Table 14.1).

The second class of self-practice was the use of personal pronouns. In English, there is only one first-person and one second-person singular pronoun, that is, *I* and *you*. However, in Japanese, there are many possibilities, and typically, one first-person pronoun and one second-person pronoun are used as pairs, implying a fixed interpersonal relationship when they are used (e.g., *watashi* and *anata*, *ore* and *omae*). In addition, English does not license pronoun drop (or ellipsis), whereas Japanese does. Therefore, the following sentence is ungrammatical in English:

   *E1 (watashi-wa)
1. *A:*   *Sonna,* *atta*   *koto*   *mo*   *hanashita*   *koto*   *mo*   *nai* *kara/*
      like   *met*   *NOM*   *also*   *spoke*   *NOM*   *also* *BE* *because*
    'Because (I've) never met (her) nor spoken (to her)'

   *E1 (watashi)
2.   *uun,*   *wakara-nai*   *kedo/*
    uh   *understand-NEG*   *but*
    'uh, (I) wouldn't know, though.'

However, this sentence is permissible in Japanese.

TABLE 14.1 The Number of Phrases in Coproduction and Observed and Ellipted First- and Second-Person Pronouns for Australians and Japanese in Friend or New Acquaintance Dyads

	Japanese		Australian	
	Friend	*New Acquaintance*	*Friend*	*New Acquaintance*
Coproduction	25.9	1.2	2.1	3.4
Observed first-person pronoun	2.0	5.4	20.4	25.8
Ellipted[a] first-person pronoun	13.7	6.2	0	0
Observed second-person pronoun	0	0	2.8	2.3
Ellipted second-person pronoun	0.4	3.1	0	0

NOTE: Measured in per-100 pause-bounded phrasal units.

a. Ellipted refers to theoretically possible minus observed numbers of personal pronouns.

To begin, the Japanese explicitly uttered first-person pronouns much less frequently than did the Australians. Most striking, the Japanese participants uttered no second-person pronouns, whereas the Australians uttered *you* at least some of the time. The Japanese participants dropped first- and second-person pronouns, whereas we failed to identify any instance of pronoun drop among the Australians. Finally, relative to the Australian participants, the Japanese produced fewer sentences with either first- or second-person subjects even when explicit utterances and ellipted instances of first- and second-person pronouns were combined.

Clearly, there were cultural differences in both sentence coproduction and pronoun use. We suggest that they are related instances of microbehavior summarized as self-practices, that is, the ways in which people position themselves in the social context. We interpreted the link between these microbehaviors in terms of the contextualization of the self: The Japanese practice is to contextualize the self in the situation of the inter-personal discourse, whereas the Australian practice of the self is to differentiate the self and the partner. We explicate this interpretation below.

Coproduction of a sentence is an instance of a joint construction of the social reality. Its process involves a series of negotiations between the interlocutors; the responsibility for the end product, the conclusion of the sentence, is shared by the participants. Such a practice of sentence construction makes it difficult to attribute, retrospectively, the re-sponsibility of the decision, as the negotiation process is completely implicit, without a distinct proposition made, evaluated, rejected, or accepted by the separate and identifi-able individuals. Thus, the more frequent coproductions in the Japanese conversation result in diffused self-other differentiation and diffused responsibility.

The relative frequency in uttering first- and second-person pronouns, on the other hand, seems connected to the contextualization of the self and other. In the context of social interaction, the typical usage of first- and second-person singular pronouns is *deictic*, that is, indexically referencing features of the speech context (e.g., *you* as the addressee in front of the speaker, *I*). According to a view suggested by Cognitive

Grammar (Langacker, 1987-1991), grammatical structures are inherently symbolic, providing for the structuring and conventional symbolization of conceptual content (Langacker, 1987, pp. 1-2). Such deictic uses of first- and second-person singular pronouns indicate relative objectification of the self and other within the speaker's scope of conception. Stated simply, the sentence that has *I* (or *you*) explicitly as its subject maximally objectifies or maximizes the prominence of the self (or the other) within the conceptual scope, just as a figure against the background. In contrast, the absence of *I* (or *you*) from the surface of the sentence can be interpreted as a decrease in the prominence of the self (or the other). This suggests that for English speakers, including Australians, the self and the conversational partner are continuously highlighted as figures in their conceptual scope; for Japanese speakers, the less-differentiated self and other remain part of the background more of the time. In this way, the use of personal pronouns may carry and maintain the cultural practice of contextualizing the person.

So far, we have shown that cultural practices that are conducive to the contextualization of the person (sentence coproduction and pronoun drop) seem to occur more frequently in one collectivist culture (i.e., Japan) than in one individualist culture (i.e., Australia). The evidence is not sufficient to conclude that these cultural practices in fact contribute to the reproduction of the cultures that are characterized by the dimensions of individualism and collectivism. To seek further evidence to support this, we conducted correlational analyses of the relationship between pronoun drop and Hofstede's individualism dimension (Kashima & Kashima, 1998). Using Hofstede's (1980, 1991) data, we computed the individualism score for a culture and for a language (the average of the national scores of cultures that use the same language, e.g., English, Spanish). We then coded each language as either licensing pronoun drop or not. The tendency to drop first- and second-person pronouns was highly correlated with individualism in both the cross-cultural and cross-linguistic analyses, $r(70) = .75$ and $r(38) = .64$. A link between sentence co-construction and individualism-collectivism should also be explored in the future. If such a correlation is observed, linguistic practices may be seen as microbehaviors that contribute to the reproduction and transmission of the cultural syndrome of individualism and collectivism.

FUTURE DIRECTIONS
AND CONCLUDING REMARKS

Empirical research using the practice-oriented perspective has only begun to identify cultural practices and analyze them in relation to characteristics of cultures recognized in prior cross-cultural research. For instance, sociolinguists and anthropological linguists have provided us in the last two decades with various clues for future investigations of cultural practice. Ellipsis (and pronoun drop in particular) has attracted much interest in linguistics (e.g., Clancy, 1986; Hinds, 1982; Huang, 1984; Li & Thompson, 1976; Shibamoto, 1984) and language development (Berman, 1990; Bloom, 1990; Greenfield & Smith, 1976; O'Grady, Peters, & Masterson, 1989; Valian, 1990, 1991). A choice of personal pronouns (e.g., *tu* vs. *vous*, *watashi* vs. *ore*) in different languages has been analyzed in relation to power and solidarity (Brown & Gilman, 1960; Mülhausler & Harré, 1990). Careful analysis of pronoun choice in different social interactions seems promising for developing our understanding of cultural practice and transmission.

We expect that numerous linguistic forms and contents can be identified and analyzed in terms of their use and cultural practice. In particular, systematic inquiries into deixis may prove fruitful. Deixis is a phenomenon in which grammatical features are directly tied to the context of utterance. As pointed out earlier, first- and second-person pronouns take on specific referents only in the context of utterance. Other examples include the use of demonstratives, tense, and specific time and place adverbs such as *now* and *then*. From a practice-oriented viewpoint, deixis is particularly interesting as it is an epitome of the situated nature of language use. If there is anything to the general tenet of the practice-oriented approach to culture, deictic practice may contribute significantly to the reproduction of a culture.

For instance, Yoshida (1980) attempted to examine the universality and relativity of the unconscious cognition of space categorization by humans through the analysis of spatial demonstratives (e.g., *here* and *there* in English) in 479 languages. He identified four common types of language: (a) 2-type, consisting of "near" and "far"; (b) 3F-type, consisting of "near," "far," and "further"; (c) 3H-type, consisting of speaker's space, hearer's space, and the other space outside these spaces; and (d) 3M-type, consisting of "near," "middle," and "far." Denny (1986) also examined the number of spatial deictic adverbs and demonstratives across cultures and considered this to be related to psychological contextualization. Furthermore, he theorized that decontextualization may depend on two factors, societal complexity and the degree to which the environment is filled with human-made objects, both of which contribute to a decrease in need for spatial deictic concepts in everyday interactions. Both studies imply that spatial demonstratives may relate to the ways in which interlocutors position themselves and objects within the context. Further analysis of the use of demonstratives in ongoing interactions in different cultural contexts may be able to uncover the role played by such linguistic practices in cultural transmission.

Language is being rediscovered as an important agent for the stability and change of psychological processes in wide areas of research. If cross-cultural psychologists are serious about the challenge of explicating "how human behaviors are shaped and influenced by social and cultural forces" (Segall et al., 1990), we can ill afford to ignore the role of language and language use in cultural transmission and reproduction. Language should be placed as a central concern for cross-cultural psychology rather than set aside as a variable most perniciously confounded with culture.

NOTE

1. Curiously enough, most cross-cultural psychologists have been silent on the topic, with Au (1983, 1992) as a notable exception, perhaps partly reflecting cross-cultural psychology's relative neglect of language in the past.

PART V

APPLIED CROSS-CULTURAL PSYCHOLOGY

Applied cross-cultural psychology has recently attracted much attention because of the increasing realization of the significant role that culture plays in social life. One of the first areas to gain attention was cross-cultural training. Brislin and Bhawuk provide a general framework in which to analyze a variety of cross-cultural training methods, in particular the culture assimilator, which Triandis helped in developing. The chapter thoughtfully appraises training methods and points to future directions for research and development.

Another area of cross-cultural significance is health and health-related behaviors. Given the great variability in life expectancy and birthrate across nations, the current surge of interest in this area is understandable. Davidson, Ahn, Chandra, Diaz-Guerrero, Dubey, and Mehryar's chapter is a fine example of culturally sensitive research in the area of population control, and specifically on the use of male contraceptive methods. The chapter outlines an exploratory cross-cultural study, whose results can inform policymakers and also provide insight into the importance of culture in health-related behaviors.

Work is yet another significant applied area. Hui and Yee give an example of tight and sophisticated empirical research that is also culturally sensitive. In their chapter, they focus on job satisfaction, a central variable in industrial and organizational psychology, and how it may be shaped by personality variables such as locus of control. The authors' finding about cultural differences in the conception of chance in the Chinese culture implies that psychological constructs developed in primarily North American contexts can be used effectively if their use is informed by cultural meanings.

- What are the goals, problems, and challenges of cross-cultural training, according to Brislin and Bhawuk?
- On the basis of the results reported by Davidson et al., what is the importance of conducting a cultural analysis of health behavior in general and of family planning in particular?
- How can constructs developed in North America be used effectively to understand organizational behavior in non-Western cultures, based on the results reported by Hui and Yee? How should a culture-specific concept be used in this process?

15

CROSS-CULTURAL TRAINING

Research and Innovations

Richard W. Brislin
Dharm P. S. Bhawuk
University of Hawaii at Manoa

In the past three decades, the field of cross-cultural training has evolved from being strictly the domain of practitioners providing orientation programs to people going abroad to a rigorous theory-driven field of inquiry, and researchers and practitioners alike have come to accept that cross-cultural training is useful for preparing people who have to work in another culture (Landis & Bhagat, 1996). Globalization of employment makes cross-cultural training even more important now than it has been in the past. This chapter presents a brief review of the literature highlighting the innovations in the field and suggests future research directions.

Cross-cultural training refers to formal efforts to prepare people for more effective interpersonal relations and for job success when they interact extensively with individuals from cultures other than their own (Brislin & Yoshida, 1994). Features of these programs are that they are formal efforts (rather than the set of informal and unplanned behaviors that everyone undertakes when they live in another country), well planned, budgeted, and staffed by experts who are knowledgeable about the wide range of issues people face when they live in other cultures. Training often takes place in a special site away from people's everyday activities, so that they can devote as much time as possible to prepare themselves to meet the criterion of "successful person" when they live in another culture.

GOALS OF CROSS-CULTURAL TRAINING PROGRAMS

Bhawuk (1990) discussed the goals of cross-cultural training programs in terms of their *end goals* and *immediate goals*. End goals refer to distal goals (i.e., goals expected of trainees in their interaction with the hosts during their sojourn). For example, a nurse would be expected to work in a clinic or hospital and follow local procedures or a student would be expected to study in the new culture and meet the standards of the host university. The immediate goals refer to proximal goals (i.e., the expected behavioral change in the trainees that can be measured at the end of the training program).

A four-part criterion of success has proved helpful as a measure of distal goals for people about to live abroad and for trainers developing programs to assist them. The first goal is that people should be exposed to training materials and exercises that increase the enjoyment they experience when living abroad and the benefits that they accrue. Enjoyment refers to a sense of happiness and excitement such that people look forward to their lives, and especially to their work, in the other country. This enjoyment includes people's interactions with hosts. The second goal is that hosts enjoy the company of the sojourners, are pleased that they are living in their country, and are positive about the contributions the sojourners are making in the workplace.

The third goal is that people are given information that helps them achieve their task-related goals. Almost all long-term sojourners have task-related goals that involve their jobs and their workplaces; for example, international businesspeople want to establish joint ventures, diplomats want to develop treaties, technical advisers want to complete projects, and so on. The fourth goal is that, after a normal period of tension referred to as culture shock, sojourners should experience no more stress in their overseas jobs than they would in their own country. Or they should not suffer from psychosomatic symptoms like headaches, nausea, sleeplessness, decreased sex drive, heart palpitations, lower back pain, and so on during their sojourn or immediately after their return from the stay abroad.

Bhawuk (1990) suggested that the proximal or immediate goals of the cross-cultural training programs should be to enable trainees to (a) learn how to learn, (b) make isomorphic attributions, and (c) handle disconfirmed expectations.

Learning how to learn refers to the trainees' ability to transfer skills from the learning situation to other situations in real life (Brislin & Pederson, 1976; Hughes-Wiener, 1986). Hughes-Wiener (1986) proposed a cyclical model of learning how to learn for cross-cultural interactions that involves four processes: concrete experience, reflection (over the experience), conceptualization (of abstract concepts), and active experimentation. One could start anywhere in the cycle, but it is easier to visualize how the cycle works if one starts with a concrete experience. For example, a sojourner experiences a situation in which a host is asking personal questions, which is a likely situation facing Westerners living in South Asia. The sojourner would reflect on this experience because it is unusual from his or her own cultural perspective, and so this situation provides the background to think about it.

Reflection over the concrete experience allows the sojourner to grasp this new knowledge (i.e., the host's inclination to ask personal questions). At this point, the sojourner needs some help to understand the reasons for the host's behavior. One explanation is that, in the host culture, the notion of privacy is different because people live in a close-knit family network; there is no such thing as private information about how much one earns, what one does for a living, and so forth. Learning this rationale helps the sojourner understand why the hosts behave in this way on the issue of privacy. The sojourner can now experiment in another situation to check his or her generalization about the notion of privacy in the host culture by asking a host national some personal questions. This would be a behavior that he or she would use to confirm the theoretical understanding of the process. Once the process is confirmed, the sojourner has a new conceptualization of privacy that applies to the host culture, and the sojourner should be able to interact with host nationals more naturally by talking about things that he or she may not have otherwise discussed. Thus, starting with a concrete experience, through reflection, conceptualization, and active experimentation, a sojourner goes on generating new knowledge and understanding about the host culture. Trainees, therefore, should be encouraged to acquire the "learning how to learn" skills in cross-cultural training programs.

Isomorphic attribution refers to a sojourner's making approximately the same judgment about the cause of a behavior as do people in the host culture (Triandis, 1975). When people make isomorphic attributions, they do not impose their own cultural perspective in deciding about the cause of a particular behavior. Instead, they use the perspective of the host culture in analyzing the behavior. In the situation discussed above, if the sojourner concludes that the host is "nosy," the sojourner is using his or her own cultural perspective about what are appropriate things to ask of others, but if the sojourner concludes that the host is being friendly, then he or she is making a correct attribution about the host's behavior. Because people's ability to make isomorphic attributions can be measured by administering critical incidents at the end of a training program, this is a measurable proximal goal.

Disconfirmed expectancies refer to situations in which sojourners expect a certain behavior from the host nationals but experience a different one. Simply stated, one's expectations are not met or confirmed. Cross-cultural training programs should prepare trainees to not come to a hurried conclusion about the cause of hosts' behavior when the hosts do not meet their expectation, because such a conclusion can lead to a negative stereotype. A negative stereotype may prejudice future interactions with hosts, resulting in interpersonal problems. Disconfirmed expectancies underlie many situations in which differences in work ethics, roles, learning styles, use of time and space, and so forth occur (Bhawuk, 1990; Brislin, Cushner, Cherrie, & Yong, 1986). Preparing sojourners for this phenomenon can be measured using cross-cultural interaction tasks.

The relationship between disconfirmed expectation and isomorphic attribution needs to be explored in future research. In most situations, it is likely that a sojourner would first encounter a behavior, often very well-meaning on the part of the host, that is unexpected and then make an incorrect attribution. For example, a Western man may shake the hands of an Eastern woman to warmly greet her, and the Eastern woman may make an incorrect attribution about this behavior—for example, that the man is rude or that he is making sexual advances. However, it is also possible that people may make incorrect attributions in situations in which the behavior is not at all unexpected, thus making future interactions problematic. For example, a customs officer may request a sojourner to open his or her suitcase, a very common occurrence at the airport, but the visitor may attribute this behavior to mistrust on the part of the officer for no apparent reason, simply because this person may never have experienced such a behavior in the past. The visitor may say something impolite, the customs officer may do something unkind, and the situation may flare up into a nasty incident. Thus, the causal link between disconfirmed expectancies and nonisomorphic attribution is not quite clear, and research is needed for a better understanding of the communication processes.

CROSS-CULTURAL TRAINING PROGRAMS: METHODS

Good cross-cultural training programs help people make isomorphic attributions, manage disconfirmed expectancies, learn "how to learn," and find success in other cultures according to the above four-part criterion. There are a number of ways to present information to trainees, and Triandis (1977b) presented a typology that has been further elaborated and refined by others (Bhawuk, 1990; Brislin, 1989; Gudykunst & Hammer, 1983). There are five basic approaches that trainers take.

Cognitive Training

In this type of training, people are given information about what to expect when living in another culture. This information can deal with diverse topics such as expectations in the workplace, supervisor-subordinate relations, schools, climate, cuisine, interpersonal relations, hobbies that can be pursued, support groups that are available, and so forth. Methods for presenting information can include lectures, group discussions, films, audiotapes, assigned readings, and any other educational media that people find useful in conveying information. The advantage of this approach is that a great deal of information can be presented economically. However, two disadvantages are that the information given can present a strain on the sojourners' memories and the pieces of facts presented do not lend themselves to be integrated in a meaningful and memorizable whole.

Self-Insight Training

In this approach, people learn about their own culture and their possible reactions to other cultures. In many cases, people have not had the opportunity to examine their own culture and to examine why they behave as they do given the guidance of their culture. Why do Americans feel that they have to speak out and make their opinions known to others, sometimes in a very forceful way? Why do Japanese feel that it is better to downplay one's own opinions, to not necessarily present them in public, and to behave according to their perceptions of their group's preferences? The advantage of self-insight training is that people from one particular country can go through the same training no matter what their country of assignment. This has important economic implications if a company is sending one or two employees to each of twenty different countries. A disadvantage is that the relation between gaining self-insight into one's own culture and the adjustments needed to find success in a specific culture is not necessarily a direct one. People can gain cultural self-insight but still be ignorant about the adjustments necessary for living in the other culture. A description of some of the popular models (e.g., Kraemer, 1973; Stewart, 1966), is provided by Brislin (1989).

Behavioral Training

In many ways, behavioral training can be considered an extension of cognitive training, discussed previously. In behavioral training, trainers help sojourners acquire overt and specific behaviors that are relevant in the other culture and replace behaviors that are not acceptable in the other culture. Behavior-modification training is necessary for habitual behaviors of which people are not usually aware, especially behaviors that are acceptable, even desirable, in one's own culture but may be offensive in another culture. For example, in Latin American cultures, people give an *abrazo*, or an embrace, to friends that is not an acceptable behavior in the United States; in Greece, when people show an open palm, called *moutza*, they are showing utmost contempt and not simply waving or saying hello (Triandis, 1994a). A *moutza* needs to be avoided, whereas an *abrazo* needs to be acquired. There are many examples of such behaviors, and the only way to learn them is through behavior modeling, by observing a model enact the behavior and then practicing the behavior many times.

Because many appropriate behaviors are specific to a certain culture, trainers must be quite knowledgeable about a number of countries other than their own. Trainees must be willing to consider modifying some behaviors that have become habitual with them, an admittedly difficult task because many people are unwilling to change behaviors. For example, sojourners may have the cognition that people do not bring up unfamiliar proposals in public meetings within the workplace, which is a common norm in some cultures. But they may not be able to keep silent at meetings or work one-on-one with other people prior to a public meeting to familiarize others with a proposal. The advantage of this method is that sojourners have the opportunity to practice actual behaviors that are likely to assist them in a number of social settings. The disadvantage of this method is that it can be costly because training materials concerned with different behaviors have to be prepared for each culture to which sojourners will be traveling. Despite its theoretical rigor and practical significance, this method has not been used much in cross-cultural training programs because it is expensive and requires a trainer to constantly work on one behavior at a time.

Experiential Training

Just as behavioral training can be viewed as an extension of cognitive training, experiential training can be viewed as an extension of concerns with multiple appropriate behaviors. In one type of experiential training, sojourners participate in simulations of another culture that are created by the training staff. For example, people use the host language, eat host food, interact with superiors and subordinates in ways typical of the target culture, seek out entertainment in the same ways as hosts, fulfill various bodily needs in culturally appropriate ways, and so forth (Trifonovitch, 1973). Training takes place at a site where a simulated version of the culture could be created. For example, Americans being trained to live in the Pacific Island societies worked in rural areas of Oahu outside the big city of Honolulu (Trifonovitch, 1973). The advantage of this approach is that people can obtain a realistic preview of their upcoming lives in the other culture. Some decide that "it is not for them," and they return home during training rather than at a later and more face-losing point during their actual assignment. The disadvantages are that it is expensive and it puts great stresses on the staff. Trainees sometimes begin their culture-shock reactions during the training and vent their frustrations on staff members. Consequently, staff members become burned out and leave the training profession.

Another type of experiential exercise is the simulation game in which trainees interact with other people following a set of guidelines provided by the trainer. Usually, trainees are divided into two groups, and each represents an imaginary culture with some simple rules. Ideally, the simulation should be able to produce an "Aha!" effect, the interaction should involve trainees emotionally, and cognition should follow affect. However, affect is usually low because of the artificial nature of the exercise; though the debriefing is useful, it seems that only some very simple conclusions like "cultures are different" and "intercultural interactions are puzzling" can be drawn from the exercises and often even the "Aha!" effect is missing (Bhawuk, 1995). It is useful to start a training program with a simulation, but its usefulness by itself is suspect in the absence of research evidence.

Attribution Training

Part of human nature is to think about and make conclusions about why people behave as they do. For example, if a man raises his voice, is he angry or simply excited about what he has to say? If a woman walking in the hall turns and goes the other way when a colleague enters the hall, is she snubbing the colleague, or did she simply remember that she was walking in the wrong direction? Conclusions about the causes of people's behaviors are called "attributions."

The purpose of attribution training is to encourage sojourners to make isomorphic attributions (Triandis, 1975), or come to the same conclusions about behaviors as do hosts. In many cases, it is not behaviors that occur among members of different cultural groups but the attributions that people make that cause misunderstandings. The training method that uses this approach is called culture assimilator.

A review of the cross-cultural training literature indicates that culture assimilators are the most researched and accepted method of cross-cultural training (Albert, 1983; Brislin & Yoshida, 1994; Landis & Bhagat, 1996; Triandis, 1994a), and in a number of studies, the effectiveness of this method has been established (Bhawuk, 1998; Fiedler, Mitchell, &

Triandis, 1971; Gudykunst, Hammer, & Wiseman, 1977; Harrison, 1992; Weldon, Carlston, Rissman, Slobodin, & Triandis, 1975).

The general acceptance of culture assimilators as training tools is reflected in the development of a number of culture-specific assimilators (Albert, 1983; Triandis, 1995a), a culture-general assimilator (Brislin et al., 1986; Cushner & Brislin, 1996), and a culture-theory-based assimilator using the concepts of individualism and collectivism (Bhawuk, 1995, 1996, 1998). Culture-specific assimilators are used to prepare people from one culture (say, the United States) to work in another culture (say, Venezuela). The culture-general assimilator (Brislin et al., 1986) is used to sensitize people to cross-cultural differences regardless of the roles they will play (e.g., businessperson, foreign student, diplomat) and the country they will live in. The culture-theory-based assimilator (Bhawuk, 1995) is designed to prepare people from a large geographic region (say, Western Europe or the United States and Canada) to work in a number of countries (say, Asia, Latin America, and Eastern Europe), in either direction (e.g., the Canadians going to Japan or the Japanese traveling to Canada).

The early culture assimilators were developed with a pair of cultures in mind, usually to prepare Americans to live in another culture, such as Thailand, Iran, Honduras, and so forth (Triandis, 1995a). These assimilators consisted of critical incidents that captured interesting, puzzling, or humorous cultural differences between the pairs of cultures (Fiedler et al., 1971). A content analysis of two recently developed culture-specific assimilators for Japan (Ito & Triandis, 1989) and Venezuela (Tolbert, 1990) supported the idea that, though culture-specific assimilators provide social context, they do not offer a cognitive framework from which one can deduce new appropriate behaviors (Bhawuk, 1995, 1996).

Triandis (1984) proposed a theoretical framework, consisting of 21 dimensions of cultural differences in social behavior, for the development of culture assimilators. He presented evidence that, by using the framework, researchers could develop culture assimilators in a shorter time. He argued that this framework could thus be used to develop culture assimilators more efficiently because, compared with the traditional method, an assimilator could be developed in about one third of the time.

Brislin et al. (1986) developed a culture-general assimilator following a similar framework, except that they used 18 themes or dimensions. The culture-general assimilator (Cushner & Brislin, 1996) uses the same format as the culture-specific assimilators—that is, critical incidents, alternatives, and explanations for the alternatives—and consists of 110 critical incidents that cover themes such as anxiety and related emotional states, prejudice and ethnocentrism, time and space, and so forth. These themes have been identified in the literature as important for the sojourners to be sensitive to. The inclusion of theoretical concepts is a definite strength of this assimilator, and there is some evidence of its effectiveness (Cushner, 1989).

Bhawuk (1995, 1996) argued that the use of 18 categories could be viewed as a weakness of this material. It can be argued that it is difficult for anybody to remember 18 disparate categories because most people's memory span breaks down somewhere around 7 or 8 categories (Anderson, 1990). One theoretical explanation offered for this limitation on human working memory is that the material must be on one's *articulatory loop*, that is, one has to be able to rehearse the material to maintain it in the working memory (Baddeley, 1986). Another related weakness of the material is that the 18 categories do not lend themselves to be integrated in an overarching theory of cross-cultural adjustment. These limitations hold for the framework proposed by Triandis (1984) as well. Therefore, it seems reasonable to develop materials that are theoretically meaningful, use fewer themes than that used by Brislin and colleagues (or proposed by Triandis, 1984), and provide an overarching theory to prepare for cross-cultural adjustment (Bhawuk, 1995).

To develop a theory-based assimilator, a parsimonious culture theory is needed that can meaningfully explain some aspect of cultural differences. Many culture theories have been discussed in the literature. Hofstede (1980) presented four constructs—power distance, masculinity, uncertainty avoidance, and individualism—that could be used to categorize cultures. Triandis and colleagues (Triandis, 1995b; Triandis & Bhawuk, 1997) have developed a theory of individualism and collectivism that can be used at both the cultural and the individual or psychological level. Fiske (1992) has identified four universal patterns of social behavior—communal sharing, equality matching, market pricing, and authority ranking—that can be used to explain similarities and differences in cultures. Schwartz (1992) presented a theory of the universal structure of value that can be used to cluster cultures into different groups and explain their similarities and differences. Triandis (1995b) presented a book-length discussion of these theories and their relationships with individualism and collectivism.

The value of the constructs of individualism and collectivism in cross-cultural training can be estimated by their effectiveness in predicting daily social behaviors across cultures (Wheeler, Reis, & Bond, 1989) and in explaining such phenomena as cultural distance, cultural influences on the self, and perception of behavior toward in-groups and out-groups (Triandis, McCusker, & Hui, 1990). Furthermore, Triandis, Brislin, and Hui (1986) proposed a practical way of using this theory in briefing people from either type of culture when they visit the other type of culture.

According to Triandis (1995b), individualism and collectivism have four universal defining attributes: (a) independent versus interdependent definitions of the self, (b) goals independent from in-groups versus goals compatible with in-groups, (c) emphasis on attitude versus norms, and (d) emphasis on rationality versus relatedness. According to Triandis, individualists have an independent self; their goals are chosen to meet their personal needs, even when they are not compatible with in-group goals; their behavior is consistent with their personal attitudes, beliefs, and values; and they base their social relationships on a careful computation of the costs and benefits of these relationships. By contrast, collectivists have an interdependent self; their goals are compatible with those of their in-group; their behavior is norm driven (e.g., they conform to social pressure and are dutiful); and they give priority to relationships even when they are costly.

Triandis (1995b) also proposed that individualism and collectivism are of two types, vertical and horizontal, depending on whether people view their selves as "same as" or "different from" others. In vertical collectivism and vertical individualism, people view their selves as different from the selves of others; India and China provide examples of vertical collectivism, whereas the United States and France exemplify vertical individualism. In horizontal collectivism and horizontal individualism, people view their selves as the same as those of others; the Israeli kibbutz and Eskimo cultures provide examples of horizontal collectivism, whereas Sweden and Australia approach horizontal individualism.

Considering the depth of research done on individualism and collectivism and that they provide a parsimonious conceptualization to explain and predict cross-cultural interaction, Bhawuk (1995) used this theory for developing the Individualism and Collectivism Assimilator. This assimilator consists of 51 critical incidents that are based on the four defining attributes of and the vertical and horizontal typology of individualism and collectivism.

The development of a theory-based assimilator provides the first step toward the inclusion of culture theories in cross-cultural training programs and, for that reason, can be considered a significant milestone in the field of cross-cultural training. According to Bhawuk (1995), a theory-based assimilator provides a threefold advantage. First, the usual structure of critical incidents is retained; second, theory can be used for explanation; and third, a manageable number of concepts can be used for explanation so that the problem of overloading the trainee's working memory is avoided.

SOME INNOVATIONS

Usefulness of More Than One Correct Answer

Brislin et al. (1986) allowed more than one correct answer among the four or five alternatives given for each of the incidents in their culture-general assimilator. This allows users to develop a more complex cognitive framework about cultural differences. It could also be argued that when participants read critical incidents that have more than one correct choice, they do not develop a strong stereotype about the target culture, which in turn allows them to be more adaptable and flexible in their view of the people of the host culture.

Usefulness of the Percentage of People Selecting the Options

In the explanation section of the Japanese culture assimilator, information regarding the proportion of the validation sample that agreed with each of the four responses was provided (Ito & Triandis, 1989). Providing such information helps the participants to see the people in the target culture as more heterogeneous. Thus, they get a more realistic picture about the target culture. This has a somewhat similar effect as having more than one correct response among the four alternatives given for each of the incidents in that participants do not build a rigid stereotype about the people of the host culture.

Assimilators on Computer

Landis has transferred a number of existing culture assimilators for use on personal computers (Cushner & Landis, 1996). This provides a medium that is convenient to many people and has also opened a new area for future growth. Effort is under way to develop culture assimilators using multimedia (Lim, Bhawuk, & Au, 1996).

SOME ISSUES

Content of Cross-Cultural Training

It could be argued that one of the goals of cross-cultural training is to make trainees more interculturally sensitive (Bhawuk, 1996). Bhawuk and Brislin (1992) presented a conceptualization of intercultural sensitivity that deals with awareness of cultural differences, knowledge of culturally appropriate behaviors, intention and ability to modify behaviors to suit the other culture, and the emotional muscle necessary to deal with the cognitive dissonance associated with behaving in a way that is different from one's own culture. Based on this conceptualization of intercultural sensitivity, training content should be based on four concepts: awareness, knowledge, actual behaviors, and emotional confrontations.

People about to have extensive intercultural interactions need to be aware that there are cultural differences to which they must adjust. Many do know this basic point; however, most of us need to be reminded that our interpersonal behaviors are programmed by our own culture and are to some degree habitual. Thus, it is easy to get carried away by the similarities of context and stimuli in another culture and ignore cultural differences. Training programs should emphasize that the feeling of bewilderment or annoyance while living abroad should be looked on as a symptom of cultural differences.

People need to learn new information, and they must realize that knowledge is what a culture defines as knowledge. There are few absolute facts outside the realms of science and engineering. "Facts" in many areas are what a culture says are facts. It is a "fact" in Japan that bosses often introduce unmarried employees to potential mates. It is a fact in the United States that this can be considered sexual harassment and the boss can be taken to court. In the example presented previously about introducing unfamiliar ideas at a meeting, the people involved had differing opinions concerning what the facts were. Is it a fact that ideas should be introduced in open meetings, or is it a fact that ideas should be introduced in one-on-one meetings to minimize embarrassment if someone is not prepared to speak out in an open meeting?

Sojourners need to understand that they must not only become more flexible in their approaches to knowledge but also modify behaviors to be more effective in other cultures. In Japan, for example, Americans must think through whether they will participate in the after-hours socializing that will be expected of them. They must think through behaviors such as making contributions in a soft manner that brings credit to their group, not to themselves. They must downplay their own preferences in favor of group consensus. There is a difference, of course, between knowledge and behaviors. Americans might know that there are fewer public displays of affection in Japan, but they must also think through whether they will give their boyfriends or girlfriends a big kiss in a public setting. Japanese might know that they should speak up in meetings in the United States and communicate their individual opinions, but this will not be easy if they have been socialized to contribute quietly and unassumingly to a group effort. Training programs often provide people with the opportunity to identify and to practice unfamiliar behaviors that will be useful in their adjustments.

When people are confronted with situations in which others behave in a manner that is inappropriate from the perspective of their own culture (e.g., the earlier example of a Japanese supervisor playing the role of matchmaker for Japanese employees will make an American observer uncomfortable) or in which they have to behave differently themselves (e.g., the American who feels limited because he or she cannot give a new idea in a meeting in Japan), they become emotionally upset. Most cross-cultural differences have the power to arouse negative emotional feelings, and training programs should help trainees prepare not only for challenges to their cognitive processes or thinking but also in developing emotional muscle to deal with expected and unexpected behavioral differences.

Culture-Specific Versus Culture-General Training

Brislin and Pederson (1976) described the debate between educators as to which formats should be taught. One view supported culture-general training, arguing that individuals learn to see the differing value structures that may be found in different cultures when they receive insight into their own culture. The main idea is that self-awareness of one's own culture may result in greater understanding of other cultures' values. The counterargument is for culture-specific training, which stresses that cross-cultural training should not only fulfill the trainees' needs for fact and language but also influence their affective behavior so that effective communication can take place in the target culture.

Triandis (1994a) identified many topics that are relevant to the effectiveness of cross-cultural interactions but are not specific to any culture. Some are general points such as people are ethnocentric in every culture, attributions made by hosts are usually different, people need to see a positive aspect in every situation, one needs to find new recreational activities in the host culture, sojourners need to avoid overdependence on the expatriate community, and so forth, but others are more specific skills that are necessary to be effective in another culture. The specific skills include learning to differentiate what is personal from what is national (e.g., an American may have to take the brunt of criticism for his or her national policy), learning to take the lead in starting a conversation with hosts to learn more about their culture, learning to live with ambiguity and to suspend judgment, and learning to transcend differences in attitudes and values. Because these are skills that are needed to be effective in many cross-cultural situations, they could be called metaskills of cross-cultural interactions. Because such metaskills exist, it can be argued that extreme positions on the use of culture-specific versus culture-general training may be irrelevant.

Rhuly (1976) pointed out that there are problems when using either the culture-general or the culture-specific training and excluding the other. Culture-general training requires more time because it involves increasing awareness of the trainees. Also, the trainee has no idea what to expect in the new culture (i.e., which behaviors are rewarded and which behaviors warrant punishment in that culture). As for culture-specific training, the generalizations given during training can leave the trainee with preconceived notions that may not be accurate. The list of dos and don'ts is easy to forget when the trainee does not understand the other culture. Bhawuk (1995, 1998) directly compared culture-specific and culture-general training material to see which is more effective, but the findings were not clearly in favor of either; on attribution-making skills, the culture-general assimilator did better than the culture-specific one, whereas on the category width scale, the culture-specific assimilator did better.

FUTURE DIRECTIONS

The theory of individualism and collectivism has been used in both the culture-general (Cushner & Brislin, 1996) and the individualism and collectivism assimilators (Bhawuk, 1995). Future research should also focus on using other such overarching theories to develop culture assimilators. Hofstede's (1980) four dimensions of culture, Schwartz's (1992) universal structure of values, and Fiske's (1992) types of socialities would be candidates for such ventures. A comparative evaluation of assimilators based on these different theories may even allow us to examine the effectiveness of each of these theories in cross-cultural training. In other words, it may be possible to test the applicability of culture theories in cross-cultural training.

In the future, culture-specific assimilators could also use individualism and collectivism and other theories to explain cultural differences. This may bridge the gap between culture-specific, culture-general, and theory-based assimilators and provide some new insights into how to develop more effective assimilators. Other types of training programs should also consider using culture theories and evaluate their applicability.

16

CULTURE AND FAMILY PLANNING

The Acceptability of Male Contraception

Andrew R. Davidson
Columbia University

Kye Choon Ahn
Yonsei University

Subhas Chandra
Charles Sturt University

Rogelio Diaz-Guerrero
National University of Mexico

D. C. Dubey
National Institute of Health and Family Welfare, India

Amir Mehryar
Institute for Research in Planning and Development, Iran

Men and women are integral partners in the act of conception. Women, however, have been the preponderant focus of birth control efforts in the 20th century. With the exception of vasectomy, the major methods of contraception available to men today (condom, withdrawal, periodic abstinence) do not differ from those available more than 400 years ago.

AUTHORS' NOTE: This research was supported by the World Health Organization Special Program of Research Development and Research Training in Human Reproduction. The opinions expressed are those of the authors and do not necessarily reflect those of the World Health Organization.

217

Two sets of reasons have been suggested for the greater emphasis on the development of female as opposed to male contraceptive methods. The first is biomedical. There has been a better understanding of female than of male reproductive physiology. Also, for males, in comparison with females, there are fewer possible sites where controlled interference in the chain of reproductive events can occur. Segal (1972) lists only four targets for new contraceptives for men: spermatogenesis, sperm maturation, sperm transport, and the chemical composition of the seminal fluid.

A second and equally important reason for the relative disinterest in new male contraceptives is the widely held belief that men would not be willing to use them. A number of authors (e.g., Attico, 1978; Diller & Hembree, 1977) have argued that the funds available for male contraceptive research lag substantially behind those for female methods because of the perception that a demand does not exist for new male methods. Prevalent stereotypes include the notion that men view family planning as a woman's problem and are neither concerned nor interested. Moreover, the role of machismo is frequently emphasized in discussions of male fertility behavior. But, in fact, the actual nature and prevalence of men's attitudes regarding fertility regulation are largely unknown.

The extent of existing stereotypes about men's disinterest in fertility regulation is surprising. The fact that in subsistence economies children are consumers as well as producers provides a prima facie case for the interest of the father in controlling fertility (Freedman, 1963). Also, some survey data available as early as 1960 suggested that the father's disinterest may have been exaggerated. Studies in India, Taiwan, Puerto Rico, and elsewhere (Freedman, 1963; Stycos, 1962) indicated roughly similar attitudes on the part of husbands and wives on many issues about reproduction.

In further contradiction of prevalent stereotypes, men have played an important role in the family planning process, despite the absence of modern contraceptives for men. The demographic transition that occurred in Europe during the last century was achieved in large part through the use of methods requiring the cooperation of men (withdrawal, abstinence, and condom) and abortion in the event of failure (Segal, 1972; Wrigley, 1969). The condom and withdrawal remain major methods in Europe, and the condom is the most common nonpermanent method of fertility regulation in Japan. Current estimates from the United Nations (1996) indicate that, worldwide, approximately 25% of the couples who use contraception rely on vasectomy, condom, or withdrawal. The widespread use of these male methods indicates the willingness of substantial numbers of men from a variety of cultures to share the responsibility for fertility control.

Only a handful of studies have attempted to directly assess whether men would be willing to use a new male contraceptive (Balswick, 1972; Gough, 1979; Keith, Keith, Bussell, & Wells, 1974; Spillane & Ryser, 1975; Wetherbee, Smith, & Benfield, 1975). Each of these studies was conducted in the United States, and each included questions about men's willingness to use a male birth control pill. The finding of greatest interest was the high percentage of men who indicated that they would be willing to use a new male contraceptive. Level of willingness ranged from 41% to 74%. Consistent with their willingness to use male methods, men overwhelmingly indicated that both sexual partners have responsibility for contraception. Finally, the background variable that was most consistently and positively related to willingness to use a male pill was level of education.

These studies demonstrate that a substantial proportion of American men indicate a willingness to try a new male contraceptive. However, key questions remain unanswered. First, to what extent do these results generalize to men from other countries, particularly developing countries? Second, what attributes of new male contraceptives would have the greatest likelihood of enhancing their acceptability?

To address these questions, we conducted comparable surveys of men in five developing countries assessing the acceptability of new male fertility-regulating methods. The fielding effort was conducted in the late 1970s and, with the exception of technical reports, the data have not been published. In addition, no subsequent cross-national survey of men's attitudes on this topic has been conducted. The present study focused on the acceptability of two existing male methods (condom, vasectomy) and two potential methods (male daily pill, male monthly injection). The potential methods were recommended for study by the World Health Organization, Male Methods of Fertility Regulation Task Force, because they represented the two most probable combinations of the key attributes—route of administration and duration of action—that would be found in a new male method.

METHODS

Sample

Countries

The study was conducted in India, Iran, Fiji, Mexico, and the Republic of Korea. (In Fiji, the study focused on the roughly 50% of the population of Indian descent, to increase the comparability of the Fijian and Indian data.) These countries were selected to achieve broad geographic distribution, reflecting differences among countries in religion and other cultural variables. There was also important variation on demographic and social indexes. Iran and Mexico had the highest birthrates, Fiji and Korea the lowest. Korea and Fiji had very high rates of literacy; Mexico ranked third, followed by India and Iran.

At the time of the survey, India had a population policy that greatly increased financial incentives to men and women with two or more children who agreed to be sterilized. The policy included threats of compulsory sterilization. Although compulsory sterilization never became national law, some states and localities put into effect a variety of strong disincentives to having more than two children. After the new policy was announced, newspapers published reports of resistance to forcible sterilization, in some instances resulting in bloodshed and fatalities as the police attempted to subdue rioting (Landman, 1977). As discussed below, the political situation probably had an effect on the Indian subjects' responses.

Sampling Regions

To investigate the effects of major-life-experience variables (e.g., urban-rural residence, education, and the constellation of characteristics associated with socioeconomic status [SES]) on the acceptability of male contraceptives, we studied contrasting groups in each country (cf. Arnold et al., 1975). Specifically, in each country, we selected samples of men from rural villages ($n = 150$) and urban-low-SES ($n = 100$) and urban-middle-SES ($n = 100$) regions.

Within each country, rural samples were selected from at least three villages. The villages were selected from one administrative region, as follows: Fiji, Southern Zone; India, Utter Pradesh; Iran, Fars Province; Mexico, State of Mexico; and the Republic of Korea, Kyunggi Province. The urban samples were selected from the following cities: Suva, Fiji; Delhi (including New Delhi); Shiraz, Iran; Mexico City; and Seoul. The cities were either in or adjacent to the administrative region from which the rural samples were drawn. Within each city, four neighborhoods, two of middle SES and two of low SES, were chosen as the sources of the urban sample.

Respondents

The population of interest was nonsterilized married men under 45 years of age. Men were randomly selected from rural and urban areas. We will refer to these men as potential users of new male contraceptives.

Characteristics of Samples

The contrasting groups sampling strategy did result in substantial variation among groups in terms of social and demographic characteristics. Within each country, the samples differed in the expected manner on measures of education, occupational status, and literacy. On these indexes, the rural group was lowest, the urban lower class was intermediate, and the urban middle class was highest.

The observed relative rankings of socioeconomic status parallel the national differences in literacy previously mentioned. The differences among nations were most pronounced when we focus on the rural groups. The rural men in Iran had an average of 1.5 years of schooling, compared with 4.7 years in Mexico, 6.8 years in India, 6.9 years in Fiji, and 7.6 years in Korea. For the urban-middle-class samples, the men in Mexico, Korea, and India were typically secondary school graduates, some of whom had attended college. In Fiji, the middle-class men had an average of slightly less than 12 years of schooling, whereas in Iran, this sample had 9.5 years of education.

The mean age of the respondents ranged from 31 (Mexico) to 35.8 (Korea). Within the countries, there was not a consistent rank ordering in terms of the average age of the rural and urban groups. Focusing on the country averages of number of living children, the means were as follows: Iran, 3.31; Mexico, 2.83; Korea, 2.82; Fiji, 2.49; and India, 2.29. The means for India and Mexico were slightly lower than expected. In India, the government's population-control policies might have led to an underreporting of the number of children. In Mexico, the lower than expected number is probably attributable to the relatively young age of the sample. Within each country, the average number of living children tended to be lowest in the middle-class sample and highest in the rural sample.

Oral contraceptives were the most frequently used methods of contraception in Fiji, Iran, and Mexico. In Korea, oral contraceptives were the second most widely used method, closely trailing the intrauterine device (IUD). In India, the condom was the most frequently used method. Condoms were also used by a substantial proportion of couples in Fiji and among the urban samples in Iran and Korea. The condom was notably unpopular in Mexico. A second male-directed method, withdrawal, was used by a small but significant proportion of the respondents in Fiji, Iran, and Korea.

Survey of Knowledgeable Sources

To gain an additional perspective on the acceptability of existing and potential male contraceptives, we also conducted interviews with 40 knowledgeable sources in each country. Knowledgeable sources consisted of physicians, family-planning field-workers, and social scientists, who by virtue of their profession and experience were in a position to judge how potential users would feel about new male contraceptives. Although this chapter focuses on the attitudes of potential users of male methods, we will briefly compare and contrast their attitudes with those of the knowledgeable sources.

Measures

The interview of potential users required between 60 and 90 minutes and had a precoded format. Men were interviewed in their residences by trained male interviewers. The questionnaire for knowledgeable sources covered the same content areas but was briefer. The procedures used for measuring acceptability have been developed and refined through previous research, much of which has been cross-cultural (Ajzen & Fishbein, 1980; Davidson & Jaccard, 1975, 1979; Davidson, Jaccard, Triandis, Morales, & Diaz-Guerrero, 1976; Davidson & Morrison, 1983; Davidson & Thomson, 1980; Marshall, 1973, 1977; Osgood, May, & Miron, 1975; Triandis, 1964, 1971; Triandis, Vassiliou, Vassiliou, Tanaka, & Shanmugam, 1972).

A special challenge for this project was the need to assess men's attitudes about contraceptive products that did not yet exist. In addition, many of the men were unfamiliar with one of the existing methods—vasectomy. As a result, it was necessary to provide the respondents with a brief description of these methods. Because these descriptions would definitely influence acceptability judgments, they were carefully designed, on the basis of consultation with biomedical scientists, to represent the best estimates of the information that would be provided to men when these methods became available. In addition to a brief description of the route of administration and duration of action, the descriptions for the pill and injection indicated that the methods were claimed to be effective, safe, and not reduce sexual desire. For the injectable method, the pain was described as equal to that of most other injections.

We relied primarily on behavioral intention measures to assess acceptability. These questions measured men's willingness to use each method of contraception on a scale that ranged from *definitely will use* (1) to *definitely will not use* (5). For the male daily pill, the monthly injection, and vasectomy, the respondents were asked "If the 'method' were available, would you use it?" The comparable question for condoms was, "Do you think you will use condoms?" The intention measure was chosen because it had very high convergent validity with other measures of acceptability. In addition, fertility and contraceptive studies in developed and developing countries have generally shown that behavioral intentions are among the best, if not the best, predictors of subsequent behavior (Ajzen & Fishbein, 1980; Davidson & Thomson, 1980; Freedman, Hermalin, & Chang, 1975; Freedman & Takeshita, 1969; Triandis, 1971).

Preliminary versions of the questionnaires were reviewed and revised at meetings of the principal investigators in an effort to decrease the probability that the content or structure of the instrument would be incompatible with the groups being studied. When the final form of the questionnaire was agreed on, it was carefully translated into the local language using the back translation method. At each stage of translation, conceptual equivalence rather than linguistic equivalence was sought.

RESULTS

Beliefs About Men Who Use Male Methods of Contraception

Survey of Potential Users

As an indirect method to assess the demand for new and improved male methods of contraception, respondents were queried on their beliefs about a man who would use a male method of contraception. It was reasoned that a poor market for new male contraceptives would exist among groups who associated predominantly negative traits with users of male contraceptives. Conversely, a better market for new male contraceptives would be expected among groups who associated primarily positive attributes with users of male contraception. The respondents were asked if they *agreed, neither agreed nor disagreed,* or *disagreed* with each of five statements. Three of the statements linked a user of a male contraceptive to a positive trait—intelligent, modern, good—and two of the statements linked a user with a negative attribute—is dominated by his wife, would be ridiculed. As shown in Table 16.1, with few exceptions, the means in each of the five countries were in the "agree" portion of the response scale for the positive traits and in the "disagree" portion of the scale for the negative attributes. That is, the respondents tended to believe that a user of a male method of birth control is an intelligent, modern, and good man, and they tended to disagree with the assertions that a male contraceptive user is dominated by his wife or that he would be ridiculed. The extremity of the average scores for some of these items is striking. For example, for the statement asserting that a male contraceptive user would be ridiculed, the mean score (3 = *disagree*) was 2.95 in Korea, 2.71 in Mexico, and 2.77 in India. Similarly, for the item stating that a male

TABLE 16.1 Beliefs About "A Man Who Uses a Male Method of Birth Control," by Country and Sampling Region

Belief	Grand Mean	Rural	Urban Low SES*	Urban Middle SES
Fiji				
Is dominated by his wife	2.49	2.53a	2.42a	2.49a
Is an intelligent man	1.35	1.18a	1.25a	1.72b
Is a modern man	2.07	2.24b	1.96a	1.94a
Is a good man	1.37	1.17a	1.35b	1.69c
Would be ridiculed	2.60	2.65b	2.71b	2.40a
India				
Is dominated by his wife	1.82	1.74a	2.19b	1.58a
Is an intelligent man	1.22	1.11a	1.45b	1.15a
Is a modern man	1.57	1.33a	2.08b	1.42a
Is a good man	1.30	1.13a	1.60b	1.24a
Would be ridiculed	2.77	2.62a	2.88b	2.87b
Iran				
Is dominated by his wife	2.41	2.30a	2.35a	2.58b
Is an intelligent man	1.44	1.62b	1.24a	1.46b
Is a modern man	1.40	1.51b	1.29a	1.39ab
Is a good man	1.52	1.63b	1.42a	1.49ab
Would be ridiculed	2.45	2.05a	2.65b	2.65b
Mexico				
Is dominated by his wife	2.78	2.68a	2.76a	2.94b
Is an intelligent man	1.37	1.33a	1.33a	1.46a
Is a modern man	1.43	1.40a	1.35a	1.57a
Is a good man	1.52	1.31a	1.48a	1.87b
Would be ridiculed	2.71	2.57a	2.74ab	2.90b
Republic of Korea				
Is dominated by his wife	2.85	2.76a	2.87ab	2.96b
Is an intelligent man	1.44	1.41a	1.41a	1.52a
Is a modern man	1.25	1.21a	1.17a	1.38b
Is a good man	2.00	1.87a	2.05ab	2.14b
Would be ridiculed	2.95	2.97a	2.94a	2.93a

NOTE: All variables scored as follows: 1 = *agree;* 2 = *neither agree nor disagree, uncertain;* 3 = *disagree.* Means in any given row without a common subscript are significantly different at the .05 level by *t* test.
*SES = socioeconomic status.

contraceptive user is dominated by his wife, the average score was 2.85 in Korea and 2.78 in Mexico.

The primary exceptions to the prevailing pattern were as follows: (a) In India, rural and urban-middle-class men tended to agree that a male contraceptive user is dominated by his wife; (b) rural Fijian men, on average, disagreed with the statement that a male contraceptive user is a modern man; and (c) the urban respondents in Korea disagreed with the statement that a male contraceptive user is a good man.

Survey of Knowledgeable Sources

Knowledgeable sources were asked to make judgments about the likelihood that men would hold certain beliefs about users of male methods of birth control. In Iran, Korea, and Mexico, the knowledgeable sources anticipated that uniformly positive beliefs would be held about men who use male methods of contraception. That is, they estimated that the majority of men would agree that a male contraceptive user is modern and smart and disagree that he is dominated by his wife. A similar pattern of responses was obtained in India and Fiji, with the exception that the knowledgeable sources estimated that a slight majority of men would not judge a male contraceptive user to be a smart man. Generally speaking, these results are quite similar to those obtained from the potential users in showing a positive belief structure about male contraceptive users.

The Relative Acceptability of Existing and Potential Contraceptives for Men

Potential Users

As discussed above, behavioral intention was selected as the primary measure of acceptability. The average scores for the intention to use each method, by country and by sampling region, are presented in Table 16.2. Although not shown in Table 16.2, we also conducted analyses of variance with post hoc comparisons to contrast, within each country and sampling group, the relative acceptability of the four methods. The differences between methods, referred to below, are all significant at the .01 level.

As shown in the table, the most consistent finding across countries was the relative unacceptability of vasectomy in relation to the condom, male daily pill, and monthly injection. The only exception was the middle-SES sample in Mexico, who judged the condom to be least acceptable. The unacceptability of vasectomy is attributable in part to the desire of most of the respondents to father additional children.

The pattern of acceptability judgments for the condom, daily pill, and monthly injection suggested two clusters of samples—one in which the condom tended to be more popular than the potential methods (Fiji and urban India) and one in which the potential methods were most popular (Mexico, Korea, Iran, and rural India). For the samples in Fiji, condoms were the most acceptable method, followed by the potential methods. In the rural and urban-low-SES Fijian samples, the potential methods were approximately

TABLE 16.2 Mean Scores on Behavioral Intentions to Use Each Male Method, by Country and Sampling Region

Belief	Grand Mean	Sampling Region		
		Rural	Urban Low SES*	Urban Middle SES
Fiji				
Condom	2.35	2.56$_b$	2.08$_{ab}$	2.30$_a$
Male daily pill	2.89	3.03$_a$	2.76$_a$	2.82$_a$
Male monthly injection	3.05	3.15$_b$	2.72$_a$	3.23$_b$
Vasectomy	4.18	4.53$_b$	3.78$_a$	4.03$_a$
India				
Condom	2.06	2.22$_b$	1.78$_a$	2.09$_{ab}$
Male daily pill	1.91	1.65$_a$	2.05$_b$	2.18$_b$
Male monthly injection	2.37	2.25$_a$	2.16$_a$	2.76$_b$
Vasectomy	3.65	3.79$_b$	3.48$_a$	3.59$_{ab}$
Iran				
Condom	3.08	3.12$_a$	3.13$_a$	3.00$_a$
Male daily pill	2.68	3.02$_b$	2.29$_a$	2.73$_b$
Male monthly injection	2.64	2.92$_b$	2.16$_a$	2.84$_b$
Vasectomy	4.34	4.29$_a$	4.45$_a$	4.28$_a$
Mexico				
Condom	3.40	3.16$_a$	3.41$_{ab}$	3.76$_b$
Male daily pill	2.56	2.82$_b$	2.54$_{ab}$	2.21$_a$
Male monthly injection	2.81	2.87$_a$	2.91$_a$	2.62$_a$
Vasectomy	3.84	4.03$_b$	3.89$_{ab}$	3.51$_a$
Republic of Korea				
Condom	2.84	3.15$_b$	2.64$_a$	2.59$_a$
Male daily pill	2.28	2.19$_a$	2.21$_{ab}$	2.49$_b$
Male monthly injection	2.50	2.46$_{ab}$	2.35$_a$	2.73$_b$
Vasectomy	4.02	4.51$_c$	3.90$_b$	3.39$_a$

NOTE: All variables scored from 1 (*definitely will use*) to 5 (*definitely will not use*). Means in any given row without a common subscript are significantly different at the .05 level by *t* test.

*SES = socioeconomic status.

TABLE 16.3 Percentage of Men in Each Country Expressing Willingness to Use Each Potential Male Method If It Were Available

Country	Intention to Use Daily Pill		Intention to Use Monthly Injection	
	Definitely Use	Probably Use	Definitely Use	Probably Use
Fiji	13%	35%	9%	33%
India	41%	37%	21%	48%
Iran	23%	32%	24%	32%
Mexico	21%	49%	16%	47%
Republic of Korea	25%	51%	18%	49%

equal in acceptability, whereas in the urban middle class, the pill was judged more acceptable than the injection. The latter acceptability ordering was also observed for the urban samples in India. However, for the rural Indian group, the male pill was the most acceptable method, followed by the condom and injection, which were ranked approximately equal in acceptability. The relative similarity of the Fijian and Indian response patterns is perhaps attributable to the similarity of the samples; in Fiji, only men of Indian heritage were interviewed.

In Korea, Iran, and Mexico, the potential methods tended to be preferred over condoms. The daily pill was judged most acceptable by all groups in Mexico, followed by the monthly injection and the existing male methods. (In the rural group, the difference between the potential methods was not significant.) The same pattern was observed for the rural and urban-low-SES respondents in Korea. The middle-SES Koreans marginally favored the pill over the condom, and the monthly injection ranked third in acceptability. The differences among these methods were very small. The injection received the greatest endorsement among the poor in Iran. The rural and urban-low-SES respondents judged the monthly injection most acceptable, the daily pill second, and the condom third. The acceptability ratings of the pill and the injection were reversed for the urban-middle-SES sample. However, the difference in ratings between the pill and injection was not significant.

Focusing on the comparative acceptability of the potential methods, the differences in ratings between the daily pill and monthly injection tended to be small and frequently were nonsignificant. The pill was judged to be more acceptable than the injection by the three groups surveyed in India, Korea, and Mexico (the largest differences were observed in India and Mexico), by the rural and urban-middle-class respondents in Fiji, and by the urban-middle-SES respondents in Iran. The injection and the pill received equivalent ratings among the rural and urban-low-SES Iranian samples.

As shown in Table 16.3, the number of respondents who stated that they would either definitely or probably use the potential male methods, if they were available, was substantial. Summing these categories, we see that a greater percentage intended to use the daily pill than the monthly injection in Fiji, India, Mexico, and Korea. In Iran, approximately equal percentages intended to try each potential method. These results are consistent with the previous analysis. There were variations by country in the percentages of respondents willing to use the potential methods. The percentages were lower in Fiji and Iran and higher in India and Korea, with Mexico occupying a middle position on this continuum. The lowest percentage of expressed willingness to use was 42% for the monthly injection in Fiji, and the highest percentage was 78% for the daily pill in India.

Survey of Knowledgeable Sources

The knowledgeable sources rated, on a scale that ranged from 1 (*like very much*) to 5 (*dislike very much*), their estimates of men's attitudes toward the two potential and two existing male methods. The most consistent finding across countries was that vasectomy was the least acceptable method. Knowledgeable sources rated the condom relatively positively, although in four of the five countries, the average rating for condom was not significantly different from that for one of the potential methods. In India, Iran, and Korea, there were no significant differences between the estimated acceptability of the condom and of the monthly injection—both were judged to be more acceptable than the daily pill. The daily pill and the condom were the most acceptable methods in Mexico, followed by the monthly injection. In Fiji, the condom was judged most acceptable, with the injection second and the pill third.

In sum, both potential users and knowledgeable sources gave the lowest acceptability ratings to vasectomy. However, potential users in Iran, Korea, Mexico, and rural India rated one of the potential methods over the condom, whereas the knowledgeable sources gave roughly equivalent ratings to the condom and one of the potential methods. The other interesting difference is the relatively high acceptability rating that knowledgeable sources, in comparison with potential users, assigned to the injectable method. Overall, the data from both samples on the beliefs about users of male contraceptives and on the direct judgments of acceptability support the continued development of new contraceptives for men.

DISCUSSION

We recognize that interviewing samples of men about hypothetical methods of birth control is a speculative venture. There is no way to accurately assess the validity of their responses concerning contraceptives in such an early biomedical development phase. We have attempted to use prudent methodological procedures—seeking data from a variety of sources and including multiple measures of our key variables—but we urge that the present findings be interpreted with considerable caution.

The findings of the survey of potential users and the survey of knowledgeable sources were clearly inconsistent with prevalent stereotypes holding that men have attitudes and values incompatible with an active role in fertility regulation. Men evidenced a clearly positive belief structure about users of male contraceptives. Although the favorableness of the results was probably inflated to some degree by men's attempt to provide socially desirable responses, the comparable findings from the survey of knowledgeable sources enhance our judgments about the validity of the data.

The two potential contraceptives, particularly the male pill, received acceptability ratings that support their continued development. In each country, the potential methods were preferred over vasectomy, and potential users preferred the male pill over the condom in Mexico, Iran, Korea, and rural India. In each country, a large percentage of the respondents indicated that they would be willing to use the potential male methods if they were available. These percentages ranged from a low of 42% for the male injection in Fiji to a high of 78% for the daily pill in India. As we noted earlier, a very similar range of willingness to use new male contraceptives was obtained in acceptability studies in the United States.

To put these numbers in perspective, contraceptives can be financially viable with a much smaller percentage of users. For example, IUDs are widely available in the U.S. market even though they are used by only approximately 2% of couples who use contraception. Similarly, the newest method of contraception available in the United States, Depo-Provera, is considered profitable with a market share of less than 5% (Davidson et al., 1997). As a result, even if men's willingness to use the potential methods is highly exaggerated, it could still be profitable to develop and market these methods.

In this chapter, we focused almost exclusively on describing national and regional variations in men's attitudes toward contraceptives, at the expense of an analysis of the broader cultural, political, and structural determinants of these attitudes. This focus reflects the applied nature of the research. However, two of these broader determinants merit further discussion. First, the government of India's fertility-control policies had an influence on the data we obtained. We have previously mentioned the possible under-reporting of the number of living children in the Indian data. In addition, the extremely positive attitudes toward the male pill, particularly in rural India, were probably attrib-utable in part to men's fears about what the alternative might be—sterilization. It should be noted that the government of India abolished the population-control policy just as the study ended.

The second of these broader attitudinal determinants is culture. Although our national and regional sampling strategy was designed to provide cultural diversity, we did not include specific measures of cultural characteristics. However, as we conducted the fieldwork and analyzed the data, we were continually struck by the extent of consistency between the two national groups that had the most similar cultures, Indians and Fijians. To increase the comparability of the Indian and Fijian data, the Fijian sample was composed of men only from the half of the population that was of Indian descent. Similarities in their patterns of responses were observed in terms of both their rated acceptability of the different methods of contraception and their beliefs about men who would use a male method of contraception. This pattern of similarity was not limited to men in the primary survey but was also evident in the data from the Indian and Fijian knowledgeable sources concerning beliefs about male contraceptive users. These findings underscore the importance of cultural factors as a determinant of contraceptive accept-ability.

In summary, the present study is part of a growing body of applied, cross-cultural research designed to improve contraceptive methods and service delivery systems. As Marshall (1977) has argued, social scientists should not only be reactive to the efforts of biomedical scientists and family planning program administrators—limiting their research efforts to understanding the knowledge, attitudes, and opinions about existing methods of contraception. Rather, they should also be making contributions much earlier in the contraceptive development sequence that can be used to guide the design of new and more acceptable fertility-regulating methods and delivery systems. Social scientists can help set the "cultural specifications" for important new technologies and products.

17

CULTURE, CONTROL BELIEFS, AND JOB SATISFACTION

C. Harry Hui
Candice Yee
University of Hong Kong

JOB SATISFACTION AND LOCUS OF CONTROL

Job satisfaction has historically been regarded as the consequence of a number of situational factors (e.g., Hackman & Oldham, 1975). More recently, effects of certain dispositional characteristics have attracted researchers' attention (e.g., Gerhart, 1987; Staw, Bell, & Clausen, 1986; Staw & Ross, 1985). Levin and Stokes (1989) found that people with greater general negative affectivity were more likely to be dissatisfied with their job. Hui, Yee, and Eastman (1995) found that employees' collectivist orientation was positively correlated with coworker satisfaction as well as general satisfaction. Gable and Topol (1989) and Hollon (1983) reported that Machiavellianism was negatively related to job satisfaction among executives and managers. Locus of control is another personality construct that has been associated with job satisfaction.

Rotter's (1966) internal-external locus of control is defined as the expectancy of personal control over life outcomes. Extensive research has linked internal control belief

AUTHORS' NOTE: We would like to thank Christina France, Josephina Ho, Kit Kengott, David Lam, and Esther Yuet-ying Lau, who made useful comments on an earlier version of this chapter.

to psychological health, self-concept, general well-being, life satisfaction (e.g., Levitt, Clark, & Rotton, 1987), and coping (e.g., Folkman, 1984). It is not surprising that internal locus of control is also conducive to a positive experience with work. Externality, on the other hand, is accompanied by a sense of powerlessness and fatalism and therefore negatively related to job satisfaction.

In the job satisfaction literature, control belief was usually treated as a bipolar construct and measured with Rotter's Internal-External Locus of Control Scale. For example, Mallinckrodt (1990) found that scores on Rotter's scale were associated with job satisfaction measures taken 1 year later. Spector and O'Connell (1994) reported similar findings. Studies using this instrument presumed that, if job satisfaction were positively related to internality, it would be negatively related to externality.

However, there are reasons to be cautious about the above assumption. First, the belief that internality and externality are two ends of a unidimensional continuum has been challenged ever since its inception. Some researchers have argued that locus of control is a multidimensional construct (Reid & Ware, 1974; Wallston, Wallston, Kaplan, & Maides, 1976). One might perceive internal control in one sphere (e.g., interpersonal) and external control in another sphere (e.g., sociopolitical). Levenson (1974) described three perceived sources of control: self (internality, "I"), powerful others ("P"), and chance ("C"). Powerful others belief is the conviction that what other people do determines one's own life experience. Chance belief is the perception that life outcomes occur in a random, unpredictable manner. Levenson argued that the three dimensions of control have their own psychological and behavioral correlates.

Second, it has been suggested that different dimensions of control are differentially related to job satisfaction. Using Levenson's IPC control conception, Butler and Burr (1980) found that, although both "C" and "P" represented external beliefs, people high in "C" were much lower in job satisfaction than those high in "P."

With a few exceptions (e.g., Cheng, 1994), there is a serious dearth of research to cross-validate the above findings in non-Western cultures. In particular, no work has been done in non-Western cultures to verify the differential effects of internality, powerful others, and chance on job satisfaction.

JOB SATISFACTION AS A FUNCTION OF
INTERNALITY AND POWERFUL OTHERS BELIEF

The Work Itself

There is a positive association between locus of control and satisfaction with the work itself (e.g., Butler & Burr, 1980; Organ & Greene, 1974). People high on internal control also have motivational, cognitive, and behavioral characteristics that would bring about satisfaction with the task itself. For example, internals gave more credit to themselves in times of success at work than externals did (Norris & Niebuhr, 1984). Silvers and Deni (1983) suggested that internal employees were more intrinsically motivated than externals. Thus good performance would become more rewarding and more satisfying for internals than for externals. Several behaviors might result from these characteristics. For example, Anderson (1977) found that internal employees engaged in more task-related or "problem-focused" coping behaviors than externals did in daily activities. Consequently, employees high in internal control actually performed better at work (Ruble, 1974; Silvers & Deni, 1983). All these characteristics contribute to a positive relation between internality and satisfaction with the task itself.

The Reward Aspect

Internality is associated with satisfaction with salary (Shukla & Upadhyaya, 1986) and satisfaction with promotion (Lester, 1987). It has been suggested that, because internals generally perform better than externals, they might experience faster promotions and hence higher satisfaction in this aspect (see Spector, 1982).

The Interpersonal Aspect

In their interactions with colleagues, internal employees take active control. This may sometimes result in positive experiences with their supervisors and peers and sometimes in negative repercussions when overly assertive and abrasive actions are taken. Consistent with this reasoning, some researchers found a positive correlation between internality and satisfaction with coworkers (Lester, 1987; Shukla & Upadhyaya, 1986). Others found no relationship (Sharma & Chaudhary, 1980), whereas Dailey (1978) even showed that internal employees rated coworkers less favorably than did external employees. The correlations were positive between internality and satisfaction with supervisors (e.g., Butler & Burr, 1980; Shukla & Upadhyaya, 1986; but see Lester, 1987). Attempts to explain why satisfaction with supervisors and coworkers might be influenced by control orientation are rare in the literature.

General Job Satisfaction

The majority of studies found a positive relationship between internality and general job satisfaction (e.g., Blegen, 1993; Dailey, 1980; Kulcarni, 1983; Oliver, 1983; Organ & Greene, 1974). However, a few others did not find any significant correlation (Freedman & Philips, 1985; Nagarathnamma, 1988).

Spector (1982) proposed three explanations for the positive relationship between internality and general job satisfaction. First, internals are more active in controlling their environment and so are more likely to resign when dissatisfied than are externals. This would result in a smaller percentage of job "stayers" who were dissatisfied internals than dissatisfied externals. Second, if internal employees are more intrinsically motivated than external employees are, they might perform better than the latter, leading to higher satisfaction with the job as a whole. Finally, internals might receive more promotions than externals do, making them happier with their jobs than externals.

The last two explanations imply that internal locus of control leads to a higher level of general satisfaction through its effects on satisfaction with the work itself and the promotion aspect. Thus, if facet satisfactions (i.e., satisfaction with individual aspects of the job) combine to determine general job satisfaction, it is possible that internality enhances general satisfaction through its positive effects on facet satisfactions.

To summarize, past studies generally reported a positive relation between a belief in internal control and general job satisfaction. With reference to the arguments suggested in previous studies, we expected that this relation comprises both direct and mediated (through job facet satisfactions) links.

Powerful Others Belief

"P" concerns how a person perceives his or her power relationships with other people. Although no empirical evidence has been found, we expect this control belief to exert a negative effect on a person's satisfaction with the social aspects at work, including satisfaction with supervisors and coworkers. However, it would not be correlated with other nonsocial aspects of satisfaction and general job satisfaction.

SPECIAL MEANING OF
"CHANCE" IN CHINESE SOCIETY

In Levenson's scale (1973a, 1973b), the term *chance* refers to the attribution to non-personal control. This usage is consistent with lexical definitions accepted in the Western world. It embodies the belief that events are random, unpredictable, and uncontrollable. In the East, however, chance and fate seem to originate from some laws or gods of nature.

In the East, the conception of chance is subtly different from that in the West. Scholars like Capra (1975) pointed out that the Chinese mind and language do not follow a Western style of abstract logical thinking. The Chinese words used to express the notion of "chance" connote the interaction between environment and human action. In Chinese thought, which is under the strong influence of Confucianism and Taoism, "chance" factors are not something in the objective reality independent from the subject or merely something "out there." Rather, "chance" is associated with the way (i.e., "Tao") or the order of nature inherent in the person-environment dynamics.

More specific, it is believed that the geometrics of gold, wood, water, fire, and soil characterize the nature of everything, both animate and inanimate. Interaction of these characteristics within the person or between people can activate dynamics of conflicting forces and complementary forces. The person needs to flexibly organize his or her action in response to the environment. The person is not being passive. The sage, as Chong Tzu said, understood the wisdom that "let everything be allowed to do what it naturally does, so that its nature will be satisfied."

According to Chinese thought, people need wisdom to manage the balance of these forces, both conflicting and complementing. This has to be done to make use of these dynamics and produce desirable outcomes. That is why some people consult fortune-tellers and geomancers on how to act differently, or they change their work or living environments to avoid undesirable events.

We therefore expected that chance belief among Chinese would neither suppress personal control nor stifle persistence in daily endeavors. At work, this belief would not lead to negative job attitudes or dampen overall job satisfaction.

A MODEL LINKING VARIOUS CONTROL BELIEFS WITH FACET SATISFACTION AND GENERAL SATISFACTION WITH ONE'S JOB

The model that we constructed on the basis of the above reasoning was constructed using a heuristic model (Figure 17.1) of the effects of control belief on job satisfaction in Chinese society. The following hypotheses summarize the relationships depicted in the model:

1. Internality will correlate with satisfaction with the work itself and reward and relational aspects of work.
2. Internality will increase general job satisfaction both directly and indirectly through its effects on facet job satisfaction.
3. Powerful others belief will not be correlated with general job satisfaction.
4. Powerful others belief will correlate negatively with satisfaction with relational aspects of work. This belief would not affect satisfaction with the nonrelational aspects.
5. Chance belief will not be correlated with job satisfaction.

Data were collected from Chinese front-line salespersons at nine outlets of a department store chain in Hong Kong. These people received questionnaires distributed via company headquarters. Out of the 576 salespersons (of whom over 70% were female), 371 completed and returned the questionnaires by mail. The response rate was 60.3%. Ages of the participants ranged from 17 to 60, with a mean of 26.

The following instruments were used:

1. A Chinese version of Levenson's IPC scale, translated by Chiu and Hong (1986). The scale was further refined with a factor analysis. The Cronbach alphas for internality, powerful others, and chance were in the range of only .57 to .67, probably because of the transcultural application of the instrument.

2. A Chinese version of Smith, Kendall, and Hulin's (1969) Job Descriptive Index (JDI), which has been used among the Chinese (e.g., Hui, Yee, & Eastman, 1995; Wu & Watkins, 1994). Made up of five subscales, it is a measurement of facet satisfaction. The reliability coefficients for the Work, Promotion, Pay, Supervisor, and Coworker subscales were .79, .70, .73, .89, and .85, respectively.

3. Chinese Job in General Scale (JIG). This 35-item instrument tapped the level of individuals' general overall job satisfaction. It was constructed specifically for the present study using Ironson, Smith, Brannick, Gibson, and Paul's (1989) approach. It consists of

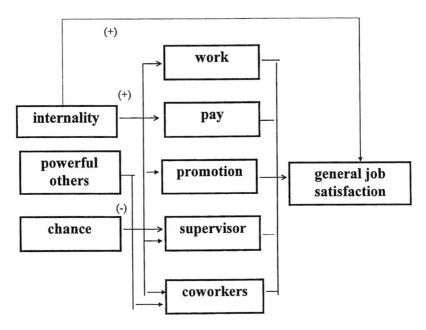

Figure 17.1. A Theoretical Model Relating Locus of Control and Job Satisfaction

adjectives and phrases that describe the general affective feelings toward the job as a whole rather than cognitive labels of particular job aspects. Examples of items are "ideal," "frustrating," "suitable for me," "disappointing," "hard but unfruitful," and "admired by others." The scale's Cronbach alpha was .91. Its split half reliability was .82.

STRUCTURAL EQUATION MODELING

A structural equation analysis (LISREL) was used to examine the model in Figure 17.1. In this structural model, the three control beliefs, "I," "P," and "C," were treated as potential exogenous variables, whereas the six measures of job satisfaction were treated as endogenous variables. The 3×6 parameters represented the potential effects of "I," "P," and "C" on the six job satisfaction measures. They were represented by parameters 1 to 18 in Figure 17.2. The potential relationships between job facet satisfaction and general satisfaction were represented by parameters 19 to 23.[1] The values of all 23 parameters were estimated in the analysis. This resulted in a just identified model. It was predicted that the parameters between "I" and the five satisfaction aspects (1-5) would be significantly positive, whereas the corresponding parameters involving "C" (13-17) would be null. Parameters 10 and 11, representing the effects of "P" on the two relational aspects of job satisfaction, would be negative, whereas parameters 7, 8, and 9 would be null. The significance of the estimated effect sizes was determined by subsequent t tests.[2]

Although structural equation analysis can be used as a test of causal relationships among variables, causality remains an assumption in this study because of the cross-

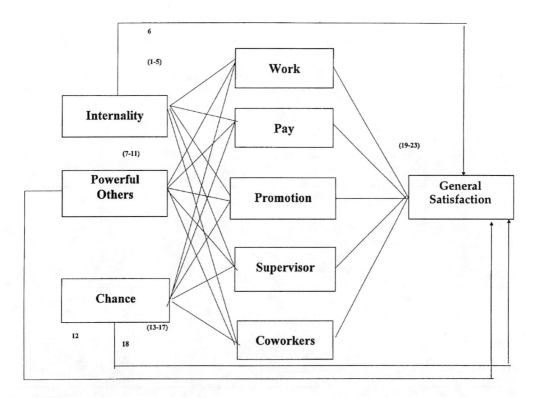

Figure 17.2. Path Analysis of the Relation Between IPC Control and Job Satisfaction: A LISREL Representation

sectional nature of our data. In this study, conceptual relationships were used to guide the interpretations of the results.

Individual parameters were estimated by the generalized least square (GLS) method. Table 17.1 shows the regression estimates and standard errors of the unconstrained paths. The goodness-of-fit indexes from the model testing suggest overall fitness of the model (.997 for both the maximum likelihood estimation and the GLS). Other indicators (e.g., adjusted goodness-of-fit index, root mean square, and chi-square) were also consistent with this finding.

Direct Effects on Facet Satisfactions

As hypothesized, "I" had positive loading on many satisfaction measures. Compared with their external counterparts, internal employees were higher on satisfaction with work itself, supervisors, coworkers, and promotion as well as general satisfaction (coefficients ranging from .11 to .18). However, internality was not related to satisfaction with pay.

The negative loading of "P" on supervisor satisfaction did not reach significance. However, "P" had a significant negative effect on coworker satisfaction (coefficient = -.14,

TABLE 17.1 Estimated Regression Weights and Standard Errors

			GLS[a] Estimation	
			---	---
Parameters	Exogenous Variables	Endogenous Variables	Regression Weight	Standard Errors
1		Work	.147**	.052
2		Pay	.059	.053
3		Promotion	.129*	.052
4	Internality	Supervisor	.109**	.035
5		Coworkers	.209***	.051
6		General satisfaction	.177***	.040
7		Work	-.050	.055
8		Pay	-.013	.055
9	Powerful	Promotion	-.074	.055
10	Others	Supervisor	-.041	.037
11		Coworkers	-.135*	.054
12		General satisfaction	.036	.041
13		Work	-.010	.055
14		Pay	-.016	.056
15		Promotion	-.006	.055
16	Chance	Supervisor	-.026	.038
17		Coworkers	-.038	.054
18		General satisfaction	-.029	.041
19	Work		.286***	.047
20	Pay		.196***	.045
21	Promotion	General Satisfaction	.085	.045
22	Supervisor		.142**	.063
23	Coworkers		.206***	.046

NOTE: Parameters shown in Figure 17.2.

a. GLS = generalized least square.

$*p < .05; **p < .01; ***p < .001.$

$p < .05$). The hypothesis that employees with a high powerful others belief would be less satisfied with relational aspects was partially supported. As predicted, "P" did not affect satisfaction with nonrelational aspects of work.

Consistent with the model, "C" was not related to facet or general job satisfaction.

Indirect Effects on General Satisfaction

It was hypothesized that "I" would affect general satisfaction both directly and indirectly. Its direct effect and indirect effect through facet satisfaction were estimated separately with LISREL (Table 17.2).

"I" had a significant indirect effect on general job satisfaction (coefficient = .12, $p < .001$). The total effect of "I" on general satisfaction, which is the sum of their direct and indirect relations, had a coefficient of .30 ($p < .001$).

TABLE 17.2 Indirect Effects of Internality Through the Five Facet Satisfactions on General Satisfaction

Job Aspect	$I^a \rightarrow FS^b$					$FS \rightarrow GS^c$
		Coefficients of Individual Effects				
Work	.147*	×	.286**	=		.042
Pay	.059	×	.196**	=		.012
Promotion	.129*	×	.085	=		.011
Supervisor	.109*	×	.142*	=		.015
Coworkers	.176*	×	.206**	=		.036
			Total indirect effects:			.116

a. I = internality.
b. FS = facet satisfaction.
c. GS = general satisfaction.
*$p < .01$; **$p < .001$.

Effects of Facet Satisfactions on General Job Satisfaction

As found in previous studies, satisfaction with specific aspects of the job affected the level of general satisfaction. Except for satisfaction with promotion, all facet satisfactions loaded significantly on general satisfaction (Table 17.1). They were related to general satisfaction in the following order of strength: work itself (coefficient = .29, $p < .001$), coworkers (coefficient = .21, $p < .001$), pay (coefficient = .20, $p < .001$), supervisors (coefficient = .14, $p < .01$), and promotion (coefficient = .09, *ns*).

CONCLUDING REMARKS

Results of the structural analysis showed that control beliefs had differential effects on different aspects of job satisfaction. The psychological mechanisms underlying their respective relationships are discussed below.

Internality

Employees high in internal locus of control experienced greater satisfaction with the task itself and had more favorable evaluations of their promotion opportunities and their supervisors and coworkers. Their overall affective response to the job was also more positive than low internals. The very belief that "I am in control" promotes a general positive outlook toward the unknown in the future. This positive outlook is sometimes referred to as "optimism" or self-efficacy. Because of this, internal employees were more satisfied with all the contexts in which control was perceived.

Powerful Others

That the powerful others belief was not associated with nonrelational job attitudes and general job satisfaction was expected. Furthermore, its negative relation with co-worker satisfaction probably resulted from the perception of possible disruptions or influences by other people at work. On the contrary, employees do not perceive their supervisors as "threatening" as they do some of their fellow workers. Although coworker collegiality has always been expected, the autocratic style of Chinese leadership has been accepted as a given. Any obstacles perceived to originate from coworkers would at the same time reduce satisfaction with coworkers and strengthen a belief in powerful others. Any obstacles perceived to originate from their supervisors might not have the same effects on satisfaction with supervisors and the "P" belief. If the above reasoning is valid, such negative reaction toward other people may be even stronger in a competitive working environment. In future studies, it will therefore be instructive to examine possible interaction effects between the powerful others belief and the nature of work relationships on work-relational satisfaction.

Chance

Chance belief had no effect on any aspects of job satisfaction. This result does not replicate Butler and Burr's (1980) finding of a negative relationship among U.S. subjects but is predicted in the Chinese setting, as "chance" among the Chinese does not indicate fatalism and helplessness. As mentioned earlier, the chance dimension in this study should be understood as the perception that there is a mystical regularity governing the world and that an individual's life also falls within this regularity. This is very akin to geomancy, a systematic study of metaphysical, personal, and physical forces in the environment. Many Chinese who believe in geomancy also believe that rules and princi-ples govern whether one will be ill or prosperous or happily married, depending on whether the harmony between the personal forces and the physical environment is attained. One can therefore "control" one's own life experiences by manipulating the physical environment (Hui, 1991). Various Chinese schools of astrology also hold similar views. A believer thinks that he or she can bring changes to life outcomes by manipulating antecedents of events. If so, people high in "C" may not necessarily be low in "I." Results even showed that "C" was positively correlated with "I" ($r = .14$, $p < .05$) in our sample. Obviously, "C" believers are not necessarily pessimistic about personal control. The nonsignificant effect on job satisfaction measures also suggests that "C" believers were not always dissatisfied at work.

The present study has identified the Chinese conception of "chance" as being differ-ent from Western external beliefs in influencing job satisfaction. Because numerous Chinese go to temples in the Chinese New Year for fortune-telling and to pray for a good year (of which career success and promotion are essential elements), it is useful to broaden our understanding of how this set of external beliefs is related to their experience at work. To do this, future research should include the development of an indigenous instrument for the measurement of the Chinese view of fate and chance.

NOTES

1. Although specific job attitudes might precede general job satisfaction, the model maintained that the five job facet attitudes were not causally related among themselves. Conceptually, employee attitudes toward a particular job aspect were affected by the respective characteristics of that job context as perceived by the employee. Therefore, one may hold very different attitudes toward different job aspects. Even if the five attitudes were correlated, their correlations might be a result of the common effects of individual characteristics, such as control orientation, as hypothesized presently, or other organizational variables not considered in this study. Technically, freeing all the parameters among the job attitudes (that is, specifying mutual causality among job attitudes) in the model would also lead to identification problems. In view of this, we treated the five job attitudes as independent of each other by fixing the betas among the job attitudes to zero.

2. We used the following equation to derive the *t* values: *t* value = (estimated value/standard error) of the parameter.

EPILOGUE

John Adamopoulos
Yoshihisa Kashima

This collection of essays by psychologists with an interest in cultural explanation contains a number of diverse approaches to the study of social psychology. In fact, the conceptual diversity found in this book may appear, at first glance, confusing, troublesome, and reflecting an unintegrated discipline. The chapters of the book deal with phenomena that vary greatly in abstraction (from concrete events and behaviors to abstract belief and meaning systems), level of explanation (from processes occurring within individuals to societal structures), and temporal properties (from immediate and short-term cognitive processes to long-term or even historical changes). In addition, some of the chapters adopt an orientation that emphasizes basic research and theory construction, whereas others explore the solution of interpersonal and social problems through the application of existing theory and knowledge.

Despite this *appearance* of diversity, however, at closer look we find significant thematic and structural convergences among the chapters. At the simplest level, they all quite obviously (though some more explicitly than others) share a concern with the role that culture—broadly defined—plays in the analysis of human social behavior. At a more complex level, most of the work and conceptual analyses reported in this book can

243

be traced to pioneering research by Harry Triandis on the subjective experience of culture and on the interplay between culture and individual behavior. Thus, while it is truly impressive that the contributions of one person led to such diversity of approaches, the common "roots" of these approaches provide common structure and integration. As explained in the introduction to this volume, the foundation of much of the work reported here rests on the notion that psychological phenomena of any scale—including those involving large collectives—can be understood by examining the manner in which individual members of a community experience their social world and by contrasting these experiences across cultures.

We see, then, that the essays appearing in this book can be characterized by both a convergence reflecting their common intellectual "roots" and theoretical assumptions and a divergence in approach reflecting differing commitments among the authors—as suggested earlier—with respect to the level of analysis and explanation, abstractness, and time frame. This divergence is a tribute to and an outcome of Triandis's approach to the study of culture: using broad strokes theoretically, avoiding disciplinary or conceptual rigidity, and emphasizing multimethod measurement. For example, his theoretical work used ideas liberally from social and cognitive psychology, anthropology, and sociology, and his research program employed a variety of experimental and quasi-experimental designs and quantitative as well as qualitative techniques.

It was inevitable that such diversity would lead to a broad spectrum of interests among his students and colleagues. In fact, many current debates among psychologists interested in the study of culture—for example, discussions about the processes involved in interpreting phenomena at the individual as opposed to the group level—are found in the diverse works of Triandis's colleagues. From a historical perspective, it is interesting that even though the label "subjective culture" appears to be out of fashion in cross-cultural psychology, the fundamental ideas associated with this label are very much current and relevant in recent research. For example, most of the descriptions of individualism and collectivism are provided within the context of "subjective culture" research—that is, the analysis of belief and values systems, social behavior patterns, norms, roles, and affective responses to social situations.

Equally important, we suggest that Triandis's "subjective culture" approach, perhaps because of its theoretical richness and independence from firm disciplinary boundaries, is sensitive even to some of the concerns of cultural (as opposed to cross-cultural) psychologists, social constructionists, and other social scientists with a more relativistic orientation. For example, the notion that culture structures the experience of the social environment—a fundamental assumption of "subjective culture" research—softens somewhat the absolutist arguments often made by experimental social psychology and offers a compromise position between absolutism on the one hand and the antiessentialist and antirealist stance of constructionism on the other.

A good measure of the significance and impact of a research tradition is often the extent to which it generates novel and challenging problems and opens new areas of investigation. We believe that the scope of the chapters in this volume represents such a measure. More important, seen in the broader context of a research tradition that provides common intellectual roots, these essays point to many interesting theoretical and research questions that have yet to be addressed. For example, some of the questions that are generated from the work reported in the various chapters and that can be explored in the future are as follows:

1. How do the basic determinants of social behavior change as not only a function of culture but also of time? It is likely that new processes will have to be developed to account for such long-term "flow" in human social behavior.
2. How do various intraindividual processes—from memory to decision making— develop over long periods of time? What exactly is the role of cultural adaptation in this case?
3. How does the regulation of various psychological and interpersonal processes (e.g., the regulation of intimacy, social power, or conflict) occur and get modified as a function of culture and the passage of time?

These are only a few of the many exciting theoretical questions that are the direct outcome of the themes developed in this volume, and they may very well underlie the key research problems investigated in the new century by the next generation of cross-cultural researchers.

REFERENCES

Ackerman, N. W. (1938). The unity of the family. *Archives of Pediatrics, 55*, 51-62.

Adamopoulos, J. (1982). Analysis of interpersonal structures in literary works of three historical periods. *Journal of Cross-Cultural Psychology, 13*, 157-168.

Adamopoulos, J. (1984). The differentiation of social behavior: Toward an explanation of universal interpersonal structures. *Journal of Cross-Cultural Psychology, 15*, 487-508.

Adamopoulos, J. (1988). Interpersonal behavior: Cross-cultural and historical perspectives. In M. H. Bond (Ed.), *The cross-cultural challenge to social psychology* (pp. 196-207). Newbury Park, CA: Sage.

Adamopoulos, J. (1991a, February). *Cross-cultural convergence in the perception of personal relationships.* Paper presented at the 20th annual meeting of the Society for Cross-Cultural Research, San Juan, Puerto Rico.

Adamopoulos, J. (1991b). The emergence of interpersonal behavior: Diachronic and cross-cultural processes in the evolution of intimacy. In S. Ting-Toomey & F. Korzenny (Eds.), *International and intercultural communication annual: Vol. 15. Cross-cultural interpersonal communication* (pp. 155-170). Newbury Park, CA: Sage.

Adamopoulos, J., & Bontempo, R. N. (1986). Diachronic universals in interpersonal structures: Evidence from literary sources. *Journal of Cross-Cultural Psychology, 17*, 169-189.

Adamopoulos, J., & Lonner, W. J. (1994). Absolutism, relativism, and universalism in the study of human behavior. In W. J. Lonner & R. Malpass (Eds.), *Psychology and culture* (pp. 129-134). Boston: Allyn & Bacon.

Adler, N. (1994). Health psychology. *Annual Review of Psychology, 45*, 229-259.

Adler, N. J., & Graham, J. L. (1989). Cross-cultural comparison: The international comparison fallacy. *Journal of International Business Studies, 20*, 515-538.

Agnew, V. (1986). Educated Indian women in Ontario: Women and ethnicity. *Polyphony, 8*(1-2), 70-72.

Ahluwalia, J. S., & McNagny, S. E. (1993). Smoking prevalence and desire to quit in inner-city African American walk-in clinic patients. *Clinical Research, 41*(4), 752A.

Ajzen, I., & Fishbein, M. (1980). *Understanding attitudes and predicting social behavior.* Englewood Cliffs, NJ: Prentice Hall.

Al-Zahrani, S. S. A., & Kaplowitz, S. A. (1993). Attributional biases in individualistic and collectivistic cultures: A comparison of Americans and Saudis. *Social Psychology Quarterly, 56,* 223-233.

Alba, J. W., & Chattopadhyay, A. (1985). The effects of context and part-category cues on the recall of competing brands. *Journal of Marketing Research, 22,* 340-349.

Alba, J. W., & Hutchinson, J. W. (1987). Dimensions of consumer expertise. *Journal of Consumer Research, 13,* 411-454.

Albert, R. D. (1983). The intercultural sensitizer or culture assimilator: A cognitive approach. In D. Landis & R. W. Brislin (Eds.), *Handbook of intercultural training: Issues in training methodology* (Vol. 2, pp. 186-217). New York: Pergamon.

Alcalay, R., Sabogal, F., Marín, G., Pérez-Stable, E., VanOss Marín, B., & Otero-Sabogal, R. (1987-1988). Patterns of mass media use among Hispanic smokers: Implications for community interventions. *International Quarterly of Community Health Education, 8*(4), 341-350.

"All Things Considered." (1996, June 12). *The Ami singers.* Washington, DC: National Public Radio.

Allen, V. L. (1965). Situational factors in conformity. In L. Berkowitz (Ed.), *Advances in experimental social psychology* (Vol. 2, pp. 133-176). San Diego, CA: Academic Press.

Allen, V. L. (1975). Social support for nonconformity. In L. Berkowitz (Ed.), *Advances in experimental social psychology* (Vol. 8, pp. 2-46). San Diego, CA: Academic Press.

Altemeyer, B. (1981). *Right-wing authoritarianism.* Winnipeg, Manitoba, Canada: University of Manitoba Press.

Altemeyer, B. (1988). *Enemies of freedom: Understanding right-wing authoritarianism.* San Francisco: Jossey-Bass.

Anderson, C. R. (1977). Locus of control, coping behaviors, and performance in a stress setting: A longitudinal study. *Journal of Applied Psychology, 62,* 446-451.

Anderson, J. R. (1990). *Cognitive psychology and its implications* (3rd ed.). New York: Freeman.

Anderson, J. R. (1991). The adaptive nature of human categorization. *Psychological Review, 98,* 409-429.

Anderson, M. (1971). *Family structure in nineteenth century Lancashire* (Cambridge Studies in Sociology, Vol. 5). Cambridge, UK: Cambridge University Press.

Andreasen, A. R. (1995). *Marketing social change.* San Francisco: Jossey-Bass.

Arnold, F., Bulatao, R., Buripakdi, C., Chung, B., Fawcett, J., Iritoni, T., Lee, S., & Wu, T. (1975). *The value of children, a cross-national study* (Vol. 1). Honolulu, HI: East-West Population Institute, East-West Center.

Arthur, W., Jr., Doverspike, D., & Fuentes, R. (1992). Recipients' affective responses to affirmative action interventions: A cross-cultural perspective. *Behavioral Sciences and the Law, 10,* 229-243.

Asch, S. (1956). Studies of independence and conformity: I. Minority of one against a unanimous majority. *Psychological Monographs, 70*(Whole No. 416).

Attico, N. (1978). Male contraception. *Public Health Reviews, 1,* 55-81.

Au, T. (1983). Chinese and English counterfactuals: The Sapir-Whorf hypothesis revisited. *Cognition, 15,* 155-187.

Au, T. (1992). Counterfactual reasoning. In G. Semin & K. Fiedler (Eds.), *Language, interaction, and social cognition* (pp. 194-213). London: Sage.

Augoustinos, M., & Walker, I. (1995, July). *Stereotypes as social representations.* Paper presented at the 5th European Congress of Psychology, Athens, Greece.

Azzi, A. E. (1992). Procedural justice and the allocation of power in intergroup relations: Studies in the United States and South Africa. *Personality and Social Psychology Bulletin, 18,* 736-747.

Azzi, A. E. (1993). Implicit and category-based allocations of decision-making power in majority-minority relations. *Journal of Experimental Social Psychology, 29*, 203-228.

Baddeley, A. D. (1986). *Working memory*. Oxford, UK: Oxford University Press.

Baha'i International Community. (1995). *The prosperity of humankind*. Haifa, Israel: Office of Public Information.

Bales, R. F., & Slater, P. (1955). Role differentiation in small decision-making groups. In T. Parsons & R. F. Bales (Eds.), *Family, socialization, and interaction process* (pp. 259-306). New York: Free Press.

Balswick, J. (1972). Attitudes of lower class males toward taking a male birth control pill. *Family Coordinator, 21*, 195-201.

Bandura, A. (1977). *Social learning theory*. Englewood Cliffs, NJ: Prentice Hall.

Bandura, A. (1986). Self-efficacy: Toward a unifying theory of behavioral change. *Psychological Review, 84*, 191-215.

Bandura, A. (1990). Perceived self-efficacy in the exercise of control over AIDS infection. *Evaluation and Program Planning, 13*, 9-17.

Banks, J. A. (1995). Multicultural education and the modification of students' racial attitudes. In W. D. Hawley & A. W. Jackson (Eds.), *Toward a common destiny: Improving race and ethnic relations in America* (pp. 315-339). San Francisco: Jossey-Bass.

Bañuelas, A. J. (Ed.). (1995). *Mestizo Christianity: Theology from the Latino perspective*. Maryknoll, NY: Orbis Books.

Bargh, J. A. (1994). The Four Horsemen of automaticity: Awareness, intention, efficiency, and control in social cognition. In R. S. Wyer & T. K. Srull (Eds.), *Handbook of social cognition* (pp. 1-40). Hillsdale, NJ: Lawrence Erlbaum.

Bargh, J. A., & Barndollar, K. (1996). Automaticity in action: The unconscious as a repository of chronic goals and motives. In P. M. Gollwitzer & J. A. Bargh (Eds.), *The psychology of action* (pp. 457-481). New York: Guilford.

Bargh, J. A., Bond, R. N., Lombardi, W. J., & Tota, M. E. (1986). The additive nature of chronic and temporary sources of construct accessibility. *Journal of Personality and Social Psychology, 50*, 869-878.

Barsalou, L. W. (1987). The instability of graded structure: Implications for the nature of concepts. In U. Neisser (Ed.), *Concepts reconsidered: The ecological and intellectual bases of categories* (pp. 101-140). Cambridge, UK: Cambridge University Press.

Barton, S. (1994). Chaos, self-organization, and psychology. *American Psychologist, 49*, 5-14.

Bartz, D. E., Hillman, L. W., Lehrer, S., & Mayhugh, G. M. (1990). A model for managing workforce diversity. *Management Education and Development, 21*(5), 321-326.

Bateson, G., Jackson, D. D., Haley, J., & Weakland, J. (1956). Toward a theory of schizophrenia. *Behavioral Science, 1*, 251-264.

Bayer, R. (1994). AIDS prevention and cultural sensitivity: Are they compatible? *American Journal of Public Health, 84*(6), 895-898.

Bazerman, M. H., & Neale, M. A. (1992). *Negotiating rationally*. New York: Free Press.

Beach, S. (1990). *Image theory: Decision making in personal and organizational contexts*. Chichester, UK: Wiley.

Bell, R. Q. (1968). A reinterpretation of the direction of effects in studies of socialization. *Psychological Review, 75*, 81-95.

Benda, B., & DiBlasio, F. A. (1994). An integration of theory: Adolescent sexual contacts. *Journal of Youth and Adolescents, 23*, 403-420.

Benjamin, R. W. (1975). Images of conflict resolution and social control: American and Japanese attitudes to the adversary system. *Journal of Conflict Resolution, 19*, 123-137.

Benveniste, E. (1971). *Problems in general linguistics* (M. E. Meek, Trans.). Coral Gables, FL: University of Miami Press. (Original work published 1966)

Berger, P. L. (1969). *A rumour of angels*. Harmondsworth, UK: Penguin.

Berkowitz, L., & Walster, E. (Eds.). (1976). *Advances in experimental social psychology: Vol. 9. Equity theory: Towards a general theory of social interaction.* New York: Academic Press.

Berman, R. A. (1990). On acquiring an (S)VO language: Subjectless sentences in children's Hebrew. *Linguistics, 28,* 1135-1166.

Berry, J. W. (1969). On cross-cultural comparability. *International Journal of Psychology, 4,* 119-128.

Berry, J. W. (1974). Ecological and cultural factors in spatial perceptual development. In J. W. Berry & P. R. Dasen (Eds.), *Culture and cognition: Readings in cross-cultural psychology* (pp. 129-140). London: Methuen.

Berry, J. W. (1975). An ecological approach to cross-cultural psychology. *Netherlands Journal of Psychology, 30,* 51-84.

Berry, J. W. (1976). *Human ecology and cognitive style: Comparative studies in cultural and psychological adaptation.* New York: Sage/Halsted.

Berry, J. W. (1979). A cultural ecology of social behavior. In L. Berkowitz (Ed.), *Advances in experimental social psychology.* New York: Academic Press.

Berry, J. W. (1980a). Ecological analyses for cross-cultural psychology. In N. Warren (Ed.), *Studies in cross-cultural psychology* (Vol. 2, pp. 157-189). London: Academic Press.

Berry, J. W. (1980b). Social and cultural change. In H. C. Triandis & R. Brislin (Eds.), *Handbook of cross-cultural psychology: Vol. 5. Social Psychology* (pp. 211-279). Boston: Allyn & Bacon.

Berry, J. W. (1983). The sociogenesis of social sciences: An analysis of the cultural relativity of social psychology. In B. Bain (Ed.), *The sociogenesis of language and human conduct* (pp. 449-458). New York: Pergamon.

Berry, J. W. (1985). Cultural psychology and ethnic psychology: A comparative analysis [International Association for Cross-Cultural Psychology presidential address]. In I. Reyes-Lagunes & Y. Poortinga (Eds.), *From a different perspective* (pp. 3-15). Lisse, The Netherlands: Swets & Zeitlinger.

Berry, J. W. (1990). The role of psychology in ethnic studies. *Canadian Ethnic Studies, 22,* 8-21.

Berry, J. W. (n.d.). *Sociopsychological costs and benefits of multiculturalism* (Working Paper No. 24). Ottawa, Canada: Economic Council of Canada.

Berry, J. W., & Annis, R. C. (Eds.). (1988). *Ethnic psychology: Research and practice with immigrants, refugees, native peoples, ethnic groups, and sojourners.* Lisse, The Netherlands: Swets & Zeitlinger.

Berry, J. W., & Dasen, P. R. (Eds.). (1974). *Culture and cognition.* London: Methuen.

Berry, J. W., & Kalin, R. (1995). Multicultural and ethnic attitudes in Canada: An overview of the 1991 national survey. *Canadian Journal of Behavioral Science, 27,* 301-320.

Berry, J. W., Kalin, R., & Taylor, D. (1977). *Multiculturalism and ethnic attitudes in Canada.* Ottawa, Canada: Ministry of Supply and Services.

Berry, J. W., & Kim, U. (1993). Indigenous psychologies: One small step towards a universal psychology. In U. Kim & J. W. Berry (Eds.), *Indigenous psychologies: Research and experience in cultural context* (pp. 77-84). Newbury Park, CA: Sage.

Berry, J. W., Kim, U., Minde, T., & Mok, D. (1987). Comparative studies of acculturative stress. *International Migration Review, 21,* 491-511.

Berry, J. W., Kim, U., Power, S., Young, M., & Bujaki, M. (1989). Acculturation attitudes in plural societies. *Applied Psychology: An International Review, 38,* 185-206.

Berry, J. W., Poortinga, Y., Segall, M., & Dasen, P. (1992). *Cross-cultural psychology: Research and applications.* New York: Cambridge University Press.

Berry, J. W., Poortinga, Y. H., Pandey, J., Dasen, P. R., Saraswathi, T. S., Segall, M. H., & Kagitcibasi, C. (Eds.). (1997). *Handbook of cross-cultural psychology* (2nd ed., Vols. 1-3). Boston: Allyn & Bacon.

Bettinghaus, E. P. (1986). Health promotion and the knowledge-attitude-behavior continuum. *Preventive Medicine, 15,* 475-491.

Bettman, J. R., & Sujan, M. (1987). Effects of framing on comparable and noncomparable alternatives by expert and novice consumers. *Journal of Consumer Research, 14,* 141-154.

Beyer, W. (1968). Individual freedom in a collectivistic society. *Social Science, 43,* 160-167.

Bhawuk, D. P. S. (1990). Cross-cultural orientation programs. In R. W. Brislin (Ed.), *Applied cross-cultural psychology* (pp. 326-346). Newbury Park, CA: Sage.

Bhawuk, D. P. S. (1995). *The role of culture theory in cross-cultural training: A comparative evaluation of culture-specific, culture general, and theory-based assimilators.* Unpublished doctoral dissertation, University of Illinois at Urbana-Champaign.

Bhawuk, D. P. S. (1996). *Development of a culture theory-based assimilator: Applications of individualism and collectivism in cross-cultural training.* Best paper proceedings at the annual conference of the Academy of Management, Cincinnati, OH.

Bhawuk, D. P. S. (1998). The role of culture theory in cross-cultural training: A multimethod study of culture-specific, culture-general, and culture theory-based assimilators. *Journal of Cross-Cultural Psychology, 29*(5), 630-655.

Bhawuk, D. P. S., & Brislin, R. W. (1992). The measurement of intercultural sensitivity using the concepts of individualism and collectivism. *International Journal of Intercultural Relations, 16,* 413-436.

Bierbrauer, G. (1994). Toward an understanding of legal culture: Variations in individualism and collectivism between Kurds, Lebanese, and Germans. *Law and Society Review, 28,* 243-264.

Blake, G. (1998, July 15-17). *Borderland stress: Local, regional, and global causes.* Paper presented at the 5th International Conference of the International Boundaries Research Unit, Durham, England.

Blass, T. (1991). Understanding behavior in the Milgram obedience experiment: The role of personality, situations, and their reactions. *Journal of Personality and Social Psychology, 60,* 398-413.

Blegen, M. A. (1993). Nurses' job satisfaction: A meta-analysis of related variables. *Nursing Research, 42,* 36-41.

Blood, R. O., & Wolfe, D. M. (1960). *Husbands and wives: The dynamics of married living.* New York: Free Press.

Bloom, P. (1990). Subjectless sentences in child language. *Linguistic Inquiry, 21,* 491-504.

Blum-Kulka, S., House, J., & Kasper, G. (1988). Investigating cross-cultural pragmatics: An introductory overview. In S. Blum-Kulka, J. House, & G. Kasper (Eds.), *Cross-cultural pragmatics: Requests and apologies* (pp. 1-34). Norwood, NJ: Ablex.

Blumberg, R. L., & Winch, R. F. (1972). Societal complexity and familial complexity: Evidence for the curvilinear hypothesis. *American Journal of Sociology, 77,* 898-920.

Bochner, S., & Hesketh, B. (1994). Power distance, individualism/collectivism, and job-related attitudes in a culturally diverse work group. *Journal of Cross-Cultural Psychology, 25,* 233-257.

Bohon, L. M., Santos, S. J., Sanchez-Sosa, J. J., & Singer, R. D. (1994). The effects of mental health video on the social skills knowledge and attitudes of Mexican immigrants. *Journal of Applied Social Psychology, 24*(20), 1794-1805.

Boldizar, J. P., & Messick, D. M. (1988). Intergroup fairness biases: Is ours the fairer sex? *Social Justice Research, 2,* 95-112.

Bond, M. H. (1987). Intergroup relations in Hong Kong: The Tao of stability. In J. Boucher, D. Dandis, & K. A. Clark (Eds.), *Ethnic conflict: International perspectives* (pp. 55-78). Newbury Park, CA: Sage.

Bond, M. H. (1988). Finding universal dimensions of individual variation in multi-cultural studies of values: The Rokeach and Chinese value surveys. *Journal of Personality and Social Psychology, 55,* 1009-1015.

Bond, M. H., & Cheung, T. (1983). College students' spontaneous self concept: The effect of culture among respondents in Hong Kong, Japan, and the United States. *Journal of Cross-Cultural Psychology, 14,* 153-171.

Bond, M. H., Leung, K., & Wan, K. C. (1982). How does cultural collectivism operate? The impact of task and maintenance contributions on rewards distribution. *Journal of Cross-Cultural Psychology, 13,* 186-200.

Bond, M. H., & Mak, A. L. P. (1996). Deriving an intergroup topography from perceived values: Forging an identity in Hong Kong out of Chinese tradition and contemporary examples. In *Conference proceedings: Mind, machine, and environment: Facing the challenges of the 21st century* (pp. 255-266). Seoul, South Korea: Ha Mun.

Bond, M. H., Wan, K. C., Leung, K., & Giacalone, R. A. (1985). How are responses to verbal insult related to cultural collectivism and power distance? *Journal of Cross-Cultural Psychology, 16,* 111-127.

Bond, R., & Smith, P. B. (1996). Culture and conformity: A meta-analysis of studies using Asch's (1952b, 1956) line judgment task. *Psychological Bulletin, 119,* 111-137.

Borneman, J. (1993). *Belonging in the two Berlins: Kin, state, nation.* Cambridge, UK: Cambridge University Press.

Botvin, G. J., Schinke, S. P., Epstein, J. A., & Diaz, T. (1994). Effectiveness of culturally focused and generic skills training approaches to alcohol and drug abuse prevention among minority youth. *Psychology of Addictive Behaviors, 8*(2), 116-127.

Botvin, G. J., Schinke, S. P., Epstein, J. A., Diaz, T., & Botvin, E. M. (1995). Effectiveness of culturally focused and generic skills training approaches to alcohol and drug abuse prevention among minority adolescents: Two-year follow-up results. *Psychology of Addictive Behaviors, 9,* 183-194.

Bourdieu, P. (1977). *Outline of a theory of practice* (R. Nice, Trans.). Cambridge, UK: Cambridge University Press.

Bourdieu, P. (1986). The forms of capital. In J. E. Richardson (Ed.), *Handbook of theory and research for the sociology of education* (pp. 241-258). New York: Greenwood.

Bourdieu, P. (1991). *Language and symbolic power.* Cambridge, UK: Polity.

Bourhis, R. Y., Moise, L. C., Perreault, S., & Senecal, S. (1997). Towards an interactive acculturation model: A social psychological approach. *International Journal of Psychology, 32,* 369-386.

Branscombe, N. R., & Wann, D. L. (1994). Collective self-esteem consequences of outgroup derogation when a valued social identity is on trial. *European Journal of Social Psychology, 24,* 641-657.

Branthwaite, A., & Jones, J. E. (1975). Fairness and discrimination: English versus Welsh. *European Journal of Social Psychology, 5,* 323-338.

Brewer, M. B. (1986). The role of ethnocentrism in intergroup conflict. In S. Worchel & W. G. Austin (Eds.), *Psychology of intergroup conflict* (pp. 88-102). Chicago: Nelson-Hall.

Brewer, M. B. (1988). A dual process model of impression formation. In T. K. Srull & R. S. Wyer, Jr. (Eds.), *Advances in social cognition* (Vol. 1, pp. 1-36). Hillsdale, NJ: Lawrence Erlbaum.

Brewer, M., & Campbell, D. T. (1976). *Ethnocentrism and intergroup attitudes: East African evidence.* New York: Halsted/Wiley.

Brewster, K. L., Billy, J. O., & Grady, W. R. (1993). Social context and adolescent behavior: The impact of community on the transition to sexual activity. *Social Forces, 71,* 713-740.

Brinberg, D., & Jaccard, J. (1989). *Dyadic decision making.* New York: Springer-Verlag.

Brislin, R. W. (Ed.). (1976). *Translation: Applications and research.* New York: Wiley/Halsted.

Brislin, R. W. (1989). Intercultural communication training. In M. Asante & W. Gudykunst (Eds.), *Handbook of international and intercultural communication* (pp. 441-457). Newbury Park, CA: Sage.

Brislin, R. W., Cushner, K., Cherrie, C., & Yong, M. (1986). *Intercultural interactions: A practical guide.* Beverly Hills, CA: Sage.

Brislin, R. W., & Pederson, P. (1976). *Cross-cultural orientation programs.* New York: Gardner.

Brislin, R. W., & Yoshida, T. (1994). *Intercultural communication training: An introduction.* Thousand Oaks, CA: Sage.

Broderick, C. B. (1993). *Understanding family process.* Newbury Park, CA: Sage.

Bronfenbrenner, U. (1979). *The ecology of human development: Experiments by nature and design.* Cambridge, MA: Harvard University Press.

Bronfenbrenner, U. (1986). Ecology of the family as a context for human development: Research perspectives. *Developmental Psychology, 22,* 723-742.

Brown v. Board of Education of Topeka, 347 U.S. 483 (1954).

Brown, R. (1976). Reference: In memorial tribute to Eric Lenneberg. *Cognition, 4,* 125-153.

Brown, R. (1986). *Social psychology: The second edition.* New York: Free Press.

Brown, R. J. (1996). Intergroup relations. In M. Hewstone, W. Stroebe, & G. M. Stephenson (Eds.), *Introduction to social psychology: A European perspective* (2nd ed., pp. 530-561). Oxford, UK: Basil Blackwell.

Brown, R., & Gilman, A. (1960). The pronoun of power and solidarity. In T. A. Sebeok (Ed.), *Style in language* (pp. 253-276). Cambridge, UK: Cambridge University Press.

Brown, R., & Lenneberg, E. (1954). A study in language and cognition. *Journal of Abnormal and Social Psychology, 49,* 454-462.

Brown, R. J., & Turner, J. C. (1979). The criss-cross categorization effect in intergroup discrimination. *British Journal of Social and Clinical Psychology, 18,* 371-383.

Brown, R. J., & Turner, J. C. (1981). Interpersonal and intergroup behaviour. In J. C. Turner & H. Giles (Eds.), *Intergroup behaviour* (pp. 33-65). Oxford, UK: Basil Blackwell.

Brown, R. J., & Wade, G. S. (1987). Superordinate goals and intergroup behaviour: The effects of role ambiguity and status on intergroup attitudes and task performance. *European Journal of Social Psychology, 17,* 131-142.

Bryk, A., & Raudenbush, S. (1992). *Hierarchical linear models.* Newbury Park, CA: Sage.

Buchignani, N. (1977). A review of the historical and sociological literature on East Indians in Canada. *Canadian Ethnic Studies, 9*(1), 86-108.

Buchignani, N., & Indra, D. M. (1985). *Continuous journey: A social history of South Asians in Canada.* Toronto, Canada: McClelland & Stewart.

Burchfield, R. W. (Ed.). (1972). *A supplement to the Oxford English dictionary* (Vol. 1). Oxford, UK: Oxford University Press.

Burgess, E. W. (1926). The family as a unity of interacting personalities. *Family, 7,* 3-9.

Butler, M. C., & Burr, R. G. (1980). Utility of a multidimensional locus of control scale in predicting health and job-related outcomes in military environments. *Psychological Reports, 47,* 719-728.

Byrne, D. (1971). *The attraction paradigm.* New York: Academic Press.

Cacioppo, J. T., & Berntson, G. G. (1994). Relationship between attitudes and evaluative space: A critical review, with emphasis on the separability of positive and negative substrates. *Psychological Bulletin, 115,* 401-423.

Cacioppo, J. T., Crites, S. L., Jr., Gardner, W. L., & Berntson, G. G. (1994). Bioelectrical echoes from evaluative categorizations: I. A late positive brain potential that varies as a function of trait negativity and extremity. *Journal of Personality and Social Psychology, 67,* 115-125.

Cacioppo, J. T., Petty, R. E., Feinstein, J. A., & Jarvis, W. B. G. (1996). Dispositional differences in cognitive motivation: The life and times of individuals varying in need for cognition. *Psychological Bulletin, 119,* 197-253.

Cacioppo, J. T., Uchino, B. N., Crites, S. L., Snydersmith, M. A., Smith, G., Berntson, G. G., & Lang, P. J. (1992). Relationship between facial expressiveness and sympathetic activation in emotion: A critical review, with emphasis on modeling underlying mechanisms and individual differences. *Journal of Personality and Social Psychology, 62,* 110-128.

Campbell, D. T. (1986). Science's social system of validity-enhancing collective belief change and the problems of social sciences. In D. W. Fiske & R. A. Shweder (Eds.), *Metatheory in social science* (pp. 108-135). Chicago: University of Chicago Press.

Campbell, D. T., & Fiske, D. W. (1959). Convergent and discriminant validation by the multitrait-multimethod matrix. *Psychological Bulletin, 56,* 81-105.

Canter, D. (Ed.). (1985). *Facet theory: Approaches to social research.* New York: Springer-Verlag.

Capra, F. (1975). *The Tao of physics: An exploration of the parallels between modern physics and Eastern mysticism.* London: Wildwood House.

Carver, C. S., & Scheier, M. F. (1990). Origins and functions of positive and negative affect: A control-process view. *Psychological Review, 97,* 19-36.

Catalano, R. F., Hawkins, J. D., Krenz, C., Gillmore, M., Morrison, D., Wells, E., & Abbott, R. (1993). Using research to guide culturally appropriate drug abuse prevention. *Journal of Consulting and Clinical Psychology, 61*(5), 804-811.

Catrambone, R., Beike, D., & Niedenthal, P. (1996). Is the self-concept a habitual referent in judgments of similarity? *Psychological Science, 7,* 158-163.

Ceci, S. J., & Bruck, M. (1995). *Jeopardy in the courtroom.* Washington, DC: American Psychological Association.

Cervantes, R. C., Gilbert, M. J., Snyder, N. S., & Padilla, A. M. (1990-1991). Psychosocial and cognitive correlates of alcohol use in younger adult immigrant and U.S. born Hispanics. *International Journal of Addictions, 25,* 687-708.

Cha, J. K., & Nam, K. D. (1985). A test of Kelley's Cube Theory of Attribution: A cross-cultural replication of McArthur's study. *Korean Social Science Journal, 12,* 151-180.

Chan, D. K. S., Triandis, H. C., Carnevale, P. J., Tam, A., & Bond, M. H. (1997). *Culture and negotiation: Effects of collectivism, relationship between negotiators, and opponent's strategies on negotiation behavior.* Manuscript submitted for publication.

Chance, J. E., & Goldstein, A. G. (1996). The other-race effect and eyewitness identification. In S. Sporer, R. S. Malpass, & G. Koehnken (Eds.), *Psychological issues in eyewitness identification* (pp. 153-176). Hillsdale, NJ: Lawrence Erlbaum.

Chemers, M. M., Oskamp, S., & Costanzo, M. (1995). *Diversity in organizations.* Thousand Oaks, CA: Sage.

Cheng, P. W., & Novick, L. R. (1992). Covariation in natural causal induction. *Psychological Review, 99,* 365-382.

Cheng, Y. C. (1994). Locus of control as an indicator of Hong Kong teachers' job attitudes and perceptions of organizational characteristics. *Journal of Educational Research, 87,* 180-188.

Chiu, C., & Hong, Y. (1986). *Chinese consumer complaint behaviors as correlates of face situations, attitudinal antecedents, and locus of control.* Unpublished bachelor's thesis, University of Hong Kong.

Chomsky, N. (1980). *Rules and representations.* New York: Columbia University Press.

Christakopoulou, S. (1995). *Koinonikoi desmoi ston psyhologiko horo kai xrono tis koinotitas: Mia diapolitistiki meleti* [Social bonds in the psychological space and time of the community: A cross-cultural study]. Unpublished doctoral dissertation, University of Athens, Greece.

Christensen, H. T. (1964). Development of the family field of study. In H. T. Christensen (Ed.), *Handbook of marriage and family* (pp. 3-32). Chicago: Rand McNally.

Cialdini, R. B., Kallgren, C. A., & Reno, R. R. (1991). A focus theory of normative conduct: A theoretical refinement and reevaluation of the role of norms in human behavior. In M. P. Zanna (Ed.), *Advances in experimental social psychology* (Vol. 24, pp. 202-235). San Diego, CA: Academic Press.

Clancy, P. M. (1986). The acquisition of communicative style in Japanese. In B. B. Schieffelin & E. Ochs (Eds.), *Language socialization across cultures* (pp. 213-250). Cambridge, UK: Press Syndicate of the University of Cambridge.

Clanet, C. (1990). *L'interculturel.* Toulouse, France: Presses Universitaires du Mirail.

Clark, H. H. (1985). Language use and language users. In L. Gardner & E. Aronson (Eds.), *The handbook of social psychology* (3rd ed., pp. 179-231). Hillsdale, NJ: Lawrence Erlbaum.

Clary, E. G., Snyder, M., Ridge, R. D., Miene, P. K., & Haugen, J. A. (1994). Matching messages to motives in persuasion: A functional approach to promoting volunteerism. *Journal of Applied Social Psychology, 24,* 1129-1149.

Claydon, L. F., Knight, T., & Rado, M. (1977). *Curriculum and culture: Schooling in a pluralistic society.* Sydney, Australia: Allen & Unwin.

Cohen, D. (1996). Law, social policy, and violence: The impact of regional cultures. *Journal of Personality and Social Psychology, 70,* 961-978.

Cohen, D., & Nisbett, R. E. (1994). Self-protection and the culture of honor: Explaining southern violence. *Personality and Social Psychology Bulletin, 20*, 551-567.

Cole, M. (1996). *Cultural psychology: A once and future discipline.* Cambridge, MA: Belknap.

Cole, M., & Scribner, S. (1974). *Culture and thought: A psychological introduction.* New York: John Wiley.

Colman, A. (1991a). Crowd psychology in South African murder trials. *American Psychologist, 46*, 1071-1079.

Colman, A. (1991b). Psychological evidence in South African murder trials. *Psychologist, 4*(11), 482-486.

Consedine, J. (1995). *Restorative justice: Healing the effects of crime.* Lyttelton, New Zealand: Ploughshares.

Cooperrider, D. L., & Pasmore, W. A. (1991). The organization dimension of global change. *Human Relations, 44*, 763-787.

Cormack, M. L. (1961). *She who rides the peacock: Indian students and social change.* London: Asian Publishing House.

Cousins, S. D. (1989). Culture and self-perception in Japan and the United States. *Journal of Personality and Social Psychology, 56*, 124-131.

Cowan, P. A., Field, D., Hansen, D. A., Skolnick, A., & Swanson, G. E. (1993). Preface. In P. A. Cowan, D. Field, D. A. Hansen, A. Skolnick, & G. E. Swanson (Eds.), *Family, self, and society: Toward a new agenda for family research* (p. ix). Hillsdale, NJ: Lawrence Erlbaum.

Cox, T., Jr. (1993). *Cultural diversity in organizations.* San Francisco: Berrett-Koehler.

Cribier, F. (1979). Les Parisiens et leur famille l'âge de la retraite. *Gérontologie, 30*, 20-30.

Cronbach, L. J., & Drenth, P. J. D. (1972). *Mental tests and cultural adaptation.* The Hague, The Netherlands: Monton.

Cross, T. L., Bazron, B. J., Dennis, K. W., & Isaacs, M. R. (1989). *Towards a culturally competent system of care* (Vol. 1). Washington, DC: Georgetown University.

Cultural contribution of other ethnic groups, The. (1969). *Report of the Royal Commission on Bilingualism and Biculturalism* (No. 4). Ottawa, Canada: Ministry of Supply and Services.

Cushner, K. (1989). Assessing the impact of a culture-general assimilator. *International Journal of Intercultural Relations, 13*, 125-146.

Cushner, K., & Brislin, R. W. (1996). *Intercultural interactions: A practical guide* (2nd ed.). Thousand Oaks, CA: Sage.

Cushner, K., & Landis, D. (1996). The intercultural sensitizer. In D. Landis & R. S. Bhagat (Eds.), *Handbook of intercultural training.* Thousand Oaks, CA: Sage.

Dailey, R. C. (1978). Relationship between locus of control, perceived group cohesiveness, and satisfaction with coworkers. *Psychological Reports, 42*, 311-316.

Dailey, R. C. (1980). Relationship between locus of control, task characteristics, and work attitudes. *Psychological Reports, 47*, 855-861.

D'Andrade, R. (1990). Some propositions about the relations between culture and human cognition. In J. W. Stigler, R. A. Shweder, & G. Herdt (Eds.), *Cultural psychology: Essays on comparative human development.* Cambridge, UK: Cambridge University Press.

D'Andrade, R. (1995). *The development of cognitive anthropology.* Cambridge, UK: Cambridge University Press.

Dasen, P. R. (1993). What's in a name? *Cross-Cultural Psychology Bulletin, 27*(2), 1-2.

Dasen, P. R., & Jahoda, G. (1986). Preface [Special issue on cross-cultural human development]. *International Journal of Behavioral Development, 9*, 413-416.

Davidson, A. R. (1989). Psychosocial aspects of contraceptive method choice. In R. Bulatao, J. Palmore, & S. Ward (Eds.), *Choosing a contraceptive: Method choice in Asia and the United States* (pp. 27-39). San Francisco: Westview.

Davidson, A. R., & Jaccard, J. J. (1975). Population psychology: A new look at an old problem. *Journal of Personality and Social Psychology, 31*, 1073-1082.

Davidson, A. R., & Jaccard, J. J. (1979). Variables that moderate the attitude-behavior relation: Results of a longitudinal survey. *Journal of Personality and Social Psychology, 37*, 1364-1376.

Davidson, A. R., Jaccard, J. J., Triandis, H. C., Morales, M. L., & Diaz-Guerrero, R. (1976). Cross-cultural model testing: Toward a solution of the etic-emic dilemma. *International Journal of Psychology, 11*, 1-13.

Davidson, A. R., Kalmuss, D., Cushman, L., Romero, D., Heartwell, S., & Rulin, M. (in press). Rates of injectable contraceptive discontinuation and subsequent unintended pregnancy among low-income women. *American Journal of Public Health.*

Davidson, A. R., & Morrison, D. M. (1983). Predicting contraceptive behavior from attitudes: A comparison of within versus across subjects procedures. *Journal of Personality and Social Psychology, 45*, 997-1009.

Davidson, A. R., & Thomson, E. (1980). Cross-cultural studies of attitude and beliefs. In H. Triandis & R. Brislin (Eds.), *Handbook of cross-cultural psychology: Vol. 5. Social psychology.* Boston: Allyn & Bacon.

Davidson, W. H. (1987). Creating and managing joint ventures in China. *California Management Review, 29*(4), 77-94.

Davis, B. J., & Voegtle, K. H. (1994). *Culturally competent health care for adolescents: A guide for the primary health care provider.* Chicago: American Medical Association.

Davison, M. (1983). *Multidimensional scaling.* New York: John Wiley.

De la Rosa, M. (1988). Natural support systems on Puerto Ricans: A key dimension for well-being. *Health & Social Work, 13*(3), 181-190.

De Miguel, A. (1990). *Los españoles.* Madrid, Spain: Ediciones Temas de Hoy.

De Vos, G. A. (1983). Achievement motivation and intra-family attitudes in immigrant Koreans. *Journal of Psychoanalytic Anthropology, 6*, 25-71.

Deaux, K., & Major, B. (1987). Putting gender into context: An interaction model of gender-related behavior. *Psychological Review, 94*, 369-389.

Deffenbacher, K. A., & Loftus, E. F. (1982). Do jurors share a common understanding concerning eyewitness behavior? *Law & Human Behavior, 6*, 15-30.

Denny, J. P. (1986). Contextualisation and differentiation in cross-cultural cognition. In J. W. Berry, S. H. Irvine, & E. B. Hunt (Eds.), *Indigenous cognition: Functioning in cultural context* (pp. 213-229). Boston: Martinus Nijhoff.

Der-Karabetian, A. (1992). World-mindedness and the nuclear threat: A multinational study. *Journal of Social Behavior and Personality, 7*, 293-308.

Deutsch, M. (1994). Constructive conflict resolution: Principles, training, and research. *Journal of Social Issues, 50*, 13-32.

Devine, P. G. (1989). Automatic and controlled processes in prejudice: The role of stereotypes and personal beliefs. In A. R. Pratkanis, S. J. Breckler, & A. G. Greenwald (Eds.), *Attitude structure and function* (pp. 181-212). Hillsdale, NJ: Lawrence Erlbaum.

Dhruvarajan, V. (1988). Religious ideology and interpersonal relationships within the family. *Journal of Comparative Family Studies, 19*(2), 274-285.

Diaz-Guerrero, R. (1975). *Psychology of the Mexican.* Austin: University of Texas Press.

Diaz-Guerrero, R. (1993). On changing the name of IACCP. *Cross-Cultural Psychology Bulletin, 27*, 3-4.

Diener, E. (1980). Deindividuation: The absence of self awareness and self regulation in group members. In P. Paulus (Ed.), *The psychology of group influence.* Hillsdale, NJ: Lawrence Erlbaum.

Digman, J. M. (1990). Personality structure: Emergence of the five-factor model. *Annual Review of Psychology, 41*, 417-440.

Dijker, A. J. (1987). Emotional reactions to ethnic minorities. *European Journal of Social Psychology, 17*, 305-325.

Diller, L., & Hembree, W. (1977). Male contraception and family planning: A social and historical review. *Fertility and Sterility, 28*, 1271-1279.

Dillon, W. R., & Goldstein, M. (1984). *Multivariate analysis*. New York: John Wiley.

Ding, D. Z. (1996). Exploring Chinese conflict management styles in joint venture in the People's Republic of China. *Management Research News, 19*(9), 45-55.

Doherty, W. J., Boss, P. G., LaRossa, R., Schumm, W. R., & Steinmetz, S. K. (1993). Family theories and methods: A contextual approach. In P. G. Boss, W. J. Doherty, R. LaRossa, W. R. Schumm, & S. K. Steinmetz (Eds.), *Sourcebook of family theories and methods* (pp. 3-10). New York: Plenum.

Donnellon, A., & Kolb, D. M. (1994). Constructive for whom? The fate of diversity disputes in organizations. *Journal of Social Issues, 50*(1), 139-155.

Dorai, M. (1993). Effets de la categorisation simple et de la categorisation croisse sur les stereotypes. *International Journal of Psychology, 28*, 3-18.

Doumanis, M. (1983). Mothering in Greece: From collectivism to individualism. *Behavioural Development Monographs*, 1-146.

Dragoti, E. (1996). Ancient crimes return to haunt Albania. *Psychology International, 7*, 1-3.

Druckman, D. (1994). Determinants of compromising behavior in negotiation. *Journal of Conflict Resolution, 38*, 507-556.

Durkheim, E. (1888). Introduction a la sociologie de la famille. *Annales De la Faculte des Lettres de Bordeaux, 10*.

Durkheim, E. (1921). La famille conjugale. *Revue Philosophique de la France et de l'Etranger, 90*, 1-14. (Original work published 1892)

Dweck, C. S., & Leggett, E. L. (1988). A social-cognitive approach to motivation and personality. *Psychological Review, 95*, 256-273.

Eagly, A. H., & Chaiken, S. (1993). *The psychology of attitudes*. Fort Worth, TX: Harcourt Brace Jovanovich.

Earley, P. C. (1997). *Creating hybrid cultures: An empirical test of international team functioning*. Unpublished manuscript, London Business School.

Edwards, D., & Potter, J. (1993). Language and causation: A discursive action model of description and attribution. *Psychological Review, 100*, 23-41.

Eisen, M., Zellman, G. L., & McAlister, A. L. (1992). A health belief model-social learning theory approach to adolescents' fertility control: Findings from a controlled field trail. *Health Education Quarterly, 19*, 249-262.

Elliot, A. J., & Church, M. A. (1997). A hierarchical model of approach and avoidance achievement motivation. *Journal of Personality and Social Psychology, 27*, 218-232.

Ellsworth, P. C. (1994). Sense, culture, and sensibility. In S. Kitayama & H. R. Markus (Eds.), *Emotion and culture: Empirical studies of mutual influence* (pp. 23-50). Washington, DC: American Psychological Association.

Elman, J. L. (1990). Finding structure in time. *Cognitive Science, 14*, 179-211.

Elman, J. L. (1995). Language as a dynamical system. In R. F. Port & T. Van Gelder (Eds.), *Mind as motion* (pp. 195-225). Cambridge, MA: MIT Press.

Engels, F. (1948). *L'origin de la famille, de la propriete privee et de l'etat*. Paris: Costes. (Original work published 1884)

Enriquez, V. (1990). *Indigenous psychologies*. Quezon City, The Philippines: Psychology Research and Training House.

Epstein, S. (1994). Integration of the cognitive and psychodynamic unconscious. *American Psychologist, 49*, 709-724.

Erber, R., & Wegner, D. M. (1996). Ruminations on the rebound. In R. S. Wyer, Jr. (Ed.), *Ruminative thoughts: Advances in social cognition* (Vol. 9, pp. 73-80). Mahwah, NJ: Lawrence Erlbaum.

Ericsson, K. A., & Charness, N. (1994). Expert performance: Its structure and acquisition. *American Psychologist, 49*, 725-747.

Ericsson, K. A., Krampe, R. T., & Tesch-Römer, C. (1993). The role of deliberate practice in the acquisition of expert performance. *Psychological Review, 100*, 363-406.

Ervin-Tripp, S. (1964). An analysis of the interaction of language, topic, and listener. *American Anthropologist, 66*, 86-102.

Esses, V. M., Haddock, G., & Zanna, M. P. (1993). Values, stereotypes, and emotions as determinants of intergroup attitudes. In D. M. Mackie & D. L. Hamilton (Eds.), *Affect, cognition, and
stereotyping: Interactive processes in group perception* (pp. 137-166). New York: Academic Press.

Fazio, R. H. (1989). On the power and functionality of attitudes. In A. R. Pratkanis, S. J. Breckler,
& A. G. Greenwald (Eds.), *Attitude structure and function* (pp. 153-179). Hillsdale, NJ:
Lawrence Erlbaum.

Fazio, R. H. (1990). Multiple processes by which attitudes guide behavior: The MODE model as
an integrative framework. In M. P. Zanna (Ed.), *Advances in experimental social psychology* (Vol.
23, pp. 75-110). San Diego, CA: Academic Press.

Fazio, R. H., Blascovich, J., & Driscoll, D. M. (1992). On the functional value of attitudes: The
influence of accessible attitudes on the ease and quality of decision making. *Personality and
Social Psychology Bulletin, 18,* 388-401.

Feather, N. T. (1980). Similarity of values systems within the same nation: Evidence from
Australia and Papua New Guinea. *Australian Journal of Psychology, 32,* 17-30.

Feather, N. T., Volkmer, R. E., & McKee, I. R. (1992). A comparative study of the value priorities
of Australians, Australian Baha'is, and expatriate Iranian Baha'is. *Journal of Cross-Cultural
Psychology, 23,* 95-106.

Feldman, J. M. (1988). Objects in categories and objects as categories. In T. K. Srull & R. S. Wyer,
Jr. (Eds.), *Advances in social cognition* (Vol. 1, pp. 53-65). Hillsdale, NJ: Lawrence Erlbaum.

Feldman, J. M. (1992). Constructive processes as a source of context effects in survey research:
Explorations in self-generated validity. In N. Schwarz & S. Sudman (Eds.), *Context effects in
social and psychological research* (pp. 49-62). New York: Springer-Verlag.

Feldman, J. M. (1994). On the synergy between theory and application: Social cognition and
performance appraisal. In R. S. Wyer, Jr., & T. K. Srull (Eds.), *Handbook of social cognition* (2nd
ed., Vol. 2, pp. 339-397). Hillsdale, NJ: Lawrence Erlbaum.

Feldman, J. M., Ah-Sam, I., McDonald, W. F., & Bechtel, G. G. (1980). Work outcome preference
and evaluation: A study of three ethnic groups. *Journal of Cross-Cultural Psychology, 11,*
444-468.

Feldman, J. M., & Hilterman, R. J. (1975). Stereotype attribution revisited: The role of stimulus
characteristics, racial attitude, and cognitive differentiation. *Journal of Personality and Social
Psychology, 31,* 1177-1188.

Feldman, J. M., & Lindell, M. K. (1990). On rationality. In I. Horowitz (Ed.), *Organization and
decision theory* (pp. 83-164). Boston: Kluwer Academic.

Feldman, J. M., & Lynch, J. G., Jr. (1988). Self-generated validity and other effects of measurement
on belief, attitude, intention, and behavior. *Journal of Applied Psychology, 73,* 421-435.

Felson, R. B. (1978). Aggression as impression management. *Social Psychology Quarterly, 41,*
205-213.

Feshbach, S. (1987). Individual aggression, national attachment, and the search for peace:
Psychological perspectives. *Aggressive Behavior, 13,* 315-325.

Fiedler, F. E., Mitchell, T. R., & Triandis, H. C. (1971). The culture assimilator: An approach to
cross-cultural training. *Journal of Applied Psychology, 55,* 95-102.

Fiedler, K. (1996). Explaining and simulating judgment biases as an aggregation phenomenon
in probabilistic, multiple-cue environments. *Psychological Review, 103,* 193-214.

Fijneman, Y. A., Willemsen, M. E., & Poortinga, Y. H. (with Erelcin, F. G., Georgas, J., Hui, H. C.,
Leung, K., & Malpass, R. S.). (1996). Individualism-collectivism: An empirical study of a
conceptual issue. *Journal of Cross-Cultural Psychology, 27,* 381-402.

Filteau, C. H. (1980). The role to the concept of love in the Hindu family acculturation process.
In K. V. Ujimoto & G. Hirabayahi (Eds.), *Visible minorities and multiculturalism: Asians in Canada*
(pp. 289-299). Toronto, Canada: Butterworth.

Fischhoff, B., Slovic, P., & Lichtenstein, S. (1980). Knowing what you want: Measuring labile
values. In T. Wallsten (Ed.), *Cognitive processes in choice and decision behavior* (pp. 117-142).
Hillsdale, NJ: Lawrence Erlbaum.

Fishbein, H. (1996). *Peer prejudice and discrimination.* Boulder, CO: Westview.

Fishbein, M., & Ajzen, I. (1975). *Belief, attitude, intention, and behavior: An introduction to theory and research.* Reading, MA: Addison-Wesley.

Fishbein, M., Bandura, A., Triandis, H., Kanfer, F., Becker, M., & Middlestadt, S. E. (1993). *Factors influencing behavior and behavior change.* Report prepared for the National Institute of Mental Health [NIMH]. Bethesda, MD: NIMH.

Fisher, J. D., & Fisher, W. A. (1992). Changing AIDS risk behavior. *Psychological Bulletin, 111,* 455-474.

Fishman, J. A. (1972). *Language and nationalism.* Rowley, MA: Newbury House.

Fiske, A. P. (1990). *Structures of social life: The four elementary forms of human relations.* New York: Free Press.

Fiske, A. P. (1992). The four elementary forms of sociality: A framework for a unified theory of human relations. *Psychological Review, 99,* 689-723.

Fiske, D. W. (1986). Specificity of method and knowledge in social science. In D. W. Fiske & R. A. Shweder (Eds.), *Metatheory in social science* (pp. 61-82). Chicago: University of Chicago Press.

Fiske, S. T., & Neuberg, S. L. (1990). A continuum of impression formation, from category-based to individuating processes: Influence of information and motivation on attention and interpretation. In M. P. Zanna (Ed.), *Advances in experimental social psychology* (Vol. 23, pp. 1-74). San Diego, CA: Academic Press.

Fiske, S. T., & Taylor, S. E. (1991). *Social cognition* (2nd ed.). New York: McGraw-Hill.

Fitzgerald, R. (Trans.). (1963). *Homer: The odyssey.* New York: Anchor.

Fitzpatrick, J. P. (1971). *Puerto Rican Americans.* Englewood Cliffs, NJ: Prentice Hall.

Foa, E. B., & Foa, U. G. (1980). Resource theory: Interpersonal behavior as exchange. In K. J. Gergen, M. S. Greenberg, & R. H. Willis (Eds.), *Social exchange: Advances in theory and research* (pp. 77-94). New York: Plenum.

Foa, U. G., & Foa, E. B. (1974). *Societal structures of the mind.* Springfield, IL: Charles C Thomas.

Fodor, J. A. (1975). *The language of thought.* New York: Thomas Y. Crowell.

Folger, R. (1977). Distributive and procedural justice: Combined impact of "voice" and improvement on experienced inequity. *Journal of Personality and Social Psychology, 35,* 108-119.

Folkman, S. (1984). Personal control and stress and coping process: A theoretical analysis. *Journal of Personality and Social Psychology, 46,* 839-852.

Fong, G. T., & Markus, H. (1982). Self-schemas and judgments about others. *Social Cognition, 1,* 191-204.

Fong, M. C. W. (1996). *Exploring attitudes towards global culture and their personality correlates.* Unpublished bachelor's thesis, Chinese University of Hong Kong.

Fontaine, J., & Schwartz, S. H. (1996, August). *Universality and bias in the structure of psychological questionnaire data.* Paper presented at the 12th Congress of the International Association for Cross-Cultural Psychology, Montreal, Quebec, Canada.

Forgas, J. P. (1995). Mood and judgment: The affect infusion model. *Psychological Bulletin, 117,* 39-66.

Foster, D. A. (1992). *Bargaining across borders.* New York: McGraw-Hill.

Fowers, B. J., & Richardson, F. C. (1996). Why is multiculturalism good? *American Psychologist, 51,* 609-621.

Frank, A. W. (Ed.). (1981). *The encyclopedia of sociology.* Guilford, CT: DRG Reference.

Frankel, M. (1981). *Partisan justice.* New York: Hill & Wang.

Freedman, R. (1963). Norms for family size in underdeveloped areas. *Proceedings of the Royal Society, 159,* 220-245.

Freedman, R., Hermann, A., & Chang, M. (1975). Do statements about desired family size predict fertility? The case of Taiwan, 1967-1970. *Demography, 12,* 407-416.

Freedman, R., & Takashima, J. (1969). *Family planning in Taiwan.* Princeton, NJ: Princeton University Press.

Freedman, S. M., & Philips, J. S. (1985). The effects of situational performance constraints on intrinsic motivation and satisfaction: The role of perceived competence and self-determination. *Organizational Behavior & Human Decision Processes, 35,* 397-416.

Freeman, J. A. (1994). *Simulating neural networks with mathematica.* Reading, MA: Addison-Wesley.

Frijda, N., & Jahoda, G. (1966). On the scope and methods of cross-cultural research. *International Journal of Psychology, 1,* 109-127.

Furnham, A. (1985). Just world beliefs in an unjust society: A cross-cultural comparison. *European Journal of Social Psychology, 15,* 363-366.

Gable, M., & Topol, M. T. (1989). Machiavellianism and job satisfaction of retailing executives in a specialty store chain. *Psychological Reports, 64,* 107-112.

Gabrielidis, C., Stephan, W. G., Ybarra, O., Pearson, V. M. S., & Villareal, L. (1997). Preferred styles of conflict resolution: Mexico and the United States. *Journal of Cross-Cultural Psychology, 28,* 661-677.

Gaertner, S. L., Dovidio, J. F., Anastasio, P A., Bachman, B. A., & Rust, M. C. (1993). The common ingroup identity model: Recategorization and the reduction of intergroup bias. In W. Stroebe & M. Hewstone (Eds.), *European Review of Social Psychology, 4,* 1-26.

Gallois, C., & Markel, N. N. (1975). Turn taking: Social personality and conversational style. *Journal of Personality and Social Psychology, 31,* 1134-1140.

Gardner, H. (1993). *Multiple intellegences: The theory in practice.* New York: Basic Books.

Geertz, C. (1973). *The interpretation of cultures.* New York: Basic Books.

Gelman, S., & Byrnes, J. P. (Eds.). (1991). *Perspectives on language and thought.* Cambridge, UK: Cambridge University Press.

Georgas, J. (1986). *Koinonike psychologia* [Social psychology] (Vol. A). Athens, Greece: University of Athens Press.

Georgas, J. (1988). An ecological and social cross-cultural model: The case of Greece. In J. W. Berry, S. H. Irvine, & E. B. Hunt (Eds.), *Indigenous cognition: Functioning in cultural context* (pp. 105-123). Dordrecht, The Netherlands: Martinus Nijhoff.

Georgas, J. (1989). Changing family values in Greece: From collectivist to individualist. *Journal of Cross-Cultural Psychology, 20,* 80-91.

Georgas, J. (1991a). Intrafamily acculturation of values in Greece. *Journal of Cross-Cultural Psychology, 22,* 445-457.

Georgas, J. (1991b, July). The relationship of family structure to allocentric and idiocentric orientation. In U. Kim (Chair), *Culture and self: Social and applied issues.* Symposium conducted at the 11th Congress of the International Association for Cross-Cultural Psychology, Liege, Belgium.

Georgas, J. (1993). An ecological-social model for indigenous psychology: The example of Greece. In U. Kim & J. W. Berry (Eds.), *Indigenous psychologies: Theory, method, and experience in cultural context* (pp. 56-78). Newbury Park, CA: Sage.

Georgas, J. (1994, July). Family structure and function in cross-cultural context. In J. Georgas (Chair), *Psychological consequences of family structure.* Symposium conducted at the 23rd International Congress of Applied Psychology, Madrid, Spain.

Georgas, J., & Berry, J. W. (1995). An ecultural taxonomy for cross-cultural psychology. *Cross-Cultural Research, 29,* 121-157.

Georgas, J., & Christakopoulou, S. (1993, July). *Psychosocial distance of the family and the neighborhood.* Paper presented at the 3rd European Congress of Psychology, Tampere, Finland.

Georgas, J., Christakopoulou, S., Poortinga, Y. H., Goodwin, R., Angleitner, A., & Charalambous, N. (1997). The relationship of family bonds to family structure and function across cultures. *Journal of Cross-Cultural Psychology, 28,* 303-320.

Gergen, K. J. (1985). The social constructionist movement in modern psychology. *American Psychologist, 40,* 266-275.

Gerhart, B. (1987). How important are dispositional factors as determinants of job satisfaction? Implications for job design and other personal programs. *Journal of Applied Psychology, 72,* 366-373.

Gerrig, R. J., & Banaji, M. R. (1994). Language and thought. In R. J. Sternberg (Ed.), *Handbook of perception and cognition: Vol. 12. Thinking and problem solving* (2nd ed., pp. 233-261). San Diego, CA: Academic Press.

Ghosh, R. (1983). Sarees and the maple leaf: Indian women in Canada. In G. Kurian & R. Srivastava (Eds.), *Overseas Indians: A study in adaptation* (pp. 90-99). Delhi, India: Vikas.

Giddens, A. (1993). *New rules of sociological method: A positive critique of interpretative sociologies.* Stanford, CA: Stanford University Press. (Original work published 1976)

Gilbert, D. T. (1989). Thinking lightly about others: Automatic components of the social inference process. In J. S. Uleman & J. A. Bargh (Eds.), *Unintended thought* (pp. 189-211). New York: Guilford.

Gilbert, D. T., & Malone, P. S. (1995). The correspondence bias. *Psychological Bulletin, 117,* 21-38.

Gillin, J. (1965). Ethos components in modern Latin American culture. In D. Heath & R. Adams (Eds.), *Contemporary cultures and societies of Latin America.* New York: Random House.

Gilmore, D. D. (1987). *Aggression and community.* New Haven, CT: Yale University Press.

Goizueta, R. S. (1995). *Caminemos con Jesús: Toward a Hispanic/Latino theology of accompaniment.* Maryknoll, NY: Orbis Books.

Gokalp, C. (1978). Le Réseau familial. *Population, 6,* 1077-1094.

Goldstone, R. L. (1995). Effects of categorization on color perception. *Psychological Science, 6,* 298-304.

Goodman, N. (1978). *Ways of worldmaking.* Indianapolis, IN: Hacket.

Gordon, C. (1968). Self-conceptions: Configurations of content. In C. Gordon & K. J. Gergen (Eds.), *The self in social interaction: Vol. 1. Classic and contemporary perspectives* (pp. 115-136). New York: John Wiley.

Goto, S. G. (1996). *Dealing with cultural diversity: An empirical test of a causal model of intergroup relations.* Unpublished doctoral dissertation, University of Illinois at Urbana-Champaign.

Gough, J. (1979). Some factors related to men's willingness to use a male contraceptive pill. *Journal of Sex Research, 15,* 27-37.

Grebler, L., Moore, J. W., & Guzman, R. C. (1970). *The Mexican-American people: The nation's second largest minority.* New York: Free Press.

Greenfield, P. M. (1997). Culture as process: Empirical methods for cultural psychology. In J. W. Berry, Y. H. Poortinga, & J. Pandey (Eds.), *Handbook of cross-cultural psychology: Vol. 1. Theory and method* (pp. 301-346). Boston: Allyn & Bacon.

Greenfield, P., & Smith, J. (1976). *The structure of communication in early language development.* New York: Academic Press.

Greenwald, A. G., & Banaji, M. R. (1995). Implicit social cognition: Attitudes, self-esteem, and stereotypes. *Psychological Review, 102,* 4-27.

Greenwald, A. G., & Pratkanis, A. (1984). The self. In R. S. Wyer, Jr., & T. K. Srull (Eds.), *Handbook of social cognition.* Hillsdale, NJ: Lawrence Erlbaum.

Gubrium, J. F., & Holstein, J. A. (1990). *What is family?* Mountain View, CA: Mayfield.

Gudykunst, W. B., & Bond, M. H. (1997). Intergroup relations across cultures. In J. W. Berry, M. H. Segall, & C. Kagitcibasi (Eds.), *Handbook of cross-cultural psychology* (2nd ed., pp. 119-162). Boston: Allyn & Bacon.

Gudykunst, W. B., & Hammer, M. R. (1983). Basic training design: Approaches to intercultural training. In D. Landis & R. W. Brislin (Eds.), *Handbook of intercultural training: Issues in theory and design* (Vol. 1, pp. 118-154). Elmsford, NY: Pergamon.

Gudykunst, W. B., Hammer, M. R., & Wiseman, R. (1977). An analysis of an integrated approach to cross-cultural training. *International Journal of Intercultural Relations, 1,* 99-109.

Gudykunst, W. B., & Ting-Toomey, S. (1988). Culture and affective communication. *American Behavioral Scientist, 31,* 384-400.

Gudykunst, W. B., Ting-Toomey, S., & Chua, E. (1988). *Culture and interpersonal communication.* Newbury Park, CA: Sage.

Gumperz, J. J., & Levinson, S. C. (1991). Rethinking linguistic relativity. *Current Antholopology, 32,* 613-623.

Guttman, L. (1968). A general nonmetric technique for finding the smallest coordinate space for a configuration of points. *Psychometrica, 33,* 469-506.

Habermann, G. M. (1996). Linguistic socialization in the languages of China. In M. H. Bond (Ed.), *Handbook of Chinese psychology.* Hong Kong: Oxford University Press.

Hackman, J. R., & Oldham, G. R. (1975). Development of the job diagnostic survey. *Journal of Applied Psychology, 60,* 159-170.

Haddock, G., Zanna, M. P., & Esses, V. M. (1993). Assessing the structure of prejudicial attitudes: The case of attitudes towards homosexuals. *Journal of Personality and Social Psychology, 65,* 1105-1118.

Hagan, J., Merkens, H., & Boehnke, K. (1995). Delinquency and disdain: Social capital and the control of right wing extremism among East and West Berlin youth. *American Journal of Sociology, 100,* 1018-1052.

Hagan, J., Rippl, S., Boehnke, K., & Merkens, H. (1998). *The interest in evil: Hierarchic self-interest and right-wing extremism among East and West German youth.* Manuscript submitted for publication.

Hall, E. T. (1966). *The hidden dimension.* New York: Doubleday.

Hall, E. T. (1973). *The silent language.* New York: Doubleday.

Hall, E. T. (1976). *Beyond culture.* New York: Doubleday.

Hamilton, D. L., Sherman, S. J., & Ruvolo, C. M. (1990). Stereotype-based expectancies: Effects on information processing and social behavior. *Journal of Personality and Social Psychology, 46,* 35-60.

Hamilton, V. L., & Sanders, J. (1988). Punishment and the individual in the United States and Japan. *Law and Society Review, 22,* 301-328.

Hanson, C., & Hanson, S. J. (1996). Development of schemata during even parsing: Neisser's perceptual cycle as a recurrent connectionist network. *Journal of Cognitive Neuroscience, 8,* 119-134.

Harackiewicz, J. M., & Elliot, A. J. (1993). Achievement goals and intrinsic motivation. *Journal of Personality and Social Psychology, 65,* 904-915.

Hardin, C., & Banaji, M. R. (1993). The influence of language on thought. *Social Cognition, 11,* 277-308.

Harrison, J. K. (1992). Individual and combined effects of behavior modeling and the culture assimilator in cross-cultural management training. *Journal of Applied Psychology, 77,* 952-962.

Hatcher, W. S. (1998, September). *Love, power, and justice.* Hasan Balyuzi memorial lecture given at the 22nd Annual Conference of the Association of Baha'i Studies, Montreal, Quebec, Canada.

Hegarty, W. H., & Dalton, D. R. (1995). Development and psychometric properties of the Organizational Diversity Inventory (ODI). *Educational and Psychological Measurement, 55*(6), 1047-1052.

Heller, C. S. (1966). *Mexican American youth: Forgotten youth at the crossroads.* New York: Random House.

Heller, W. M., & Mahmoudi, H. (1992). Altruism and extensivity in the Baha'i religion. In P. M. Oliner, S. P. Oliver, L. Baron, L. A. Blum, D. L. Krebs, & M. Z. Smolenska (Eds.), *Embracing the other: Philosophical, psychological, and historical perspectives on altruism* (pp. 420-432). New York: New York University Press.

Henderson, G. (1994). *Cultural diversity in the workplace.* Wesport, CT: Praeger.

Herbst, P. G. (1952). The measurement of family relationships. *Human Relationships, 5,* 3-35.

Herbst, P. G. (1954). Conceptual framework for studying the family. In O. A. Oeser & S. B. Hammond (Eds.), *Social structure and personality in a city.* New York: Macmillan.

Hewstone, M., & Brown, R. J. (1986). Contact is not enough: An intergroup perspective on the contact hypothesis. In M. Hewstone & R. J. Brown (Eds.), *Contact and conflict in intergroup encounters* (pp. 1-44). Oxford, UK: Basil Blackwell.

Higgins, E. T. (1989). Knowledge accessibility and activation: Subjectivity and suffering from unconscious sources. In J. S. Uleman & J. A. Bargh (Eds.), *Unintended thought* (pp. 75-123). New York: Guilford.

Higgins, E. T. (1996). Ideals, oughts, and regulatory focus: Affect and motivation from distinct pains and pleasures. In P. M. Gollwitzer & J. A. Bargh (Eds.), *The psychology of action* (pp. 91-114). New York: Guilford.

Higgins, E. T., & King, G. (1981). Accessibility of social constructs: Information processing consequences of individual and contextual validity. In N. Cantor & J. J. Kihlstrom (Eds.), *Personality, cognition, and social interaction* (pp. 69-121). Hillsdale, NJ: Lawrence Erlbaum.

Higgins, E. T., King, G. A., & Mavin, G. H. (1982). Individual construct accessibility and subjective impressions and recall. *Journal of Personality and Social Psychology, 43,* 35-47.

Hill, J. H., & Mannheim, B. (1992). Language and world view. *Annual Review of Anthropology, 21,* 381-406.

Hill, R., & Rodgers, R. (1964). The developmental approach. In H. Christensen (Ed.), *Handbook of marriage and the family* (pp. 171-211). Chicago: Rand McNally.

Hilton, D. J. (1995). The social context of reasoning: Conversational inference and rational judgment. *Psychological Review, 118,* 248-271.

Hinds, J. (1982). *Ellipsis in Japanese.* Edmonton, Canada: Linguistic Research.

Hinton, G. E., & Anderson, J. A. (Eds.). (1981). *Parallel models of associative memory.* Hillsdale, NJ: Lawrence Erlbaum.

Hoch, S. J. (1984). Availability and interference in predictive judgment. *Journal of Experimental Psychology: Learning, Memory, and Cognition, 10,* 649-662.

Hoffman, D. M. (1996). Culture and self in multicultural education: Reflections on discourse, text, and practice. *American Educational Research Journal, 33,* 545-570.

Hofstadter, R. (1955). *Social Darwinism and American thought.* Boston: Beacon.

Hofstede, G. (1980). *Culture's consequences: International differences in work-related values.* Beverly Hills, CA: Sage.

Hofstede, G. (1991). *Cultures and organizations: Software of the mind.* London: McGraw-Hill.

Holland, A., & Andre, T. (1987). Participation in extracurricular activities in secondary school. *Review of Educational Research, 57,* 437-466.

Hollins, E. R. (Ed.). (1996). *Transforming curriculum for a culturally diverse society.* Mahwah, NJ: Lawrence Erlbaum.

Hollon, C. J. (1983). Machiavellianism and managerial work attitudes and perceptions. *Psychological Reports, 52,* 432-434.

Holyoak, K. J., & Gordon, P. C. (1983). Social reference points. *Journal of Personality and Social Psychology, 44,* 881-887.

Homans, G. C. (1976). Commentary. In L. Berkowitz & E. Walster (Eds.), *Advances in experimental social psychology* (Vol. 9, pp. 231-244). San Diego, CA: Academic Press.

Hooper, J. (1986). *The Spaniards: A portrait of the new Spain.* New York: Viking.

Horner, M. S. (1970). Femininity and successful achievement. In J. M. Bardwick, E. Donvan, M. S. Horner, & D. Gutmann (Eds.), *Feminine personality and conflict* (pp. 45-74). Pacific Grove, CA: Brooks/Cole.

Horowitz, S. V., & Boardman, S. K. (1994). Managing conflict: Policy and research implications. *Journal of Social Issues, 50,* 197-211.

Huang, J. (1984). On the typology of zero anaphora. *Ohak Yongu [Language Research], 20,* 85-105.

Hughes-Wiener, G. (1986). The "learning how to learn" approach to cross-cultural orientation. *International Journal of Intercultural Relations, 10,* 485-505.

Hui, C. H. (1991). Religious and supernaturalistic beliefs. In S. K. Lau, M. K. Lee, P. S. Wan, & S. L. Wong (Eds.), *Indicators of social development: Hong Kong 1988* (pp. 103-143). Hong Kong: Chinese University of Hong Kong.

Hui, C. H., & Triandis, H. C. (1986). Individualism-collectivism: A study of cross-cultural researchers. *Journal of Cross-Cultural Psychology, 17,* 225-248.

Hui, C. H., Yee, C., & Eastman, K. L. (1995). The relationship between individualism-collectivism and job satisfaction. *Applied Psychology: An International Review, 44,* 276-282.

Humana, C. (1986). *World human rights guide.* London: Pan.

Hunt, E. B., & Agnoli, F. (1991). The Whorfian hypothesis: A cognitive psychology perspective. *Psychological Review, 98,* 377-389.

Hunt, E. B., & Banaji, M. R. (1986). The Whorfian hypothesis revisited: A cognitive science view of linguistic and cultural effects on thought. In J. W. Berry, S. H. Irvine, & E. B. Hunt (Eds.), *Indigenous cognition: Functioning in cultural context* (pp. 57-84). Boston: Martinus Nijhoff.

Huo, Y. J., Smith, H. J., Tyler, T. R., & Lind, E. A. (1996). Superordinate identification, subgroup identification, and justice concerns: Is separatism the problem, is assimilation the answer? *Psychological Science, 7,* 40-45.

Hutchins, E., & Hazelhurst, B. (1993). *How to invent a lexicon: The development of shared symbols in interaction.* University of California, San Diego, Department of Cognitive Science.

Institutos Nacionales de la Salud. (1993). *Rompa con el vicio* (NIH Publication No. 94-3001). Washington, DC: National Cancer Institute.

Ironson, G. H., Smith, P. C., Brannick, M. T., Gibson, W. M., & Paul, K. B. (1989). Construction of a job in general scale: A comparison of global, composite, and specific measures. *Journal of Applied Psychology, 74,* 193-200.

Isasi-Díaz, A., & Tarango, Y. (1992). *Hispanic women: Prophetic voices in the church.* Minneapolis, MN: Fortress Press.

Isen, A. W., & Diamond, G. A. (1989). Affect and automaticity. In J. S. Uleman & J. A. Bargh (Eds.), *Unintended thought* (pp. 124-152). New York: Guilford.

Isenberg, D. J. (1986). Group polarization: A critical review and meta-analysis. *Journal of Personality and Social Psychology, 50,* 1141-1151.

Islam, R. M., & Hewstone, M. (1993). Dimensions of contact as predictors of intergroup anxiety, perceived outgroup variability, and outgroup attitude: An integration model. *Personality and Social Psychology Bulletin, 19,* 700-710.

Ito, K., & Triandis, H. C. (1989). *Cultural assimilator for Japanese visiting in the United States.* Urbana: University of Illinois, Department of Psychology.

Jaccard, J. (1975). A theoretical analysis of selected factors important to health education strategies. *Health Education Monographs, 3,* 152-166.

Jaccard, J. (1981). Attitudes and behavior: Implications of attitudes towards behavioral alternatives. *Journal of Experimental Social Psychology, 17,* 286-307.

Jaccard, J. (1995). *Adolescent contraceptive behavior: Conceptual and applied issues.* Paper presented at conference, Improving contraceptive use in the United States: Assessing past efforts and setting new directions. Bethesda, MD, October 5-6.

Jaccard, J., & Becker, M. (1985). Attitudes and behavior: An information integration perspective. *Journal of Experimental Social Psychology, 21,* 440-465.

Jaccard, J., Radecki, C., Wilson, T., & Dittus, P. (1995). Methods for identifying consequential beliefs: Implications for understanding attitude strength. In R. Petty & J. Krosnick (Eds.), *Attitude strength: Antecedents and consequences.* Hillsdale, NJ: Lawrence Erlbaum.

Jaccard, J., & Wood, G. (1986). An idiothetic analysis of consumer decision making. In D. Brinberg & R. Lutz (Eds.), *Perspectives on methodology in consumer research.* New York: Springer-Verlag.

Jackson, S. E. (1991). Team composition in organizational settings: Issues in managing an increasingly diverse work force. In S. Worchel, W. Wood, & J. A. Simpson (Eds.), *Group process and productivity* (pp. 138-173). Newbury Park, CA: Sage.

Jackson, S. E., & Associates. (1992). *Diversity in the workplace.* New York: Guilford.

Jackson, S. E., & Ruderman, M. N. (1995). *Diversity in work teams.* Washington, DC: American Psychological Association.

Jahoda, G. (1980). Theoretical and systematic approaches in cross-cultural psychology. In H. C. Triandis & W. W. Lambert (Eds.), *Handbook of cross-cultural psychology* (pp. 69-142). Boston: Allyn & Bacon.

Jahoda, G. (1982). *Psychology and anthropology.* London: Academic Press.

Jahoda, G. (1992). *Crossroads between culture and mind.* London: Harvester Wheatsheaf.

Jahoda, G., & Krewer, B. (1997). History of cross-cultural and cultural psychology. In J. W. Berry, Y. H. Poortinga, & J. Pandey (Eds.), *Handbook of cross-cultural psychology: Vol. 1. Theory and method* (2nd ed.). Boston: Allyn & Bacon.

James, K. (1993). The social context of organizational justice: Cultural, intergroup, and structural effects on justice behaviors and perceptions. In R. Cropanzano (Ed.), *Justice in the workplace* (pp. 21-50). Hillsdale, NJ: Lawrence Erlbaum.

James, K., Chen, D. L., & Cropanzano, R. (1996). Culture and leadership among Taiwanese and U.S. workers: Do values influence leadership ideals? In M. N. Ruderman, M. W. Hughes-James, & S. E. Jackson (Eds.), *Selected research on work team diversity* (pp. 33-52). Greensboro, NC: Center for Creative Leadership/American Psychological Association.

James, L. R. (1998). Measurement of personality via conditional reasoning. *Journal of Organizational Research Methods, 1,* 131-163.

James, W. (1950). *The principles of psychology* (Vols. 1-2). New York: Dover. (Original work published 1890)

James, W. (1970). The moral equivalent of war. In R. A. Wasserstrom (Ed.), *War and morality.* Belmont, CA: Wadsworth. (Original work published 1910)

Jayakody, R., Chatters, L. M., & Taylor, R. J. (1993). Family support to single and married African American mothers: The provision of financial, emotional, and child care assistance. *Journal of Marriage and the Family, 55,* 261-276.

Jaynes, J. (1976). *The origins of consciousness in the breakdown of the bicameral mind.* Boston: Houghton Mifflin.

Jessor, R. (1991). Risk behavior in adolescence: A psychosocial framework for understanding and action. *Journal of Adolescent Health, 12,* 579-605.

Jordan, B. (1989). Cosmopolitical obstetrics: Some insights from the training of traditional midwives. *Social Science and Medicine, 28,* 925-944.

Judd, C. M., & Krosnick, J. A. (1989). The structural bases of consistency among political attitudes: Effects of political expertise and attitude importance. In A. R. Pratkanis, S. J. Breckler, & A. G. Greenwald (Eds.), *Attitude structure and function* (pp. 99-128). Hillsdale, NJ: Lawrence Erlbaum.

Jussim, L. (1991). Social perception and social reality: A reflection-construction model. *Psychological Review, 98,* 54-73.

Kagan, S. (1977). Social motives and behaviors of Mexican-Americans and Anglo children. In J. L. Martinez (Ed.), *Chicano psychology* (pp. 45-86). New York: Academic Press.

Kagan, S., & Zahn, G. L. (1983). Cultural differences in individualism? Just artifact. *Hispanic Journal of Behavioral Sciences, 5,* 219-232.

Kagitcibasi, C. (1990a, July). *A critical appraisal of individualism and collectivism: Towards a new formulation.* Paper presented at the Conference on Individualism and Collectivism: Psychocultural Perspectives from East and West, Seoul, South Korea.

Kagitcibasi, C. (1990b). Family and socialization in cross-cultural perspective: A model of change. In J. Berman (Ed.), *Cross-cultural perspectives: Nebraska Symposium on Motivation* (pp. 135-200). Lincoln: University of Nebraska Press.

Kagitcibasi, C. (1994). A critical appraisal of individualism and collectivism. In U. Kim, H. C. Triandis, C. Kagitcibasi, S.-C. Choi, & G. Yoon (Eds.), *Individualism and collectivism* (pp. 52-65). Thousand Oaks, CA: Sage.

Kagitcibasi, C. (1996). *Family and human development across cultures.* Mahwah, NJ: Lawrence Erlbaum.

Kahn, C. H. (1979). *The art and thought of Heraclitus.* Cambridge, UK: Cambridge University Press.

Kahneman, D. (1973). *Attention and effect.* Englewood Cliffs, NJ: Prentice Hall.

Kahneman, D., Slovic, P., & Tversky, A. (1982). *Judgment under uncertainty: Heuristics and biases.* Cambridge, UK: Cambridge University Press.

Kalin, R., & Berry, J. W. (1980). Geographic mobility and ethnic tolerance. *Journal of Social Issues, 112,* 129-134.

Kalin, R., & Berry, J. W. (1982). The social ecology of ethnic attitudes in Canada. *Canadian Journal of Behavioural Science, 14,* 97-109.

Kanfer, R. (1990). Motivation theory and industrial-organizational psychology. In M. D. Dunnette & L. Hough (Eds.), *Handbook of industrial and organizational psychology: Vol. 1. Theory in industrial and organizational psychology* (pp. 75-170). Palo Alto, CA: Consulting Psychologists Press.

Kanfer, R. (1996). Self-regulatory and other non-ability determinants of skill acquisition. In P. M. Gollwitzer & J. A. Bargh (Eds.), *The psychology of action* (pp. 404-421). New York: Guilford.

Kanfer, R., & Ackerman, P. L. (1989). Motivation and cognitive abilities: An integrative aptitude/ treatment interaction approach to skill acquisition [Monograph]. *Journal of Applied Psychology, 74,* 657-690.

Kashima, E. S., & Kashima, Y. (1997). Practice of the self in conversations: Pronoun drop, sentence co-production, and contextualization of the self. In K. Leung, Y. Kashima, U. Kim, & S. Yamaguchi (Eds.), *Progress in Asian social psychology* (pp. 165-179). Singapore: Wiley.

Kashima, E. S., & Kashima, Y. (1998). Culture and language: The case of cultural dimensions and personal pronoun use. *Journal of Cross-Cultural Psychology, 29,* 461-486.

Kashima, Y. (1994). The production and reproduction of the "person": Toward a situated practice theory of cultural change and beyond. *Proceedings of Asian psychologies: Indigenous, social, and cultural perspectives.* Seoul, South Korea: Chung-Ang University, Department of Psychology.

Kashima, Y. (1995). Introduction to the special section on culture and self. *Journal of Cross-Cultural Psychology, 26,* 603-605.

Kashima, Y., & Callan, V. J. (1994). The Japanese work group. In H. C. Triandis, M. D. Dunnette, & L. Hough (Eds.), *Handbook of industrial and organizational psychology* (2nd ed., Vol. 4, pp. 609-646). Palo Alto, CA: Consulting Psychologists Press.

Kashima, Y., & Kerekes, A. (1994). A distributed memory model of averaging phenomena in person impression formation. *Journal of Experimental Social Psychology, 30,* 407-455.

Kashima, Y., Siegal, M., Tanaka, K., & Kashima, E. S. (1992). Do people believe behaviours are consistent with attitudes? *British Journal of Social Psychology, 31,* 111-124.

Kashima, Y., Woolcock, J., & King, D. (1998). The dynamics of group impression formation: The tensor product model of exemplar-based social category learning. In S. Read & L. Miller (Eds.), *Connectionist models of social behavior and inference* (pp. 71-109). Hillsdale, NJ: Lawrence Erlbaum.

Kashima, Y., Yamaguchi, S., Kim, U., Choi, S.-C., Gelfand, J. M., & Yuki, M. (1995). Culture, gender, and self: A perspective from individualism-collectivism research. *Journal of Personality and Social Psychology, 69,* 925-937.

Kassin, S. M., Ellsworth, P. C., & Smith, V. (1989). The "general acceptance" of psychological research on eyewitness testimony. *American Psychologist, 44,* 1089-1098.

Katigbak, M. S., Church, A. T., & Akmine, T. X. (1996). Cross-cultural generalizability of personality dimensions: Relating indigenous and imported dimensions in two cultures. *Journal of Personality and Social Psychology, 70,* 99-114.

Katz, I., & Hass, R. G. (1988). Racial ambivalence and American value conflict: Correlational and priming studies of dual cognitive structures. *Journal of Personality and Social Psychology, 55,* 893-905.

Keefe, S. E., & Padilla, A. M. (1987). *Chicano ethnicity.* Albuquerque: University of New Mexico Press.

Keith, L., Keith, D., Bussell, R., & Wells, J. (1974). *Attitudes of men toward contraception.* Paper presented at the 1st Annual Conference of the World Population Society, Washington, DC.

Kelly, G. A. (1955). *A theory of personality: The psychology of personal constructs.* New York: Norton.

Keltner, D., Young, R. C., & Buswell, B. N. (1997). Appeasement in human emotion, social practice, and personality. *Aggressive Behavior, 23,* 359-374.

Kessler, R. C., Price, R. H., & Wortman, C. B. (1985). Social factors in psychopathology. *Annual Review of Psychology, 36,* 531-572.

Khosla, R. (1982). The changing familial role of South-Asian women in Canada: A study in identity transformation. In K. V. Ujimoto & G. Hirabayashi (Eds.), *Asian Canadians regional perspective. Selections from proceedings: Asian Canadian 1981 Symposium V* (pp. 178-184). Guelph, Ontario, Canada: University of Guelph Press.

Kim, U. (1994). Individualism and collectivism: Conceptual clarification and elaboration. In U. Kim, H. C. Triandis, C. Kagitcibasi, S.-C. Choi, & G. Yoon (Eds.), *Individualism and collectivism: Theory, method, and applications* (pp. 19-40). Thousand Oaks, CA: Sage.

Kim, U., & Berry, J. W. (Eds.). (1993). *Indigenous psychologies: Research and experience in cultural context.* Newbury Park, CA: Sage.

Kim, U., Triandis, H. C., Kagitcibasi, C., Choi, S.-C., & Yoon, G. (Eds.). (1994). *Individualism and collectivism: Theory, method, and applications.* Thousand Oaks, CA: Sage.

Kirkbride, P. S., Tang, S. F., & Westwood, R. I. (1991). Chinese conflict preferences and negotiating behavior: Cultural and psychological influences. *Organization Studies, 12*(3), 365-386.

Kluckhohn, F., & Strodtbeck, F. (1961). *Variations in value orientations.* Evanston, IL: Row, Peterson.

Kluger, A. N., & DeNisi, A. (1996). The effects of feedback interventions of performance: A historical review, a meta-analysis, and a preliminary feedback intervention theory. *Psychological Bulletin, 119,* 254-284.

Knight, G. P., Kagan, S., & Buriel, R. (1981). Confounding effects of individualism in children's cooperation-competition motive measures. *Motivation and Emotion, 5,* 167-178.

Knowles, E. S. (1988). Item context effects on personality scales: Measuring changes the measure. *Journal of Personality and Social Psychology, 55,* 312-320.

Knowles, E. S., & Byers, B. (1996). Reliability shifts or measurement reactivity: Driven by content engagement or self-engagement? *Journal of Personality and Social Psychology, 70,* 1080-1090.

Knowles, E. S., Coker, M. C., Cook, D. A., Diercks, S. R., Irwin, M. E., Lundeen, E. J., Neville, J. W., & Sibiky, M. E. (1992). Order effects within personality measures. In N. Schwarz & S. Sudman (Eds.), *Context effects in social and psychological research* (pp. 221-236). New York: Springer-Verlag.

Korten, D. C. (1993). A not so radical agenda for a sustainable global future. *Convergence, 26,* 57-66.

Kosterman, R., & Feshbach, S. (1989). Toward a measure of patriotic and nationalistic attitudes. *Political Psychology, 10,* 257-274.

Kowalski, R. M., & Wolfe, R. (1994). Collective identity orientation, patriotism, and reactions to national outcomes. *Personality and Social Psychology Bulletin, 20,* 533-540.

Kozan, M. K. (1989). Cultural influences on styles of handling interpersonal conflicts: Comparisons among Jordanian, Turkish, and U.S. managers. *Human Relations, 42*(9), 787-799.

Kraemer, A. (1973). *Development of a cultural self-awareness approach to instruction in intercultural communication* (Report No. 73-17). Arlington, VA: Human Resources Research Office.

Krebs, D. L., & Miller, D. T. (1985). Altruism and aggression. In G. Lindzey & E. Aronson (Eds.), *The handbook of social psychology* (3rd ed., Vol. 2, pp. 1-72). New York: Random House.

Krewer, B., & Jahoda, G. (1993). Psychologie et culture: Vers une solution du "Babel." *International Journal of Psychology, 28,* 367-375.

Kroeber, A. L., & Kluckhohn, C. (1952). *Culture: A critical review of concepts and definitions* (Vol. 147). Cambridge, MA: Peabody Museum.

Kroonenberg, P., & Kashima, Y. (1997). Rules in context: A three-mode principal component analysis of Mann et al.'s data on cross-cultural differences in respect for others. *Journal of Cross-Cultural Psychology, 28,* 463-480.

Kruglanski, A. W. (1980). Lay epistemologic process and contents: Another look at attribution theory. *Psychological Review, 87,* 70-87.

Kruglanski, A. W. (1996). Goals as knowledge structures. In P. M. Gollwitzer & J. A. Bargh (Eds.), *The psychology of action* (pp. 599-618). New York: Guilford.

Kruglanski, A. W., & Webster, D. M. (1996). Motivated closing of the mind: "Seizing" and "freezing." *Psychological Review, 103,* 263-283.

Ku, L., Sonenstein, F. L., & Pleck, J. H. (1993). Neighborhood, family, and work: Influences on the premarital behaviors of adolescent males. *Social Forces, 72*(2), 479-503.

Kuhl, J., & Beckmann, J. (Eds.). (1994). *Volition and personality.* Seattle, WA: Hogrefe & Huber.

Kuhn, M. H., & McPartland, T. S. (1954). An empirical investigation of self-attitudes. *American Sociological Review, 19,* 68-76.

Kulcarni, A. V. (1983). Relationship between internal vs. external locus of control and job satisfaction. *Journal of Psychological Researches, 27,* 57-60.

Kunda, Z. (1990). The case for motivated reasoning. *Psychological Bulletin, 108,* 480-498.

Kunda, Z., & Thagard, P. (1996). Forming impressions for stereotypes, traits, and behaviors: A parallel-constraint satisfaction theory. *Psychological Review, 103,* 284-308.

Kuroda, S. -Y. (1992). Reflection on *cogito:* Or, from *congitat, ergo est* to *cogito, ergo es.* In L. Tasmowski & A. Zribi-Hertz (Eds.), *Hommages a Nicolas Ruwet* (pp. 621-633). Ghent, Belgium: Communication and Cognition.

Ladson-Billings, G. (1995). Toward a theory of cultural relevant pedagogy. *American Educational Research Journal, 32,* 465-491.

Lakatos, I. (1970). Falsification and the methodology of scientific research programmes. In I. Lakatos & A. Musgrave (Eds.), *Criticism and the growth of knowledge* (pp. 91-195). Cambridge, UK: Cambridge University Press.

Landis, D., & Bhagat, R. (Eds.). (1996). *Handbook of intercultural training.* Thousand Oaks, CA: Sage.

Landman, L. (1977). Birth control in India: The carrot and the rod. *Family Planning Perspectives, 9,* 101-110.

Langacker, R. W. (1987-1991). *Foundations of cognitive grammar* (Vols. 1-2). Stanford, CA: Stanford University Press.

Laslett, P., & Wall, R. (Eds.). (1972). *Household and family in past time.* Cambridge, UK: Cambridge University Press.

Laudan, L. (1977). *Progress and its problems: Toward a theory of scientific growth.* Berkeley: University of California Press.

Laughlin, P. R. (1988). Collective induction: Group performance, social combination processes, and mutual majority and minority influence. *Journal of Personality and Social Psychology, 58,* 254-267.

Lave, J., & Wenger, E. (1994). *Situated learning: Legitimate peripheral participation.* Cambridge, UK: Cambridge University Press.

Lee, D. (1950). Notes on the conception of the self among the Wintu Indians. *Journal of Abnormal and Social Psychology, 45,* 538-543.

Leong, F. T. L. (1996, January 12-13). *Acculturation and Asian values in the United States.* Paper presented at the Conference on Global Organizations, Hong Kong University of Science and Technology, Hong Kong.

Lerner, M. (1980). *The belief in a just world: A fundamental delusion.* New York: Plenum.

Lester, D. (1987). Correlates of job satisfaction in police officers. *Psychological Reports, 60,* 550.

Leung, K. (1987). Some determinants of reactions to procedural models for conflict resolution: A cross-national study. *Journal of Personality and Social Psychology, 53,* 898-908.

Leung, K. (1988a). Some determinants of conflict avoidance. *Journal of Cross-Cultural Psychology, 19*, 125-136.

Leung, K. (1988b). Theoretical advances in justice behavior: Some cross-cultural inputs. In M. H. Bond (Ed.), *The cross-cultural challenge to social psychology* (pp. 218-229). Newbury Park, CA: Sage.

Leung, K. (in press). Negotiation and reward allocations across cultures. In P. C. Earley & M. Erez (Eds.), *New perspectives on international industrial/organizational psychology*. San Francisco: Jossey-Bass.

Leung, K., & Bond, M. H. (1984). The impact of cultural collectivism on reward allocation. *Journal of Personality and Social Psychology, 47*, 793-804.

Leung, K., & Bond, M. H. (1989). On the empirical identification of dimensions for cross-cultural comparisons. *Journal of Cross-Cultural Psychology, 20*, 133-151.

Leung, K., & Bond, M. H. (1998, August 9-14). *Cultural beliefs about conflict and peace.* Paper presented at the 24th International Congress of Applied Psychology, San Francisco, CA.

Leung, K., Chiu, W., & Au, Y. (1993). Sympathy and support for industrial actions: A justice analysis. *Journal of Applied Psychology, 78*, 781-787.

Leung, K., & Iwawaki, S. (1988). Cultural collectivism and distributive behavior. *Journal of Cross-Cultural Psychology, 19*, 35-49.

Leung, K., & Li, W. (1990). Psychological mechanisms of process-control effects. *Journal of Personality and Social Psychology, 75*, 613-620.

Leung, K., & Lind, A. (1986). Procedural justice and culture: Effects of culture, gender, and investigator status on procedural preferences. *Journal of Personality and Social Psychology, 50*, 1134-1140.

Leung, K., & Morris, M. W. (1996). *Justice through the lens of culture and ethnicity.* Unpublished manuscript, Chinese University of Hong Kong.

Leung, K., & Park, H. (1986). Effects of interactional goal on choice of allocation rule: A cross-national study. *Organizational Behavior and Human Performance, 37*, 111-120.

Leung, K., & Stephan, W. G. (in press). Justice perception in intercultural relations. *Applied and Preventative Psychology.*

Leung, K., & Wu, P. G. (1990). Dispute processing: A cross-cultural analysis. In R. W. Brislin (Ed.), *Applied cross-cultural psychology* (pp. 209-231). Newbury Park, CA: Sage.

Levenson, H. (1973a). Multi-dimensional locus of control in psychiatric patient. *Journal of Consulting and Clinical Psychology, 41*, 397-404.

Levenson, H. (1973b). Perceived parental antecedents of internal, powerful others, and chance locus of control orientations. *Developmental Psychology, 9*, 260-265.

Levenson, H. (1974). Activism and powerful others: Distinctions within the concept of internal-external control. *Journal of Personality Assessment, 38*, 377-383.

Levin, I., & Stokes, J. P. (1989). Dispositional approach to job satisfaction: Role of negative affectivity. *Journal of Applied Psychology, 74*, 752-758.

Levine, J. M., & Moreland, R. L. (1992). Small groups and mental health. In D. N. Ruble, P. R. Costanzo, & M. E. Oliveri (Eds.), *The social psychology of mental health* (pp. 126-165). New York: Guilford.

LeVine, R. A., & Campbell, D. T. (1972). *Ethnocentrism.* New York: John Wiley.

Levinson, D., & Malone, M. J. (1980). *Toward explaining human nature.* New Haven, CT: Human Relations Area Files.

Levitt, M. J., Clark, M. C., & Rotton, J. (1987). Social support, perceived control, and well-being: A study of an environmentally stressed population. *International Journal of Aging and Human Development, 25*, 247-258.

Levitt, M. J., Weber, R. A., & Guacci, N. (1993). Convoys of social support: An intergenerational analysis. *Psychology and Aging, 8*, 323-326.

Lewis, M., & Brooks-Gunn, J. (1979). *Social cognition and the acquisition of self.* New York: Plenum.

Leyens, J. -P., Yzerbyt, V., & Corneille, O. (1996). The role of applicability in the emergence of the overattribution bias. *Journal of Personality and Social Psychology, 70,* 219-229.

Li, C. N., & Thompson, S. A. (1976). Subject and topic: A new typology of language. In C. N. Li (Ed.), *Subject and topic* (pp. 457-594). New York: Academic Press.

Liebrand, W. B., Messick, D. M., & Wolters, F. J. (1986). Why are we fairer than others? A cross-cultural replication and extension. *Journal of Experimental Social Psychology, 22,* 590-604.

Lim, K. H., Bhawuk, D. P. S., & Au, K. Y. (1996). *Preparing managers for international assignments: Using a multimedia individualism-collectivism culture assimilator.* Grant proposal, Center for International Business Education and Research.

Lind, E. A. (1994). Procedural justice and culture: Evidence for ubiquitous process concerns. *Zeitschrift fur Rechtssoziologie, 15,* 24-36.

Lind, E. A., & Tyler, T. R. (1988). *The social psychology of procedural justice.* New York: Plenum.

Lipman-Blumen, J. (1972). How ideology shapes women's lives. *Scientific American, 226,* 34-42.

Liu, J. H. (in press). Social representations of history: Preliminary notes on content and consequences around the Pacific Rim. *International Journal of Intercultural Relations.*

Liu, J. H., Wilson, M. S., McClure, J., & Higgins, T. R. (1997). *Social identity and the perception of history: Cultural narratives of Aotearoa/New Zealand.* Unpublished manuscript, Victoria University of Wellington, New Zealand.

Loftus, E. F. (1993). The reality of repressed memories. *American Psychologist, 48,* 518-534.

Lonner, W. J. (1980). The search for psychological universals. In H. C. Triandis & W. W. Lambert (Eds.), *Handbook of cross-cultural psychology: Vol. 1. Perspectives* (pp. 143-204). Boston: Allyn & Bacon.

Lonner, W. J. (1992). Does the Association need a name change? *Cross-Cultural Psychology Bulletin, 26,* 1.

Lonner, W. J., & Adamopoulos, J. (1997). Culture as antecedent to behavior. In J. W. Berry, Y. H. Poortinga, & J. Pandey (Eds.), *Handbook of cross-cultural psychology* (2nd ed., Vol. 1, pp. 43-84). Boston: Allyn & Bacon.

Lonner, W. J., & Berry, J. W. (Eds.). (1986). *Field methods in cross-cultural research.* Beverly Hills, CA: Sage.

Lucy, J. A. (1992). *Language diversity and thought: A reformulation of the linguistic relativity hypothesis.* Cambridge, UK: Cambridge University Press.

Lucy, J. A., & Wertsch, J. V. (1987). Vygotsky and Whorf: A comparative analysis. In M. Hickmann (Ed.), *Social and functional approaches to language and thought.* Orlando, FL: Academic Press.

Luk, C. L., & Bond, M. H. (1993). Personality variation and values endorsement in Chinese University students. *Personality and Individual Differences, 14,* 429-437.

Lyons, J. (1977). *Semantics.* Cambridge, UK: Cambridge University Press.

Mackie, J. A. (1976). *The Chinese in Indonesia.* Hong Kong: Heinemann.

MacWhinney, B., & Bates, E. (1978). Sentential devices for conveying givenness and newness: A cross-cultural developmental study. *Journal of Verbal Learning and Verbal Behavior, 17,* 539-558.

Madden, T. J., Ellen, P. S., & Ajzen, I. (1992). A comparison of the theory of planned behavior and the theory of reasoned action. *Personality and Social Psychology Bulletin, 18,* 3-9.

Magaffey, W., & Barnett, C. R. (1962). *Cuba: Its people, its society, its culture.* New Haven, CT: Human Relations Area Files.

Mallinckrodt, B. (1990). Satisfaction with a new job after unemployment: Consequences of job loss for older professionals. *Journal of Counseling Psychology, 37,* 149-152.

Mannino, F. V., & Shore, M. F. (1976). Perceptions of social support by Spanish-speaking youth with implications for program development. *Journal of School Health, 46,* 471-474.

Marín, G. (1993). Defining culturally appropriate community interventions: Hispanics as a case study. *Journal of Community Psychology, 21,* 149-161.

Marín, G. (1996). Perceptions by Hispanics of channels and sources of health messages regarding cigarette smoking. *Tobacco Control, 5,* 125-130.

Marín, G. (in press-a). Changes across three years in self-reported awareness of product warning messages in a Hispanic community. *Health Education Research.*

Marín, G. (in press-b). Expectancies for drinking and excessive drinking among Mexican Americans and nonHispanic whites. *Addictive Behaviors.*

Marín, G., Allen, D., Burhanstipanov, L., Connell, C., Gielen, A., Lorig, K., Morisky, D., Tenney, D., & Thomas, S. (1995). A research agenda for health education among special populations. *Health Education Quarterly, 22*(3), 346-363.

Marín, G., Amaro, H., Eisenberg, C., & Opava-Stitzer, S. (1993). The development of a relevant and comprehensive research agenda to improve Hispanic health. *Public Health Reports, 108,* 546-550.

Marín, G., & Gamba, R. J. (in press). Changes in awareness of environmental health warning signs in cohorts of Hispanics and nonHispanic whites. *Interamerican Journal of Psychology/ Revista Interamericana de Psicología.*

Marín, G., & Pérez-Stable, E. (1995). Effectiveness of disseminating culturally appropriate smoking cessation information: Programa Latino Para Dejar de Fumar. *Journal of the National Cancer Institute Monographs, 18,* 155-163.

Marín, G., Posner, S., & Kinyon, J. (1993). Alcohol expectancies among Hispanics and non-Hispanic whites: Role of drinking status and acculturation. *Hispanic Journal of Behavioral Sciences, 15,* 373-381.

Marín, G., & Triandis, H. C. (1985). Allocentrism as an important characteristic of the behavior of Latin Americans and Hispanics. In R. Diaz-Guerrero (Ed.), *Cross-cultural and national studies* (pp. 85-104). Amsterdam: Elsevier.

Marín, G., Triandis, H. C., Betancourt, H., & Kashima, Y. (1983). Ethnic affirmation versus social desirability: Explaining discrepancies in bilinguals' responses to a questionnaire. *Journal of Cross-Cultural Psychology, 14,* 173-186.

Marín, G., & VanOss Marín, B. (1990). Perceived credibility of channels and sources of AIDS information among Hispanics. *AIDS Education and Prevention, 2,* 156-163.

Marín, G., VanOss Marín, B., Otero-Sabogal, R., Sabogal, F., & Pérez-Stable, E. J. (1989). The role of acculturation on the attitudes, norms, and expectancies of Hispanic smokers. *Journal of Cross-Cultural Psychology, 20,* 399-415.

Marín, G., VanOss Marín, B., Pérez-Stable, E. J., Sabogal, F., & Otero-Sabogal, R. (1990a). Changes in information as a function of a culturally appropriate smoking cessation community intervention for Hispanics. *American Journal of Community Psychology, 18,* 847-864.

Marín, G., VanOss Marín, B., Pérez-Stable, E. J., Sabogal, F., & Otero-Sabogal, R. (1990b). Cultural differences in attitudes and expectancies between Hispanic and non-Hispanic white smokers. *Hispanic Journal of Behavioral Sciences, 12*(4), 422-436.

Markides, K. S., Costley, D. S., & Rodriguez, L. (1981). Perceptions of intergenerational relations and psychological well-being among elderly Mexican Americans: A causal model. *International Journal of Aging and Human Development, 13,* 43-52.

Markides, K. S., & Krause, N. (1985). Intergenerational solidarity and psychological well-being among older Mexican-Americans: A three-generations study. *Journal of Gerontology, 40*(3), 390-392.

Marks, N. F., & McLanahan, S. S. (1993). Gender, family structure, and social support among parents. *Journal of Marriage and the Family, 55,* 481-493.

Markus, H. (1977). Self-schemas and processing information about the self. *Journal of Personality and Social Psychology, 35,* 63-78.

Markus, H., & Kitayama, S. (1991). Culture and the self: Implications for cognition, emotion, and motivation. *Psychological Review, 98,* 224-253.

Marshall, J. (1973). Fertility regulating methods: Cultural acceptability for potential adopters. In G. Duncan, E. Hilton, P. Kreager, & A. Lumsdaine (Eds.), *Fertility control methods: Strategies for introduction.* New York: Academic Press.

Marshall, J. (1977). Acceptability of fertility regulating methods: Designing technology to fit people. *Preventive Medicine, 6,* 65-73.

Martin, L. L., Harlow, T. F., & Strack, F. (1992). The role of bodily sensations in the evaluation of social events. *Personality and Social Psychology Bulletin, 18,* 412-419.

Martin, L. L., & Tesser, A. (1996). Some ruminative thoughts. In R. S. Wyer, Jr. (Ed.), *Ruminative thoughts: Advances in social cognition* (Vol. 9, pp. 1-48). Mahwah, NJ: Lawrence Erlbaum.

Martin, S. (1975). *A reference grammar of Japanese.* New Haven, CT: Yale University Press.

Maynard, S. K. (1989). *Japanese conversation: Self-contextualization through structure and inter-actional management.* Norwood, NJ: Ablex.

Mazlish, B. (1982). American narcissism. *Psychohistory Review, 10,* 185-202.

Maznevski, M. L., & DiStefano, J. J. (1996, August). *The mortar in the mosaic: A new look at composition, process, and performance in decision-making groups.* Paper presented at the annual meeting of the Academy of Management, Boston.

McClintock, C. G. (1978). Social values: Their definition, measurement, and development. *Journal of Research and Development in Education, 12,* 121-137.

McGuire, W. J. (1960). A syllogistic analysis of cognitive relationships. In C. I. Hovland & M. J. Rosenberg (Eds.), *Attitude organization and change: An analysis of consistency among attitude components* (pp. 65-111). New Haven, CT: Yale University Press.

McGuire, W. J., & McGuire, C. V. (1988). Content and process in the experience of self. In L. Berkowitz (Ed.), *Advances in experimental social psychology* (Vol. 21, pp. 97-144). New York: Academic Press.

Mead, G. H. (1962). *Mind, self, and society.* Chicago: University of Chicago Press. (Original work published 1934)

Medin, D. L., Goldstone, R. L., & Gentner, D. (1993). Respects for similarity. *Psychological Review, 100,* 254-278.

Mesquita, B., Fridja, N., & Scherer, K. (1997). Culture and emotion. In J. W. Berry, P. R. Dasen, & T. S. Saraswathi (Eds.), *Handbook of cross-cultural psychology* (2nd ed., Vol. 2, pp. 255-298). Boston: Allyn & Bacon.

Messick, D. M., Bloom, S., Boldizar, J. P., & Samuelson, C. D. (1985). Why are we fairer than others? *Journal of Experimental Social Psychology, 21,* 480-500.

Michel, A. (1970). La famille urbaine et la parente en France. In R. Hille & R. Konig (Eds.), *Families in East and West* (pp. 436-437). The Hague, The Netherlands: Mouton.

Milgram, S. (1974). *Obedience to authority.* New York: Harper & Row.

Miller, J. G. (1984). Culture and the development of everyday social explanation. *Journal of Personality and Social Psychology, 46,* 961-978.

Miller, J. G. (1997). Theoretical issues in cultural psychology. In J. W. Berry, Y. H. Poortinga, & J. Pandey (Eds.), *Handbook of cross-cultural psychology* (2nd ed., Vol. 1, pp. 85-128). Boston: Allyn & Bacon.

Miller, P. J., & Hoogstra, L. (1992). Language as tool in the socialization and apprehension of cultural meanings. In T. Schwartz, G. M. White, & C. A. Lutz (Eds.), *New directions in psychological anthropology* (pp. 83-101). Cambridge, UK: Cambridge University Press.

Milliken, F. J., & Martins, L. L. (1996). Searching for common threads: Understanding the multiple effects of diversity in organizational groups. *Academy of Management Review, 21*(2), 402-433.

Minturn, L., & Lambert, W. (1964). *Mothers of six cultures.* New York: John Wiley.

Mischel, W., & Shoda, Y. (1995). A cognitive-affective system theory of personality: Reconceptu-alizing situations, dispositions, dynamics, and invariance in personality structure. *Psychological Review, 102,* 246-268.

Misra, G., & Gergen, K. J. (1993). On the place of culture in the psychological sciences. *International Journal of Psychology, 28,* 225-243.

Mittelman, B. (1944). Complementary neurotic reactions in intimate relationships. *Psychoanalytic Quarterly, 13,* 479-491.

Moghaddam, F. M., & Studer, C. (1997). Cross-cultural psychology: The frustrated gadfly's promises, potentialities, and failures. In D. Fox & I. Prillentensky (Eds.), *Critical psychology* (pp. 185-201). Thousand Oaks, CA: Sage.

Monahan, J., & Walker, L. (1988). Social science research in law: A new paradigm. *American Psychologist, 43,* 465-474.

Montandon, A. (Ed.). (1995). *Dictionnaire raisonné de la politesse et du savoir-vivre.* Paris: Editions du Seuil.

Moore, D. B. (1993). Shame, forgiveness, and juvenile justice. *Criminal Justice Ethics, 12,* 3-25.

Morris, M. W., & Peng, K. (1994). Culture and cause: American and Chinese attributions for social and physical events. *Journal of Personality and Social Psychology, 67,* 949-971.

Moscovici, S. (1985). Social influence and conformity. In G. Lindzey & E. Aronson (Eds.), *The handbook of social psychology* (3rd ed., Vol. 2, pp. 347-412). New York: Random House.

Mülhausler, P., & Harré, R. (1990). *Pronouns and people: The linguistic construction of social and personal identity.* Cambridge, MA: Blackwell.

Muninjaya, A. A. G., & Widarsa, T. (1993-1994). Development of culturally appropriate educational material to improve home case management of diarrhea in rural Lombok, Indonesia. *International Quarterly of Community Health Education, 14*(3), 237-243.

Munroe, R. L., & Munroe, R. H. (1997). A comparative anthropological perspective. In J. W. Berry, Y. H. Poortinga, & J. Pandey (Eds.), *Handbook of cross-cultural psychology: Vol. 1. Theory and method* (pp. 171-213). Boston: Allyn & Bacon.

Murdock, P. M. (1949). *Social structure.* New York: Free Press.

Murillo, N. (1976). The Mexican-American family. In C. A. Hernandez (Ed.), *Chicanos: Social and psychological perspectives.* St. Louis, MO: Mosby.

Murphy, G. L., & Medin, D. L. (1985). The role of theories in conceptual coherence. *Psychological Review, 92,* 289-316.

Murray, N., Sujan, H., Hirt, E. R., & Sujan, M. (1990). The influence of mood on categorization: A cognitive flexibility interpretation. *Journal of Personality and Social Psychology, 59,* 411-425.

Muslim Public Affairs Council. (1996). The Krasniqi case. *Islamic Information & News Network, 8*(10).

Muslims in Dallas hold series of demonstrations demanding justice in Krasniqi case. (1995, September 22). *Muslim World Monitor.*

Na, E. Y., & Loftus, E. (1996). *Attitudes towards law and prisoners, conservative authoritarianism, attribution, and internal-external locus of control: Korean and American law experts and non-experts.* Paper presented at the 50th Anniversary Conference of the Korean Psychological Association, Seoul, South Korea.

Nagarathnamma, B. (1988). Job satisfaction as a function of locus of control and neurotics. *Journal of the Indian Academy of Applied Psychology, 14,* 12-15.

Naidoo, J. C. (1980a). East Indian women in the Canadian context: A study in social psychology. In K. V. Ujimoto & G. Hirabayashi (Eds.), *Visible minorities and multiculturalism: Asians in Canada* (pp. 193-218). Toronto, Canada: Butterworth.

Naidoo, J. C. (1980b). New perspectives on South Asian women in Canada. In N. A. Nyiri & T. Miljan (Eds.), *Unity in diversity: The proceedings of the interdisciplinary research seminar at Wilfrid Laurier University* (Vol. 2, pp. 199-226). Waterloo, Ontario, Canada: Wilfrid Laurier University Press.

Naidoo, J. C. (1980c). Women of South Asian and Anglo-Saxon origins: Self-perceptions, socialization, achievement, aspirations. In C. Stark-Adamec (Ed.), *Sex roles: Origins, influences, and implications for women* (pp. 50-69). Montreal, Canada: Eden Press.

Naidoo, J. C. (1985a). Contemporary South Asian women in the Canadian mosaic. *International Journal of Women's Studies, 8*(4), 338-350.

Naidoo, J. C. (1985b). A cultural perspective on the adjustment of South Asian women in Canada. In I. R. Lagunes & Y. H. Poortinga (Eds.), *From a different perspective: Studies of behavior across cultures* (pp. 76-92). Lisse, The Netherlands: Swets & Zeitlinger.

Naidoo, J. C. (1986). Value conflicts of South Asian women in multicultural Canada. In L. H. Ekstrand (Ed.), *Ethnic minorities and immigrants in a cross-cultural perspective* (pp. 132-146). Lisse, The Netherlands: Swets & Zeitlinger.

Naidoo, J. C. (1987). Women of South Asian origins: Status of research, problems, future issues. In M. Israel (Ed.), *The South Asian diaspora in Canada: Six essays* (pp. 37-58). Toronto, Canada: Multicultural History Society of Ontario.

Naidoo, J. C. (1992a). Between East and West: Reflections on Asian Indian women in Canada. In R. Ghosh & R. Kanungo (Eds.), *South Asian Canadians: Current issues in the politics of culture* (pp. 81-90). India: Shastri Indo-Canadian Institute.

Naidoo, J. C. (1992b). Mental health of visible ethnic minorities in Canada. *Psychology and Developing Societies, 4*(2), 165-186.

Naidoo, J. C. (1994). *Research on South Asian women in Canada: Selected annotated bibliography with surname index, 1972-1992.* Waterloo, Ontario, Canada: Wilfrid Laurier University Printing Services.

Naidoo, J. C. (1996a, August). *Canadian Asian women in transition: Issues and problems of cultural value continuity, change, and conflict in family life.* Paper presented at the 13th Congress of the International Association for Cross-Cultural Psychology, Montreal, Quebec, Canada.

Naidoo, J. C. (1996b, August). *South Asian Indian women in Canada: Religious identification and adaptation.* Paper presented at the 26th International Congress of Psychology, Montreal, Quebec, Canada.

Naidoo, J. C., & Davis, J. C. (1988). Canadian South Asian women in transition: A dualistic view of life. *Journal of Comparative Family Studies, 19,* 311-327.

Naisbitt, J., & Aburdene, P. (1990). *Megatrends 2000: Ten new directions for the 1990's.* New York: Avon.

Naroll, R. (1983). *The moral order.* Beverly Hills, CA: Sage.

Nathan, D., & Snedeker, M. (1995). *Satan's silence.* New York: Basic Books.

Naylor, J. C., Pritchard, R. D., & Ilgen, D. R. (1980). *A theory of behavior in organizations.* San Diego, CA: Academic Press.

Neisser, U., Boodoo, G., Bouchard, T. J., Jr., Boykin, A. W., Brody, N., Ceci, S. J., Halpern, D. F., Loehlin, J. C., Perloff, R., Sternberg, R. J., & Urbina, S. (1996). Intelligence: Knowns and unknowns. *American Psychologist, 51,* 77-101.

Newman, L. S., & Uleman, J. S. (1989). Spontaneous trait inference. In J. S. Uleman & J. A. Bargh (Eds.), *Unintended thought* (pp. 155-188). New York: Guilford.

Ng, S. H. (1984). Equity and social categorization effects on intergroup allocations of reward. *British Journal of Social Psychology, 23,* 165-172.

Nimkoff, M. F., & Middleton, R. (1960). Types of family and types of economy. *American Journal of Sociology, 66,* 215-225.

Nisbett, R. E., & Wilson, T. D. (1977). Telling more than we can know: Verbal reports on mental processes. *Psychological Review, 84,* 231-259.

Nobles, W. W., & Goddard, L. L. (1993). An African-centered model of prevention for African-American youth at high risk. In L. L. Goddard (Ed.), *An African-centered model of prevention for African-American youth at high risk* (Vol. 6, pp. 115-129). Rockville, MD: Substance Abuse and Mental Health Services Administration.

Norem, H., Ardyth, A., & Johnson, D. W. (1981). The relationship between cooperative, competitive, and individualistic attitudes and differentiated aspects of self-esteem. *Journal of Personality, 49,* 415-426.

Norris, D. R., & Niebuhr, R. E. (1984). Attributional influences on the job performance-job satisfaction relationship. *Academy of Management Journal, 27,* 424-431.

Oakes, P. J., & Turner, J. C. (1980). Social categorization and intergroup behaviour: Does minimal intergroup discrimination make social identity more positive? *European Journal of Social Psychology, 10,* 295-301.

Ochs, E. (1986). Introduction. In B. B. Schieffelin & E. Ochs (Eds.), *Language socialization across cultures* (pp. 1-13). Cambridge, UK: Cambridge University Press.

O'Grady, W., Peters, A. M., & Masterson, D. (1989). The transition from optional to required subjects. *Journal of Child Language, 16*, 513-529.

Ohbuchi, K. I., & Takahashi, Y. (1994). Cultural styles of conflict management in Japanese and Americans: Passivity, covertness, and effectiveness of strategies. *Journal of Applied Social Psychology, 24*, 1345-1366.

Oliver, J. E. (1983). Job satisfaction and locus of control in two job types. *Psychological Reports, 52*, 425-426.

Organ, D. W., & Greene, C. N. (1974). The perceived purposefulness of job behavior: Antecedent and consequences. *Academy of Management Journal, 17*, 69-78.

Orlandi, M. A. (Ed.). (1992). *Cultural competence for evaluators* (Vol. 1). Rockville, MD: U.S. Department of Health and Human Services, Office of Substance Abuse Prevention.

Osgood, C. E. (1971). Explorations in semantic space: A personal diary. *Journal of Social Issues, 27*, 5-64.

Osgood, C. E., May, W. H., & Miron, M. S. (1975). *Cross-cultural universals of affective meaning.* Urbana: University of Illinois Press.

Osgood, C. E., Suci, G., & Tannenbaum, P. (1957). *The measurement of meaning.* Urbana: University of Illinois Press.

Ouchi, W. G., & Jaeger, A. M. (1978). Type Z organization: Stability in the midst of mobility. *Academy of Management Review, 3*, 305-314.

Padilla, E. (1964). *Up from Puerto Rico.* New York: Columbia University Press.

Pancer, S. M., McMullen, L. M., Kabatoff, R. A., Johnson, K. G., & Pond, C. A. (1979). Conflict and avoidance in the helping situation. *Journal of Personality and Social Psychology, 37*, 1406-1411.

Panter, A. T., Tanaka, J. S., & Wellens, T. R. (1992). The psychometrics of order effects. In N. Schwarz & S. Sudman (Eds.), *Context effects in social and psychological research* (pp. 249-264). New York: Springer-Verlag.

Parsons, T. (1943). The kinship system of contemporary United States. *American Anthropologist, 45*, 22-38.

Parsons, T. (1949). The social structure of the family. In R. N. Anshen (Ed.), *The family: Its functions and destiny.* New York: Harper.

Parsons, T. (1965). The normal American family. In S. M. Farber (Ed.), *Man and civilization: The family's search for survival* (pp. 34-36). New York: McGraw-Hill.

Patterson, G. R., McNeal, S., Hawkins, N., & Phelps, R. (1967). Reprogramming the social environment. *Journal of Child Psychology and Psychiatry, 8*, 181-195.

Pearson, A. M. (1996). *"Because it gives me peace of mind": Ritual fasts in the religious lives of Hindu women.* Albany: State University of New York Press.

Pearson, V. M. S., & Stephan, W. G. (in press). Preferences for styles of negotiation: A comparison of Brazil and the U.S. *International Journal of Intercultural Relations.*

Pelham, B. W. (1993). The idiographic nature of human personality: Examples of the idiographic self-concept. *Journal of Personality and Social Psychology, 64*, 665-677.

Pérez-Stable, E. J., Sabogal, F., Marín, G., VanOss Marín, B., & Otero-Sabogal, R. (1991). Evaluation of the Guía Para Dejar de Fumar: A Spanish language self-help guide to quit smoking. *Public Health Reports, 106*, 564-570.

Pérez-Stable, E., VanOss Marín, B., & Marín, G. (1993). A comprehensive smoking cessation program for the San Francisco Bay Area Latino community: Programa Latino Para Dejar de Fumar. *American Journal of Health Promotion, 7*(6), 430-442, 475.

Peristiany, J. G. (Ed.). (1965). *Honor and shame: The values of Mediterranean society.* London: Weidenfeld & Nicolson.

Peterson, B. E., Doty, R. M., & Winter, D. G. (1993). Authoritarianism and attitudes towards contemporary social issues. *Personality and Social Psychology Bulletin, 19*, 174-184.

Pettigrew, T. F. (1979). The ultimate attribution error: Extending Allport's cognitive analysis of prejudice. *Personality and Social Psychology Bulletin, 5,* 461-476.

Pettigrew, T. F. (1998). Intergroup contact theory. *Annual Review of Psychology, 49,* 65-85.

Petty, R. E., & Cacioppo, J. T. (1990). Involvement and persuasion: Tradition versus integration. *Psychological Bulletin, 107,* 367-374.

Petty, R. E., & Krosnick, J. (1995). *Attitude strength: Antecedents and consequences.* Hillsdale, NJ: Lawrence Erlbaum.

Piaget, J. (1955). *The language and thought of the child.* Cleveland, OH: Meridian Books.

Picard, D. (1995). *Les rituels du savoir-vivre.* Paris: Editions du Seuil.

Pierson, H. D., & Bond, M. H. (1982). How do Chinese bilinguals respond to variations of interviewer language and ethnicity? *Journal of Language and Social Psychology, 2,* 123-139.

Pike, K. L. (1967). *Language in relation to a unified theory of the structure of human behavior.* The Hague, The Netherlands: Mouton.

Pinker, S. (1990). Language acquisition. In D. N. Osherson & H. Lasnik (Eds.), *Language: An invitation to cognitive science* (Vol. 1, pp. 199-241). Cambridge: MIT Press.

Pomazal, R. P., & Jaccard, J. (1976). An informal approach to altruistic behavior. *Journal of Personality and Social Psychology, 33,* 317-336.

Poortinga, Y. H. (1990). Towards a conceptualization of culture for psychology. *Cross-Cultural Psychology Bulletin, 24,* 2-10. (Reprinted in *Innovations in cross-cultural psychology,* pp. 3-17, by S. Iwawaki, Y. Kashima, & K. Leung, Eds., 1992, Amsterdam: Swets & Zeitlinger)

Poortinga, Y. H. (1997). Towards convergence? In J. W. Berry, Y. H. Poortinga, & J. Pandey (Eds.), *Handbook of cross-cultural psychology: Vol. 1. Theory and method* (pp. 347-387). Boston: Allyn & Bacon.

Poortinga, Y. H., & Van de Vijver, F. (1994). IACCP or IACP? *Cross-Cultural Psychology Bulletin, 8,* 3-4.

Port, R. F., & Van Gelder, T. (1995). *Mind as motion.* Cambridge: MIT Press.

Portes, A. (1998). Social capital: Its origins and applications in modern sociology. *Annual Review of Sociology, 24,* 1-24.

Pound, E. (1933). *Confucian analects.* London: Peter Owen.

Pozo, C., Carver, C. S., Wellens, A. R., & Scheier, M. F. (1991). Social anxiety and social perception: Construing others' reactions to the self. *Personality and Social Psychology Bulletin, 17,* 355-362.

Pratkanis, A. R. (1989). The cognitive representation of attitudes. In A. R. Pratkanis, S. J. Breckler, & A. G. Greenwald (Eds.), *Attitude structure and function* (pp. 71-98). Hillsdale, NJ: Lawrence Erlbaum.

Pratto, F., Liu, J. H., Levin, S., Sidanius, J., Shih, M., & Bachrach, H. (1996). *Social dominance orientation and legitimization of inequality across cultures.* Unpublished manuscript, Stanford University, Stanford, CA.

Pratto, F., Sidanius, J., Stallworth, L. M., & Malle, B. F. (1994). Social dominance orientation: A personality variable predicting social and political attitudes. *Journal of Personality and Social Psychology, 67,* 741-763.

Pratto, F., Tatar, D. G., & Conway-Lanz, S. (1996). *Who gets what and why: Determinants of social allocations.* Manuscript submitted for publication.

Pruitt, D. G., & Carnevale, P. J. (1993). *Negotiation in social conflict.* Buckingham, UK: Open University Press.

Pryor, J. B., & Stoller, L. M. (1994). Sexual cognition in men high in the likelihood to sexually harass. *Personality and Social Psychology Bulletin, 20,* 163-169.

Pusch, M. (1979). *Multicultural education: A cross-cultural training approach.* Yarmouth, ME: Intercultural Press.

Putnam, R. D. (1995). Bowling alone: America's declining social capital. *Journal of Democracy, 6,* 65-78.

Quinn, N., & Strauss, C. (1993). *A cognitive framework for a unified theory of culture.* Durham, NC: Duke University, Department of Anthropology.

Ralston, H. (1992). Religion in the life of South Asian immigrant women in Atlantic Canada. *Research in the Social Scientific Study of Religion, 4,* 245-260.

Ramirez, A. G., MacKellar, D. A., & Gallion, K. (1988). Reaching minority audiences: A major challenge in cancer reduction. *Cancer Bulletin, 40*(6), 334-343.

Ratner, C. (1991). *Vygotsky's sociohistorical psychology and its contemporary applications.* New York: Plenum.

Razí, Z. (1993). The myth of the immutable English family: Past and present. *Journal of Historical Studies, 140,* 3-44.

Read, S. J. (1987). Constructing causal scenarios: A knowledge structure approach to causal reasoning. *Journal of Personality and Social Psychology, 52,* 288-302.

Reddy, M. A. (Ed.). (1995). *Statistical record of Hispanic Americans* (2nd ed.). New York: Gale Research.

Redfield, J. M. (1975). *Nature and culture in the Iliad: The tragedy of Hector.* Chicago: University of Chicago Press.

Reid, D. J., Killoran, A. J., McNeill, A. D., & Chambers, J. S. (1992). Choosing the most effective health promotion options for reducing a nation's smoking prevalence. *Tobacco Control, 1,* 185-197.

Reid, D. W., & Ware, E. E. (1974). Multidimensional of internal versus external control: Addition of a third dimension and non-distinction of self versus others. *Canadian Journal of Behavioral Sciences, 6,* 131-142.

Report of the Royal Commission on the Status of Women in Canada. (1970). Ottawa, Canada: Ministry of Supply and Services.

Resnick, L. B., Levine, J. M., & Teasley, S. D. (Eds.). (1991). *Perspectives on socially shared cognition.* Washington, DC: American Psychological Association.

Retschitzky, J., Bossel-Lagos, M., & Dasen, P. (Eds.). (1989). *La recherche interculturelle.* Paris: L'Harmattan.

Rhuly, S. (1976). *Orientations to intercultural communication.* Chicago: Science Research Associates.

Rieu, E. V. (Trans.). (1950). *Homer: The Iliad.* Harmondsworth, UK: Penguin.

Roberts, R. N. (1990). *Culturally competent programs for families of children with special needs.* Washington, DC: Georgetown University Child Development Center.

Roccas, S. (1997). *The effects of group and individual characteristics and their interaction on identification with groups.* Unpublished doctoral dissertation, Hebrew University, Jerusalem, Israel.

Rodgers, R. H., & White, J. M. (1993). Family development theory. In P. G. Boss, W. J. Doherty, R. LaRossa, W. R. Schumm, & S. K. Steinmetz (Eds.), *Sourcebook of family theories and methods* (pp. 225-254). New York: Plenum.

Rodin, J. (1985). The application of social psychology. In G. Lindzey & E. Aronson (Eds.), *The handbook of social psychology* (3rd ed., Vol. 2, pp. 805-882). New York: Random House.

Rogers, E. (1983). *Diffusion of innovations.* New York: Free Press.

Rogoff, B. (1990). *Apprenticeship in thinking: Cognitive development in social context.* New York: Oxford University Press.

Rogoff, B., & Chavajay, P. (1995). What's become of research on the cultural basis of cognitive development? *American Psychologist, 50,* 859-877.

Rokeach, M. (1973). *The nature of human values.* New York: Free Press.

Rosch, E. (1977). Human categorization. In N. Warren (Ed.), *Studies in cross-cultural psychology* (Vol. 1, pp. 1-49). San Diego, CA: Academic Press.

Rosch, E. (1988). Coherences and categorization: A historical view. In F. S. Kessel (Ed.), *The development of language and language researchers: Essays in honor of Roger Brown* (pp. 373-392). Hillsdale, NJ: Lawrence Erlbaum.

Rosenau, J. N. (1997). *Along the domestic-foreign frontier: Exploring governance in a turbulent world.* Cambridge, UK: Cambridge University Press.

Ross, A. D. (1961). *The Hindu family in its urban setting.* Toronto, Canada: University of Toronto Press.

Ross, L. (1977). The intuitive psychologist and his shortcomings: Distortions in the attribution process. In L. Berkowitz (Ed.), *Advances in experimental social psychology* (Vol. 10, pp. 173-220). New York: Academic Press.

Rosser, C. C., & Harris, C. (1968). *The family and social change.* London: Routledge & Kegan Paul.

Rotter, J. B. (1954). *Social psychology and clinical psychology.* Englewood Cliffs, NJ: Prentice Hall.

Rotter, J. B. (1966). Generalized expectancies for internal versus external control of reinforcement. *Psychological Monographs, 80*(1), 609.

Roussel, L. (1976). La famille après le mariage des enfants. *Travaux et documents, Cahier. no 78.* Paris: PUF.

Ruble, D. N., Costanzo, P. R., & Oliveri, M. E. (1992). *The social psychology of mental health.* New York: Guilford.

Ruble, T. L. (1974). Effects of one's locus of control and the opportunity to participate in planning. *Organizational Behavior & Human Performance, 16,* 63-73.

Rumelhart, D. E., Hinton, G. E., & Williams, R. J. (1986). Learning internal representations by error propagation. In D. E. Rumelhart, J. L. McClelland, & the PDP Research Group (Eds.), *Parallel distributed processing: Explorations in the microstructure of cognition* (Vol. 1, pp. 318-362). Cambridge, MA: MIT Press.

Rumelhart, D. E., McClelland, J. L., & the PDP Research Group. (Eds.). (1986). *Parallel distributed processing: Explorations in the microstructure of cognition* (Vol. 1). Cambridge, MA: MIT Press.

Russell, B. (1972). *A history of Western philosophy.* New York: Simon & Schuster. (Original work published 1945)

S. v. Gqeba and Others, No. 53/89 (Supreme Court of South Africa, Eastern Cape Local Division, 1990).

S. v. Sibisi and Others, No. 187/87 (Supreme Court of South Africa, Witwatersrand Local Division, 1989).

Sabogal, F., Marín, G., Otero-Sabogal, R., VanOss Marín, B., & Pérez-Stable, E. J. (1987). Hispanic familism and acculturation: What changes and what doesn't? *Hispanic Journal of Behavioral Sciences, 9,* 397-412.

Safilios-Rothschild, K. (1970). The study of family power structure: A review of 1960-69. *Journal of Marriage and the Family, 32,* 539-552.

Sagiv, L., & Schwartz, S. H. (1995). Value priorities and readiness for outgroup social contact. *Journal of Personality and Social Psychology, 69,* 437-448.

Sampson, D. L., & Smith, H. P. (1957). A scale to measure world-minded attitudes. *Journal of Social Psychology, 45,* 99-106.

Sampson, E. E. (1988). The debate on individualism: Indigenous psychologies of the individual and their role in personal and societal functioning. *American Psychologist, 43,* 15-22.

Sampson, R., & Laub, J. (1993). *Crime in the making: Pathways and turning points through life.* Cambridge, MA: Harvard University Press.

Sattler, D. N., & Kerr, N. L. (1991). Might vs. morality explored: Motivational and cognitive bases for social motives. *Journal of Personality and Social Psychology, 60,* 756-765.

Saussure, F. de. (1959). *Course in general linguistics* (W. Baskin, Trans.). New York: McGraw-Hill.

Schieffelin, B. B., & Ochs, E. (Eds.). (1986). *Language socialization across cultures.* Cambridge, UK: Press Syndicate of the University of Cambridge.

Schliemann, A., Carraher, D., & Ceci, S. J. (1997). Everyday cognition. In J. W. Berry, P. R. Dasen, & T. S. Saraswathi (Eds.), *Handbook of cross-cultural psychology* (2nd ed., Vol. 2, pp. 177-216). Boston: Allyn & Bacon.

Schmitt, M. J., Schwartz, S. H., Steyer, R., & Schmitt, T. (1993). Measurement models for the Schwartz Values Inventory. *European Journal of Psychological Assessment, 9,* 107-121.

Schneider, W., & Shiffrin, R. M. (1977). Controlled and automatic human information processing: I. Detection, search, and attention. *Psychological Review, 84,* 1-66.

Schwartz, S. H. (1990, July). Thoughts in response to cross-cultural applications and critiques. In H. C. Triandis (Chair), *Value theory applications and critique.* Symposium conducted at the 10th Congress of the International Association for Cross-Cultural Psychology, Nara, Japan.

Schwartz, S. H. (1992). Universals in the content and structure of values: Theoretical advances and empirical tests in twenty countries. In M. P. Zanna (Ed.), *Advances in experimental social psychology* (Vol. 25, pp. 1-65). San Diego, CA: Academic Press.

Schwartz, S. H. (1994a). Are there universal aspects in the content and structure of value? *Journal of Social Issues, 50,* 19-45.

Schwartz, S. H. (1994b). Beyond individualism/collectivism: New cultural dimensions of values. In U. Kim, H. C. Triandis, C. Kagitcibasi, S.-C. Choi, & G. Yoon (Eds.), *Individualism and collectivism: Theory, method, and applications* (pp. 85-119). Thousand Oaks, CA: Sage.

Schwartz, S. H., & Ros, M. (1995). Values in the West: A theoretical and empirical challenge to the individualism-collectivism cultural dimension. *World Psychology, 1,* 99-122.

Schwartz, S. H., & Sagiv, L. (1995). Identifying culture specifics in the content and structure of values. *Journal of Cross-Cultural Psychology, 26,* 92-116.

Schwartz, S. H., Struch, N., & Bilsky, W. (1990). Values and intergroup social motives: A study of Israeli and German students. *Social Psychology Quarterly, 53,* 185-198.

Schwartz, S. H., Verkasalo, M., Antonovsky, A., & Sagiv, L. (1997). Value priorities and social desirability: Much substance, some style. *British Journal of Social Psychology, 36,* 3-18.

Schwarz, N. (1990). Feelings as information: Informational and motivational functions of affective states. In E. T. Higgins & R. M. Sorrentino (Eds.), *Handbook of motivation and cognition: Foundations of social behavior* (Vol. 2, pp. 527-561). New York: Guilford.

Schwarz, N. (1994). Judgment in social context: Biases, shortcomings, and the logic of conversation. In M. P. Zanna (Ed.), *Advances in experimental social psychology* (Vol. 26, pp. 123-162). San Diego, CA: Academic Press.

Schwarz, N., Bless, H., Strack, F., Klumpp, G., Rittenauer-Schatka, H., & Simons, A. (1991). Ease of retrieval as information: Another look at the availability heuristic. *Journal of Personality and Social Psychology, 61,* 195-202.

Segal, S. J. (1972). Contraceptive research: A male chauvinist plot? *Family Planning Perspectives, 4,* 21-29.

Segalen, M. (1986). *Historical anthropology of the family.* Cambridge, UK: Cambridge University Press.

Segall, M. H. (1993). Cultural psychology: Reactions to some claims and assertions of dubious validity. *Cross-Cultural Psychology Bulletin, 27*(3), 2-4.

Segall, M. H., Campbell, D. T., & Herskovits, M. J. (1964). *The influence of culture on visual perception.* Indianapolis, IN: Bobbs-Merrill.

Segall, M. H., Dasen, P. R., Berry, J. W., & Poortinga, Y. H. (1990). *Human behaviour in global perspective: An introduction to cross-cultural psychology.* New York: Pergamon.

Segall, M. H., Lonner, W. J., & Berry, J. W. (1998). Cross-cultural psychology as a scholarly discipline: On the flowering of culture in behavioral research. *American Psychologist, 53,* 1101-1110.

Seleskovitch, D. (1976). Interpretation, a psychological approach to translation. In R. Brislin (Ed.), *Translation: Applications and research* (pp. 92-116). New York: Wiley/Halsted.

Seville statement on violence. (1994). *American Psychologist, 49,* 845-846.

Sharan, S., Hare, P., Webb, C., & Hertz-Lazarowitz, R. (Eds.). (1980). *Cooperation in education.* Provo, UT: Brigham Young University Press.

Sharma, U., & Chaudhary, P. N. (1980). Locus of control and job satisfaction among engineers. *Psychological Studies, 25,* 126-128.

Shehan, C. L., & Lee, G. R. (1960). Roles and power. In J. Touliatos, B. F. Perlmutter, & M. A. Straus (Eds.), *Handbook of family measurement techniques* (pp. 420-441). Beverly Hills, CA: Sage.

Sherif, M. (1966). *Group conflict and cooperation: Their social psychology.* London: Routledge & Kegan Paul.

Sherzer, J. (1987). A discourse-centered approach to language and culture. *American Anthropologist, 89,* 259-309.

Shibamoto, J. S. (1984). Subject ellipsis and topic in Japanese. In S. Miyagawa & C. Kitagawa (Eds.), *Studies in Japanese language use* (pp. 233-265). Edmonton, Canada: Linguistic Research.

Shiffrin, R. M., & Schneider, W. (1977). Controlled and automatic human information processing: II. Perceptual learning, automatic attending, and a general theory. *Psychological Review, 84,* 127-190.

Shotter, J. (1993). *Cultural politics of everyday life: Social constructionism, rhetoric, and knowing of the third kind.* Buckingham, UK: Open University Press.

Shukla, A., & Upadhyaya, S. B. (1986). Similar jobs: Dissimilar evaluations. *Psychologia, 29,* 229-234.

Shweder, R., Markus, H. R., Minow, M. L., & Kessel, F. (1997). The free exercise of culture. *Items, 51,* 61-67.

Shweder, R., & Sullivan, M. (1993). Cultural psychology: Who needs it? *Annual Review of Psychology, 44,* 497-523.

Sidanius, J. (1993). The psychology of group conflict and the dynamics of oppression: A social dominance perspective. In W. McGuire & S. Iyengar (Eds.), *Current approaches to political psychology* (pp. 183-219). Durham, NC: Duke University Press.

Silvers, M., & Deni, R. (1983). Rating of importance of job factors by office employees as a function of internal-external control scores. *Psychological Reports, 53,* 323-326.

Singelis, T. M., & Brown, W. J. (1995). Culture, self, and collectivist communication: Linking culture to individual behavior. *Human Communication Research, 21,* 354-389.

Sinha, D. (1988). The family scenario in a developing country and its implications for mental health: The case of India. In P. R. Dasen, J. W. Berry, & N. Sartorius (Eds.), *Health and cross-cultural psychology: Toward applications* (pp. 48-70). Newbury Park, CA: Sage.

Sinha, D. (1997). Indigenising psychology. In J. W. Berry, Y. H. Poortinga, & J. Pandey (Eds.), *Handbook of cross-cultural psychology: Vol. 1. Theory and method* (pp. 129-169). Boston: Allyn & Bacon.

Sinha, D., & Bharat, S. (1985). Three types of family structure and psychological differentiation. *International Journal of Psychology, 20,* 693-708.

Sinha, J. B. P., & Verma, J. (1987). Structure of collectivism. In C. Kagitcibasi (Ed.), *Growth and progress in cross-cultural psychology* (pp. 123-129). Lisse, The Netherlands: Swets & Zeitlinger.

Sjostrom, B. R. (1988). Culture contact and value orientations: The Puerto Rican experience. In E. Acosta-Belén & B. R. Sjostrom (Eds.), *The Hispanic experience in the United States* (pp. 163-186). New York: Praeger.

Smith, E. R. (1994). Procedural knowledge and processing strategies in social cognition. In R. S. Wyer, Jr., & T. K. Srull (Eds.), *Handbook of social cognition* (2nd ed., Vol. 1, pp. 99-152). Hillsdale, NJ: Lawrence Erlbaum.

Smith, E. R. (1996). What do connectionism and social psychology offer each other? *Journal of Personality and Social Psychology, 70,* 893-912.

Smith, P. B., & Bond, M. H. (1998). *Social psychology across cultures* (2nd ed.). Hemel Hempstead, England: Prentice Hall.

Smith, P. B., Peterson, M. F., Leung, K., & Dugan, S. (in press). Individualism-collectivism and the handling of disagreement: A 23-country study. *International Journal of Intercultural Relations.*

Smith, P. C., Kendall, L. M., & Hulin, C. C. (1969). *The measurement of satisfaction in work and retirement.* Chicago: Rand McNally.

Smith, S. (1995). Family theory and multicultural family studies. In B. Ingoldsby & S. Smith (Eds.), *Families in multicultural perspective* (pp. 5-35). New York: Guilford.

Snyder, M., & Ickes, W. (1985). Personality and social behavior. In G. Lindzey & E. Aronson (Eds.), *The handbook of social psychology: Vol. 2. Special fields and applications* (3rd ed., pp. 883-948). New York: Random House.

Snyder, M., & Swann, W. B., Jr. (1978). Behavioral confirmation in social interaction: From social perception to social reality. *Journal of Experimental Social Psychology, 14,* 148-162.

South Asians: Success and strength in unity. (1983, August 25). *Toronto Star,* pp. C1, C4.

Spector, P. E. (1982). Behavior in organizations as a function of employee's locus of control. *Psychological Bulletin, 91,* 482-497.

Spector, P. E., & O'Connell, B. J. (1994). The contribution on personality traits, negative affectivity, locus of control, and Type A to the subsequent reports of job stressors and job strains. *Journal of Occupational and Organizational Psychology, 67,* 1-11.

Spillane, W., & Ryser, P. (1975). *Male fertility survey: Fertility knowledge, attitudes, and practices of married men.* Cambridge, MA: Ballinger.

Spiro, M. E. (1965). A typology of social structure and the patterning of social situations: A cross-cultural study. *American Anthropologist, 67,* 1097-1119.

Srull, T. K., & Gaelick, L. (1983). General principles and individual differences in the self as a habitual reference point: An examination of self-other judgments of similarity. *Social Cognition, 2,* 108-121.

Srull, T. K., & Wyer, R. S., Jr. (1989). Person memory and judgment. *Psychological Review, 96,* 55-84.

Stacey, J. (1990). *Brave new families: Stories of domestic upheaval in the late twentieth century American.* New York: Basic Books.

Stanton, M. E. (1995). Patterns of kinship and residence. In B. Ingoldsby & S. Smith (Eds.), *Families in multicultural perspective* (pp. 97-116). New York: Guilford.

Statistics Canada. (1991). *Distribution of South Asian population (visible minority dataset): Mother tongue groups, age, gender, labour force activity, income, and education.* Ottawa, Canada: Ontario Ministry of Citizenship, Culture, and Recreation Research and Data Group.

Staub, E. (1988). The evolution of caring and nonaggressive persons and societies. *Journal of Social Issues, 44,* 81-100.

Staub, E. (1989). *The roots of evil.* Cambridge, UK: Cambridge University Press.

Staw, B. M., Bell, N. E., & Clausen, J. A. (1986). The dispositional approach to job attitudes: A lifetime longitudinal test. *Administrative Science Quarterly, 31,* 56-77.

Staw, B. M., & Ross, J. (1985). Stability in the midst of change: A dispositional approach to job attitudes. *Journal of Applied Psychology, 70,* 469-480.

Stephan, W. G. (1985). Intergroup relations. In G. Lindzey & E. Aronson (Eds.), *Handbook of social psychology* (3rd ed., Vol. 2, pp. 599-658). New York: Random House.

Stephan, W. G., Ageyev, V., Coates-Shrider, L., Stephan, C. W., & Abalakina, M. (1994). On the relationship between stereotypes and prejudice: An international study. *Personality and Social Psychology Bulletin, 20,* 277-284.

Stephan, W. G., & Stephan, C. (1985). Intergroup anxiety. *Journal of Social Issues, 41,* 157-176.

Stephan, W. G., & Stephan, C. (1989). Antecedents of intergroup anxiety in Asian-Americans and Hispanic-Americans. *International Journal of Intercultural Communication, 13,* 203-219.

Stephan, W. G., Ybarra, O., & Bachman, G. (1998). *Prejudice toward immigrants.* Manuscript submitted for publication.

Stephan, W. G., Ybarra, O., Martinez, C. M., Schwartzwald, J., & Tur-Kaspa, M. (in press). Prejudice towards immigrants to Spain and Israel: An integrated threat theory analysis. *Journal of Cross-Cultural Psychology.*

Sternberg, R. J., Wagner, R. K., Williams, W. M., & Horvath, J. A. (1995). Testing common sense. *American Psychologist, 50,* 912-927.

Stevahn, L., Johnson, D. W., Johnson, R. T., & Real, D. (1996). The impact of a cooperative or individualistic context on the effectiveness of conflict resolution training. *American Educational Research Journal, 33,* 801-825.

Stewart, E. (1966). The simulation of cultural differences. *Journal of Communication, 16,* 291-304.

Stillman, F. A., Bone, L. R., Rand, C., Levine, D. M., & Becker, D. M. (1993). Heart, body, and soul: A church-based smoking-cessation program for urban African Americans. *Preventive Medicine, 22*(3), 335-349.

Stycos, J. (1962). A critique of the traditional Planned Parenthood approach in underdeveloped areas. In C. Kiser (Ed.), *Research in family planning.* Princeton, NJ: Princeton University Press.

Sue, D. W. (1991). A model for cultural diversity training. *Journal of Consulting & Development, 70,* 99-105.

Sussman, S., Dent, C. W., Stacy, A. W., Sun, P., Craig, S., Simon, T. R., Buyrton, D., & Flay, B. R. (1993). Project Towards No Tobacco Use: 1-year behavior outcomes. *American Journal of Public Health, 83,* 1245-1250.

Szapocznik, J., Kurtines, W., & Hanna, N. (1979). Comparison of Cuban and Anglo-American cultural values in a clinical population. *Journal of Consulting and Clinical Psychology, 47*(3), 623-624.

Szapocznik, J., Scopetta, M. A., Aranalde, M. A., & Kurtines, W. (1978). Cuban value structure: Treatment implications. *Journal of Consulting and Clinical Psychology, 46*(5), 961-970.

Taft, R. (1974). Ethnically marginal youth and culture conflict. In J. L. M. Dawson & W. J. Lonner (Eds.), *Readings in cross-cultural psychology* (pp. 268-276). Hong Kong: University of Hong Kong Press.

Taft, R. (1977). Coping with unfamiliar cultures. In N. Warren (Ed.), *Studies in cross-cultural psychology* (Vol. 1, pp. 121-151). London: Academic Press.

Tajfel, H. (Ed.). (1978). *Differentiation between social groups: Studies in the social psychology of intergroup relations.* London: Academic Press.

Tajfel, H. (1981). *Human groups and social categories.* Cambridge, UK: Cambridge University Press.

Tajfel, H. (1982). Social psychology of intergroup relations. *Annual Review of Psychology, 33,* 1-39.

Tajfel, H., & Turner, J. C. (1979). An integrative theory of intergroup conflict. In W. G. Austin & S. Worchel (Eds.), *The social psychology of intergroup relations* (pp. 33-47). Belmont, CA: Wadsworth.

Tanabe, K. (1963). The process of litigation: An experiment with the adversary system. In A. T. von Mehren (Ed.), *Law in Japan: The legal order in a changing society* (pp. 73-110). Cambridge, MA: Harvard University Press.

Tanford, S., & Penrod, S. (1984). Social influence model: A formal integration of research on majority and minority influence processes. *Psychological Bulletin, 95,* 189-225.

Taylor, S. E., & Fiske, S. T. (1978). Salience, attention, and attribution: Top of the head phenomena. In L. Berkowitz (Ed.), *Advances in experimental social psychology* (Vol. 11, pp. 250-289). San Diego, CA: Academic Press.

Tedeschi, J. T., & Felson, R. B. (1994). *Violence, aggression, and coercive actions.* Washington, DC: American Psychological Association.

Tesser, A. (1978). Self-generated attitude change. In L. Berkowitz (Ed.), *Advances in experimental social psychology* (Vol. 11, pp. 290-338). San Diego, CA: Academic Press.

Tetlock, P. E. (1992). The impact of accountability on judgment and choice: Toward a social contingency model. In M. P. Zanna (Ed.), *Advances in experimental social psychology* (Vol. 25, pp. 331-376). San Diego, CA: Academic Press.

Thibaut, J., & Walker, L. (1975). *Procedural justice: A psychological analysis.* Hillsdale, NJ: Lawrence Erlbaum.

Thomas, R. R., Jr. (1992). Managing diversity: A conceptual framework. In S. E. Jackson & Associates (Eds.), *Diversity in the workplace* (pp. 306-317). New York: Guilford.

Tinsley, C., & Brett, J. (1997, August). *Managing workplace conflict: A comparison of conflict frame and outcomes in the U.S. and Hong Kong.* Paper submitted to the Academy of Management meeting, Boston.

Tolbert, A. S. S. (1990). *Venezuelan culture assimilator: Incidents designed for training U.S. professionals conducting business in Venezuela.* Unpublished doctoral dissertation, University of Minnesota.

Tomasello, M., Kruger, A. C., & Ratner, H. H. (1993). Cultural learning. *Behavioral and Brain Sciences, 16,* 495-511.

Toren, N., & Grifel, A. (1983). A cross-cultural examination of scientists' perceived importance of work characteristics. *Social Science Research, 12,* 10-25.

Touliatos, J., Perlmutter, B. F., & Straus, M. A. (1990). *Handbook of family measurement techniques.* Newbury Park, CA: Sage.

Trafimow, D., Triandis, H. C., & Goto, S. G. (1991). Some tests of the distinction between the private self and the collective self. *Journal of Personality and Social Psychology, 60,* 649-656.

Trapnell, P. D. (1994). Openness versus intellect: A lexical left turn. *European Journal of Personality, 8,* 273-290.

Triandis, H. C. (1964). Exploratory factor analyses of the behavioral component of social attitudes. *Journal of Abnormal and Social Psychology, 68,* 420-430.

Triandis, H. C. (1971). *Attitude and attitude change.* New York: John Wiley.

Triandis, H. C. (1972). *The analysis of subjective culture.* New York: Wiley-Interscience.

Triandis, H. C. (1975). Culture training, cognitive complexity, and interpersonal attitudes. In R. W. Brislin, S. Bochner, & W. Lonner (Eds.), *Cross-cultural perspectives on learning* (pp. 39-77). Beverly Hills, CA: Sage.

Triandis, H. C. (1976). Approaches toward minimizing translation. In R. W. Brislin (Ed.), *Translation: Applications and research* (pp. 229-243). New York: Wiley/Halsted.

Triandis, H. C. (1977a). *Interpersonal behavior.* Monterey, CA: Brooks/Cole.

Triandis, H. C. (1977b). Theoretical framework for evaluation of cross-cultural training effectiveness. *International Journal of Intercultural Relations, 1,* 19-45.

Triandis, H. C. (1980). Introduction. In H. C. Triandis et al. (Eds.), *Handbook of cross-cultural psychology* (Vol. 1). Boston: Allyn & Bacon.

Triandis, H. C. (1984). A theoretical framework for the more efficient construction of culture assimilator. *International Journal of Intercultural Relations, 8,* 301-330.

Triandis, H. C. (1988). Collectivism and individualism: A reconceptualization of a basic concept in cross-cultural psychology. In G. K. Verma & C. Bargley (Eds.), *Personality, attitudes, and cognitions* (pp. 60-95). London: Macmillan.

Triandis, H. C. (1989). The self and social behavior in differing cultural contexts. *Psychological Review, 96,* 506-520.

Triandis, H. C. (1990). Cross-cultural studies of individualism and collectivism. In J. Berman (Ed.), *Nebraska Symposium on Motivation, 1989: Cross-cultural perspectives* (Vol. 37, pp. 41-133). Lincoln: University of Nebraska Press.

Triandis, H. C. (1991, July). *Individualism and collectivism theory as a framework for understanding the convergence of the East and West European systems.* Invited keynote address presented at the International Association for Cross-Cultural Psychology, Debrecen Conference, Debrecen, Hungary.

Triandis, H. C. (1993). Collectivism and individualism as cultural syndromes. *Cross-Cultural Research, 27,* 155-180.

Triandis, H. C. (1994a). *Culture and social behavior.* New York: McGraw-Hill.

Triandis, H. C. (1994b). Theoretical and methodological approaches to the study of collectivism and individualism. In U. Kim, H. C. Triandis, C. Kagitcibasi, S.-C. Choi, & G. Yoon (Eds.), *Individualism and collectivism: Theory, method, and applications* (pp. 41-51). Thousand Oaks, CA: Sage.

Triandis, H. C. (1995a). Culture specific assimilators. In S. M. Fowler (Ed.), *Intercultural sourcebook: Cross-cultural training methods* (Vol. 1, pp. 179-186). Yarmouth, ME: Intercultural Press.

Triandis, H. C. (1995b). *Individualism and collectivism.* Boulder, CO: Westview.

Triandis, H. C. (1996). The psychological measurement of cultural syndromes. *American Psychologist, 51,* 407-415.

Triandis, H. C., & Bhawuk, D. P. S. (1997). Culture theory and the meaning of relatedness. In P. C. Earley & M. Erez (Eds.), *New perspectives on international industrial/organizational psychology* (pp. 13-52). New York: New Lexington Free Press.

Triandis, H. C., Bontempo, R., Betancourt, H., & Bond, M. (1986). The measurement of the etic aspects of individualism and collectivism across cultures. *Australian Journal of Psychology, 38,* 257-267.

Triandis, H. C., Brislin, R. W., & Hui, C. H. (1986). Cross-cultural training across the individualism and collectivism divide. *International Journal of Intercultural Relations, 12,* 269-289.

Triandis, H. C., & Gelfand, M. J. (1998). Converging measurement of horizontal and vertical individualism and collectivism. *Journal of Personality and Social Psychology, 74,* 118-128.

Triandis, H. C., Kurowski, L. L., & Gelfand, M. J. (1994). Workplace diversity. In H. C. Triandis & M. D. Dunnette (Eds.), *Handbook of industrial and organizational psychology* (Vol. 4, pp. 769-827). Palo Alto, CA: Consulting Psychologists Press.

Triandis, H. C., Lambert, W. W., Berry, J. W., Lonner, W. J., Heron, A., Brislin, R., & Draguns, J. (Eds.). (1980). *Handbook of cross-cultural psychology* (Vols. 1-6). Boston: Allyn & Bacon.

Triandis, H. C., Leung, K., Villareal, M. J., & Clack, F. L. (1985). Allocentric versus idiocentric tendencies: Convergent and discriminant validation. *Journal of Research in Personality, 19,* 395-415.

Triandis, H. C., Marín, G., Hui, C. H., Lisansky, J., & Ottati, V. (1984). Role perceptions of Hispanic young adults. *Journal of Cross-Cultural Psychology, 15,* 297-320.

Triandis, H. C., Marín, G., Lisansky, J., & Betancourt, H. (1984). *Simpatía* as a cultural script of Hispanics. *Journal of Personality and Social Psychology, 47,* 1363-1375.

Triandis, H. C., McCusker, C., & Hui, C. H. (1990). Multimethod probes of individualism and collectivism. *Journal of Personality and Social Psychology, 59,* 1006-1020.

Triandis, H. C., & Vassiliou, V. (1972). A comparative analysis of subjective culture. In H. C. Triandis (Ed.), *The analysis of subjective culture* (pp. 299-335). New York: John Wiley.

Triandis, H. C., Vassiliou, V., Vassiliou, G., Tanaka, Y., & Shanmugam, A. (1972). *The analysis of subjective culture.* New York: John Wiley.

Trifonovitch, G. (1973). On cross-cultural orientation techniques. *Topics in Culture Learning, 1,* 38-47.

Tse, D. K., Francis, J., & Walls, J. (1994). Cultural differences in conducting intra- and intercultural negotiations: A Sino-Canadian comparison. *Journal of International Business Studies, 25,* 537-555.

Turnbull, C. M. (1972). *The mountain people.* New York: Simon & Schuster.

Tversky, A. (1977). Features of similarity. *Psychological Review, 84,* 327-352.

Tyler, T. R., & Bies, R. J. (1990). Interpersonal aspects of procedural justice. In S. J. Carroll (Ed.), *Applied social psychology in business settings* (pp. 77-98). Hillsdale, NJ: Lawrence Erlbaum.

Tyler, T. R., Boeckmann, R. J., Smith, H. J., & Huo, Y. J. (1997). *Social justice in a diverse society.* Boulder, CO: Westview.

Tyler, T. R., Lind, E. A., & Huo, Y. J. (1997, May-June). *Cultural values and authority relations.* Paper presented at the annual meeting of the Law and Society Association, St. Louis, MO.

Uba, L. (1992). Cultural barriers to health care for Southeast Asian refugees. *Public Health Reports, 107,* 544-548.

United Nations. (1996). *Levels and trends of contraceptive use as assessed in 1994.* New York: United Nations Publication.

Ury, W. L., Brett, J., & Goldberg, S. B. (1988). *Getting disputes resolved.* San Francisco: Jossey-Bass.

Uzoka, A. F. (1979). The myth of the nuclear family. *American Psychologist, 34,* 1095-1106.

Vaidyanathan, P., & Naidoo, J. (1990). Asian Indians in Western countries: Cultural identity and the arranged marriage. In R. Bleichrodt & P. Drenth (Eds.), *Contemporary issues in cross-cultural psychology* (pp. 37-49). Amsterdam: Swets & Zeitlinger.

Valian, V. (1990). Null subjects: A problem for parameter-setting models of language acquisition. *Cognition, 35,* 105-122.

Valian, V. (1991). Syntactic subjects in the early speech of American and Italian children. *Cognition, 40,* 21-81.

Vallacher, R. R., & Nowak, A. (1994). *Dynamical systems in social psychology.* San Diego, CA: Academic Press.

Valsiner, J. (1988). Ontogeny of co-construction of culture within society organized environmental settings. In J. Valsiner (Ed.), *Child development within culturally structured environments* (Vol. 2, pp. 283-297). Norwood, NJ: Ablex.

Van Avermaet, E., & McClintock, C. G. (1988). Intergroup fairness and bias in children. *European Journal of Social Psychology, 18,* 407-427.

Van de Vijver, F., & Leung, K. (1997). Methods and data analysis of comparative research. In J. W. Berry, Y. H. Poortinga, & J. Pandey (Eds.), *Handbook of cross-cultural psychology: Vol. 1. Theory and method* (pp. 257-300). Boston: Allyn & Bacon.

VanOss Marín, B., Marín, G., Pérez-Stable, E. J., & Hauck, W. W. (1994). Effects of a community intervention to change smoking behavior among Hispanics. *American Journal of Preventive Medicine, 10*(6), 340-347.

VanOss Marín, B., Marín, G., Pérez-Stable, E. J., Otero-Sabogal, R., & Sabogal, F. (1990). Cultural differences in attitudes toward smoking: Developing messages using the theory of reasoned action. *Journal of Applied Social Psychology, 20,* 478-493.

VanOss Marín, B., Pérez-Stable, E. J., Marín, G., Sabogal, F., & Otero-Sabogal, R. (1990). Attitudes and behaviors of Hispanic smokers: Implications for cessation interventions. *Health Education Quarterly, 17*(3), 287-297.

Varela, J. A. (1971). *Psychological solutions to social problems.* New York: Academic Press.

Vassiliou, G. (1966). *Diereunesis metavleton ypeiserhomenon eis tin psychodynamikin tis hellenikis oikogeneias* [Exploration of factors related to the psychodynamics of the Greek family]. Athens, Greece: Athenian Institute of Anthropos.

Vega, W. A. (1992). Theoretical and pragmatic implications of cultural diversity for community research. *American Journal of Community Psychology, 20,* 375-391.

Verma, J. (1986). Perceived causes of norm violation as a function of individualism and collectivism. *Psychological Studies, 31,* 169-176.

Vidmar, N. J., & Schuller, R. A. (1989). Juries and expert evidence: Social framework testimony. *Law and Contemporary Problems, 52,* 133-176.

Vygotsky, L. S. (1978). *Mind in society: The development of higher psychological processes.* Cambridge, MA: Harvard University Press.

Wadley, S. S. (1977). Women and the HIndu tradition. *Signs: Journal of Women in Culture and Society, 3*(1), 113-125.

Wagatsuma, H. (1977). Problems of language in cross-cultural research. *New York Academy of Sciences Annals, 285,* 141-150.

Wagenheim, K. (1972). *Puerto Rico: A profile.* New York: Praeger.

Wagley, C. (1968). *The Latin American tradition.* New York: Columbia University Press.

Walker, I., & Pettigrew, T. F. (1984). Relative deprivation theory: An overview and conceptual critique. *British Journal of Social Psychology, 23,* 301-310.

Wallston, B. S., Wallston, K. A., Kaplan, G. D., & Maides, S. A. (1976). Development and validation of the Health Locus of Control (HLC) scale. *Journal of Consulting and Clinical Psychology, 44,* 580-585.

Wänke, M., Schwarz, N., & Bless, H. (1995). The availability heuristic revisited: Experienced ease of retrieval in mundane frequency estimates. *Acta Psychologica, 412,* 1-8.

Watson, W. E., Kumar, K., & Michaelsen, L. K. (1993). Cultural diversity's impact on interaction process and performance: Comparing homogeneous and diverse task groups. *Academy of Management Journal, 36,* 590-602.

Wegner, D. M. (1994). Ironic processes of mental control. *Psychological Review, 101,* 34-52.

Weiner, M. (1995). *The global migration crisis: Challenge to states and to human rights.* New York: HarperCollins.

Weiss, M. G., & Kleinman, A. (1988). Depression in cross-cultural perspective. In P. R. Dasen, J. W. Berry, & N. Sartorius (Eds.), *Health and cross-cultural psychology* (Vol. 10, pp. 179-206). Newbury Park, CA: Sage.

Weissberg, R. P., & Elias, M. J. (1993). Enhancing young people's social competence and health behavior: An important challenge for educators, scientists, policy makers, and funders. *Applied and Preventive Psychology, 2,* 179-190.

Weldon, D. E., Carlston, D. E., Rissman, A. K., Slobodin, L., & Triandis, H. C. (1975). A laboratory test of effects of culture assimilator training. *Journal of Personality and Social Psychology, 32,* 300-310.

Weldon, E., Jehn, K. A., Chen, X. M., & Wang, Z. M. (1996, August). *Conflict management in US-Chinese joint ventures.* Paper submitted to the Academy of Management meeting, Boston.

Wertsch, J. B. (1991). *Voices of the mind: A sociocultural approach to mediated action.* Hemel Hempstead, UK: Harvester Wheatsheaf.

Wertsch, J. B., & Hickmann, M. (1987). In M. Hickmann (Ed.), *Social and functional approaches to language and thought.* Orlando, FL: Academic Press.

Westwood, R. I., Tang, S. F., & Kirkbride, P. S. (1992). Chinese conflict behavior: Cultural antecedents and behavioral consequences. *Organizational Development Journal, 10*(2), 13-19.

Wetherbee, H., Smith, M., & Benfield, W. (1975). The pill for men: Attitudes of college students. *Medical Marketing and Media, 10,* 31-36.

Wheeler, L., Reis, H. T., & Bond, M. H. (1989). Collectivism-individualism in everyday social life: The middle kingdom and the melting pot. *Journal of Personality and Social Psychology, 57,* 79-86.

White, P. W. (1988). Causal reasoning: Origins and development. *Psychological Bulletin, 104,* 36-52.

Whiting, B., & Whiting, J. W. M. (1975). *Children of six cultures: A psycho-cultural analysis.* Cambridge, MA: Harvard University Press.

Whiting, J. W. M., & Child, I. L. (1953). *Child training and personality.* New Haven, CT: Yale University Press.

Whorf, B. L. (1956). *Language, thought, and reality* (J. B. Carroll, Ed.). Cambridge: MIT Press.

Wierzbicka, A. (1991). *Cross-cultural pragmatics: The semantics of human interaction.* Berlin: Mouton De Gruyter.

Wilkinson, R. G. (1996). *Unhealthy societies: The afflictions of inequality.* London: Routledge.

Wilkinson, R. G., Kawachi, I., & Kennedy, B. P. (1998). Mortality, the social environment, crime, and violence. *Sociology of Health and Illness, 20,* 578-597.

Wilson, T. D., Dunn, D. S., Kraft, D., & Lisle, D. J. (1989). Introspection, attitude change, and attitude-behavior consistency: The disruptive effects of explaining why we feel the way we do. In L. Berkowitz (Ed.), *Advances in experimental social psychology* (Vol. 22, pp. 287-344). San Diego, CA: Academic Press.

Wilson, T. D., & Schooler, J. W. (1991). Thinking too much: Introspection can reduce the quality of preferences and decisions. *Journal of Personality and Social Psychology, 60,* 181-192.

Winett, R. A. (1995). A framework for health promotion and disease prevention programs. *American Psychologist, 50,* 341-350.

Winkleby, M. A., Flora, J. A., & Kraemer, H. C. (1994). A community-based heart disease intervention: Predictors of change. *American Journal of Public Health, 84*(5), 767-772.

Wiseman, R. L. (Ed.). (1995). *Intercultural communication theory.* Thousand Oaks, CA: Sage.

Woehr, D. J., & Feldman, J. M. (1993). Processing objective and question order effects on the causal relation between memory and judgment: The tip of the iceberg. *Journal of Applied Psychology, 78,* 232-241.

Wolf, E. R. (1956). San José: Subcultures of a "traditional" coffee municipality. In J. Steward (Ed.), *The people of Puerto Rico* (pp. 171-264). Urbana: University of Illinois Press.

Wolfram, S. (1991). *Mathematica: A system for doing mathematics by computer.* Reading, MA: Addison-Wesley.

Wood, W., Lundgren, S., Ouellette, J. A., Busceme, S., & Blackstone, T. (1994). Minority influence: A meta-analytic review of social influence processes. *Psychological Bulletin, 115,* 323-345.

Wrigley, E. A. (1969). *Population and history.* London: Weidenfeld & Nicholson.

Wu, K. F. J., & Watkins, D. (1994). A Hong Kong validity study of the Job Description Index. *Psychologia, 37,* 89-94.

Wyer, R. S., Jr. (Ed.). (1996). *Ruminative thoughts: Advances in social cognition* (Vol. 9). Mahwah, NJ: Lawrence Erlbaum.

Yoshida, S. (1980). Typology and universality of the cognition of space division through the analysis of demonstratives. *Bulletin of the National Museum of Ethology, 5,* 833-950.

Young, M., & Wilmott, P. (1968). *Family and class in a London suburb.* London: Routledge & Kegan Paul.

Yu, E. S. (1980). Chinese collective orientation and need for achievement. *International Journal of Social Psychiatry, 26,* 184-189.

Zhang, Q. W. (1994). An intervention model of constructive conflict resolution and cooperative learning. *Journal of Social Issues, 50,* 99-116.

Index

ABOUT THE EDITORS

John Adamopoulos is Professor of Psychology at Grand Valley State University in Allendale, Michigan. He was born in Greece and received his undergraduate degree in psychology from Yale University, where he studied cross-cultural psychology with Leonard W. Doob. He completed his Ph.D. at the University of Illinois under the direction of Harry C. Triandis. His research focuses on the emergence of interpersonal meaning across cultures and time, and he also has interests in the critique of theoretical systems in the area of psychology and culture. He has been Editor of the *Cross-Cultural Psychology Bulletin* and is currently an Associate Editor of the *Journal of Cross-Cultural Psychology*.

Yoshihisa Kashima is Senior Lecturer in Psychology at the School of Psychological Science, La Trobe University, Melbourne, Australia. He lived in Japan until he finished his law degree at the University of Tokyo. He then went to the University of California, Santa Cruz, for his psychology degree and completed his Ph.D. at the University of Illinois, Urbana-Champaign, under the guidance of Harry Triandis. He was an Associate Editor of the *Journal of Cross-Cultural Psychology* and is currently Secretary-General of the Asian Association of Social Psychology and an Associate Editor of the *Asian Journal of Social Psychology*. He lives in the multicultural city of Melbourne, Australia, living and breathing cross-cultural psychology.

ABOUT THE CONTRIBUTORS

Kye Choon Ahn is Professor of Sociology at Yonsei University, Seoul, Republic of Korea.

John W. Berry is Professor of Psychology at Queen's University, Kingston, Ontario, Canada. He has been a Lecturer at the University of Sydney for 3 years, a Fellow of the Netherlands Institute for Advanced Study, and a Visiting Professor at the Université de Nice and the Université de Genève. He is Past President of the International Association for Cross-Cultural Psychology and has been an Associate Editor of the *Journal of Cross-Cultural Psychology*. He is the author or editor of 25 books in the areas of cross-cultural, social, and cognitive psychologies and is particularly interested in the application of cross-cultural psychology to public policy and programs in the areas of acculturation, multiculturalism immigration, health, and education. He received the 1998 D. O. Hebb Award from the Canadian Psychological Association for contributions to psychology as a science.

Dharm P. S. Bhawuk, a citizen of Nepal, is Assistant Professor of Management at the College of Business Administration, University of Hawaii at Manoa. His research interests include cross-cultural training, intercultural sensitivity, diversity in the workplace, individualism and collectivism, and political behavior in the workplace. He has published several empirical papers in the *International Journal of Intercultural Relations, International Journal of Psychology, Cross-Cultural Research,* and *Journal of Management.* He has also published a number of book chapters and is a coeditor of the book *Asian Contributions to Cross-Cultural Psychology* (1996). He has received many awards and honors, including the

Best Paper Award from the International Division of the Academy of Management (1996), the Distinguished Service Award from the East-West Center (1989), and the Lum Yip Kee Outstanding MBA Student Award from the College of Business Administration, University of Hawaii (1990).

Michael Harris Bond is a Canadian-born social psychologist who has taught, researched, and practiced in Hong Kong for the past 24 years. His first cross-cultural posting was in California, where he learned about comparative accents and semantics; his second was in Japan, where he learned about *mochii,* positive discrimination, restraint, and crowding. He is the coauthor with Peter Smith of *Social Psychology Across Cultures* (2nd edition, 1998).

Richard W. Brislin joined the faculty of the College of Business Administration, University of Hawaii, in 1996, and now directs the Ph.D. program in International Management. Previously, he was Senior Fellow and Project Director of Intercultural Programs at the East-West Center in Honolulu, Hawaii. His current research interests include cross-cultural training programs, mentoring for career development, and leadership. He has consulted with Sage Publications for more than 15 years. One of his books, *The Art of Getting Things Done: A Practical Guide to the Use of Power,* was a Book-of-the-Month-Club selection in 1992. He is also the codeveloper of some of the most widely used cross-cultural training materials, published as *Intercultural Interactions: A Practical Guide* (2nd ed., 1996).

Darius K.-S. Chan is Associate Professor at the Chinese University of Hong Kong. His research interests include attitudes and behavior consistency, AIDS and social behavior, cross-cultural methodology, and conflict resolution across cultures. He has published articles in various journals such as *Psychology and Health, Public Health Reports, International Journal of Psychology, Journal of Cross-Cultural Psychology, European Journal of Social Psychology, Journal of Applied Social Psychology, Journal of Experimental Social Psychology,* and *Psychology of Women Quarterly.*

Subhas Chandra is Assistant Professor at Charles Sturt University, Bathurst, New South Wales, Australia.

Andrew R. Davidson is Professor and the Vice Dean at the Columbia University, Joseph L. Mailman School of Public Health. He completed his Ph.D. at the University of Illinois under the guidance of Harry C. Triandis. His research focus is fertility decision making and the acceptability and use of contraceptive methods. He has served as a member of the National Institutes of Health study section on demographic and social behavior and as an adviser to the United Nations World Health Organization special program in human reproduction. He is a Fellow of the American Psychological Association and was a National Science Foundation Predoctoral Fellow.

Rogelio Diaz-Guerrero is Professor Emeritus at the National University of Mexico in Mexico City.

D. C. Dubey is a social scientist with the National Institute of Health and Family Welfare, New Delhi, India.

Jack M. Feldman is Professor of Psychology at the Georgia Institute of Technology in Atlanta. His interests focus on judgment processes and on how the judgments people construct might, or might not, guide their lives. A desire to both understand and benefit those lives led him to the study of social and industrial psychology under the patient (and at times exasperated) guidance of Harry Triandis. He has conducted research on stereotyping, performance appraisal, motivation, and judgment, evaluation, and decision processes, as often as possible in cross-cultural contexts.

James Georgas is Professor of Social Psychology at the University of Athens in Greece. His current research interests are the impact of the structure and function of the family on psychological variables across cultures, and theory and methodology in cross-cultural research. He is Secretary-General of the International Association for Cross-Cultural Psychology.

C. Harry Hui is Senior Lecturer in the Department of Psychology at the University of Hong Kong. He teaches and does research in industrial and organizational psychology. Items from the INDCOL (Individualism-Collectivism) Scale he developed are now widely used in many measures of individualism and collectivism. His current work focuses on the assessment of employee attitudes and aptitudes.

James Jaccard is Professor of Psychology at the University of Albany, State University of New York. He is Director of the Center for Applied Psychological Research. His research focuses on the prevention of unintended pregnancies and the prevention of alcohol-impaired driving in adolescents.

Emiko S. Kashima is Lecturer in Psychology at the Swinburne University of Technology, Melbourne, Australia. With her experience as a high school exchange student in Minnesota, she was destined to become a cross-cultural psychologist. She graduated from the Sacred Heart University, Tokyo, and completed her Ph.D. at the University of Illinois, Urbana-Champaign, under Harry Triandis. Her research interests include the processes of identity construction in the context of culture and language use.

Arielle Lehmann recently completed her doctoral dissertation in the social psychology program of the Department of Psychology at the Hebrew University of Jerusalem. She studied motivations in close friendships and their relations to values. Until moving recently to London, she was the Academic Coordinator of the social psychology course in the Open University of Israel, for which she wrote a social psychology textbook on small groups.

Kwok Leung is Professor and Chairman of the Department of Psychology at the Chinese University of Hong Kong. He was an Associate Editor of the *Journal of Cross-Cultural Psychology* and is an Associate Editor of the *Asian Journal of Social Psychology*. He is the current President of the Asian Association of Social Psychology. His research interests include justice, conflict, cross-cultural psychology, and research methodology.

Harold A. Litardo is a doctoral student in the Psychology Department at the University of Albany, State University of New York. His research focuses on delinquency and crime-related behaviors of adolescents.

Walter J. Lonner is Professor of Psychology at Western Washington University in Bellingham, Washington. He has been involved in cross-cultural psychology for about 33 years. Founding Editor and currently Senior Editor of the *Journal of Cross-Cultural Psychology*, he has served as President of the International Association for Cross-Cultural Psychology (IACCP) and is also an Honorary Fellow of IACCP. He has coauthored or coedited more than 15 books, most of which have a cross-cultural focus. In addition, he is coeditor (with J. W. Berry) of the Sage Publications series **Cross-Cultural Psychology**. In 1998, he was President of the Silver Jubilee Congress of IACCP, which was held at his university.

Roy S. Malpass is Professor of Psychology and Director of Criminal Justice at the University of Texas at El Paso. He was Editor of the *Journal of Cross-Cultural Psychology* from 1982 to 1986. He is Past President of the Society for Cross-Cultural Research and Past President of the International Association for Cross-Cultural Psychology. He was Founding President of the Division of Psychology and Law of the International Association for Applied Psychology. He is also the founder of two Internet discussion lists: Psylaw-L, for specialists in psychology and law, and xcul, for cross-cultural psychology. His current work focuses on cross-race face recognition, decision processes in eyewitness identification, and the evaluation of fairness in lineups and photo spreads.

Gerardo Marín is Professor of Psychology and Senior Associate Dean at the College of Arts and Sciences at the University of San Francisco. He has published widely in the areas of stereotyping, health promotion, and culturally appropriate research and interventions. His two most recent books are *Research with Hispanic Populations* and *Readings in Ethnic Psychology*. He is currently researching predictors of cigarette smoking among Hispanic children.

Amir Mehryar is a researcher at the Institute for Research Planning and Development, Tehran, Iran. He has served as a consultant to the United Nations World Health Organization special program in human reproduction and numerous other international organizations.

Josephine C. Naidoo is Professor Emerita of Psychology at Wilfrid Laurier University in Waterloo, Ontario, Canada. She has engaged in research and published work related to South Asian immigrant women in Canada, multicultural issues, racism, and indigenous psychology. She has served on federal and provincial government studies of ethnic minorities and on the International Association for Cross-Cultural Psychology as Secretary-General. Recently, she conducted studies in South Africa, testing the generality of her Canadian findings for populations in the South Asian diaspora.

Sonia Roccas is a Lecturer at the Open University of Israel. She received her Ph.D. in social psychology from the Hebrew University of Jerusalem in 1997 and recently spent a postdoctoral year at Ohio State University. Her main research is in the areas of group identification, intergroup relations, and human values.

Shalom H. Schwartz is Leon and Clara Sznajderman Professor of Psychology at the Hebrew University of Jerusalem. His current research, based on a project in more than 60 nations, concerns the nature of individual human values and dimensions of culture—their antecedents, their consequences, and changes in them. Recent publications include studies of culture and change in East-Central Europe, relations of values to work, organizational behavior, violence, voting, religion, gender, and worries, and a critical review of cross-cultural research on values.

Choi K. Wan is a senior researcher in the Center for Applied Psychological Research at the University of Albany, State University of New York. He conducts research on quantitative methods, decision making, and health-related behaviors.

Candice Yee received a master's degree in social psychology from the University of Hong Kong. Her research interest focused on the relationship between person and job characteristics and job satisfaction. Since graduation, she has held a range of human resources appointments with several multinational companies and specializes in employee communication, skills assessments, and people development.